THE OUTLINE OF KNOWLEDGE

EDITED BY

JAMES A. RICHARDS

PART I

HISTORY OF LITERATURE
By Francis Rolt-Wheeler
Introduction by Edward J. Wheeler

PART II

ENGLISH POETRY

VOLUME XI

J. A. RICHARDS, INC.
NEW YORK

Copyright 1924
J. A. RICHARDS, INC.
MANUFACTURED IN U. S. A.

Typesetting, Paper, Printing, Binding and Cloth
By THE KINGSPORT PRESS
Kingsport, Tenn.

CONTENTS

PART ONE

HISTORY OF LITERATURE

CHAPTER		PAGE
I	The Growth of Language	2
II	Writing	8
III	Sacred Book of the Ancients	15
IV	Sacred Books in Historic Times	26
V	The Classic Epics	34
VI	The Epics of the Orient	43
VII	The Northern Epics	55
VIII	The Epics Chivalry	70
IX	Dante and Milton	82
X	The Development of the Drama	90
XI	Essayists and Historians	104
XII	The Novel and the Short Story	108

PART TWO

ENGLISH POETRY

Geoffrey Chaucer	125
Robyn Hode	158
Richard Rowlands	209
Thomas Nashe	213
Edmund Spenser	214
Michael Drayton	219
John Lyle	222
Sir Philip Sidney	222
Thomas Lodge	224
Anthony Munday	226
Sir Walter Raleigh	227
Christopher Marlowe	228
Robert Greene	229
Richard Barnfield	230
Thomas Campion	230
Ben Jonson	232
John Donne	236
Richard Corbet	243
Francis Beaumont	244
William Drummond	247
George Wither	248
Thomas Dekker	250

CONTENTS

	PAGE
Anonymous	251
Robert Herrick	254
Joshua Sylvester	258
George Herbert	259
Henry Vaughan	260
Francis Bacon, Viscount St. Alban	262
James Shirley	263
Thomas Carew	264
Sir John Suckling	264
Sir William D'Avenant	265
Richard Lovelace	265
Edmund Waller	267
James Graham, Marquis of Montrose	268
Richard Crashaw	269
Thomas Jordan	271
Abraham Cowley	272
Andrew Marvell	273
John Dryden	273
Matthew Prior	283
Isaac Watts	284
Lady Grisel Baillie	284
John Gay	286
Henry Carey	287
Alexander Pope	289
Thomas Gray	318
William Collins	328
George Sewell	329
John Logan	330
Henry Fielding	332
Samuel Johnson	333
Oliver Goldsmith	334
Adam Austin	344
William Cowper	344
Richard Brinsley Sheridan	358
Michael Bruce	359
George Halket	360
William Hamilton of Bangour	361
Samuel Rogers	364
William Blake	365
Susanna Blamire	366
William Wordsworth	367
Samuel Taylor Coleridge	391
Robert Southey	414
Charles Lamb	417
Elizabeth Barrett Browning	419
John Keats	435
Percy Bysshe Shelley	451
John Milton	463

HISTORY
OF
LITERATURE

CHAPTER I

THE GROWTH OF LANGUAGE

STRANGE kinships are seen between the physical frame of man and of the brute. Still stranger ties appear linking the man of art to a world invisible, but it is in the realm of Literature that reason, man's finest gift, attains its sublimest flight. When primitive man haltingly stammered the first articulate words of the human race, little could he realize that those syllables which forever unshackled the trammels of brutehood should branch into a thousand lines and lead to the creation of those masterpieces which form the priceless heritage of the present time.

Yet these few stammered sounds most truly form a lofty verbal ancestry, for Literature is the child of Language, and Language, like some inspired architect, builds into its imperishable walls the word-gems garnered through the ages. The depth and copiousness of meaning that lies in words, just in the terms themselves, is vaster than is realized. Children of the mind, they reflect the manifold richness of man's faculties and affections. They incarnate man's unconscious, passionate creative energy. They bring the eternal provocations of personality. They are the sanctuary of the intuitions and they paint humanity in all its thoughts, longings, aspirations, struggles and its failures.

How all-permeative a force is this same Language, this wonder-working grouping together of mere words! It is the vehicle of every thought, the expression of every life; it forms alike the merry prattle of childhood and the ripe comfort of old age; it is the same in cradle-song and battle-cry, and half a dozen sentences may exalt the mind to its utmost height or plunge it to degradation. And yet the pean of joy and the dirge of grief, the shout of triumph and the despondent utterances of despair alike are but a few consonantal sounds and still fewer vowels strung together in a certain order.

That there must be order is evident and clear. With the same organs of speech the whole world over, there are tens of thousands of dialects of tongues mutually incomprehensible. Yet order exists. "We may define Language," suggests A. H. Sayce, in his "Introduction to the Science of Language," "as consisting of certain modulations of the voice, variously combined and arranged, which serve as symbols for the thoughts or feelings we wish to express. The sounds that we utter must have a meaning before they can become language, otherwise they will be mere cries, or gibberish, less worthy of the name of Language than even the howling of a dog upon the prairie or the wild song of a forest bird. Language is the outward expression and embodiment of thought—the garment, so to speak, with which the mind clothes itself when it would reveal itself to another or even, it may be, to itself."

Language is something more than this. The essential difference which separates man's means of communication in kind as well as in degree from that of the lower animals is that, while the latter is instinctive, the former is, in all its parts, arbitrary and conventional. No man can become possessed of any existing language without learning it; no animal (that we know of) has any expression which he learns that is not the direct gift of Nature to him.

This distinct possession, moreover, that which marks so wide a gulf, is universal in its scope. There is no race or tribe, however isolated or no matter how savage, known to-day, that is dumb or does not own some articulate speech. Life is so much bigger a thing to man than to beast that he had to talk about it.

Articulate speech is largely influenced, and indeed determined, by the organs of articulation. The vocal mechanism is a wind instrument of which the lungs, compressed by the thorax, may be considered as bellows. The trachea, or windpipe, leads from the bronchial tubes in the lungs to the pharynx or upper part of the throat, situated behind the mouth cavity, and the larynx is placed in the opening of the trachea into the pharynx or throat. The larynx can be closed by a valve known as the epiglottis, which prevents the food from entering the trachea when swallowing.

Efforts have been made at various times to assign the origin of speech to attempts on the part of primitive man to mimic the sounds about him, or to evolve words from mere interjectional cries. These are known as the onomatopoetic and interjectional schools, or as Max Muller expressed the idea in an undying phrase, the "bow-wow" and "pooh-pooh" theories. A list of such words could readily be made up, names of birds like "bobolink" and "cuckoo"; of sounds, like "crack" and "whizz," but while these have contributed to the language, any

THE GROWTH OF LANGUAGE

effort to ascribe all roots to such beginnings have proved futile. The interjectional theory, once a vogue among philologists, has dropped out of sight, it could not stand the test of analysis.

The Science of Language, in its present-day form, rather ignores the question of the real origin of the primal sounds and gives its whole endeavor to the tracing of the roots which underlie the words of all languages. If the question be asked, "Whence came these roots?" Muller again must be called on for reply. "I have said," he declares, "intentionally very little about roots; at least very little about the nature of the origin of roots, because I believe that in the Science of Language we must accept roots simply as ultimate facts, leaving to the physiologist and the psychologist the question as to the possible sympathetic or reflective action of the five senses upon the motor nerves of the organs of speech."

The essential lies not in the pedantic argument as to the birthplace of the root, but in the realization that the roots are vital, are alive. Language is not a cunning conventionalism arbitrarily agreed upon; it is an internal necessity, begotten of a lustful longing to express man's secret sense of his ability to interpret Nature.

It is not to be thought that the power to trace back words to a small number of roots in any way portrays a paucity of language, for Leibnitz has computed the possible word-combinations in an alphabet of twenty-four letters, no word to be more than three syllables long, as being 620,448,401,733,239,439,360,000. When to these are added inflectional changes and differences of intonations, it will be seen that the vocabulary is ample. The average business man's vocabulary will contain at most about 3,000 words.

The changes in these roots, in their grouping and in their relation each to each are what really constitute the development of Language. These changes are of two kinds: Phonetic, which deals with changes of the sound, and Semantic, which deals with the changes of the meaning. The former has led to the greatest number of corruptions which have crept into the language—*e.g.*, "John's book," instead of "John his book," the latter to the modernizing of words and phrases. New knowledge gives new meaning to old terms, and this to so great an extent that even for the Elizabethan era, in many cases, a glossary of obsolete words or of words whose meaning has been greatly altered is found necessary.

It is these constant changes, be they phonetic or semantic, whether they partake of the nature of sound or meaning, which render the classification of language a task of extreme difficulty, especially in the more debased dialects. By carefully comparing similarities and variances of structure (the morphological plan) and by observing the inter-relations of vocabularies and word-systems (the genealogical basis) and connoting the results of these two, an outline which is correct as a general whole can be secured. The latest, and perhaps the one that most clearly views the whole field, is that used by W. L. Tucker in his "Introduction to the History of Language." With minor changes, it is as follows:

The Science of Language, however, is by no means confined to this type of work. It has a vast purview and more and more is becoming a weapon of research into the important field of psychology. The philologist no longer studies the words alone, but the man behind the words; not the grammar alone, but the logic behind the grammar; not the phrase alone, but the philosophy behind the phrase. In this sense the Science of Language is largely a product of the last century.

"It is a young and growing science," says Max Muller, "that puts forth new strength with every year, that opens new prospects, new fields of enterprise on every side and rewards its students with richer harvests than could be expected from the exhausted soil (?) of the older sciences. The whole world is open, as it were, to the student of language. There is virgin soil close to our door and there are whole continents still to conquer, if we step beyond the frontiers of the ancient seats of civilization. And even were the old mines exhausted, the Science of Language would create its own materials, and as with the rod of the prophet, smite the pictured rocks of the desert to call from them new streams of living speech."

Philology has emblazoned upon its roll many illustrious names, extending from hoary antiquity to the present day, but as a science the synthetic conception had its first and foremost representative in Friedrich August Wolf, and it was by him admirably outlined in an essay published in 1807 and, significantly enough, dedicated to Goethe, "Darstellung der Alterthumwissenschaft." "Wolf conceived of philology as the biography of a nation," says Hanns Oertel in his "Lectures on the Study of Language." "He does not study the works of the ancients for their own sakes, but in order to become acquainted through them with those who produced them. Wolf proposed to do for these nations just what the biographer does for an individual. To him and his school philology is not a history of the literature, or of the art, or of the religion of a given nation, but a history of its life which rests upon the inter-relation and combined action of all these factors.

"Even while Wolf's conception of philology reigned supreme," Oertel remarks in another portion of the same work, "we find analytical tendencies in Wolf's great rival, G. Hermann. Not for his results, but for his aims Hermann must be mentioned among the pioneers of the analytic treatment of languages. It was he who elevated grammatical studies from the ancillary position they had held and won for them relative independence. But he also introduced an abstract, logical method which derives its system not from the observed concrete facts of a language, but from logical and philosophic speculation.

"There are faint traces of a historical view in both Hermann and Wolf, but the first practical demonstration on a large scale of the application of the historical treatment to grammar was given in Jacob Grimm's monumental German grammar, the first volume of which appeared in 1819. Under Grimm's treatment it was inevitable that the interest of the investigator tracing the successive stages in the history of a given language, noting gains, losses and mutations, should become focused upon this process of evolution which was going on before his very eyes, and that thus both a firm basis and a strong incentive should be furnished for a study of the dynamic problems of speech."

This is very largely the point of view of Franz Bopp in his "Ueber J. Grimm's Deutsche Grammatik," wherein he writes, "A grammar in the higher, scientific use of the word must be both the history and the natural science of a language. It must, as far as possible, historically trace the road along which a language has risen to its perfection or sunk to low estate (this states the historical problem), but especially it should, after the manner of the natural sciences, investigate the laws according to which its development or its decay or its rebirth out of former ruins has taken place (this is the dynamic aspect of the problem)."

The compendium of August Schleicher (1861) sums up all that had accrued in comparative grammar in the thirty years that had followed Bopp's work, but Schleicher did more than this. He originated the idea of inferentially constructing a parent language on the basis of actually existing cognate languages and dialects.

The comparative treatment, so conceived, differs from the historical treatment, not in aim but in method. In fact, it joins hands with the latter and endeavors to extend its scope beyond the line of the earliest historical records into the prehistoric past. The basis upon which most philological work rests is the direct evidence of extant records, literary remains, monuments, etc. The historical method taught the student to arrange these so that by an unbroken line the most recent ones should be connected with the oldest. But with these oldest direct records the historical method came to a halt, because direct testimony was exhausted. It was here, then, that the comparative method of dealing with cognate languages supplied a means by which the still earlier prehistoric periods might be opened up; that a proper setting might be furnished to these oldest historical periods and a sequence be established which, for want of evidence, otherwise would have been broken.

Wilhelm von Humboldt caused the whole of philologic attention to be centered on grammatical structure, a matter so technical that a reaction against it was led by F. Eucken, who voiced the conception of Language as an independent organism.

This naturalistic attitude was brought back to its true relation by H. Steinthal, who led the psychological reaction. He was the first to place linguistics on a true psychological basis, and his chiefest work lay in his recognition that linguistic phenomena as a whole were different from the pyschological phenomena of a single individual.

Steinthal was the first true herald to recognize the fact that the phenomena of the mind which manifest themselves in recognized speech are variant from those which may be peculiar to a single person, and in grouping these speech-relations with the phenomena of custom, he proclaimed a new principle in philology Speech is only possible where there are hearers, but the reflex action upon speech of the hearer formerly had been overlooked. In his "Logik and Psychologie" Steinthal puts this matter very succinctly when he says, "it is the important fate of the human soul not to exist as an independent individual but to exist as a member of some community, which from the beginning, both in body and soul, forms part of some people. By birth every man belongs to some society which materially influences his psychical development. So that the individual cannot be fully comprehended without reference to the community within which he was born and lives."

It is this same conception which so largely enters into the question of the acceptance of words. Hanns Oertel, in the volume previously quoted, presents this at some length. He says, in part, "Inasmuch as every social phenomenon owes its existence not only to individual creation but also to communal acceptance (in fact, it does not become a social phenomenon except by such acceptance), it can easily be seen that a proper valuation of linguistic facts is only obtained by treating them as social phenomena. The individual does not create his language, but he receives in childhood a ready-made set of symbols which he must henceforth use as best he can. And, in gradually appropriating these definite symbols during the formative period of his mental life, they are used as a supporting trellis around which the latter grows up.

"The forms of every language represent certain characteristic groups of associations, relations, emotions; and the child, in learning to use them intelligently, is forced to arrange his mental contents in the same groups in which the preceding generations arranged theirs. For this reason language serves as the most important assimilative factor by which minds of new generations are forced into uniformity with those of their ancestors. The social value of Language lies in this fact—that it makes psychical heredity possible."

THE GROWTH OF LANGUAGE

It is the life in Language and its transmissibility that have led to Literature. "One must not," writes Wilhelm von Humboldt, "consider a language as a product dead and formed but once; it is an animate being and ever creative. Human thought elaborates itself with the progress of the intelligence, and of this thought Language is a manifestation. An idiom therefore cannot remain stationary; it walks, it develops, it grows up, it fortifies itself, it becomes old and it reaches decrepitude."

There is, however, a certain danger in this readiness for change in Language, the danger of a too constant flux. In the earliest times this was in part avoided by the memory powers of the story-tellers and later the reciters of sacred hyms and liturgies. With a superstitious reverence attaching to the text, most strenuous endeavors were made to preserve even the accent along the conventional channels. This was of great value, the more so as the memory, thus trained from childhood and transmitted hereditarily through generations, became stored to an extent that the modern Occidental types would hardly believe possible. It is, even in these days, when memory is not so cultivated, no such difficult task to learn ten thousand lines of verse, and even the vocabulary of ten thousand lines, preserved in their purity, would go far to keep the standard of a language to its level.

But the increasing diversity of life and the extension of relation to more distant countries speedily pointed out the necessity not only of communication but also of permanent communication. Speech and Language were all very well in their way, but the residuum of knowledge had grown so great, the interests of life had so expanded that some methods of fixing the evanescent speech became obligatory. From mere gibberish and harsh cry had evolved Language, and the need for the perpetuation of Language pointed the way to writing.

CHAPTER II

WRITING

The essential difference between Speech and Writing is that the former appeals to the ear, the latter to the eye. "The first endeavors at the communication of thought to the eye," says W. L. Tucker in his "Introduction to the History of Language," "would naturally take the shape of drawings or sketches, such as those executed by the American Indians or the Australian aboriginals. These would represent a whole scene, which each observer would interpret for himself according to his own lights and the greater or less detail and precision of the delineation. Doubtless within a particular tribe or community there would grow up certain traditional principles to assist in both the execution and the reading of a drawing, but even more beyond doubt is the fact that such sketches would only express the concrete elements in very simple notions, leaving undetermined—so far as the drawing was a drawing and nothing else—anything abstract or any conditions of time, place, fact or contingency. They therefore necessarily admitted of various and often contradictory interpretations."

The distinction between a picture and a pictograph is not always clearly borne in mind. Suppose, for example, that the subject which was to be represented was the seizure of a young girl by a warrior who has braved the dangers of an enemy's camp and is carrying her away in his canoe. This would make a clear scene in a true picture. In the background would appear the tent from which the girl was taken, with her father issuing therefrom, brandishing a spear in rage; in the foreground the warrior with the girl in his arms, and near by, the canoe. But the details of time and all abstract conceptions would have to be omitted, for the picture could not portray them. It is well known how difficult it is even for the greatest artists to depict subtle ideas and how impossible to portray a consecution of such.

Suppose, however, that the artist drew a succession of single signs. Thus he might depict first figure of a warrior, then his totem sign to show to what tribe he belonged, then a canoe, then three suns, then a tent with a different totem sign on it, then a hawk, then a girl, then a snake, then an eagle with the girl on his back, then a shower of arrows, then a canoe with two figures in it. The story thus pictographically represented would declare that a warrior whose totem sign was shown had taken a three days' journey by canoe to a hostile camp. He had then scouted about the hostile camp like a hawk until he located the tepee in which the girl he sought was to be found. Then, like a snake, he had crept into the tepee, and taking the girl in his arms, had fled as swiftly as an eagle, and, although pursued by a shower of arrows, had escaped unharmed and had returned to his home with the girl in his canoe. It is readily seen how much more complete is the story when told pictographically than the story told pictorially, and at the same time it becomes evident that picture-writing belongs to a far earlier stage than writing by pictographs.

In neither of these cases is there any connection between symbol and individual sound or indeed between symbol and speech at all. It is thought, not language, which puts on the visible shape. This fact is made abundantly clear by the reflection that this picture-writing, as a medium of communication, would be just as effective between the deaf-and-dumb who have never known any language or between foreigners whose languages would be mutually unintelligible. Like gesture, it has no reference to the operations of the vocal apparatus and makes no attempt to indicate them.

The Eskimo medium of communication was midway between the two. In part it consisted of pictographs, in part it was a picture and in part it endeavored to express the more difficult conceptions by the use of pictured gestures. Thus a man points to himself for the meaning "I," but he points away from himself to mean "go." Thus a man pointing to himself, followed by a man pointing away from himself, means "I go" (not two men as a pure picture would imply). Here, then are three stages in the transmission of communication: First, the picture; second, the pictured gestures in succession; third, the pictograph. But none of these bore relation to sound, only to idea.

The case is not very different with the "knot-writing," which was practiced at a remote period of Chinese history, and which, as quipu-writing, was found by the Spaniards in regular use among the officials of the Incas of Peru. "The quipu," as described by Tucker, "was a cord, measuring from two feet upward, from which hung a parti-colored fringe of threads. These were knotted and intertwined in various conventional ways and, partly by the colors and sequence of the threads, partly by the disposition and number of the knots, they could be employed so as to convey official messages and preserve records. This, of course, necessitated the representation not only of material objects, but also of abstract notions. For the latter purpose the colors were employed. Thus white stood for "silver" or "peace," red for "gold" or "war."

"Here we take a distinct step beyond the sketch writing of the North American Indian, inasmuch as we must assume for the Peruvian method the existence of a previous understanding or code of interpretation between the parties employing the device. Whatever the origin of the practice, the connection between thought on the one hand and colors and knots on the other became purely artificial and conventional, and instruction for both reader and '"writer" was as necessary as it is with the modern alphabetical system.

"We can therefore perhaps hardly deny that this quipu method was a form of writing. That it was utterly inadequate and helplessly dependent on special materials is no doubt an immense advantage, but hardly touches the essence of the matter. More to the point is the fact that it was purely symbolical of ideas and not of the sound in which those ideas were orally conveyed. It was not made up of signs with distinct phonetic values, but of signs with notional values in the rough. Given, therefore, the secret of a knot or color, it would have been possible for persons of entire different languages to write the same thought identically in quipu. In other words, it has, like picture-writing, no relation to speech, but only to thought."

Like the picture, the quipu led nowhither. It possessed no vitality in itself, and the increasing boundaries of its usefulness increased its complexity and made it the more ungainly to handle. As a mere record of official acts its limitations were not so apparent, for the same round of duties were recorded over and over again. But no sooner was an attempt made to extend it to the purposes of common life than it was found too cumbersome. In a word, from the quipu no Literature could have evolved.

The pictograph, on the other hand, bore within itself the possibilities of growth. It was but little removed from the ideogram, which was simply the depiction of an idea, but which differed from the pictograph in that the latter would convey one idea—tho that idea might be expressed in a phrase of many words—while the ideogram set forth the one word alone. At first, of course, there were as many ideograms as there were concrete concepts, and under such a system the entire concrete group could be adequately transcribed. Naturally the ideograms in different nations would be different. Thus the Egyptian ideogram for water was taken from the rippling Nile in flood and consequently was three wavy lines horizontally set above the other, but the Aztec ideogram was that of water being poured from a jug.

Various writers, moreover, familiarized with various types, would make variant ideograms for the same thought, and this would lead to a confusion of ideas. But, as time passed on, that one which seemed more easily differentiated from the others or which was easier to draw would secure popular favor. Thus while the original pictographs and even the first ideograms might have been in part mutually translatable, the one set of conventionalized symbols might have little in common with another. Such a change is seen in the accompanying developments of "mountain." The chiefest difficulty, however, lay in the representation of purely abstract ideas. Thus for example, how was such an important concept as "if" to be expressed by a picture which should be recognized as being "if"?

Curiously enough, the chief present difficulty of language was the true beginning of writing. Every family of speech has a number of homonyms; that is to say, words which sound alike but have different meanings. Sometimes they are even spelt alike. Thus there is a "box" hedge, a "box" on the ear, a "box" of toys, a "box" of a coach, and the last word itself as a homonym for a coach is also one for him who teaches a special study or sport. Sometimes they are spelt differently, such as "piece" and "peace," "to," "too" and "two," "sail" and "sale," and hundreds more. Thus in Chinese, for example, the sound "hua" has twenty-six different definite meanings.

The ideogram for one meaning of these homonyms thus came to be associated in each language with the sound of the word used. As, for example, a square box meant a box containing certain articles, but it also came to mean the other senses of "box" also. This led to a great deal of confusion until the device was adopted of using the ideogram for a square "box" in all its meanings, but putting a leaf beside it to show it was a "box" hedge, or a wheel beside it, to show that what was meant was the "box" of a coach. (The reader will understand that this English example is for the purpose of showing the method and is not a concrete case.)

In Chinese, to give an example of actual happening, the word "hua," among its many meanings, represented "prince" and "cold water." Of these the more important was "prince," wherefore the ideogram for "hua" alone meant prince, and when the sense of "cold water" was desired to be expressed, this was done by adding the symbol of water. Further confusion might arise, however, by reading into the symbol of water its own meaning, and thus perhaps "prince" "water" might imply that it was a royal bath. Therefore to show that this explanatory symbol was not to be read but was merely to point out the manner in which the "hua" should be read, the sign for water was written in the old, unabbreviated ideogram, the sign for "hua" in the new shortened form. This was as far as true Chinese ever reached, and modern Chinese has developed from this arrested system. The Hittite hieroglyphs never reached as far.

In Egypt, however, while a similar process went on, a different order of things arose in the idea of prefixes and suffixes. If, for example, the addition of a letter meant "father" and of another letter "mother" and so forth, it was easy to see that each letter possessed a value. Chinese never conceived a smaller unit than a word, but Egyptian truly realized the meaning of a syllable. The development of this was that the initial consonantal sound sign of a certain group of similar-sounding syllables came to be placed in front of all such syllables and thence naturally passed to a representation of the consonantal sound itself.

It was by this means that a true alphabet came tentatively into existence. "Nevertheless," points out Tucker, "tho purely alphabetical sounds appear on very antique monuments, the ancient Egyptians themselves never came to employ them purely and consistently. The older methods of ideography and of syllable phonograms continued still to blend with the incomparably more convenient device for which the way had been shown. The consistent use of alphabetical characters triumphed only when an alien people borrowed for the purposes of its own language the best expedients at which Egypt had arrived."

These people were unquestionably the Phenicians. That the Babylono-Phenician alphabet came from Egypt was a tradition of antiquity, and there seems little doubt, since the researches of De Rouge, that the tradition can be deemed substantiated. There are excellent remains of the cursive hieratic writing—that is to say, the general correspondence writing hand of the priests and merchants of early times, and it seems sure that it was from this that the alphabet was formed. The hieroglyph, intended for carving, was unsuitable, and the later demotic or commercial writing of Egypt had not been developed.

The Phenicians, like all trading peoples, found it necessary to possess a lingua franca, and it is fair to assume that there were dialects and differences in the historic script. Even to the script of the Moabite stone every letter of the Roman alphabet can be traced, and to other hieratics the resemblance is closer still. The Phenicians were radical in their adoptive measures, casting aside all determinant ideograms and variants. In this reforming of the language Cadmus is given by tradition the greatest credit. But without knowing definitely to whom the credit may be ascribed, it was little short of wonderful that the true idea of one sign for one sound should have arisen from the confused Egyptian system and that there should have been formed a true alphabet of twenty-two letters.

But one part of the old heritage remained—the alphabet was syllabic in that it had no vowels. Thus "T" might mean "Ta," or "Te," or "Ti," "To." This was not of so much difficulty in Phenician, but when the alphabet was adopted by the Greeks, with their intensely orotund language, they dropped four of the extra sibilants

WRITING

which stood for non-Greek sounds and took them to represent the vowels "a," "e," "i" and "o."

The subject of writing material and its influence upon the development of writing is another subject of too vast a scope for treatment here. It is seen in the change between the hieroglyph carved upon the temple wall and the hieratic writing intended for thin and flimsy papyrus, but its most remarkable development was in the Assyrian cuneiform. This has not been touched upon in the previous consideration of the development of writing, since it bore no relation to the final result.

The famous wedge-shaped cuneiform inscriptions of the Assyrians were simply a device to draw on wet clay. In the valley of the Tigris and Euphrates was no stone and all cities were built of clay. There was no papyrus, and all the writing was on clay. There was not even pebble for seals—all were made of clay. The principal difficulty of such writing is that the clay pushes up before the stylus and mars the whole. Therefore it must be done by stamping rather than writing. Had the Assyrians possessed an alphabet at this time the stamping would have been no difficulty, but they did not; they were still drawing pictures. Therefore no set of stamps could be made, for the reason that each new concept would require a different stamp.

Almost all things can be expressed or drawn in a fashion by straight lines, and therefore the Assyrians had little steles or punches made of three different lengths. With these they stamped in the moist clay the figure they desired to produce. As writing progressed and the eye and hand became familiarized, stroke after stroke of the ideogram was left out, until the barest skeleton remained, no longer a picture but a symbol which had to be learned just as did the alphabet. But it never attained an alphabetical form, and created as it was for a certain environment of time and place, it had no means of historical perpetuation. Chinese has lived on in a changed form to this day, Egyptian lives in the English alphabet through its adoption by Phenician channels, but Assyrian cuneiform and the Central American hieroglyphs are as extinct as the dodo.

Thus came Writing into the world and thus it developed. Taking upon itself the changed circumstances of race and time, of material and of concept, Writing has gone on and on, becoming with each succeeding change more potent in its influence on the race. It is the foundation of all knowledge, the keystone of all civilization. The part of human information which is secured from observation, untrained by reading, is infinitesimal. Remove at one fell swoop all the books upon the earth, sweep away all records, expunge from the minds of all men the power or even the thought of transmitting their thoughts, and what would remain? No railroad could run without time-table and telegraphic dispatch, and with all trains stopped, the cities would be deserted, for no food supplies could reach; factories would close, mills shut down, industries pass into oblivion, scholarship be forgotten and law become annulled. All these great civilizations of the present day would dwindle, and knowledge would collapse like a house of cards, but for the great foundation stones of the Science of Language and the Art of Writing.

CHAPTER III

SACRED BOOKS OF THE ANCIENTS

THE earliest Literature of the world, and the most important because of its bearing upon the development of man, is the Literature of the Sacred Books. Every nation that reached the scale of civilization wherein Literature was possible had its Sacred Books, and these were not only the best known and most revered of the writings of those nations, but they were also the means of crystallizing and conserving the very language itself.

In the Sacred Books, the earlier one particularly, almost all the knowledge and thought of the time is to be found. They contain philosophy and versification; they portray science and depict art; they discuss economics and relate parable; they wax denunciatory or glide into a pastoral. No two literary styles could be more unlike, for example, than the Lamentations of Jeremiah and the idyll of the Book of Ruth; nothing more diverse in character than the list of legal observances in Leviticus and the love-poetry of the Song of Solomon; nothing more utterly dissimilar than the medical directions concerning leprosy laid down in the Pentateuch and the visionary fantasies of Ezekiel.

These illustrations as to the diversity of matter to be found in the Sacred Books of the world have been taken from the Hebrew Bible, the Old Testament, for the double reason that it is the most familiar to the reader and is, perhaps, the oldest. It might be more correct to say that parts of it are older than any other sacred books for the reason that the Hebrew Bible is not so much a rewritten story of old traditions as a compilation of the old traditions themselves placed side by side.

The difference between this ancient plan and the modern method is well stated by James Robertson in his "Book by Book," wherein he says, "Whereas a modern historian, after consulting his authorities and verifying his facts, relates occurrences in his own words, with a reference to the sources from which he has drawn, we have here the very words of the authorities: family registers, lists of places, fragments of old poetry, stories of bygone days and details of the lives of ancient heroes, minute regulations of social life or ritual service are all strung upon the one thread of the history, but their individuality is not obliterated."

Much turns, therefore, on the identity of this compilatory historian. But his identity is legion! No manuscript in the world has gone through such vicissitudes as the Hebrew Bible, none has passed through so many hands. Despite the storm of controversy that has raged concerning the exegesis of the Old Testament, an effort will be made to state here what is generally admitted concerning its authorship.

The first five books, commonly ascribed to Moses and generally known as the Pentateuch, are to be considered as of more importance than the other books. From the earliest times tradition speaks of these books as "the law of Moses," altho it is particularly to be noticed that in the books themselves the Mosaic origin is not claimed. Certain passages are declared to have been set down by Moses, but certain other passages are assigned to different sources.

Not infrequently those things supposed to have been written by Moses are obviously spoken advice to Aaron and the priestly tribe, counsel given to the elders or the decrees of an assembly of the elders. In the sense, therefore, that Moses was the dictator of the Jewish people at this period, and that judicial and religious codes were drafted by him, it may be said that he was the inspirer of the formation of the Pentateuch; and work belonging to the Mosaic period, accomplished at the behest and with the advice of the great lawgiver himself, according to Oriental ideas, would be ascribed to him. Thus the first period of the Old Testament is the compiling of the Pentateuch under the eye of, if not by the hand of Moses.

The second period was that during which the Hebrew nation was governed first by the judges (a modified theocracy) and later by the great monarchs Saul, David and Solomon, thence splitting into the divided kingdoms. It was the golden age of the Hebrew race and their greatness found its way into their literature in two channels—the historical book of the Old Testament and the poetical books. The books of Joshua, Judges, Samuel, Kings and Chronicles (with Ruth and Esther) relate the history of that time; the books of Job, Psalms, Proverbs, Ecclesiastes and the Song of Solomon reveal the development of the national spirit. Temple observances multiplied and the old knowledge of the Pentateuch began to fall into disuse. The later reigns, with their idolatrous desecrations, brought things to such a pass that a great sensation was caused in the days of Josiah, when Hilkiah the priest discovered in some hiding-place the lost and almost forgotten "temple manuscript of the law." Soon after, falls upon Israel the darkness of the Babylonian captivity.

The third period extends from the time of Ezra and the return of the exiles to the destruction of Jerusalem by Titus (70 A.D.). "It is

SACRED BOOKS OF THE ANCIENTS

introduced," says J. Paterson Smyth in his "The Old Documents and the New Bible," "by the touching scene in the eighth chapter of Nehemiah, the thousands of returned exiles that September morning in the 'broad place that was before the water gate' in Jerusalem, with their ruined temple in the distance, and Ezra the scribe, from the pulpit of wood, reading to them out of his Hebrew manuscript the almost forgotten words of Moses. But the glory is departed of the ancient days; the holy tongue sounds strangely in ears accustomed so long to the speech of their Chaldean masters, and in the simple words of the prophet, 'all the people wept when they heard the law.'"

During the Babylonian captivity, banished from their temple, the Jews had originated synagogues, and after their return Ezra brought into being "The Great Synagogue," as it was called. This group of scholars collected all the manuscripts of the law, of the historical books, of the poetical books and of the prophecies which had been made just prior to and during the Babylonian captivity. Of these they made the complete Jewish Bible and the "decreed books" or the "canon" of the Old Testament was closed, so that no books written afterward would be received as inspired. This is the complete Hebrew Bible, or Old Testament, of which a Greek translation, called the Septuagint, was made in Alexandria at the order of Ptolemy Philadelphus, then king of Egypt.

The fourth period is that of the Massoretes. After the destruction of the temple naught remained to the Jews but their traditions, and for five centuries the scribes labored over the Talmud, which is a traditional explanation (Mishna) of the Law of Moses, and a series of commentaries (Gemara) upon that tradition. But during this period a number of oral regulations had been handed down regarding the right method of reading the text, the accuracy of certain passages, etc., and these were called the Massorah or the Tradition.

Owing to the dispersion of the Jewish race, it became continuously more important to commit these to writing, and the scribes who did so were called the Massoretes, wherefore the text which these scholars have handed down is known as the Massoretic text. The greater part of this work was done between 500 A.D. and 1000 A.D. The value of the work of the Massoretes is twofold. First, they carefully revised a text, pointing out obvious inaccuracies, and, secondly, they invented a system of vowel-points. The early texts were written without vowels, without divisions between the words and could only be read by oral tradition. Thus, for example, "THLRDSMSHPRD'SHLLNTWNT" would appear at first sight almost unreadable, but if the phrase, "The Lord is my shepherd, I shall not want," was in mind, the consonants would serve as a sufficient guide.

The Massoretes also actually invented their entire vowel system, which could be added outside the letters, so that the actual text need not be changed, and then divided the words from each other. Of the earlier types there are none, and the earliest dated manuscript is one of 916 A.D. There is one in the British Museum which may be a few, a very few years older. Thus, strange as it may seem, the world possesses an earlier complete copy of the Koran, the latest of the great Sacred Books, than it does of the complete Hebrew Bible, the earliest. An ancient Syriac commentary, that of St. Ephraem, refers to a "palimpsest" or document written upon the second time after the earlier writing had grown faint. This may be as early as the second century, and portions of the original writing have been restored by the use of chemicals.

The Old Testament is so well known and contains so many points of view that it is difficult to select a quotation that shall be typical of its spirit, but perhaps the direct commandments of Moses might be regarded as presenting a fair example as found in Exodus xx, 1-17. The first two commandments and their effect upon the people follow:

"So Moses went down unto the people and spake unto them:

"'And God spake all these words, saying,

"'"I am the Lord thy God, which have brought thee out of the land of Egypt, out of the house of bondage.

"'"Thou shalt have no other gods before me.

"'"Thou shalt not make unto thee any graven image, or any likeness of anything that is in heaven above, or that is in the earth beneath, or that is in the water under the earth:

"'"Thou shalt not bow down thyself to them, nor serve them: for I the Lord thy God am a jealous God, visiting the iniquity of the fathers upon the children unto the third and fourth generation of them that hate me;

"'"And shewing mercy unto thousands of them that love me, and keep my commandments."'

"And all the people saw the thunderings, and the lightnings, and the noise of the trumpet and the mountain smoking (Mt. Sinai); and when the people saw it, they removed, and stood afar off.

"And they said unto Moses, 'Speak thou with us, and we will hear: but let not God speak with us, lest we die.'"

Reaching as far back as the twenty-fourth century B.C., documents dealing with the old dynasties are found in the ancient books of China. They are reverenced as Sacred Books and must so here be treated, but they are scarcely Sacred Books in the sense that they

SACRED BOOKS OF THE ANCIENTS

deal with sacred subjects. Indeed, it may be stated that no such array of books exists in the world in which there is less religious philosophy than in the Sacred Books of China.

The first and greatest in historical importance of these books is called the Shu, and since the period of the Han dynasty, the Shu King. Its documents commence with the reign of Yao in the twenty-fourth century B.C. and they come down to those of King Hsiang of the Kau dynasty (651-619 B.C.). Only second in importance is the Shih, or the Book of Poetry, often called the Shih King. It contains in all 305 pieces, five of which are of the time of the Shang dynasty (1766-1123 B.C.). The others belong to the dynasty of Kau from the time of its founder, King Wan (1231 B.C.), to King Ting (586 B.C.). The book as a whole is divided into four parts, the last of which is occupied with "Odes of the Temple and the Altar."

The third book is the Yi, commonly called the Book of Changes. "This is often thought the most ancient, but wrongly so, since no portion of the text is older than the time of King Wan," says James Legge in the introduction to his translation of the Shu King, "There were and indeed are in it trigrams ascribed to Fu-hsi, who is generally considered as the founder of the Chinese nation and whose place in chronology should probably be ascribed to the thirty-fourth century 2.3." The eight trigrams are again increased to sixty-four hexagrams, all compounded of a strange and arbitrary arrangement of long and short lines. "But what ideas Fu-hsi attached to the primary lines," says Legge again, "what significance he gave to his trigrams, what to the sixty-four hexagrams and why their number should stop there—of none of these points is there any knowledge from him." Copious notes were made on these figures by Wan and his equally famous son, the Duke of Kau, but the interpretations are forced and not infrequently contradictory.

The fourth of the great books is the Li-Ki, or Record of Rites. But this is scarcely more than the official register of the Kau dynasty. It enumerates the various office-holders of the empire and describes their duties, together with the proper ceremonies for installation and matters of that kind. It is not more religious than a "Court Circular" or a "Congressional Record."

The fifth and last King, or Sacred Book, is ascribed to Confucius himself. This is the Khun Khiu, but it consists merely of the annals of his native state Lu from 722-481 B.C. These are the five Kings. To them are usually added the four Shu, books of four philosophers. These are the Lun Yu, containing conversations between Confucius and his disciples; the works of Mencius; the Ta Hsio, which is ascribed to Tsang-Tze, and the Kung Yung to the son of the latter, Tze-Tze.

China's greatest statesman, K'ung-foo-tseu, better known as Confucius, was born about 550 B.C. and as a conserver of tradition and an economist probably never has known a peer. He was certainly for many years Minister of Justice and tradition states that he was also Prime Minister. Absolutely different in type from the great medieval statesman, Cardinal Richelieu, his policies were identical. He aggrandized the monarchy at the expense of the nobility, centralized the government and regarded his actions as being Destiny incarnate.

Confucius was a sublime moralist, but not a religionist. The name of any supreme being only appear once in his entire writings. "The most marked feature in the religion of the Chinese before this time," says John Lord, "was the worship of ancestors, and this worship he did not seek to change. He did not like to talk of spiritual things, professing no interest in the working out of abstruse questions, either of philosophy or theology. Hence he did not aspire to throw any new light on the great problems of human condition and destiny; nor did he speculate, like the Ionian philosophers, on the creation or end of things. He confined his attention to outward phenomena—to the world of sense and matter—to forms, precedents, ceremonies, proprieties, rules of conduct, filial duties and duties to the State, enjoining temperance, honesty and sincerity as the cardinal and fundamental laws of private and national prosperity. He was a man of the world, and all his teachings have reference to respectability in the world's regard. He doubted more than he believed."

Among these books of the distant ages past is the papyrus of the Egyptian "Book of the Dead." It is best known from texts and citations placed in mummy cases as advice or protection to the spirit of the man and woman who was awaiting judgment. One of the most famous examples is the Egyptian "Final Judgment" of Ani, a scribe who has just died.

But little less ancient in date and possessing a hoariness of antiquity which makes it seem even further back in the history of man is the Vedic literature of India, which ranges from about 2000 B.C. to 700 B.C. It has been transmitted to the Western world but recently and, indeed, is by no means yet thoroughly understood. The importance of these books and of other ancient literary treasures of the Oriental nations can scarcely be overestimated.

"To watch in the Sacred Books of the East," says Max Muller in his introduction to "The Upanishade," in a prefatory article which is indeed an introduction to that great series of translations grouped under the title "Sacred Books of the East," "to watch in these books the dawn of the religious consciousness in man must always remain one of the most inspiring and hallowing sights in the whole history of the world; and he whose heart cannot quiver with the first quivering rays of human thought and human faith as revealed in these ancient documents is, in his own way, as unfit for these studies as, from another side, is the man who shrinks from copying and collating ancient manuscripts or toiling through volumes of tedious commentary."

Altho it must be admitted that the present day cannot reread into that ancient literature the potency of spell it once possessed, it can secure a general conception of what the Vedic Literature was and the scheme of its general purport. Maurice Bloomfield, one of the most modern and profound authorities on Sanscrit, has, in his "Religion of the Veda," illumined certain aspects of the immense field.

"At the beginning of our knowledge of India," he says, "we are face to face with an extensive poetical literature in set meters. This is crude on the whole, even when compared with classical literature times. Yet it shows, along with uncouth naiveté and semi-barbarous turgidity, a good deal of beauty and elevation of thought. Vedic Literature includes hymns, prayers and sacred formularies offered by priests to the gods in behalf of rich lay sacrificers; charms for witchcraft, medicine and other homely practices, manipulated by magicians and medicine-men, in the main for plainer people. From a later time come expositions of the sacrifices, illustrated by legends, in the manner of the Jewish Talmud. Then speculations of a higher sort, philosophic, cosmic, psycho-physical and theosophic, gradually growing up in connection with and out of the simpler beliefs. Finally there is a considerable body of set rules for conduct in every-day secular life at home and abroad; that is, a distinct literature of customs and laws. This is the Veda as a whole.

"The Veda consists of considerably more than a hundred books, written in a variety of slightly differentiated dialects and styles. Some of the Vedic books are not yet published (1908) or even unearthed. At the base of this entire canon lie four varieties of metrocal composition, or, in some cases, prayers in solemn prose. These are known as the four Vedas in the narrower sense: The Rig-Veda, the Yajur-Veda, the Sama-Veda and the Atharva-Veda.

"The Rig-Veda is a collection of priestly hymns addressed to the gods of the Vedic Pantheon. The enduring interest of the Rig-Veda in literature lies in those old priestly poets' vision of the beauty, the majesty, the power of the gods and in the myths and legends told of them. Its mythology, on one side at least, is primitive in conception and constructive under our very eyes. How a personal god developed by personification out of a visible fact in Nature, no literary document teaches as well as the Rig-Veda.

"The Yajur-Veda represents the exceeding growth that began to cumber the simpler ceremonial of the Rig-Veda and it details an interminable ceremonial full of symbolic meaning down to its smallest minutiæ. The Sama-Veda is unimportant and is only of interest as revealing the manner in which the earlier Vedic utterances were changed and modified to suit the use of musical instruments in the constantly increasing complexity of worship. The Atharva-Veda consists almost entirely of popular charms, for health, for prosperity, for victories, to keep peace, to win love, to secure revenge, conjurations against demons, sorcerers and enemies, and a thousand others, representing to the people the need of keeping the temples well supplied and the priests contented."

As an addenda to these appear the Brahmanas, an exegesis of certain parts of the Veda proper, which in the main are bulky prose statements and explications of the greater and the lesser sacrifices and defining their theological meaning. They are important because they are written in a connected prose, being probably the first prose of the world, because they are an inexhaustible mine for the history of the priesthood and because they are a storehouse of the myths and stories India has cherished from the beginning of time.

At the end of the Brahmanas comes a class of texts known as the Aranyakas, the transitional scriptures of the first forest hermits, who saw the symbol in the sacrifice, the reason in the ritual and prepared the way for the great Upanishads. These latter, which have become fateful for all subsequent higher Hindu thought, consist of contemplative meditations setting forth the philosophy and theosophy which was characteristic of the later literature.

In order to show the gradual development of conception between these three stages, the ancient Rig-Veda, the later Brahmanas and the comparatively recent Upanishads, the following examples are given. It will be noted that the form of the first is a hymn, of the second a legend and of the third a philosophy in the form of a parable.

From a hymn to the dawn in the Rig-Veda, I, 113:

"The sisters' pathway is the same unending,
Taught by the gods, alternately they tread it;
Fair shapes, of different forms, and yet one-minded,
Night and Morning clash not nor yet do linger."

From the Brahmana, Maitrayani Sanhita, 10-13:

"The mountains are the eldest children of Prajapati (the Creator). They were winged (birds). They kept flying forth and settling where they liked. At that time the earth was unstable. Indra (God) cut off their wings. By means of the mountains he made firm the earth. The wings became clouds. Therefore these clouds ever hover about the mountains. For this is their place of origin."

From the Khandogya-Upanishad, VIII, 7-12 (abbreviated):

"Indra and Virokana approached Prajapati and dwelt there as pupils thirty-two years. Then Prajapati asked them: 'For what purpose have you dwelt here?'

"They replied: 'A saying of yours is being repeated—the Self which is free from sin, free from old age, from death and grief, from hunger and thirst, which desires nothing but what it ought to desire and imagines naught but what it ought to imagine, that it is which we must search out, that it is which we must try to understand. He who has searched out that Self, and understands it, obtains all worlds and all desires. Now we have both dwelt here because we wish for that Self.'

"Prajapati said to them: 'He who moves about happy in dreams he is the Self.'

"But Indra saw this difficulty. Altho it is true that Self is not blind, yet it is as if they struck him (the Self) in dreams, as if they chased him. He becomes even conscious, as it were, of pain and sheds tears. He came again as a pupil to Prajapati.

"He lived with him two more periods of thirty-two years and then Prajapati said: 'When a man being asleep, reposing and in perfect rest sees no dreams, that is the Self.'

"But Indra saw this difficulty. In truth he thus does not know his Self, that he is I, nor does he know anything that exists. He is gone to utter annihilation. He came again as a pupil to Prajapati.

"He lived with him another five years and then Prajapati said: 'The body is mortal and always held by death. It is the abode of that Self which is immortal and without body. When in the body, the Self is held by pleasure and pain. But when he is free of the body (that is, when he knows himself different from the body) then neither pleasure nor pain touches him. Thus does that serene being, arising from this body, appear in its own form as soon as it has approached the highest light (the knowledge of Self). He, in that state, is the Highest Person. He moves about there, never minding that body into which he was born. He who behaves thus all his life reaches the world of Brahman and does not return, yea, he does not return.'"

The reader will note immediately the change, not only in phraseology but, in what is more important still, the name of the God of Gods. In the Vedas proper it is Indra, in the later Upanishads it is Brahman. Indra, in the true Vedic age, was a personification of one of the powers of Nature, but Brahm, or Brahma, is described in the Laws of Menu as being "an eternal, unchangeable, absolute being, the soul of all beings, who, having willed to produce various beings from his own divine substance, created the waters and placed in them a productive seed."

"But Brahmanism," says John Lord in his "Beacon Lights of History," "became corrupted. Like the Mosaic Law, under the sedulous care of the sacerdotal orders it ripened into a most burdensome ritualism. The Brahmanical caste became tyrannical, exacting and oppressive. With the supposed sacredness of his person and with the laws made in his favor, the Brahman became intolerable to the people."

An introspective philosophy of great subtlety proved the curse of the Brahmans. Finding themselves unable to teach the people their metaphysical abstractions, they multiplied their sacrifices and sacerdotal rites and even permitted a complicated polytheism. Siva and Vishnu became worshiped, as well as Brahma and a host of other gods unknown to the earlier Vedas.

Intimately connected with the ceremonies of the Vedas is the Code of Menu, which in its present form dates back to about the fifth century B.C. Some parts of it were doubtless current at a considerably earlier date, as the gods mentioned are principally Vedic. Originally it merely represented certain rules and precepts, probably by different authors, which were observed by a particular tribe or school of Brahmans called Menavas. Ultimately, however, the code was accepted by the Hindu people generally, and it plainly reveals the strenuous rules by which the Brahmans sought to perpetuate an organized system of caste which should definitely define and maintain their own superiority.

Under these circumstances Buddhism arose as a protest against Brahmanism. It was effected by a prince who goes by the name of Buddha (the Enlightened), but whose true name was Gautama Siddartha. The word Gautama was borrowed by the Sakyas after their settlement in India from one of the ancient Vedic bard families. The foundation of present-day knowledge of Sakya Buddha is from a life of him by Asvaghosha, in the first century of the modern era, but this is simply a rewritten form of an earlier history. The commentaries of Buddhaghosa, two or three centuries later, form the basis of the teachings of later Buddhism.

"At first sight," says John Caird in his "Religions of India," "no religious event in the history of mankind seems more unaccountable than the rapid, widely extended and enduring success of the religion which owes its origin to Gautama. Promulgated at first by a solitary teacher in a country in which Brahmanism had for more than a thousand years dominated the thoughts and lives of men, it succeeded in a short time in overthrowing the ancient faith and in transforming the social life of India. Its conquests have been greater, more extended and more lasting than those of any other

SACRED BOOKS OF THE ANCIENTS

religion, and even now, twenty-four centuries from the birth of its founder, Buddhism is, nominally at least, the religion of five hundred millions of the human race."

This success, no doubt, was largely due to the firm monastic system which was built up by Gautama. He not only preached a faith, but created the greatest order of mendicant monks in the world to carry it on. First issued by Prince Gautama (557-477 B.C.), Buddhism spread steadily and with but little change until the time of the conversion of the great monarch Asoka (259 B.C.), when it was, in a sense, made the state religion. It was during the reign of Asoka at a council known as the Council of Palalysutra (242 B.C.) that the cannon of the Buddhist Scriptures was settled, including the Vinaya-Pitaka, the Sutta-Pitaka and the Abhidhamma-Pitaka. The Book of the Great Decease or the Maha-Parinibbana Sutta, is one of the oldest of the books, dating from not more than one hundred years after the death of Gautama, and it is of special interest as showing the nature and the principles of the order that was founded to carry Buddhism all over the world.

Among the later forms of Hindu sacred literature are the Puranas, which present a comparatively modern field for investigation. They are eighteen in number, besides several smaller productions of a similar kind called Upa or Minor Puranas.

Their purpose seems to be to check the growth of Buddhism by stimulating the worship of Vishnu and Siva. They are acknowledged by all scholars to be the most modern of the Sacred Books, the oldest dating from the period of the Koran and the later books being as recent as the sixteenth century. The mythology of the Puranas is much more developed than that of the Maha-bhrarata, in which Vishnu and Siva are apparently regarded merely as great heroes. In medieval times there was much sectarian feeling between the worshipers of Brahma, Krishna, Vishnu and Siva, each sect being jealous of its favorite system and devoted to its favorite god. Hence the Puranas, which were compiled about this time, were each of them devoted to the exaltation of the particular deity who happened to be the favorite of the compiler. In modern times Silva is the most popular object of worship with Brahmans, while Krishna is the favorite god of the lower classes. It is this idea which has contributed so much to the loss of the high ideals of religion so apparent to students of life in Modern Hindustan.

CHAPTER IV

SACRED BOOKS IN HISTORIC TIMES

MEANWHILE, branching out from the parent stock about the time of the first Vedic hymns, the Iranians developed a nation and a language of their own. Handed down from the Chaldean astrologers, influenced by those forces which are found in the Vedic hymns and changed by the Median magi who became the holders of the tradition, the Iranian concept found its unifier in Zarathustra or Zoroaster, as he is more generally known. The date of his birth is largely conjectural, but it seems probable that he lived a century or two before Gautama. The religion thus centralized by Zoroaster became one of the greatest and certainly the finest until Christian thought appeared. But of it little remains.

In the Asian East, in the southeastern inaccessible Persian mountains, live remnants of that ancient, mighty people, holding this great creed in the tenacity of the remembrance of their proud past, the few remaining followers of that great religion which reigned over Persia before its conquest by the Mohammedans. This people is known as the Parsees (Parsis). "As the Parsees are the ruins of a people," points out James Darmestetter in the introduction to his translation of "The Zend-Avesta," "so are their sacred books the ruins of a religion. There has been no other great belief in the world that ever ever left such poor and meager monuments of its past splendor."

Like to the excavation of ruins, however, is the story of the recovery, or rather the discovery, of the Avesta. The credit for this is due to a young Frenchman, Anquetil du Perron, who, in 1754, chanced to see in the Bodleian Library at Oxford a few pages in the Pahlavi character and who sacrificed everything to give this ancient language and this unknown literature to the world. Unfortunately, however, Du Perron was as egotistic and volatile as he was courageous and determined, and when he came to give his labors to the public he interlarded his work with copious references to himself, to his adventures and—alas for him—sarcastic comments on the ignorance and blindness of the English, who had done nothing to further progress in this regard. He was bitterly opposed by Sir William Jones, afterward the founder of the Royal Asiatic Society, who declared that the entire matter was a forgery and held up Du Perron to the obloquy of the learned world.

The controversy between Jones and Du Perron raged throughout the lifetime of the latter, tho, toward the last, the English scholar was compelled to admit that his assertion of deliberate forgery had been in error. Yet nothing more definite was known about the Avesta until Le Page Renouf, in his studies of Sanskrit, traced an affinity to the language of the Zoroastrian books, and interpreting them from this aspect, secured an authoritative translation. Soon after the ancient Persian inscriptions at Persepolis and Behistun were deciphered, revealing the existence at the time of the first Achemenian kings of a language closely connected with the early Pahlavi texts, and the last doubts as to the authenticity of the Avesta were removed.

The Zend-Avesta, as it is generally called (tho it is really the Avesta—the books, and the Zend—the commentary), is divided in its usual form into two parts. The first part, or Avesta properly so called, contains the Vendidad, the Visperad and the Yasna. The Vendidad is a compilation of religious laws and of mythical tales, the Visperad is a collection of litanies for the sacrifice and the Yasna is composed of litanies of the same order and of five hymns or Gathas written in a special dialect older than the general language of the Avesta. The second part, generally known as the Khorda-Avesta, or Small Avesta, is composed of short prayers, which are recited not only by the priests but by all the faithful at certain moments of the day, month or year and in presence of the different elements; these prayers are the five Gah, the thirty formulas of the Sirozah, the three Afrigan and the six Nyayis. But it is also usual to include in the Khorda-Avesta, altho forming no real part of it, the Yasts or hymns of praise and glorification to the several Izads and a number of fragments, the most important of which is the Hadhakht Nosk.

The loftiness of the aspirations of this creed does not appear so strongly in the later developments, but is found in its purest form in the earlier portion of the work, especially in the five Gathas, which, as has been said, are so markedly of a more ancient character than their dialect is even distinctly different. "In these Gathas," says A. V. Williams Jackson, perhaps the most interpretative authority the Avesta yet has produced, "we see before our eyes the prophet of the new faith speaking with the fervor of the Psalmist of the Bible. In them we feel the thrill of ardor that characterizes a new and struggling religious band; we are warmed by the burning zeal of the preacher of a church militant. The end of the world cannot be far away; the final overthrow of Anra-Mainyu (Ahriman the Evil One) by Ahura-Mazda (Ormuzd, the Holy Spirit) is assured; the establishment of a new order of things is certain; at the founding of this 'kingdom' the resurrection of the dead will take place and the life eternal will be entered upon."

One of the earliest of the Gathas is the Gatha Ustavaiti, and the following phrases of prayer from Yasna, xliv, show the nature of the books. The following are merely the first seven of a long invocation, first for knowledge as to the world itself, and, secondly, for information as to the best mode of spreading right and confuting wrong:

"This I ask Thee, O Ahura (God)! Tell me aright; when praise is to be offered, how shall I complete the praise of One like You, O Mazda (Lord)?

"This I ask Thee, O Ahura! Tell me aright; how, in pleasing Him, may we serve the Supreme One of the better world?

"This I ask Thee, O Ahura! Tell me aright; who gave the sun and stars their way? Who established that whereby the moon waxes and whereby she wanes save Thee? Who, as thus skillful, hath made sleep and the zest of waking hours?

"This I ask Thee, O Ahura! Who hath fashioned Aramaiti, the Beloved One?"

It is especially observable that while the Parsees of the present day are largely known as fire-worshipers, in the earlier portion of the Avestas, fire, while sacred, takes no such place as it does in the later Pahlavi texts. The Avesta, as has been said, was not written by Persians for Persians, but by Median magi for the use of the priestly body. Pahlavi is the medieval language of Persia. But the Persians had been in contact with many surrounding nations, and consequently not only their language but their ideas were of a heterogeneous character. It is this which has made the chiefest Pahlavi work, the Bundahis, a document of such transcendent interest.

The work in question is probably a free translation and commentary (the whole intermingled) of a book called Damdad Nask, belonging to the Avesta, which is lost, and it is of value as having been the storehouse whence many of the ancient philosophers found support for their theories. "The term Bundahis ('creation of the beginning')," says E. W. West in his translation "Pahlavi Texts," "is applied by the Parsees to a Pahlavi work which, in its present state, appears to be a collection of fragments relating to the cosmogony, mythology and legendary history taught by the Mazdayasnian tradition, but which cannot be considered, in any way, a complete treatise upon these subjects.

"The work commences by describing the state of things in the beginning, the good spirit being in endless light and omniscient and the evil spirit in endless darkness and with limited knowledge. Both produced their own creatures, which remained apart in a spiritual or ideal state for 3,000 years, after which the evil spirit began his op-

SACRED BOOKS IN HISTORIC TIMES

position to the good creation under an agreement that his power was not to last more than 9,000 years, of which only the middle 3,000 were to see him successful."

Thus, at the beginning of the Christian era, many diverse religions and philosophies were abroad, but all of them debased from their original purity. The finest of them all, Zoroastrianism, based upon the teaching of the Avesta, had degenerated through the Pahlavi texts and had suffered in the Macedonian conquest. The religions of China, with the rationalism of Taoism, the moral precepts and rules of life of Confucianism and the ceremonial observances of Chinese Buddhism, touched but little upon the Western world and they contained no life in themselves to set up a rivalry.

The Greek theogony also had become debased through familiarity. Anthropomorphic legends and myths had gone far to unify men with gods and gods with men. At the beginning of the Christian era Zeus or Jupiter was but a name, Athene or Minerva a poetic conception, Demeter or Ceres a holiday goddess of the early loved but not revered type of the modern Santa Claus. Iranian subtlety, Hebraic religion and Hellenic philosophy were all familiar, but were regarded as systems of thought, not religion.

The utter dearth of Sacred Literature in the Roman Empire formed a most marvellous setting for the shining forth of that finest of all religious writings, the New Testament. Like the Old Testament, it is in no sense the work of one writer, but rather is a selected group of writings from a mass of manuscripts which had arisen in the first three centuries of the Christian era. Just as the authority of the Old Testament rests upon the men who in Ezra's time decided what was to be allowed a place in the Old Testament canon, so a church council in 398 A.D. decided which gospel was to be admitted and what one thrown out, or whether a certain epistle was to be deemed genuine or spurious. But the decisions of this council were not so much with regard to the value of the documents considered as to their authenticity, a subject on which they would be well adapted to pudge.

The New Testament is divided into four parts, the Synoptic Gospels, those of St. Matthew, St. Luke and St. Mark, which give a synopsis of the life of Jesus of Nazareth, the writings ascribed to St. John including the Gospel, the Epistles and the Apocalypse; the Epistles written by St. Paul (which usually include the Epistle to the Hebrews, tho this probably was written by Apollos) and the Epistles of St. James, St. Peter and St. Jude. Each of these writers possesses a marked individuality, their style varies and even the language in which they wrote is different, for the Gospel of St. Matthew evidently was written originally in a Hebrew dialect (approximating

Aramaic), St. Luke is Hellenistic Greek and the writings of St. John are Hebraic Greek. These differences do not appear to any great extent in the authorized version, for the reason that the English therein, being a trifle archaic to a modern ear, stamps its own peculiarity upon its utterances rather than reveals the distinctions of the original authors.

Certain marked peculiarities stand out which may be commented on. Thus the Gospel of St. Matthew, written in the Aramaic vernacular commonly spoken in Palestine, was addressed to the Jews. Therefore the incidents of Christ's life are not related chronologically but in such wise as to show forth more strongly the fulfillment of ancient Jewish prophecies for the Messiah. It is a Jewish appeal to Jews. The Gospel according to St. Mark is a biography, pure and simple. It was probably the first written of the Gospels and, in generally accepted opinion, formed a basis for the writing of the Gospels of St. Matthew and St. Luke. The Gospel according to St. Luke is a Gospel to the Gentiles or non-Jews. It is written to display the human side of the life of Jesus of Nazareth, and therefore it is in St. Luke that the narrative of the Childhood is found. The author was a physician and seems to have been a personal friend of Mary the Mother of Jesus.

Far other is the Gospel according to St. John. It is not a synoptic gospel, does not aim to give the incidents of a Life as such, but rather mentions incidents to illumine some doctrinal or ethical point. It is obviously a supplemental gospel and implies a knowledge among its readers of a previous gospel, either oral or written. Its objective is the portrayal of the divine side of the Christ, as its great philosophic introduction in the first chapter witnesses. The Revelation of St. John, different in many ways, still possesses primarily this purposed elucidation of the divinity of Christ. It is no idle metaphor to say that battle has raged around this book, and this is the last place to enter the lists either for or against the higher criticism.

The Epistles, both Pauline and extra-Pauline, reveal upon the surface their origin and their purpose. They are letters written by the founder or the erstwhile teacher of a church, to the congregation from which he has been sundered. They are hortatory and advisory, dealing with all manners of subjects, from interpretations of difficult passages in the Gospels to minute directions as to how to behave in church. But, taken as a whole, it can be stated without fear of contradiction, that the Old Testament and the New Testament together stand in a position of unchallenged supremacy for loftiness of thought and chastity of diction among the Sacred Books of the world.

What may be deemed perhaps as characteristic an utterance as can be found in the New Testament is that of the Beatitudes, in the fifth chapter of St. Matthew's Gospel. The passage is as follows:

"And, seeing the multitudes, He (Jesus) went up into a mountain; and when He was set, His disciples came unto Him.

"And He opened His mouth and taught them, saying:

"'Blessed are the poor in spirit, for theirs is the Kingdom of Heaven.

"'Blessed are they that mourn, for they shall be comforted.

"'Blessed are the meek, for they shall inherit the earth.

"'Blessed are they which do hunger and thirst after righteousness, for they shall be filled.

"'Blessed are the merciful, for they shall obtain mercy.

"'Blessed are the pure in heart, for they shall see God.

"'Blessed are the peacemakers, for they shall be called the children of God.

"'Blessed are they which are persecuted for righteousness sake, for theirs is the Kingdom of Heaven.

"'Blessed are ye, when men shall revile you, and persecute you, and shall say all manner of evil against you falsely for My sake.

"'Rejoice and be exceeding glad, for great is your reward in Heaven: for so persecuted they the prophets who were before you.'"

That any Sacred Book should be written in an attempt to improve upon the sayings of the Founder of Christianity seems surprising today, and the Koran was regarded in the Middle Ages as a most blasphemous volume. But it must never be forgotten that the Koran was not intended as a sequence to the New Testament, it was not so written, but began as the sayings of a true and earnest religious reformer who was afire with zeal to put to an end the gross idolatries of his countrymen.

The old religion of the Arabs was Sabeanism, or the worship of the hosts of heaven, Seth and Enoch being considered as prophets of the faith, but this comparatively simple star worship had been greatly corrupted, and a number of fresh deities, superstitious practises and meaningless rites had been introduced. "The Arab," says E. H. Palmer in his translation of the Qur-An (Koran), "peopled the vast solitudes amidst which he dwelt with supernatural beings, and fancied that every rock and tree and cavern had its ginn or presiding genius."

The degrading polytheism of the Arabs in the sixth century of the Christian era, the multitude of their idols, the grossness of their worship and the degrading morals which usually accompany a false theology called for the reformer and the latter was found in Mohammed. The great Arabian prophet was born in 570 A.D. in Mecca, a member of the tribe to whom was entrusted the keeping of the worshipped Black Stone, reputed to have fallen from heaven at the same time as Adam. Mohammed therefore belonged to the highest Arabian aristocracy, but was afflicted with ill health. His ecstasies and his visions, often of the most fantastic character, were largely influenced by his weak condition, and while, as a subject to epilepsy, he fell into fits and trances his followers deemed divine, the morbid state influenced his teaching.

But he burned to tell his countrymen of their false idolatry and to lead them to the worship of a purer faith, and one day, in his fortieth year, after he had spent a month in solitude, he convinced himself that he had seen a vision of the Angel Gabriel, who declared to him that he was chosen prophet of Allah, the one and only God, and that the burden of leading his country on to the right paths devolved upon him. For nearly fourteen years he preached the gospel of faith, of purity of morals and of obedience to a high mental discipline, his only success in all those years being the conversion of thirteen people, most of them relatives and of the rest, one, a slave. He became deeply hated by the people of Mecca and at last fled to Medina. This was the Hegira, 622 A.D., the year from which the Mohammedans date the present era. It is the year one of the East.

Arrived at Medina, Mohammed changed his tactics. He gave forth (in his own words) that "different prophets have been sent by God to illustrate His different attributes: Moses His providence, Solomon His wisdom, Christ His righteousness, but I, the last of the prophets, am sent with the sword. Let those who promulgate my faith enter into no arguments or discussions, but slay all who refuse obedience. Whoever fights for the true faith, whether he fall or conquer, will assuredly receive a glorious reward, for the sword is the key of heaven. All who draw it for the defense of the faith shall receive temporal and future blessings. Every drop of their blood, every peril and hardship will be registered on high as more meritorious than fasting or prayer. If they fall in battle their sins shall be washed away and they shall be transported to Paradise to revel in eternal pleasures and in the arms of black-eyed houris."

He had struck the keynote. The impulsive emotionalism of the Arabs leaped in response to the cry of a "holy war," and the sterner their leader grew, the more he demanded conquest, the more obedient they became. When, on one occasion, he ordered them to a campaign in the extreme of summer and a captain protested, "It is hot," he vouchsafed no other answer than "Hell is hotter." Success hung over his troops at every onset until they believed themselves invincible, and so believing, overran all the contiguous country.

In the strictest sense of the word the Japanese have no Sacred Books. Buddhism and Confucianism have millions of followers, but the books of those faiths are but adaptations of the Upanishads and the King. Shintoism, the only purely Japanese cult, and which has its origin among the Aryan aborigines known as the Ainos, possesses nothing but the Norito and the Kojiki. The Norito are rituals of worship, merely disconnected and fragmentary services. A few of them show a certain rough grace.

But the religious observances prior to the introduction of Buddhism were of a very trifling character. "There was not even a shadowy idea of any code of morals," says Basil H. Chamberlain in "Things Japanese," "or any systematization of the simple notions of the people concerning things unseen. There was neither heaven nor hell, only a kind of neutral-tinted Hades. Some of the gods were good, some were bad, nor was the line between man and gods at all clearly drawn."

Against a fully formed and ornate Buddhism, strong in its own strength, with ceremonial, priestly systems and a gorgeous ceremonial, Shintoism had no chance to compete. In order to gain a good foothold, the Buddhist missionaries showed themselves interested in Shintoism, added the Shinto gods to the Japanese Buddhist Pantheon, carefully collected the Shinto legends and wove them into a book which is neither Shinto nor Buddhist, neither Japanese nor Chinese, but a fearful commixture of all of these, called the Kojiki, or Records of Great Matters. It was completed 712 A.D. "The Kojiki," comments W. G. Aston in his "History of Japanese Literature," "is a very poor production, whether we consider it as literature or as a record of facts. The language is a curious mixture of Chinese and Japanese, which there has been little attempt to endue with artistic quality."

No Sacred Books have been given to the world since that date. Hundreds of thousands of commentaries, of exegeses, of translations and comparative versions have been made; a vast apologetic literature hangs as a fog over them, but new Sacred Books there are none. Each century has seen, of course, some religious sect arising. Full many of these claim divine revelations, affirm that angels have foregathered with their founders and that a peculiar holiness attaches to their writings, but Sacred Books of the character of the Vedas, the Avestas, the Hebrew and Christian Scriptures and the Koran the modern ages have seen none. Whether the last "revelation" has been made, whether the silence is due to the abolition of superstition by accessible education, or whether a succeeding age will witness the rise and growth of some great faith and greater sacred literature is a question to which Time holds the only possible reply.

CHAPTER V

THE CLASSIC EPICS

Epic poetry is a phrase much changed from its older usages. Formerly a definition of some rigidity, it has now been extended to embrace such diverse elements as the battle-songs of Homer and the romances of Tasso, the folk-lore of the Kalevala and the polish of Ariosto, the floridity of the Ramayana and the austere somberness of Dante and Milton. Indeed, in common usage the epic has come to mean little more than a poem of considerable length, of definite unity of purpose, of loftiness of theme and of excellence of diction.

It is undoubted, therefore, that every literature that is worthy the name will contain such epics, as it is relevant to treat these great epics as developments of that literature and characteristic phases therein. Thus, in English literature, it is no injustice to treat Beowulf, Layamon, Chaucer, Spenser, Milton and Tennyson by their epics as the great figures in the development of English letters, rather than Sidney, Herrick, Suckling, Wordsworth, Shelley and Keats. The Sacred Books have carried the gradual development in the conception of man from his first written language to the ripeness of the New Testament as revealing his thoughts, worthy of transmission to posterity; the development of the epic will trace his conception of the values of secular thought and literary style.

Aristotle truly, in the fragmentary discussion of the epic which he left in his "Poetics," defined it as "that poetic imitation which is narrative in form and employs a single meter." He declared that "it should have for its object a single action, whole and complete, with a beginning, a middle and an end"; that "the beginning and the end must be capable of being brought within a single view"; that "the characters presented should be of a lofty type and consistently presented"; that "in the development both of the plots and of the characters the poem should present permanent truths rather than actual realities," and that "the subject matter should deal with probable impossibilities rather than probable possibilities."

"These statements," comments Irene T. Myers in "A Study of Epic Development," "are for the most part broad in application. Aristotle recognizes a difference between Nature's actual product and the ideal for which she strives; he believes that the ideal while frequently transcending the natural, is but the conception of Nature's intention,

THE CLASSIC EPICS

and that, as an expression of the real truth of things, it constitutes the material with which the poet should deal."

It has of late become the literary custom to speak of all the Hindu literature as being immeasurably more ancient than Semitic or Ionic; much in the same manner as a preceding generation accorded such veneration to the Chinese. But Confucius is not as old as the Israelitish monarch Solomon, and both Homer and Hesiod probably are his predecessors. The same is true of the Osirid hymns of ancient Egypt; their compilation is later than the Homeric period. So also, while the Mahabharata and the Ramayana of Hindu literature are of ancient date, there seems no adequate reason for withholding from Homer that position of priority he so long has held, and the great collection of the "blind poet of Chios" therefore will come first in point of treatment among the great epics of the world.

Homer is but little less mythical than the persons whereof he writes in the Trojan War. It is certain that he was rather the compiler than the author of the Iliad and the Odyssey, for he seems to have come rather at the end than at the beginning of a poetical epoch. Two causes have perpetuated the belief that Homer's home was in the island of Chios, one that a later so-called "Homeric hymn" speaks of its author as having been a blind old man living in Chios, the other that the Homeridæ, who claimed to be the descendants of Homer, lived in Chios. It is to be remembered that the Homeric poetry, strictly speaking, is not Greek at all, but Asian. The Iliad and the Odyssey had their first origin on the Ionian coast of Asia Minor, and Athens is only mentioned casually as a small but "well-built town."

The Iliad is so-called because it is the Poem of Ilion, or Troy, a city of Mysia, in the northwest of Asia Minor. It relates many of the events connected with the siege and capture of that city, but only touches on a small portion of the group of legends which had arisen about that war. It is enlarged and remodeled, evidently by several hands, from a shorter poem, which must have been extremely ancient, on the "Wrath of Achilles." This was probably little more than a lay or war song and was used as the central basis around which the rest of the Iliad was gathered. The siege lasted ten years, but the Iliad tells merely the events of a few days during the last year.

The cause of the war was the seizure of Helen, wife of Menelaus, King of Sparta, by Paris (also called Alexander), son of Priam, King of Troy. Helen was known as the fairest woman of the time, and it is a curious evidence of the barbarity of the times that during her youth, when she was wooed by a number of suitors, all of whom were kings and princes of neighboring tribes, her father bound these suitors with an oath to join in assisting her future husband, whoever he might be, should she be taken from him by force by a disappointed suitor. When, therefore, Paris forcibly captured her after her marriage to Menelaus, Agamemnon, King of Mycenae (the Myceneans were the strongest of all the tribes and were the progenitors of the Greeks), called together these aforetime suitors from Asia, Greece and all the isles and sailed with many ships to besiege Troy, to recapture Helen and avenge King Menelaus of Sparta.

It was a long siege, for the reason that within their walls the Trojans seemed invulnerable, and they did not dare to come out to fight a pitched battle against the Greek (or Mycenean) army because of Achilles, a warrior so terrible that none of the Trojans could face him, not even Hector, the greatest of the besieged people. During the war Achilles took to his tent a captive damsel, Briseis, and this girl King Agamemnon claimed for him in place of his own captive, whom the oracles had ordered to be returned. Achilles, angered in the highest degree, but scorning to take arms against the leader of his host and thereby foment civil warfare, withdrew from the army.

At this point the Iliad begins: "Sing, goddess, the wrath of Achilles." Its action is complicated by the constant interposition, now on one side, now on the other, of the gods and goddesses. In consequence the fate of battle changed ever, and even on Olympus the gods watched breathlessly; but with Achilles away, disaster hovered nearer and nearer the army of the Greeks. But, tho he knew of their losses, Achilles, angered at King Agamemnon, remained in his tent. At last his friend Patroclus, fearing that final ruin would come upon the army, besought Achilles at least to allow him to wear the famous armor, saying that the sight of it alone would strike such terror into the hearts of the Trojans that victory might return to the Greek side.

In Achilles' armor Patroclus performed prodigies of valor, but at last he found himself confronting Hector, and this greatest of the Trojans, more than a match for any save Achilles, slew Patroclus. The news of the death of Patroclus roused Achilles from his moodiness. Calling upon his mother, Thetis, one of the goddesses of the sea, to aid him, he secured a wonderful suit of armor from Vulcan, the god of the forge and patron of armorers, in place of the armor which had become the prize of Hector by the death of Patroclus.

In this armor Achilles rushed to the field alone, the Greeks following him in a confused but eager mass. Before his onrush the Trojans fell back, broke into flight and retreating helter-skelter to the gates of Troy, losing a man at every step through the vengeance of Achilles. Alone the hero would have followed into the town and stormed the citadel, but Apollo, taking the form of a warrior, engaged him in combat, then fled, drawing away Achilles long enough for the Trojans to shut the gates. Hector, who felt that he had ordered the advance to the fatal field, stood without the gate to resist Achilles.

THE CLASSIC EPICS

But when he saw the form of Achilles thundering down upon him, the heart of Hector forsook him and he fled, the Greek champion pursuing. At last, in order to give him courage, Athene appeared in the form of his brother Deiphobus, and seeing that they were two to one, Hector thought there might be a chance of resistance against Achilles. But as soon as the combat was joined Athene disappeared, leaving the battle to Hector. The issue was not long doubtful and Hector fell.

With more barbarity than would have been expected in a mighty warrior, Achilles scorned Hector's dying plea that his body should have due burial and exulted over his fallen foe by telling him of the disgrace that awaited his corpse. Then fastening the body to his chariot wheels, he dragged it back and forth before the gates of Troy. At last the aged Priam, King of Troy, humbling himself, went to Achilles' tent to beg the body of his son. The Iliad closes with a recital of the funeral ceremonies of the Trojans over the mighty Hector.

The second great Homeric epic, the Odyssey, does not take up the story where the Iliad left off, but deals entirely with the wanderings of Odysseus, or Ulysses as he is better known, and of the adventures he sustained on his voyage home from Troy, caused by his having offended Poseidon (Neptune), the god of the sea. When the Odyssey begins, ten years have elapsed since the surrender of Troy (the story of which is told in the Æneid, to be dealt with later), seven years of which Ulysses has spent on an island with a nymph Calypso, who loves him and has detained him there against his will. In the meantime his faithful wife, Penelope, altho besieged by a ravening host of suitors who quartered themselves upon her, wasting her sustenance, has refused all proffers, and when at last they become urgent, she promised to choose a second husband so soon as she should have finished weaving a certain shroud. But as she unraveled at night what she had woven by day, the web was long in finishing.

Observant of this loyalty, Zeus (Jupiter, chief of the gods) sent his messenger Hermes (Mercury) to Calypso to order her to let Ulysses go. The warrior escaped on a raft, but the sea god still pursuing his enmity wrecked the raft and Ulysses only reached the shore by the aid of the sea goddess Ino. He swam to the island of the Phacians, where King Alcinous entertained him, in return for which Ulysses told all his adventures, from the time of the fall of Troy until his arrival at the island of Calypso. In this recital the hero described the Cyclops and the one-eyed giant Polyphemus; the island of the enchantress Circe, who turned all his crew into swine until he compelled her to restore them to human form; the rocks where sat the sweet-voiced sirens who lure men to their deaths; the perilous passage between the hundred-headed Scylla and the whirlpool Charybdis, and how at last all his comrades perished because they had slain the sacred oxen of the Sun God.

King Alcinous, recognizing the greatness of the warrior, gave him a ship and men, and Ulysses landed on his own island of Ithaca. None recognized him, save his old nurse and Argus, the faithful dog, who creeping to his master's side, licked his hand and died. Ulysses, helped by Athene (Minerva, goddess of wisdom), then plotted the destruction of the suitors. Under the inspiration of the goddess, Penelope, who had at last been forced to finish her web by the suitors, announced that she would wed the suitor who could shoot an arrow through a certain mark, with the bow of Eurytus, which none but Ulysses could bend.

The suitors accordingly all tried and failed, but Ulysses, disguised as an old beggar man, took the bow they handed him for trial in jest, shot the mark, and then turning on the suitors, threw off his disguise, called on his son Telemachus and slaughtered every man in the hall. He then revealed himself to his wife and resumed the kingship.

Of a widely different character, but not the less deserving of fame among the founders of great epic poetry, was Hesiod, perhaps a century later in date than Homer. He is certainly earlier than the seventh century before Christ and is usually coupled with Homer, tho it is scarcely likely that he was contemporary. He was a Boeotian shepherd, a man with an intensely practical mind, and his two great masterpieces, "Work and Days" and the "Theogony," are didactic, not imaginative.

In the "Works and Days" there are really three parts. "These," R. C. Jebb suggests in his "Greek Literature, " "may once have been distinct. They comprise the introductory poem addressed to his brother Perses, the Works proper, and then the Days or Calendar. Hesiod and his younger brother Perses had divided the property left by their father, but Perses had got the larger share—according to the story of Hesiod—by bribing the judges, and accordingly 'lived in luxurious idleness,' while Hesiod faced poverty. Hesiod pointed out in his verse that Justice, so wronged, has taken refuge with her father, Zeus (Jupiter), who may be expected to avenge. He illustrated the injustice of the 'might is right' idea by a fable—the first in Greek literature—'the hawk and the nightingale.' It is in this part of his work also that Hesiod described the five ages of the world —the Age of Gold, the Age of Silver, the Age of Bronze, the Age of the Heroes (apparently an afterthought so as to fit in with the Homeric conceptions) and the Age of Iron, in which the poet had the sorrow to live."

He warned the unjust brother that he was laying up disaster of a deeper character because he would not work. The need of constant attention to duty and the worth of labor was strongly presented, and the poet took the opportunity of writing in verse a practical manual on farm industry, rules for sowing, for plowing, for reaping, with the required propitiary prayers for all the various operations. Thence by a natural sequence the poem went on to deal with the right times and seasons for the doing of these things and the lucky and unlucky "days" upon which to begin them. The need for this knowledge is shown to be very great, for amid such a host of gods and goddesses as there were in the Greek Pantheon it was difficult to avoid offending some of them.

In his "Works and Days" Hesiod shows himself to be especially careful of the honor to be shown the gods, and it is therefore not surprising that his next great work should be a "Theogony." This is no more original than his agricultural rules, no more determinative than his compilation of suitable prayers, but it is of vast importance because of its attempt to gather together into a collected whole the hymns, legends, traditions and folk-lore about the gods.

The "Theogony" falls naturally into two parts, the first describing the creation of the visible world, the second relating the manner wherein the life of the gods came forth from the earth itself and how they gave birth to the demigods, the demigods to heroes and the heroes to men. Chaos, the yawning abyss, composed of Void, Mass and Darkness all in confusion, was preëxistent to all else. From this confusion came forth Gaea (Earth) and Eros (Love) and with these two forces removed, Chaos produced Tartarus (Darkness) and Erebus (Night). Next came Uranus (Heaven), who through the influence of Eros took Gaea to wife, and these became the parents of the elder gods and of the gigantic Titans. Cronus, one of these elder gods, begot Zeus, who in turn rose against his father. Cronus was helped by the Titans, Zeus by the Cyclops, and at the last Cronus was defeated and Zeus became king of the Olympian gods and the father of heroes.

It has already been pointed out that the Iliad and the Odyssey touch on but two small sections of the Trojan siege and its after happenings, and not a few readers have been puzzled by their inability to find in these two great Homeric pieces and in the "Theogony" of Hesiod many events which have been the themes of modern poets, sculptors and artists, which themes, none the less, point back to the siege of Troy. These also belong to the group of legends and myths concerning the Trojan War, which the two great epicists left untouched, but which were worked up by the school of Cyclic poets in the period between 776 B.C. and 550 B.C. They were so called because they took the legends and wove them together in such wise as to be continuous, rearranging, where necessary, the chronology to do so.

They are enumerated by Jebb, and the most important groups are six in number. These are: (1) The Cyprian Lays, written by Stasinus of Cyprus, relating the preparations for the siege of Troy and the first nine years of the siege up to the very point where the Iliad begins. (2) The Lay of Ethiopia, by Arctinus of Miletus, telling how the Amazons or tribe of women warriors came to the help of Troy, how their queen was killed by Achilles and how Achilles was treacherously slain by Paris, whose capture of Helen had caused the Trojan War; it is so called because the Ethiopian prince Memnon is the central figure. (3) The Sack of Troy by the same author, a supplement to the preceding. (4) The Little Iliad, by Lesches of Mitylene; this somewhat overlaps the work of Arctinus in that it continues the Iliad down to the fall of Troy, but it is devoted mainly to the exploits of Ajax and Philoctetes. (5) The Homeward Voyages, by Agias of Troezen; this gives the adventures of the various heroes in their return from Troy during the ten years which elapsed until Homer's poem begins with Ulysses on Calypso's island. (6) The Lay of Telegonus, by Eugammon of Cyrene; this told how Telegonus, the son of the enchantress Circe, born to her shortly after Ulysses' departure from the island, was sent by his mother to avenge her because Ulysses had made her free all her captives, and how at last Ulysses was slain by him in Ithaca.

It cannot be said that Virgil in his Æneid becomes a serious rival to Homer, both because it is clear that he is a copyist and because it is defaced by political flatteries. As a poem, however, it is perhaps finer in detail and infinitely more lovely in thought. The old Homeric epic is thoroly archaic, and as was noted in Achilles' barbaric triumph over the fallen Hector and the pusillanimous grudge of certain of the gods, is lacking in many of the better instincts of a later time; but Virgil is not wanting here. "In soundness of judgment," says Lord, "in tenderness of feeling, in chastened fancy, in delineation of character, in matchless beauty of diction and in splendor of versification it has never been surpassed by any poem in any language and proudly takes its place among the imperishable works of genius."

Publius Virgilius Maro (70-19 B.C.) was born near Mantua, of comparatively humble birth. His life, unlike that of the other great epic poets, was unmarked by special grief or disadvantage. He was first brought to the notice of the emperor by his skill as a veterinarian in the imperial stables, and there his multifarious learning (he studied privately assiduously) procured him the reputation of a sorcerer. On his father's death he returned to the little farm, where Mæcenas, a Roman noble, now become his patron, and at his instance, in order to ennoble the art of husbandry which was falling into disuse, Virgil wrote the most beautiful poem in the Latin language, the "Georgics." They are largely modeled on Hesiod's "Works and

Days," but are infinitely superior. The unparalleled success of the Georgics led to the Æneid.

It is at least to Virgil's credit that his purpose in the selection of this theme was of the loftiest. "Availing himself of the pride and superstition of the Roman people," says Henry Thompson in his "History of Roman Literature," "the poet traces the origin and establishment of the 'Eternal City' to those heroes and actions which had enough in them of what was human and ordinary to excite the sympathies of his countrymen, intermingled with persons and circumstances of an extraordinary and superhuman character to awake their awe. No subject could have been more happily chosen. It has been admired also for its perfect unity of action, for while the episodes command the richest variety of description, they are always subordinate to the main object of the poem, which is to impress the divine authority under which Æneas settled first in Italy."

Æneas was described in the Æneid as having been one of the princes of Troy who had stayed in the city almost to the end of the siege, but having been warned by the ghost of Hector in a dream, determined upon flight. He left shortly before the taking of Troy, bearing his aged father, Anchises, on his shoulder, carrying in one hand the gods of his household, while with the other he led his little son Julius (Ascanius). By this Virgil desired to depict his hero as having been loyal to his city, as having been pious to his gods and as showing filial affection and domestic devotion. His wife, Creusa, was separated from him in the course of the escape and he could not turn back to seek her.

He first landed at Thrace, where he commenced to build a home to form the nucleus of a city to be called Ænos, but the omens were unpropitious. He sought the oracle at Delphi, and misinterpreting the cryptic response, went to Crete. Thence he was driven away by pestilence. He determined then to sail for Italy, but the passage became perilous in the extreme and on the voyage Anchises died. A storm arose, preventing his landing, and he was blown to the north shore of Africa, where he was warmly welcomed by Dido, Queen of Carthage.

The queen, knowing the noble blood than ran in the veins of her guest, and fired besides by his youth and comeliness, was found only too willing to share her throne with him, but as the wedding preparations were in progress Mercury appeared, sent by Jupiter, to warn Dido against marrying Æneas, as mighty Jove had other fate in store for him, and Dido, disappointed and her pride in arms, destroyed herself. Æneas then hastily sailed away and landed in Sicily.

Here the sailors, who had grown tired of going from place to place with no settled home, endeavored to burn the fleet. At this Æneas consulted the Sibyl at Cumae, who conducted him to the infernal regions, where he saw his father, Anchises, and the ghost told him his future fate in Italy. On his return to earth Æneas set sail, landing in Latium. Here he made an alliance with the King Latinus, married his daughter Lavinia, and built Lavinium. A rejected suitor, Turnus, king of the Rutuli, made war on Latinus and in the battle both kings were slain. With the death of Turnus the Æneid closes. Livy, later, made Æneas the king of the Latins and of the Rutuli and thence the father of the founders of Rome.

The "Metamorphoses" of Publius Ovidius Naso (43 B.C.-17 A.D.), an interminable series of narratives drawn from classical mythology, are wonderfully rich in flights of fancy, and in certain places the tenderness of feeling shown is as unexpected as it is delightful. His versification is fluent, too fluent indeed, losing in force what it gains in ease. That he was not a great epic writer was because he had no great theme to treat, no purpose to fulfil.

A truer epic is the "Pharsalia" of Lucan, who was tortured and slain at the age of twenty-seven from a false accusation of conspiracy against Nero. The "Pharsalia" is full of faults; indeed, no really great work exists wherein weaknesses are so numerous. Yet while its plan is artificial and its characters are indistinct and undifferentiated, it does possess a real and splendid strength.

"Among the shades of the poetical coloring, none tends to give the 'Pharsalia' so peculiar an air as the originality of its supernatural machinery," says Wm. Spalding in his "Italy." "The beautifully cold mythology of Greece has here no place; the supreme powers which hover above the field of civil slaughter are the native divinities and native dead of Rome and Latium. In the beginning of the contest terrible portents in heaven and in earth affright the people; the Etruscan rites elicit no prophetic answer; a raving woman rushes through the streets of the city prophesying uncertain horrors; the ghost of Sylla rises in the field of Mars, and the last supernatural terrors which close around Pompey are summoned by the spells of a Thessalian witch, whose incantation forms one of the most strongly painted scenes in the circle of Roman poetry.

The republican Lucan was succeeded by Statius, the court poet of Domitian. His chief work, the "Thebias," an epic poem in ten books, on the story of the two sons of Œdipus, is by no means his best production, tho far the most labored. It has a want of symmetry and coherence, which, with its long-drawn diffuseness and its exaggerated monotony of horror and cruelty, makes it wearisome to read. Yet poor as the epic seems, it is the last; the Goths were knocking at the gates of Rome, as yet only as individuals, but later to come in hordes. Greece was about to become Byzantine, and Rome barbarian, and the literature of the Classic Age dwindled and sank and died.

CHAPTER VI

THE EPICS OF THE ORIENT

VERY different in character, but not less great, are the epics of the Orient. Of these two are Hindu and the third Persian. Between them is a marked difference, not only the difference between the true ancient hero-epic and the modern romance-epic, but also a wide difference in philosophic viewpoint. Language holds few things sweeter than the love-verse of the Persians, but for nobility of theme not even Homer himself can surpass the two great epics of the Hindus, the Ramayana and the Maha-bharata.

The subject of both epics is a war undertaken to recover the wife of one of the warriors who was carried off by the hero on the other side. In this the Ramayana corresponds in thought to the Iliad, but Sita, the chaste and beautiful wife of Rama, is a thousandfold more lofty in conception than the fickle Helen of Troy, and Savitri, in the Maha-bharata, is perhaps the finest wifely character in the whole realm of Literature ancient or modern. Her importunacy of the dread god of Death for the body of her husband as he trod the gloomy wastes to his own sad abode is one of the most beautiful passages ever penned.

The Ramayana is held to be one of the most sacred of all the Hindu productions. Like other works of the same class, it boldly lays claim to supernatural powers, declaring that "Whoever reads or hears the Ramayana will be freed from all sin. The Ramayana heals diseases, removes all fear of enemies, compensates for the loss of wealth or fame, prevents loss of life and secures all that is desired."

The plot and unity of the poem show it to have been originally the work of one man, but his name is lost to the historian, and there are three different versions now in existence. The one best known and most popular among Europeans is ascribed to Valmiki himself; but Tulasi-dasa, who was born 1544 A.D., and Vyasa took the crude legend which had for generations been repeated from father to son, and remodeled and finished it, each in his own peculiar style. The Ramayana seems almost interminable, consisting of 24,000 slokas or verses, and the brief abstract which follows and which is taken partly from the transcription by E. A. Reed in "Hindu Literature," scarcely does more than touch the mere outlines of the plot.

In the midst of unparalleled magnificence there lived in Ayodhya (Oude) a childless king, Dasaratha. Altho descended from the sun, his line threatened to become extinct, for there was no heir to his throne, and in despair the raja resolved to perform a stupendous sacrifice in order to propitiate the gods.

The gods, pleased with the sacrifice, went in a body to Brahma to intercede with him on behalf of the raja and to present a petition of their own. This latter was the ridding the world of the hideous ten-headed demon Ravana.

But Ravana aforetime had secured from Brahma the promise that he should not be slain by gods, by other demons or genii. Brahma having bestowed this promise, found himself in a dilemma, but he conducted the gods to the home of Vishnu, on an island in the sea of milk. The great Vishnu, the lord of all the world, was gracious to his divine petitioners and answered: "Be no longer alarmed; your foe shall fall before my feet. Ravana in his pride of power did not ask Brahma to preserve him from men or from monkeys, for he deemed them beneath his notice. I will myself be born as the son of Dasaratha. You shall assist me by assuming the form of monkeys, and together we will overthrow this terrible enemy of gods and men."

Soon after the conclave of the gods had received from Vishnu a favorable answer to their petition, the principal wives of Dasaratha bore him four sons, Rama, Bharata, Lakshmana and Satru-ghna.

Each nation has an undoubted right to its own ideal, but the personal appearance which is ascribed to Rama hardly accords with modern ideas of beauty. He is represented as being of "a beautiful color like green grass, with fine, glossy hair and a large head. His nose was like that of the green parrot, his legs resembled plantain trees and his feet were red as the rising sun."

The raja Janaka, who ruled over a neighboring province, was the possessor of the wonderful bow of Siva, and no man could handle the great bow or the heavy arrows of the vindictive god. Janaka therefore issued a proclamation that he who could bend this bow should receive in marriage his beautiful daughter Sita, whose fame as the loveliest of living creatures is presented as world-wide.

When the bow was brought into the royal presence for the suitors' trial it lay in a great car, which moved upon eight wheels and was drawn by five thousand strong men; but Rama stepped forward and took the bow that none could lift from the car with his right hand and with the other hand bent the bow nearly double, so that it broke with a crash. The feat was unparalleled, and after lengthy ceremonies and with much pomp Sita was given in marriage to this wonderful warrior.

Rama thus being wed, in accordance with custom his father, the rajah, desired that he be installed as vice-rajah, that he might learn the ways of government, but Kaikeyi, the youngest and most beautiful wife of Dasaratha, mother of Bharata, had been burning with jealous rage ever since the joy and feasting over Rama's marriage began, and now the great preparations to install him as vice-rajah made her resolve to defeat him if possible. She remembered that some years before, when the rajah was wounded in battle, she had nursed him tenderly, and in his gratitude he had promised her any two boons she might ask. The jealous mother then reminded the rajah of the two favors which he had promised when she had saved his life by her care and which she now claimed. "The first favor," she said, "is that my son Bharata be installed this day instead of Rama and the second is that Rama may be banished to the forest of Dandaka (a forest infested by demons), to lead the life of a hermit and to clothe himself in deerskins and in the bark of trees for fourteen years."

The rajah sought by every means in his power to avert the calamity, but Kaikeyi calmly told Rama herself, knowing that to keep his father's promise inviolate he would willingly go into exile. When Sita heard her husband's resolve, however, no argument could dissuade her from accompanying him into the forest, and followed by the tears of all the people of the city, they left luxury for hardship, plenty for privation, safety for danger.

The plot of Kaikeyi failed in part, however, for Bharata resolutely refused to profit by his mother's evil and followed Rama into the forest, beseeching him to return. But Rama stated that he had taken a vow to obey his father, and tho that father had died upon his leaving the court, still he would stay away the fourteen years. Whereon Bharata took the sandals that Rama had been wearing, ordered that the royal canopy should be spread above them and vowed that he, in the dress of a devotee, would administer the affairs of the realm in the name of Rama till his brother should return.

The perils of the forest at first appeared little to the loving husband and wife, for all the woodland creatures became tame, but the Rakshasas, or forest demons, hated them. At last one of these, determined to separate the pair, assumed the guise of a young woman and permitted herself to be found by Rama while engaged in the chase. His kindly sympathy she endeavored to transform to love, but he pointed out that, come what may, he would be faithful to Sita. Then in anger the she-demon ran to the tent to slay Sita, but Lakshmana, who had been left to guard his sister-in-law, cut off the nose and ears of the assailant with his sword, and she, returning to her base form, fled howling into the forest. The other Rakshasas joined in an attack on Rama, but the latter seized the bow of Vishnu and, single-handed, conquered the army of demons. The credit of the demon world was at stake, and an appeal was made to Ravana, the demon king of Ceylon, the enemy of gods and men. There were ten hideous heads upon his colossal form and twenty strong arms bade defiance to his foes. Each frightful head wore a golden serpent as a crown. He was taller than the Himalayas, and reaching upward, he could stop the stars in their courses. Such was the fear he inspired, that every living thing shuddered and shrunk out of sight upon his approach. Even the winds crept silently by and the angry sea forgot to rave and only moaned in terror when he looked upon her billows.

The she-demon, displaying her wound and calling for vengeance, adroitly suggested to Ravana that the woman Sita was the most lovely of the daughters of the earth and so inflamed the demon-king's imagination that he himself called his chariot and started for the distant forest. Arrived there, he bade one of his followers assume the shape of a fawn of gold and thus decoy Rama from Sita's side. Then assuming Rama's voice and calling for help, Lakshmana was drawn away and Sita was left alone.

Ravana approached the hut in the guise of a mendicant priest and the princess willingly told him her story. Then the mighty rajah of the Rakshasas said to her, "I am Ravana, the terror of the world. I have assumed this lowly form only to gain admission to your presence, for my power is known throughout the universe. You shall be the chief of all my wives and five thousand handmaids shall attend you."

The princess scorned him and threatened him with the wrath of Rama until the demon-god was angered and showed himself to her in his true form, vast as a mountain and terrible as Yama, the King of Death. His red eyes glared upon her and his enormous body seemed to be covered with bristles of fire. With his ten horrible heads and twenty terrible arms he stood before her like a black, angry cloud flashing with lightnings. With one pitiful cry of "Rama! Rama!" she fainted at his feet, and he, lifting her from the ground, carried her to his chariot.

A vulture, who had been fatally wounded by the demon-king in an attempt to snatch the woman from his arms, revealed to Rama who was his foe, and armed with this information, the bereaved husband hastened to the King of the Monkeys for assistance. He arrived at an opportune moment, and being so fortunate as to be able to help Sugriva, the king, he secured his powerful aid, and Hanuman, the great monkey general, was sent on a reconnoisance. As J. Talboys Wheeler says in his "History of India," "The narrative of Rama's alliance with the monkeys exercises a weird influence upon the imagination. . . . The mind is called up to deal with nondescript beings, half monkey and half man; having long tails and walking upon all fours, and yet performing funeral rites for a deceased rajah and installing a successor upon the throne with all the forms of ceremony of human beings."

Hanuman crept through the city of Lanka in the form of a cat until he found Sita, still resisting the bribes and endearments of Ravana. The captive would not escape, desiring only to be rescued by Rama, so in part revenge on the demon-king, Hanuman ravaged a grove of mango-trees and then set the city on fire, returning to Rama and Sugriva with the report of his success.

At last the expedition was ready and an innumerable host of monkeys awaited the word of command to march upon Lanka. The rajah had given the control of his troops into the hands of Rama, who was commander general, while Lakshmana and Sugriva were his chiefs of staff. The vast army extended in length a thousand miles. Over a bridge made by the aid of a sea goddess the hosts marched to the island capital of the demon-king. The forces joined in combat immediately.

Finding that the tide of battle was going against his troops Ravana marched to the field in person at the head of powerful re-enforcements. As the terrible conflict continued Rama and Ravana came face to face in the fight and were soon engaged in single combat. The god Indra looked down from heaven, and seeing that Rama was without a chariot, sent him his own, with armor and weapons, and also his charioteer. As the terrible duel progressed, the other gods became so absorbed in the fight that they could not refrain from joining in the fray.

As the fight grew more and more desperate the combatants drew closer, and at last an arrow hissing from Rama's bow cut off one of Ravana's heads; but like the hydra whose heads were severed by Hercules, another immediately grew in its place. Again and again he cut a heat from the demon, only to see it renewed by the time he could draw his bow again.

"Then Matali to Rama cried:
'Let other arms the day decide.
Launch at the foe thy dart whose fire
Was kindled by the Almighty Sire.'
He ceased, and Raghu's son obey.
Upon his string the hero laid
An arrow like a snake that hissed,
Whose fiery flight had never missed.
By Brahma's self on him bestowed
When forth to fight Lord Indra rode.

. . . .

"He laid it on the trusted cord
And turned the point at Lanka's lord,

> And swift the limb-dividing dart
> Pierced the huge chest and cleft the heart,
> And dead he fell upon the plain,
> Like Vritra by the Thunderer slain."

But when all men looked to see Sita restored to favor, her husband, the victim of false Hindu ideas of honor, would not receive her, and when she came, all gladness and rejoicing to meet him, he repulsed her and declared that revenge and not rescue had been the cause of his attack upon the demon-king.

Thereupon Sita, desiring not to live, ordered that a funeral pyre be built, and sadly averring her spotless innocence, she passed into the flames and the pyre burnt on amidst the cries and lamentations of the multitude, when lo! the god of fire came forth from the flames, bearing Sita in his arms. Giving her to Rama, Agni said: "Take her as your wife. She is without a stain. I know the hearts of all, and had she the shadow of a stain upon her chastity she would never have passed in safety from me." Then Rama placed his arm around her, and declaring that his sternness had been but for the purpose of securing this evidence of her innocence, restored to her rightful place the queen. Then, the fourteen years of exile being accomplished, he returned in triumph to his own kingdom.

At last, however, it began to be whispered in the capital that a woman who had spent months of her life at the court of the demon-king was unfit to be the queen of Ayodhya. "The king knew," writes Miss Reed, "his wife as pure as the snow upon the peak of Himalaya; he knew that she was as far above immorality as that icy coronal was above the dust in the vale at its feet, but this divine Rama had not the manliness to stand by his devoted wife and banished her to the forest under the guise of having her seek the counsel of a sage.

"Over long stretches of desert and through wild jungle the exiled wife struggled on her unknown way, tho the birds in pity dipped their pinions in the waters of the Ganges and fanned her feverish face that she might not faint with the heat, and the royal tiger walked beside her to protect her from the hungry wolves in the wilderness. But at last she fell fainting by the way and was found in a swoon by Valmiki the sage, who lifting her tenderly in his arms, carried her to his hermitage." That very night Sita gave birth to two boys whom she named Lava and Kusa.

The two sons of Sita were carefully educated by Valmiki. Before they were twenty years of age they had attained to physical and mental manhood. One day, however, they seized a horse, made sacred as a sacrifice for the king, and refused to give him up. An army sent to capture them was defeated by these two sons of Rama, whereupon the rajah himself went to meet them, and learning that their mother's

THE EPICS OF THE ORIENT

name was Sita and realizing that these two stalwart warriors were his own sons, was overcome with emotion and gladly assented when the sage urged him to be reconciled to his wife.

Rama made the condition, however, that Sita should again go through the ordeal of fire. But Sita's love had cooled, and when she was persuaded to come forth by Valmiki, instead of invoking the god of fire, as before, she said: "Oh, Earth, if I have never turned my thoughts toward any man but Rama; if my truth and purity are known to thee; I beseech of thee to open a passage for me and receive me into thy bosom, for I will never again behold the face of and living creature."

On hearing these terrible words a thrill of horror ran through the multitude, the earth thus appealed to slowly heaved and opened and out of the newly formed abyss arose a splendid throne, supported by four of the sacred serpents. Then the beautiful goddess of the earth came from the chasm, wearing a robe of molten silver, and led Sita to the throne and took a seat beside her. The glad earth slowly closed and the gods sang praises to the enthronized. But the terror-stricken spectators, turning their eyes upon Rama, beheld him groveling upon the ground in agony. At length the aged and heart-broken king returned to the palace, taking his sons with him, but Sita he never saw again.

Of less poetical value, but of greater worth as pseudo-history, is the "Great War of Bharata," or the Mahabharata. It is the most gigantic poetic work in literature, consisting of two hundred and twenty thousand lines, while the Iliad and Odyssey combined contain only about thirty thousand. Unlike the Ramayana, it is not a single poem; it is an immense collection of Hindu mythology, legend and philosophy. To relate the details of the thread of fratricidal war that links the whole together would be purposeless. In spirit and in treatment it compares with the Ramayana. There is an apparently authentic tradition to the effect that the Kauravas, who were the sons of the blind Rajah Dhrita-rashtra, engaged in a long bitter rivalry with their cousins, the Pandavas, who were the sons of Rajah Pandu, and that it was this rivalry between the two branches of the royal house that led to the great war from which the Mahabharata derives its name.

But there is occasionally a germ of sentiment which ought to be preserved, such as the victory of love over death in the beautiful legend of Savitri and Satyavan. This little poem is well worthy of the attention which has been given it by various scholars, the condensation hereinafter partly follows E. A. Reed's excellent description in "Hindu Literature," partly Sir Edwin Arnold's famous and beautiful setting in "Indian Idylls." Of all the myths of the Mahabharata it is perhaps the purest and most touching.

King Asva-pati had as his only daughter the beautiful Savitri, who was so lovely, so rich and so scornful of her suitors that none dared to ask for her hand, and the princess at last was given the right to travel and choose her own lord. But the rajahs in their luxurious courts wearied her, and she was returning to her home when she stopped at a hermitage, where the aged hermit and his wife were tended by a handsome youth, their only son. The princess looked upon him thoughtfully, then proceeded on her journey homeward.

One day the Maha-raja sat in his council hall with the sage Narada. They were talking in low tones of the affairs of state when the king's daughter was announced. Standing before the sage, with her face crimsoned with blushes, she said, "Father, I have been long away; I have visited the courts of princes; I have offered sacrifice in the sacred groves, and I found in one of these the banished king of Chalva, who lost his throne and kingdom because of blindness. Their loyal son ministers to their wants; he brings them fruit and game for food; he feeds their sacrificial fire and pulls the sacred kusa grass. Him I have chosen."

Then said Narada, "Not he, my child—thou canst not choose the banished Satyavan. He is both brave and noble; a grander youth ne'er trod a kingly court, but o'er his head there hangs a fearful fate. He is doomed to die, and in a year the gods decide that he must go."

But the girl replied, "A loyal heart can choose but once and a loyal sire will not revoke his promise.

Elaborate preparations were made for the wedding and before many weeks passed the bridal train left the city for the hermitage, and the exiled king and hermit blessed the union. But no sooner were the rajah and his queen gone than Savitri laid aside her costly jewels and her silken robes and donned the rough garments that befitted her new station as a hermit's wife. She could not wear a finer robe than he; she could not see her hands decked with gold and gems while his were rough with toil.

The little family dwelt in their forest home in sweet content, but Savitri carried a fearful dread—a counting of the days when the death decree should be fulfilled. This she bore alone, saving the others pain. Each night the sun went down she knew that one day less remained to Satyavan. At last the days had nearly fled and her songs were hushed in tearful prayers. When the time was nearly come she sat beneath a great tree like a beautiful statue for three long days and nights, mutely imploring the gods to save from death's decree the man she loved.

The fateful day dawned at last and found her weak and faint, but she would not taste of food. Only one plea she made—that she might go with Satyavan when he went out into the forest to cut the sacred wood for the evening sacrifice, and tho he tenderly remonstrated, she

THE EPICS OF THE ORIENT

pleaded still and he set out, ax in hand through the wilderness, making a path for the woman's feet that patiently followed his own.

Afar from home they gathered fruits and flowers for the evening sacrifice, and all the while the anxious wife watched with aching heart every look and motion of her lord. At last he reeled in sudden pain and cried, "I cannot work," and falling at her feet, lay still.

Suddenly at her side she saw a fearful shape, that seemed neither god nor man, tall and dark with visage grim, his garments crimson as if with blood, his eyes glowing like burning coals in their deep sockets. In one hand he bore a long black noose and bent over Satyavan. As the specter leaned above her husband the trembling princess prayed to know who he was and why he came. He answered, "I am Yama, the god of death, and I am come to bear away the soul of Satyavan."

"But," pleaded the wife, "'tis thy messengers that bear away the soul of men. Why is it, mighty chief, that thou hast come?"

"Because Prince Satyavan was the grandest, noblest of his race," replied the god, "and none save Yama's self was worthy to bear his soul away," and bending lower still he fitted the dreadful noose and drew out the soul of Satyavan. Then silently he strode away toward the southland with his prize.

But the stricken princess hastened on behind the fearful King of Death. At last he turned.

"Go back," he said. "Why dost thou follow in my steps?"

But she replied: "Wherever my lord is borne, there I shall surely go; he is my life, my all; I cannot leave him, and I must go with thee. By reason of my wifely love thou wilt let me come."

And still she followed on until the King of Death himself felt pity for the faithful wife, and turning back he said: "Return, my child, to life and health. Thy wifely love is good, but the kingdom of Yama is not the place for thee. Still, I will grant thee any boon that thou dost crave, except this life that I am bearing away."

Then said Savitri, "Let the blind and banished king, my husband's father, have both his sight and throne restored."

"It shall be so," returned the god. "I grant thee this, but now turn back; our way is long and dark; already thou art weary and thou wilt die upon the road."

"I am not weary," said Savitri; "I cannot tire while I am near to Satyavan. Wherever he is borne, there must I go."

And the tireless feet toiled patiently on behind the King of Death until he turned again and said: "Darkness is coming on; soon thou canst not find thy way alone. I will give to thee another boon—anything except this life—and then thou must return."

Quickly the princess thought of her own sire, whose only child now followed Death—thought of his lonely home and coming age, and she said, "Give to my father princely sons to bear his royal name."

"So shall it be," returned the mighty king, "and now I have granted thy wishes, go back to life and light."

But she only answered plaintively, "I cannot go, great king. I cannot leave my lord. Thou hast taken him and my heart is in thy hand. I must surely come with thee."

At last they came to a cavern, dark and damp as death itself, and here again Yama turned upon the pitiful figure in the darkness behind him and this time demanded fiercely, "Art thou still upon my path? In pity for thy grief I will give anything thou will except this life within my hand."

Then answered Savitri, "Give me children—the sons of Satyavan. Let me bear to him loyal heirs of his goodness and his truth."

Death smiled grimly. Should he be conquered yet by this little Hindu wife? But he answered: "Yama hath promised thee, and I must grant thee even this."

Then with rapid strides he entered the great vault of the cavern, while the startled bats and owls made the place more hideous with their cries. But still he heard the patter of patient feet behind him, and his burning eyeballs blazed in the darkness upon Savitri. "Go back," he said. "Thou shalt return; I will bear no longer with thy persistent following!"

"I would go back, oh, mighty Yama, if I could," wailed the weary wife, "but in your hands you carry my own life. 'Tis only my helpless frame that follows thee, and now I am so weak with grief and fear that I must come nearer to Satyavan"; and the tired head drooped upon the dark, cold hand of Death, close to the life she craved. The pitiless king felt the touch of tear-wet cheeks and clinging hair, and again his heart was softened by her faithful love.

"Thou art innocence itself and tenderness and truth," said Yama. "Thou hast taught me lessons new of woman's fidelity. Ask any boon thou wilt and it shall be thine."

Then at his feet she fell in joy. "This time, oh, king," she cried, "thou hast excepted nothing, and I ask not wealth, nor throne, nor heaven itself. I crave my heart, my life—give me my Satyavan!"

The fire in his eyes beamed more softly as he said: "Fair queen, thou art the brightest gem of womankind. Here, take thy Satyavan. Saved by his peerless wife, he long shall live and reign with her, and his line shall be upheld by princely sons who shall call thee mother. Go now, my child, time hasteth, and long hast thou been with me." Then turning gloomily away, he went down—down into the darkness of the cavern. But the glad wife, holding her precious treasure close to her heart, retraced her steps back through the darkness of cavern and wood, her torn feet climbing the ascending pathway, fearing nothing, knowing nothing, save that in her arms she carried her beloved.

THE EPICS OF THE ORIENT

The greatest of the modern epics of the East unquestionably is the Shah-Namah of Firdusi, who wrote in the beginning of the eleventh century. It is a valuable Persian classic, but despite the fact that it possesses a national aspect is not truly national. At this time the ancient Oriental Epics and the Classic Epics were thoroly familiar, and most of the incidents in the Shah-Namah will be found to be adaptations (either conscious or unconscious) therefrom. Moreover, it lacks a consistent story and a coherent whole.

It tells the wondrous birth of the hero Rustem, how that he was brought up by a Simurgh (roc?), a mighty bird who caught elephants for its young. (Compare the Song of Gudrun.) The hero, leading the Persian hosts, secured a determinative victory over the Turanian invaders and forced them to an assurance that they would return to their own territory and refrain from further attempts upon the peace of Persia. But the old Persian king died, his boastful successor, Kai-Kaus, taking his place, and the newly crowned monarch, not content with peace and having heard of the riches of the Tartar hordes, defied the hosts of Mazinderan.

Rustem opposed the campaign, and the king led his hosts without the presence of his famous warrior. The Tartar chieftain, however, called the army of "White Demons" to his aid (compare the Maha-bharata), the braggart king was taken prisoner and blinded and the royal prisoner was placed in custody in the capital city of the Land of the Demons. Rustem, loyal despite the monarch's slight, set out to rescue him, passing through six fearful perils (compare the Labors of Hercules), only to be confronted at the last with the task of storming the mountain-dwelling of the White Demon single-handed. This, however, he did, and after a fearful struggle slew the hated chief of the demons. Having—with the blood of the White Demon—cured his king's blindness, Rustem returned to the court.

Out hunting one day, having lain down to sleep as night fell, some Tartar horseman stole his famous horse Rakush. The warrior traced the steed to Samenegan, the capital of Turan, and quietly entered the city of his foes and demanded the steed from the king. But while the search was proceeding, Rustem met the daughter of the Turanian king, and mutual love hastened the bridal. The Tartar bride, as time went on, grew jealous of the Persian home-longings of Rustem, and when her son was born she sent word to the father that it was a girl to avoid his taking the boy away. Therefore a matter of no interest, the child was kept hidden, and the boy grew to manhood without ever having been seen by his father.

This son was Sohrab, a hero almost as great as Rustem. Seeing this complication, the Tartars ingeniously fomented war with Persia and Rustem returned to his native soil to head the army, leading it against a force commanded—all unknowingly to him—by his son.

Sohrab, fatally wounded by Rustem, revealed his parentage, and Rustem was stricken with grief at the knowledge of his having slain his only son and his realization of his wife's deceit.

The latter part of the story—hundreds of thousands of lines in length—tells of the jealousy of the king against Rustem, of his sending against him in combat the hero Isfendiyar, of the death of Isfendiyar and of the later treachery against Rustem by which the hero's fall was compassed. Such is the baldest suggestion of an outline of the greatest epic of "The Homer of Iran," whose own independence and scorn of petty courtiers was not less haughty than that of the hero whose labors he told so well.

CHAPTER VII

THE NORTHERN EPICS

It is one of the especial characteristics of great epic poetry that it takes its tone and its breadth from the people wherein it was born; that it is not, like a lyric, a pretty conception which might be equally true in all climes and among all races, but that it is intensely national and profoundly interpretative of a people's life. Herein lies its value. Thus the exotic beauty of the epics of the Orient harps too much on pleasure, and its sweetest lines ripple in indolence and love of ease. Love is tender rather than lofty and duty is philosophic rather than intuitive.

A far different note is struck when the Sagas of the frozen north become heard. The abandonment to luxury held out and hoped for in the Hindu poems is in strong contrast to the rigorous sense of "honor at any price" and the Viking disregard of the softer shades of personal comfort. The Greek Epics treat of heroes, the Oriental of monarchs, but the northern sagas ring with the clash of battle and the Berserk cries of warriors. The most primitive and perhaps the purest form is found in the Icelandic Eddas.

During the latter part of the ninth century Iceland, the remotest corner of Europe, was discovered and peopled by a number of noble and high-minded families who had emigrated from Norway, seeking freedom from the despotism of Harold the Fair-Haired. They carried with them the ancient heirlooms of the Teutonic race: its language, manners, religion and its love for song and poetry and for the beauties and sublimity of nature. There the ice-crust often cracks and Hecla casts forth its flames, and as from their frozen swamps hot springs rise on high, so poetry defied the ice.

In the year 1643 Brynjolf Sveinsson, bishop of Skalholt, discovered a number of manuscripts, and, supposing them to have been collected by Saemund (born 1056, died 1133), he called the work "Edda Saemundar hinns froda"—*i.e.*, "Edda of Saemund the Wise." The name "Edda" signifies in Icelandic "great-grandmother," and had been applied before, particularly to a work supposed to have been written by Snorre Sturleson (born 1178, died 1241), the author of "Heimskringla," the great history of the North. Snorre's collection was was before Sveinsson's discovery, and is somewhat like the Edda of

Saemund, but of later origin. The two Eddas have therefore been distinguished from each other by the terms "Elder Edda," or the Edda of Saemund, and "Younger Edda," or the Edda of Snorre Sturleson. The Elder Edda is in two parts, the first dealing with the gods and the second with the hero stories, and the Younger Edda is a commentary.

The Volsunga Saga, called so after Volsung, the sire of Sigurd (the German Siegfried), the hero of all the Nibelung stories, is partly a paraphrase in prose of the songs of the Elder Edda and was probably collected during the twelfth century. This work is of great importance, as its compiler knew some of the songs of the Edda that have been lost, and it contains also an account of Sigurd's ancestors, not to be found in the Elder Edda. The manuscripts of the Volsunga Saga give also the Ragnar Lodbrok Saga, which seems to owe its existence, at least partly, to the purpose of glorifying the Norwegian dynasty. The Thidrek or Vilkina Saga, including the Niflunga Saga, collected toward the middle of the thirteenth century, was composed from the saga-lore of Germany and bears the impress of some of the later romantic tales in many of its parts.

The Nornagest Saga from the fourteenth century is based on the songs of the Elder Edda. The title of the saga is derived from "Gest," a native of the town Graening in Denmark. His life depended on a candle which a kind Norn had given to him, and he was therefore called "Nornagest" (the guest of the Norn). He lived three hundred years and related as an eye-witness Sigurd's (Siegfried's) deeds and death and other incidents of the Nibelung story to King Olaf Tryggvason.

There is a strong temptation to tell in some detail the story of the Volsunga Saga and to compare it with the story of the Nibelungen Lied that follows, to show the differences (which are great) and to trace the causes of these dissimilarities. But such would be outside the scope of this work. It must suffice to consider the story of the Nibelungen Lied as the principal and the finest type of the saga-cycle of the Volsungs and the Nibelungs.

The Nibelungen Lied, the great medieval epic of Germany, was composed in its present shape at the end of the twelfth or the beginning of the thirteenth century. Yet the beginning must be sought at an epoch when most of the German tribes, proud of their freedom, still hunted through the primeval forests; when the king was little more than the chosen leader in war; when Odin and Thor were worshipped; when the sacred trees had not yet fallen under the ax of the Christian missionaries and the martial spirit of the warriors was kindled to higher flames by the joys that waited on them at the feasts of Valhal. It is based on the combination and blending of four different sources: 1. The Frankish saga-cycle, or the saga-cycle of the

THE NORTHERN EPICS

Lower Rhine, whose hero is Siegfried, of Santen on the Lower Rhine. 2. The saga-cycle of Burgundy, whose heroes are Gunther, king at Worms, and his brothers, Gernot and Giselher. Their mother is called Ute (meaning ancestress); their sister is Kriemhild; Gunther's wife is Brunhild; his chief vassals are Hagen and Volker. 3. The Ostrogothic saga-cycle, whose hero is Dietrich von Bern; his principal vassal and weapon-master is old Hildebrand. 4. The saga-cycle of Etzel, or Attila, king of the Huns, with his allies and vassals; among the latter, Rüdiger von Bechlaren is the most distinguished. In the form in which it has been transmitted, the epic is divided into two parts, each of them containing nineteen songs. The first part may be named Kriemhild's Love, the second Kriemhild's Revenge.

The epic opens with the dream of Princess Kriemhild of Worms, a dream of eagles and a falcon, which betokened woe. As Vilmar says in his "History of German Literature":

"The shadows of this dream move henceforth athwart the serene heaven of Kriemhild's life and love; darker and ever darker they hover over the spring days of her first and only love, darker and ever darker over the gay sports and magnificent feasts at the time of her marriage; with a pale glimmer the sun shines through the gloomy semi-darkness, until glowing red he approaches his decline, and at last with bloody, glaring splendor sinks into eternal night."

The fame of Kriemhild's beauty reached the ears of Siegfried, a mighty warrior who had conquered the keepers of the Nibelung hoard and possessed the treasure. He excelled all comers at the tournament held at Worms, but especially added to his fame by leading a small band of Burgundians to victory against the allied forces of the Saxons and the Danes. Thus fanned by his exploits and her beauty, the love of Siegfried and Kriemhild grew daily.

One day Gunther, the brother of Kriemhild, was urged by his friends to select a consort worthy of himself and of the glory of his country, and none but the mighty Brunhild, the Amazon Queen of Isenland, would suit him. As soon as Siegfried heard this, he endeavored to dissuade Gunther from such a dangerous plan by telling him of the martial prowess and unconquerable strength of Brunhild. Yet the king was determined that none other should be queen at Worms, and seeing this, Siegfried agreed to help him, providing Gunther would give him his sister Kriemhild in marriage.

There was, of course, no possibility of Gunther's success by his own powers, but through the aid of Siegfried and the use by the latter of the cap of darkness and other charms from the Nibelung hoard, which Siegfried in one of his adventures had secured, Gunther was made to appear a hero of heroes. In order not to outshine Gunther during his wooing, Siegfried passed himself off as a vassal. The bridal feast was to be celebrated at Gunther's court, but the surprise and annoyance of the stately Brunhild was great when she found her sister-in-law about to be married at the same time to this supposed vassal.

That very night the warlike queen tried to force her husband to reveal the cause of the other marriage, but he would not, and Brunhild bound him fast with her magic girdle till he should speak. The next day Gunther appealed to Siegfried, who at evening, donning the cap of darkness, wrested from Brunhild the magic charms she had possessed, leaving her no stronger than any other woman. Then Siegfried and Kriemhild journeyed home and lived many years in perfect happiness.

Brunhild, however, had not forgotten Siegfried, and feigning to have a great desire to see Kriemhild, Gunther complied with her wish to invite Siegfried and his wife to a great festival at Worms. At the festival a question of precedence arose and Brunhild taunted her guest with being the wife of a vassal. Kriemhild's knowing Siegfried's powers, replied angrily, and in the quarrel ensuing, in the heat of her passion, wrongly interpreting the events of the bridal night, asserted that Brunhild had been Siegfried's paramour, showing her the magic girdle and a ring.

Bitter hostility arose and partisans of each queen waited constantly upon their weapons until "Grim Hagen," an ally of Brunhild, feigning friendship to Siegfried, learned the secret of the only place on the hero's body where he was vulnerable. Then, despite his reputation as a hero, he treacherously slew the warrior hated by his queen. After the body had been buried, Kriemhild took up her dwelling near the minster and went every day to Siegfried's grave, but no one could console her. During three years and a half she did not speak a word to her brother Gunther nor cast her eyes on blood-stained Hagen, but scattered precious gifts from the Nibelung hoard among rich and poor.

When Hagen saw what great power she could wield by her generosity, and how many knights were willing to become her vassals, he was greatly alarmed and stealthily had the hoard sunk in the Rhine, where, according to popular belief, it still remains. Thirteen years had passed since Siegfried's death, but Kriemhild bewailed his loss as vehemently as ever. She was about to withdraw to an abbey when suddenly new tidings came over the Rhine which changed her resolution.

This was the proposal of marriage from Etzel (Attila), King of the Huns, whose former wife, a saga-woman, had just died. Kriemhild would not listen to his suit until a promise of revenge on Hagen awakened her interest and she gave consent. Thenceforward Kriemhild, who had been queen of the Nibelungs (because Siegfried possessed the treasure and the name), now became the most bitter enemy of the Nibelungs, of which Hagen had become the leader. For twenty-six years after Siegfried's death no opportunity for revenge arrived, but at last her plans were ready and a great festival was held in Hungary which the Nibelungs attended.

Kriemhild endeavored now to execute her plans of vengeance, all unknown to King Etzel, and she found a willing tool for her bloody schemes in Blödel, Etzel's brother, who was won over by the queen's magnificent promises of reward. While Blödel departed with his warriors to attack the yeomen at their quarters, Kriemhild went to join her lord at the royal banquet. After a long and desperate combat, in which Blödel fell by Dankwart's hand, all the Burgundian yeomen and twelve knights, except Dankwart, were slain by the Huns.

The rest of the poem is a recital of desperate and bloody carnage. Dankwart, Hagen's brother, streaming with blood, cut his way to the banquet and stirred Hagen to revenge. The grim chief of the Nibelungs smote off the head of Kriemhild's child, Ortlieb, and threw it in the mother's lap, raising the Huns to the extremest pitch of fury at thus seeing their prince slaughtered before his mother's eyes at a banquet. Each side, desiring to see the other slaughtered to a man, refused to give way, and all the Nibelungs were slain except Hagen, Gunther and Volker.

In the conflict other tribes and allies who were guests at the festival had been drawn in and these were hurled against the two heroes, Hagen and Volker. At last Volker was slain by Hildebrand, the sole remaining warrior of the band of Amelungs, who was himself severely wounded. This left of the Nibelungs only Hagen and Gunther, the brother of the queen. At last, through the equally famous hero, Dietrich of Bern, Hagen and Gunther were both taken alive, tho severely wounded, and were cast into separate cells.

The queen, filled with joy at the thought that now at last revenge might be accomplished, went to Hagen's cell and promised to spare his life if he would reveal the place where the Nibelung hoard had been concealed. Hagen, undaunted despite his fetters, declared that as long as one of his lords should live he would not disclose the secret. The frenzied queen at once had Gunther's head cut off, in order to remove this supposed obstacle, and she herself bore it by the hair to Hagen. When the latter had recovered from the horror with which the deed filled his soul he vowed that never would he reveal to her where the treasure lay.

Kriemhild, once the very type of meek and gentle womanhood, seized the sword Balmung and with one stroke killed her ancient foe lying before her helpless in bonds. Etzel was struck with dismay at the ghastly deed, and Hildebrand, furious at seeing the mighty hero thus dealt with by the frenzied woman, grasped his sword and killed the queen.

XI

Thus begun as a simple love story does the Lay of the Nibelungs take to itself more and more somber colors till the scene closes upon murder requited by murder and revenge drowned in a red rain of slaughter. The pessimistic philosophy of it is seen in its last lines:

> "The royal feast was ended in sorrow and in pain;
> As joy draws ever sorrow behind it in its train."

Of mighty streams of poetry Germany has two, the one roaring through the rocks, foaming and bellowing in eddies and deep abysses —the Nibelungen Lied—the other flowing on clear and smooth, yet deep and strong, through pleasing landscapes—the poem of Gudrun. G. T. Dippold, in his "Great Epics of Medieval Germany," treats this most ably. The following summary is largely from his abstract:

The Lay of Gudrun comprises the sagas of three generations in thirty-two songs, which according to the custom of the age were called adventures, is divided into three sections. The first two form, as it were, an introduction to the story of Gudrun.

The epic opens with the carrying away by a griffin of Hagen, son of Sigelband, a king in Holland. The boy, then only seven years old, soon after escaped from the griffin and was brought up by three lovely girls who also had been carried to the griffin's island. As soon as he reached his full strength Hagen gave battle to the giant birds, slew them all and in a ship which arrived most opportunely returned to his home, where he married the youngest of the girls and became a famous warrior. After, his wife bore him a daughter of the greatest beauty, named Hilde, who was stolen from her home by King Hetel, the monarch of the Hegelings, with his staunch kinsman the hero, Wat of Sturmland.

It is of their daughter, Gudrun, fairest of all the daughters of men, that the true epic deals. As in Hilde's case, the father looked angrily on all suitors to her hand. There were many of these, but the chiefest were Siegfried, King of Moorland; Hartmut, son of King Ludwig of Normandy, and Herwig, King of Seeland. Hartmut, disguised, came to the court and endeavored to win by sympathy where he had failed by position, but Gudrun advised him to flee. Of a sudden Herwig of Seeland invaded Hetel's realm with three thousand knights and a fierce combat took place near the castle gate, the fight being stopped by Gudrun, who stepped forward and announced herself ready to become betrothed to Herwig.

When Siegfried of Moorland learned that Gudrun had been betrothed to Herwig, angrily remembering the scornful rejection of his suit, he at once mustered a large army and set sail for Herwig's country, which he devastated with merciless hand. Herwig sent messengers to Gudrun, and Hetel, followed by Wat, Morung and Horant, with a powerful host, set out to aid Herwig. After long and

THE NORTHERN EPICS

fierce fighting, Siegfried was compelled to take refuge in a fortress situated by a large river, where he was besieged.

In the meantime Hartmut had been informed by spies that Hetel with his great vassals had left his country, and the Normans landed an army, while Hartmut sent messengers to the royal castle again to woo Gudrun. The maiden told them artlessly and frankly that she was affianced to Herwig and therefore could not listen to the proposals of another man. Thereupon the Normans attacked the castle, which was taken and destroyed after a fierce struggle. Gudrun, with sixty-two maidens, was carried away captive by the Normans.

For thirteen years Gudrun remained faithful to her betrothed Herwig and would not listen to Hartmut until one winter day, when Gudrun and Hildburg were on the beach, being forced to wash for the cruel Gerlind, as had been their weary lot for many years past, there appeared on the waves a strange bird, swimming toward them, probably a swan maiden or a mermaid, skilled in foretelling the future. The bird spoke to Gudrun in a human voice and told her that all the youth of the country having now grown up to be warriors, a huge army had landed in the hope of finding Gudrun, and bade her come to the beach next morning.

The next day on reaching the beach they cast many a wistful glance toward the sea, hoping to espy the promised aid from their native land. All at once they perceived on the waves a little skiff and two men sitting in it, who rowed toward the shore. Gudrun and Hildburg shivered with cold, having been sent out in the snow barefoot, and were ashamed not only of their scant attire but also of being seen washing by their friends. They were about to flee, but the two knights, who were no other than Herwig and Ortwein, besought them by their maiden honor to await their approach.

Gudrun tested them by saying that she was dead, but seeing their grief, revealed herself, and Herwig, enraptured at seeing his bride, clasped her in his arms and kissed her tenderly. He intended to take her with him at once, but Ortwein opposed such a step, saying that it would be craven not to rescue all the noble maidens who had shared her fate. Then the two knights took leave of the maidens, promising them to be on the next morning with eighty thousand men before the gates of the Norman castle.

At sunrise the combat began in front of the castle, from whose battlements Gudrun gazed down upon the host. The Normans fought with desperate valor, but Wat raged like a furious lion among his foes and Hartmut distinguished himself greatly. Herwig assailed King Ludwig with great rage, but was struck down by the latter and only saved from instant death by his vassals who hastened to his rescue. Ashamed of his defeat in the sight of his fair bride, Herwig followed the fierce old Norman king, who was about to withdraw into his castle, and challenged him to combat. Ludwig turned round to face his adversary, and after a bitter fight was slain by Herwig. Thus the latter revenged the death of King Hetel on the Wülpensand.

Meanwhile Hartmut and Wat had met and Gudrun called from the castle window to Herwig to separate the two rival chiefs. Herwig asked Wat to cease the contest, but Wat, however chivalrous he might be to women, did not allow them to interfere in matters of warfare, and as Herwig thrust himself between the two champions, Wat dealt him such a blow that he fell to the ground. His vassals bore him away. Hartmut and eighty of his knights were made prisoners of war and Wat entered the hall.

"Then old Sir Wat the champion of them, became aware,
With gnashing teeth in fury he made his entrance there.
His ell-long beard was floating about, his eyes were glaring.
All stood in mortal terror of Wat's grim rage unsparing."

He gave no quarter, showed no mercy, himself slew the cruel Gerlind and did not even spare the children in the cradle, while any rebuke of his barbarity only enraged him the more. A full vengence thus having been wreaked, they joyfully set sail for the land of the Hegelings with Gudrun and her retinue. They also carried with them Hartmut and the other prisoners, besides a large and rich booty.

Gudrun's true nature found itself in securing a kind reception for Ortrun, Gerlind's daughter, and in pleading for the freeing of Hartmut and the other Norman captives from their bonds. The preparations for the wedding of Herwig and Gudrun immediately were begun on a large scale. Ortwein, Gudrun's brother, was charmed by the now captive Norman princess Ortrun, and Hartmut wedded Hildburg, who had shared Gudrun's captivity in such a faithful manner. Herwig's sister was married to Siegfried. After the wedding feasts of the four kings were ended they departed with their wives into their own countries. Thus, after years of bloody warfare, peace and tranquility were at last established among these wild seafaring tribes.

Scarcely less great than the famous epics of Homer, equal in power to the Volsunga Saga and the Nibelungen Lied and of an antiquity extending to almost 3,000 years, is the Kalevala. "This great Finnish epic," says Wm. Sharp, "is in a sense the most important national epic in existence. In it are reflected not only the manners, beliefs and superstitions of a race, but the very soul of that race. The Finnish pulse beats in the Kalevala, the Finnish heart stirs throughout its rhythmic sequences, the Finnish brain

THE NORTHERN EPICS

molds and adapts itself within these metrical limits." Steinthal places it second in his list of the four great epics of the world, giving the Iliad the first place, and Jacob Grimm declares that only the epics of India are worthy of being compared to it.

Even Max Muller is momentarily weaned from his Sanskrit devotion to praise it. "A Finn is not a Greek," he says, "and Wainamoinen was not an Achilles; but, if the poet may take his colors from that nature by which he is surrounded, if he may depict the men with whom he lives, the Kalevala possesses merits not dissimilar from those of the Iliad and will claim its place as the fifth national epic of the world, side by side with the Ionian songs, the Mahabharata, the Shah-namah and the Nibelungen Lied."

The main body and frame of the Kalevala is compounded of four cycles of folk songs. The poem itself deals with three heroes, Wainamoinen, Ilmarinen and Lemminkainen, with a later (and Christian) addition concerning Mariatta, a virgin who had a child of wondrous birth. The theme of the narrative is the struggles and adventures of these three heroes with the mythical darksome Laplanders from two lands of terror, "Pohjola, a land of the cold north," and "Luomela, the land of death." The poem proper, which begins with the creation of the world, ends with the final triumph of Wainamoinen and his comrades.

Beside the four divisional cycles of the three heroes, there are seven distinct romances and fables woven into the general fabric—namely, The Tale of Aino, The Fishing for the Mermaid, The Wooing of the Daughter of the Air, The Golden Bride, The Wooing of the Son of Kojo, The Captivity and Deliverance of the Sun and Moon and The Story of the Virgin Mariatta. Like all the great epics of this character, it has existed from time immemorial in the form of lays and ballads and it is but recently that these have been collected and woven together. The Kalevala dates back to an enormous antiquity. John Martin Crawford, whose translation of the Finnish epic is unsurpassed, and from whose version the passages to be quoted hereafter are taken, points out that in it Russians, Swedes and Germans have no existence.

It is most distinctly and aggressively national. "In this great national epic," says Wm. Sharp, "we hear, almost as distinctly as the voices of men and women and the sharp antagonism of forces bodily and spiritual, the lone cry of the wind, the dashing of solitary seas and the cry of the wild swan along the unfrequented lakes."

One very noticeable feature of the poem is the stress which is laid upon magical power. "It might have been expected from the character of the people," comments John A. Porter in his "Selections from the Kalevala," "but still it stands out here as in no other people's poems or legends. Wainamoinen, the hero the god of poetry and music, accomplishes nearly everything by magic. His songs disarm his antagonists, they appease the eagle of the storm, they throw a whole people into a deep sleep, they give warmth to the new sun and moon which Ilmarinen forges out of copper, they give life to the new wife made out of gold and silver," and they make the world fair to live in as the Master sings. It is not verbose and discursive as certain of the Indian and Persian epics, but in true northern style, has a story to tell and does so with direct phrase and abundance of incident. The Iliad possesses a certain sameness, the Odyssey adventures are grouped around a very simple story, but the Kalevala is richer in excitement than the two of them together.

Wainamoinen, in the very beginning of things, was born of the Daughter of the Ether. He began his work as world-magician at birth, and finding the earth treeless, planted first forests and then grain. The forests spread so rapidly that they threatened to engulf the grain, so he destroyed the forests, leaving only small parts of them, notably the birch trees, for the birds to rest in. Then he began his magic song, and as the melodic phrases fell the world about him grew up to a golden age of peace and contentment.

But the fame of Wainamoinen reached at last to Lapland. A young braggart, Youkahainen, who had learned some few of the rudimentary principles of magic and some simple magic songs, determined to go and oust the great master singer Wainamoinen and rob him of his laurels. Driving madly, he reached the boundaries of Finland, and seeing before him an aged man, he sought to force the traveler out of the road, and refusing to turn his horses, the sleighs crashed together.

Youkahainen immediately broke into a violent diatribe against Wainamoinen for not getting out of his way and threatened to bring down a curse on him by a magic song. The old magician smiled and bade him sing, but the braggart found his powers naught. The boasting Laplander, to show his lore, sang of the ways of the fish beneath the sea, of the birds in the air and all the lore of his time; but Wainamoinen told him to sing of the creation of world and of the happenings in the kingdoms of the gods, asking for philosophy instead of children's tales.

Youkahainen then tried to veil his ignorance by a boastful recital of his presence when the first rocks were made and when the sea was gathered together and assumed almost as much authority as tho he were the Creator himself. At this Wainamoinen, who throughout the whole poem is very reverent to Ukko, the one God and the Creator, became angered, revealed himself and began to sing. First he sang of the inner life of the world and how all things came to have their being; turning the magic songs, he sang Youkahainen's horses into birds, the sleigh into reeds that grew beside the frozen river, the

THE NORTHERN EPICS

harness into shackles wherewith to bind the boastful Laplander and the ground about where he stood into a bog in which Youkahainen sank until he cried in despair for help. Wainamoinen would not free himself until he promised his sister, The Maid of the Rainbow, in marriage to the old magician. This plan, however, was foiled by the cleverness of the girl herself, and Wainamoinen instead wooed another beautiful Northland maid, the daughter of Louhi, a great enchantress. The mother refused, however, to consider his suit, saying she would not give her except to the man who could make the Sampo, a curious charm of fertility.

This, however, Wainamoinen could not do, but Ilmarinen, the great blacksmith, after producing many undesired but wonderful things, at last brought forth the Sampo from his forge, but the girl declared she was still too young to wed. Wainamoinen and Ilmarinen returned home, and hearing of their departure, a lover, also a hero but of a different moral caliber, appeared. This was Lemminkainen. He went through many adventures in order to show his right to be considered a suitor for Louhi's daughter, but failed in the last, which was the slaying of the giant pike which guarded the River of Death.

Wainamoinen and Ilmarinen, having heard of Lemminkainen's attempt, returned to the wooing, agreeing to abide by the maid's decision. The girl chose Ilmarinen. Wainamoinen, despite his grief, praised the girl for her bravery and sagacity in refusing even the master magician of the world for the sake of youth. The marriage festivities were lengthy and glorious, but suddenly in the midst of them appeared Lemminkainen, full of spite, who in revenge drew his sword, cut off the head of the father of the bride and fled.

He was pursued, but reached a fair island in the sea, called the Island of Refuge. There this handsome but evil-minded young hero won the hearts of all the girls on the island and forced them all to submit to his pleasure. Despite his ruining them, they became deeply attached to him, all save one, a spinster, whose features were extremely plain, and in jealousy she called down a curse upon his homeward voyage, and Lemminkainen's craft accordingly was sunk in a violent storm, and he reached home after unparalleled hardship to find his home burned and his mother slain by the people of Louhi.

In the meantime there arose a hero of magic power, Kullervo, of gigantic stature. (This is a story within a story, really a different epic entirely.) He could not be slain, even in babyhood, but his huge size made him so clumsy that all he touched went askew. Being angered one day by Ilmarinen's wife, for whom he was herding cattle, he went through the forest, gathered together all the bears and wolves, helped the wild beasts to slay the flock, and then drove the herd of bears and wolves home at the milking time. He called Ilmarinen's wife to the milking and waited to see her devoured.

Ilmarinen's wife having been slain through the evil doings of Kullervo, the blacksmith resolved to secure her younger sister. But he was refused because the girl feared some mishap such as fell upon her sister and because Louhi, having the Sampo, was content. Ilmarinen returned to Wainamoinen and pointed out that they must secure the Sampo, and an expedition accordingly was contrived, in which Lemminkainen joined. Suddenly the boat in which the three heroes were ran aground, but Wainamoinen, looking into the water, declared it to be a huge pike. Lemminkainen raised his huge sword, but failed to arouse the monster; Ilmarinen whirled his new forged blade about his head and brought it resounding upon the body of the fish, who slept on undisturbed; but Wainamoinen, drawing from its scabbard the Sword of Fire worn by Ukko the Creator, severed the monster's head from its body.

Of the bones of the great pike Wainamoinen made a most wonderful harp, the strings being from the hair of the horses of Hisi, the God of Terror. Many heroes and minstrels tested the instrument, but none could master it till Wainamoinen took the harp and began to play. As he played the waters stilled, the winds came to rest, the clouds hung motionless and all nature hushed to listen. Then Wainamoinen changed his theme and sleep fell on all the land, a slumber deep and dreamless, during which Ilmarinen rent apart the mountain wherein the Sampo treasure was hidden and they departed in silence.

But Ilmarinen was so rejoiced over the recovery of the treasure that he broke the silence. The Northland people woke and saw the ship sailing away. Straightway Louhi summoned the mighty serpent from the bottom of the sea to seize the ship, but Wainamoinen reached into the water and grasped the huge creature by the ears, holding the head out of water until the water-dweller begged for mercy and promised to seek the bottom and never rise again. As the tale quaintly tells, this must be true because he has never risen since. Louhi sought other means of redress, including the capture of the sun and moon, but learning that wonderful magic fetters were being forged for her from which she could not escape, and finding that at last the heroes could doom her to perpetual confinement, she released the sun and moon from their captivity and returned to her Northland home, leaving Wainamoinen and Ilmarinen masters of the situation.

The Mariatta story, which follows immediately upon the final defeat of Louhi, tells of a maiden, spotlessly pure and wondrously beautiful, who one day, standing beneath the rowan tree, heard a voice from the tree, and a berry craved to nestle in her bosom. Deeming no harm, she plucked the berry, and the spirit of the tree passing within her, she knew another life had come. Her parents, deeming her a daughter of shame, expelled her roughly, and when her time had come, no shelter could she find save a stable, wherein stood one

THE NORTHERN EPICS

of the steeds of Hisi, King of Terror. But the girl appealed to the steed for aid, and he wrapped her with his fiery breath until the numbness crept from out her limbs, and in the stable the child was born and vanished at the moment of birth.

The despairing mother traveled far, seeking news of her babe, until the sun led her to the child with songs of praise. The mother then desired the child brought up for baptism (this is a modern intrusion), but as he was of no parental lineage, questions were asked, and when Mariatta told her tale it was put for decision before the judges, of whom Wainamoinen was the chief. Wainamoinen gave his word against the child and ordered that he be slain by having his head dashed against a tree.

Then the two-weeks child began to sing of magic and revealed secrets of the world that no one, not even Wainamoinen, knew, and, moreover, told of happenings in the early life of the magician which he fain would have kept dark. The judges declared that a child of such wondrous powers must be the child of some unusual birth, and avowed their belief that the Spirit of the World took the form of the rowan berry.

Wainamoinen knew and realized his time had come, that the old was passing away and giving place to new. He called to him his famous copper boat, and declaring that he went to seek the Sampo and the wonderful harp that was made from the bones of the magic pike, sailed away toward the fiery sunset, singing as he went the "Lament of Wainamoinen." On he sailed to the lurid west, the glow growing deeper and deeper and the song fainter and fainter until the dusk fell, the night came and the light in the sky and the "Song of Wainamoinen" died away forever.

The Kalevipoeg, which may be called the national epic of Esthonia, contains the adventures of a mythical hero of gigantic size, who ruled over the country in the days of its independence and prosperity. There seems no reason to dissociate him from the Kullervo of the Finnish poem. The Kalevipoeg consists of twenty cantos and contains about nineteen thousand lines. The story truly differs in many important particulars from the Kalevala, but the meter and general character is similar, and the type of the adventures is after the same pattern. An excellent prose rendering of the Kalevipoeg is given in "The Hero of Esthonia" by W. F. Kirby. It is not to be deemed of the same antiquity as the Kalevala, but should rank as one of the great national epics of Europe.

Russian Literature is singularly destitute of any one great epic work. Only one, "The World of Igor's Armament," has survived from antiquity. "This precious relic," says Leo Wiener in his "Anthology of Russian Literature," "is not only interesting for its intrinsic poetical merit, permitting us to guess the possibilities of the Russian untutored mind before the introduction of the repressive Byzantinism, but it serves as a guide in redating much of the oral literature of the present day."

The poem tells the story of the expedition of Igor Soyatoslavich against the Polovtses. It is written in a gloomy key and returns again and again to a strain of melancholy, begun almost with the first words in the description of the unfavorable omen of an eclipse. In all the disasters that follow reference is made to this eclipse, and not a little of the despairing speech of the soldiery lies in their realization of the worst of their forebodings. The battles open unfavorably, the Russians are defeated, the hero is captured and when, at the close of the poem, he makes his escape from prison, it is only to find his own province in a state of discontent and unrest.

The following passage, taken from the third section or canto of the poem, gives perhaps as clear a conception of the general style of the whole as any part that could be chosen:

"Igor leads his soldiers to the Don:
The birds in the thicket forbode his misfortune;
The wolves bristle up and howl a storm in the mountain clefts;
The eagles screech and call the beasts to a feast of bones;
The foxes bark for the crimson shields;
O Russian land, you are already beyond the mound!
Night is long and murky;
The Dawn withholds its light;
Mist covers the fields;
The nightingale's song is silent;
The cawing of crows is heard;
The Russians bar the long fields with their crimson shields;
Seeking honor for themselves and glory for the Prince."

The bridge between the saga and the epic of chivalry is found in such a work as Beowulf. While it has resemblance to Scandinavian mythic poetry, still it is vastly more direct, the style is not metaphorical, but simple, almost austere. Yet "the very silence of the poem is thunder, through it we hear the tread of the dragon." Its argument is most direct. Hrothgar, king of the Gar-Danes, built a splendid hall called Heorot, which he was never able to occupy because a monster from the fen, the dragon Grendel, broke into it a few nights after its completion and devoured thirty of the king's thanes. Beowulf, the hero of the Geats in Sweden, with fourteen companions sails across the sea. He is warmly welcomed by Hrothgar and takes his place in the hall. Grendel attacks the place and one of the defenders is slain, but Beowulf mortally wounds the monster, tearing out his arm. The next night the monster's co-mate comes up out of the fen and Beowulf slays that dragon also. A third dragon, fifty years later, is encountered at his home in Sweden, but he is slain himself in ridding his country of that danger.

The importance of the poem is ably stated by Geo. Saintsbury. He says in his "Short History of English Literature," "If we take into consideration the fact that Beowulf is the very oldest poem in the language, that it has no known predecessors and has the whole literature of romance for its successors, it is seen that it is a very venerable document indeed, well worth the envy of the nations to whom it does not belong. Even if it were no older than its M.S., Beowulf would be the senior of the Chanson de Roland by nearly a century, the Poema del Cid by two, the Nibelungen Lied by three. In reality it is elder of the eldest of these by half a millennium. Some of those who love England least have been fain to admit that we have the best poetry in Europe. It is thanks mainly to Beowulf that our poetry can claim the oldest lineage and poetical coat armor from the very first."

CHAPTER VIII

THE EPICS OF CHIVALRY

The word "Chivalry" brings to mind far other thoughts than the rude northern sagas presented. Courtliness, devotion, efflorescence of speech and an overpowering sense of personal dignity appear as striking characteristics, and while "knighthood" as such now seems in retrospect artificial and stilted, it must be remembered that such a figure as the Chevalier Bayard, "sans peur et sans reproche," was rightly little less than a demigod in a time when all save the knights were so brutish and so ignorant. The two great cycles of Chivalry were the Carlovingian (Charlemagne) and the Arthurian, of which the former took definite shape the earlier. The most notable product of the Carlovingian cycle is the Chanson de Roland.

The Chanson de Roland, or Song of Roland, which is the most famous and the most beautiful of the Chansons de Geste (Songs of Great Deeds) of France, was written late in the eleventh or early in the twelfth century. It is but one of the many romances that circled about Charlemagne and his twelve peers of paladins, of whom the chief was Roland. They were sung by the trouveres, and while a few might have been in manuscript copies, undoubtedly the larger number were transmitted orally. The copy of the Chanson de Roland in the Bodleian Library at Oxford evidently was such a manuscript. It has a peculiar interest to the English race, by reason of its relation to the battle of Hastings. It appears that a certain warlike minstrel by name Taillefer (Cleave-Iron) begged of Duke William the privilege of striking the first blow at the English. The boon was granted, and Taillefer, bearing harp and sword, singing this very Chanson de Roland, rode singly to the English line, where he fought bravely until he was slain.

Not the least curious feature of the Charlemagne cycle is that the chiefest part of it is not the record of a success but of a failure; it is not a song of victory but of a disaster. Certainly nothing stranger could appear in history than that a conqueror should be immortalized by one of the few most utter reverses his arms had ever sustained. Charlemagne, at a time when a large part of Europe was under his hand, turned covetous eyes to Spain, and after a five years' campaign the Moorish governor of Saragossa led him to believe that the city could be captured. Charlemagne acted on the hint and besieged the town. After nine months, on the payment of a large sum in gold, however, Charlemagne raised the siege and returned through the Pyrenees to France. He left a strong army, under Roland, to guard the rear of the main force.

On the return, however, an army whom tradition declared to have been Moors led by Basque guides, ambushed the rear guard in a small defile at Roncesvalles and overwhelmed them. Three of the Paladins—Roland, Olivier and Archbishop Turpin—were with this group. Olivier, who was brave but prudent, advised Roland to blow his horn as soon as the dilemma was observed, but Roland, in a foolhardy manner refused, deeming themselves able to win through alive. The battle waged furiously, but the odds were overpowering and at last none remained alive but the three Paladins.

On seeing their dire plight and noting that Olivier was wounded, Roland became willing to wind the horn, but this time Olivier objected, for the reason that Charlemagne could not reach them in time to save them, and since there was no hope of turning the day, they might as well die without having had the shame of calling for help. But Archbishop Turpin came up to stop the quarrel between the two knights. He blamed Roland for his recklessness in not having summoned help before in time to prevent defeat, but urged him to do so now, not in the hope of help but merely that their bodies might be given Christian burial and that their deaths should be revenged.

Roland blew the horn so that it was heard by the main army, many miles away. Charlemagne was for turning immediately, but Ganelon, who hated Roland and who treacherously had laid the trap of the ambush into which Roland had fallen, declared that the emperor must have been mistaken, for Roland would never lower his pride to call for aid. But the horn was heard again, very faintly, and Charlemagne, who had long suspected Ganelon, ordered him bound, and rode back.

The three Paladins had stood long against the host until Olivier was thrust through the back by a foul lance-thrust from a Saracen leader. Seeing him wounded, Roland, half fainting with grief, rode to his side, and Olivier, blinded and not seeing who was coming, with a dying stroke smote Roland, wounding him sorely. A moment after Olivier died.

Roland, despite his wound, rode to the side of Archbishop Turpin, who had fought gallantly, but whose strength was nearly spent. Still the fight raged on, tho four hundred men slain lay around the archbishop, till human power could do no more, and despite the aid of Roland, the militant churchman fell at the point of death. Covering his comrade with his shield, Roland with his single blade beat back the host confronting him until the archbishop died and he was left alone, tho he had received his death blow and was all but gone.

Roland staggered to a rock and thrice tried to shatter his blade upon it that the Paynim might not have the trophy, but the blade remained undented and he fell, still holding it. For some time none dared approach the dying Paladin, till at last a Moor came near and wrenched the sword from the rigid grasp. A last flicker of life leapt in the exhausted frame, and summoning strength, Roland brought his heavy, gem-studded horn on the Saracen's skull, crushing it in. As he did so he heard the trumpets of the army and staggered to his feet in welcome just as force came crashing down the slope, but fell headlong, dead, before his comrades reached him. Fell was the slaughter which followed, for filled with fury Charlemagne hurled his troops upon the entire countryside and left not a Moor alive in the province to tell the tale.

The great national epic of England unquestionably is the Arthurian cycle, for King Arthur and the Knights of the Round Table seem to be regarded with a sense of possession such as no other English poems educe. "For nearly a thousand years," says Richard Jones, "the Arthurian legends have furnished unlimited literary material, not to English poets alone but to all Christendom. These Celtic romances, having their birthplace in Brittany and Wales, had been growing and changing for some centuries before the fanciful 'Historia Bretonum' of Geoffrey of Monmouth, Bishop of St. Asaph, flushed them with color and endued them with new life."

The Arthurian Epic is composed of five separate and widely distinct cycles, which seem to have remained apart for many centuries. These were as follows: (1) The Merlin cycle, wherein Arthur and Guinevere appear, but in which all the importance is assigned to Merlin, Arthur merely being a chieftain of some importance in Wales. (2) The Round Table Cycle, which is markedly different in every particular from the Merlin cycle, the Welsh being primitive and barbarous and the Round Table being chivalric. (3) The Holy Grail cycle, which, in its origin had nothing whatever to do with knights or even with the Quest, but was purely a religious tale to emphasize the teaching of the Real Presence. (4) The Launcelot cycle, which had its origin in the Norman trouveres and which may have been purely fantastic, or at least the figure from whom it is drawn is unknown. (5) The Tristram cycle, which again is old and barbarous, but seems to be a Cornish legend not known till later times in Wales and Brittany. It is one of the oldest cycles.

Owing to the manner in which these tales and legends were told, it was unavoidable that a certain confusion should arise, and often for the sake of continuity the adventures of the one knight would be engrafted on the other and the whole gradually would be made to

THE EPICS OF CHIVALRY

conform more and more to the growing sense of chivalry, so that even barbarous stories would begin to possess the knightly gloss. Then in 1145 the fluent bishop put out the "Historia," wherein he had worked various legends and cycles into a certain whole, taking for his central theme the Merlin saga and for his basis of unity the idealized conception of Arthur, who as a popular leader of the Celts against the Saxons had been handed down to posterity as a mighty leader. "The figure of Arthur," says Ten Brink, "now stood forth in very brilliant light, a chivalrous king and hero, endowed and guarded by supernatural powers, surrounded by brave warriors and a splendid court, a man of marvelous life and a brave death."

Robert Wace immediately translated the Latin "Historia Bretonum" into French, but included in it a full form of the Round Table legend, making King Arthur the founder of knighthood. It is readily seen what a wonderful advance this would be in the history of the tale. Knighthood was almost a religion at this time and other than Charlemagne and his twelve peers, it seemed to have no originator. So that the conception of Arthur and his Table Round met instant favor. Layamon in his "Brut d'Angleterre" reproduced Wace, his version indeed being set forth as no more than a translation. But aside from its philological interest, Layamon made some marked changes in the Arthurian legend, especially in his enlarging those portions of it which dealt with the Holy Grail. It remained for Walter Map to give the one touch that was needed to accord a due perspective to the whole.

The legends were discursive and vague, but they had within them the roots of noble things. This Walter Map saw, and being a priest, he determined to carry out in the form of these legends the teaching of the Church. It was just at the time of the Trans-substantiation argument, and the Holy Grail story, with which Map as an ecclesiastic would be thoroly familiar, afforded him the very means he sought. When the great stories of courts and people could be so arranged as to make it appear that the whole order and glory of Christian chivalry was devoted on a Quest which constantly kept before their eyes the Holy Grail and the Real Presence, it made a teaching in parable which nothing could have bettered.

"At that day," points out S. Humphreys Gurteen, "no one knew whence Arthur came, what the Round Table meant, how Merlin was able to predict so much and how Lancelot and Tristram grew to be so strong." So Map, who, as has been said, was a poet-priest, determined that where so many miracles were happening religion must be called in to give them reason—it would not be wise to allow the idea to spread that miracles could come save by the orthodox channels—and true ideals must be connected with spiritual subjects.

One of the Apochryphal gospels mentioned the Cup, the Holy Cup which had been used at the Last Supper, and tradition told that Joseph of Arimathea had brought this to England, together with one of the thorns from the Crown of Thorns, which planted at Glastonbury had grown. (It is not generally known that a slip from the veritable old Glastonbury Thorn is growing in the gardens of the Cathedral at Washington, D. C.) Thus, by weaving together the finest legends of the people, by infusing them with the loftiest sentiments of chivalry and inspiring them with a fine spiritual purport, Map made his "Roman de la Mort Artus" perhaps the first great popular work in England. Sir Thomas Mallory's "Morte d'Arthur" is interesting and has been the basis for nearly all later work, but as compared with the earlier writer is badly done.

Aside from the great storehouse, Map's work, the Welsh Arthurian stories are both found in bardic and popular literature. Owen Jones, the rescuer of Welsh literary archeology, at the close of a long life of astonishing singleness of purpose produced in 1807 "The Mywyrian Archaiology of Wales." In this invaluable collection are the remains of the bards Llywarch Hen, Aneurin and Taliessin. As Gurteen says in "The Arthurian Epic," "Llywarch Hen, when a youth, served together with Geraint in the army under Arthur, and Aneurin was the grandson." The popular literature was collected or rather was translated by Lady Charlotte Guest, who set forth a collection of Mabinogion or Welsh Children's Stories, which are of immense importance in folk-lore and which bear an especial relation to the subject in hand for the reason that three of the stories therein retailed are portions of the old Arthurian romances.

The fifth cycle, that of the Tristram stories, has never worked in homogeneously into the Arthurian group, and indeed only seems to have been incorporated therewith in earlier years because of a poem on the subject by Chretien de Troyes, which is now lost, and the admirable work in German by Gottfried von Strassburg. This extremely lengthy production is full and well told, but throughout its purport barbarous. Gottfried gives it the due color by making the passionate love of the two due to a magic potion, a point that Tennyson most lamentably overlooks, making his poem, "The Last Tournament," almost as disastrous to the spirit of this cycle as his Merlin and Vivian is to the Merlin cycle. An excellent piece of work called "Tristran in Brittany," by Lauriston Ward, catches the true spirit of the theme. "The essence of the story," says Howard Maynadier in his "The Arthur of the English Poets," "is that the love of Tristram and Iseult was great enough to burn their guilt away. This it is which has made the wild Celtic tale of passion, immoral and barbarous, into a love romance that is immortal."

It is to be deemed most regrettable that the great modern poet in his "Idylls of the King" should have, in two of the five cycles so

THE EPICS OF CHIVALRY

greatly misrepresented them from their earlier and purer forms. It cannot be too strongly insisted upon that in the earlier legend Vivian was a pure, fair girl who had won the heart of Merlin, who lived in the enchanted garden that Merlin had made for her, and that her only charm was the hold her winsome love had over the mighty sage, then in his youth. And in Tennyson's story of Tristram and Iseult he has made them lovers whose sin is that of gross desire rather than an irresistible impulsion under a magic draught.

It is the sadder when the superb beauty of King Arthur's last words to his repentant queen Guinevere, lying at his feet, are remembered. In the hands of so great a poet as Tennyson, what might not the old Arthurian epic had become, if instead of writing dainty verse about the Table Round, he had put all his splendid powers into an epic worthy of his name?

One of the finest developments of a part of the Arthurian epic, the Holy Grail, is the magnificent spiritual poem of Parzival by Wolfram von Eschenbach, who is but little short of a place of honor among the greatest poets of mankind. The poem was written between 1200 and 1215, and its power is in the highest degree surprising when the loftiness of the sentiments, the value of a spiritual faith, the setting aside of formalism are remembered. Not even Martin Luther himself had more truly the spirit of the reformer than Wolfram.

The story, of course, is well known, how the young Parzival is brought up in such innocence and purity, and being warned by an angel hermit not to ask too many questions in his youth, he chances to come to the Temple of the Holy Grail. There he sees the wondrous mystery, but asks no questions, not knowing that a spell is on the king, awaiting merely the query of an innocent boy to cast it off. He joins the Round Table, but is suddenly denounced there for his failure to realize the Holy Grail, and deeming himself unworthy, he renounces the knightly fellowship. His adventures all tending to promote humility, his repentance and at last his sincere trust in God cause him to be permitted to approach the temple again. He enters, sees the wondrous vision and asks the required question. Later he is made head of the knights of the Holy Grail, as is his son Lohengrin after him.

Bayard Taylor, in his "Studies of German Literature," gives an excellent description of the mental and moral characteristics of Wolfram. "The author's peculiar genius is manifested in every part of the poem," he says, "and thus the work has a spiritual coherence which distinguishes it from all other epics of the age. . . . I must confess that the more I study the poem, the more I find a spiritual meaning shining through its lines. The perfect innocence and purity of Parzival as a boy are wonderfully drawn; the doubts of his age of manhood, the wasted years, the trouble and gloom which blood over him suggest a large background of earnest thought; and altho the symbolism of the Holy Grail may not be entirely clear, it means at least this much—that peace of soul comes only through faith and obedience."

The Ossian saga-cycle belongs within this group, but it is in truth not an epic, being but a collection of ballads. The battle between Finn McCoul (MacCuhhool) and Conn of a Hundred Battles is an incident, not a central theme, and even the theological utterances of St. Patrick will not bind all together. Yet fragments, like the Lament of Deirdru, are exceptionally fine.

The Borza-Briez of Brittany is not dissimilar. It is yet almost entirely unknown, but Hersort de la Villemarque is bringing it to the place of attention so richly deserved.

After the storminess of Beowulf and the monotonous fluency of Caedmon, it is as a wonderful effulgent visitant that Geoffrey Chaucer (1340-1400) appears upon the horizon. John Dryden's appreciation of him is worth quoting: "He must have been a man of a most wonderful comprehensive nature, because, as it has truly been observed of him, he has taken into the compass of his 'Canterbury Tales' the various manners and humours (as we now call them) of the whole English nation in his age. Not a single character has escaped him. All his pilgrims are severally distinguished from each other, and not only in their inclinations but in their very physiognomies and persons. The matter and the manner of their tales and of their telling are so suited to their different educations, humors and calling, that each of them would be improper in any other mouth." It is true doubtless that this delineation of Chaucer would read with better grace from Dryden had he not attempted to transliterate the "Canterbury Tales" into eighteenth century English and mangled it in the attempt.

The essential vitality and dramatic note, however, is well sounded by John Richard Green in his "History of the English People," wherein he says, "No poetry was ever more human that Chaucer's; none ever came more frankly and genially home to men than his 'Canterbury Tales.' It is the first time in English poetry that we are brought face to face, not with characters or allegories or reminiscences of the past, but with living and breathing men, men distinct in temper and sentiment, as in face or custom or mode of speech; and with this distinctness of each maintained throughout the story by a thousand shades of expression and action. It is the first time, too, that we meet with the dramatic power which not only creates each character, but combines it with its fellows; which not only adjusts each tale or jest to the temper of the person who utters it, but

THE EPICS OF CHIVALRY

fuses all into a poetic unity. It is life in its largeness, its variety, its complexity which surrounds us in the 'Canterbury Tales.'"

The "Canterbury Tales" are set in a framework of very simple device. The Tabard Inn at Southwark, then an outlying suburb of London, was a great rendezvous for pilgrims who were journeying to the shrine of St. Thomas a Becket, at Canterbury—that Saxon archbishop who had been murdered by the minions of Henry II. A most diverse company is gathered, and as a substantial dinner smokes upon the Saxon-English board, mine host proposes that as they start upon their way the morning following, that each pilgrim shall tell two stories to relieve the tedium of the ride. The tales themselves constitute the rest, but the prologue, containing a description of those who sat even at mine host's table, is the most precious passage of the whole. Among this list is found the true philosophy of the English society of that time. The temptation to name some of them is not to be resisted.

> A Knight ther was, and that a worthy man
> That from the tyme that he ferst bigan
> To ryden out, he lovede chyvalrie
> Trouthe and honour, fredom and curtesie,
> And of his port (deportment) as meyke as he is mayde.
> He never yit no vilonye ne sayde
> In al his lyf unto no maner wight.
> He was a verray perfight gentil knight.

> A Clerk ther was of Oxenforo also,
> That into logik hadde longe i-go.
> For him was lever have at his beddes heed
> Twenty bookes, clothd in bleak and reed,
> Of Aristotl, and of his philosophie
> Then robus riche, or fithul or sawtrie (psaltery).

> Ther was also a Doctour of Physik
> In al this world ne was there non him lyk
> To speke of physik and of surgerye;
> For he was groundud in astronomye.
> He knew the cause of every maladye,
> Were it of cold, or hete; or moist or drye,
> And where thei engendrid, and of what humour;
> He was a verrey parfight practisour.
> And yit he was but esy in dispence;
> He kepte that he wan in pestilence.
> For gold in physik is a cordial;
> Therfore he lovede gold in special.

The great epic of Spain, the Poema del Cid, borrows its framework from the Chanson de Roland, and in point of time it antedates the completed Arthurian epic. Its authorship is doubtful, for the Per Abbat, who endeavors in the closing lines to convey the impression that he is the author of the whole, is but an intruder. The Cid, or Ruy Diaz de Bivar, appears on the pages of history at first merely as a free lance, a man who sold his sword to the highest bidder.

The Moorish king of Saragossa welcomed him warmly, and for eight years the Cid fought under the Moorish banner against Moor and Christian alike. But he was keen enough to see that this could not long continue, and when the Moors began to threaten Spain as a whole, the Cid left Saragossa. He held the Moors back till his death, which occurred in 1099, and his widow, Ximena, held the city for three years longer. Then, seeing that further resistance would be impossible with the leader gone, she set fire to the city and retired, taking with her the body of the great warrior.

But it would not be fair to the mirror of Spanish chivalry to represent him only as a freebooter whose deeds struck the popular fancy. As J. Fitzmaurice Kelly points out in his "Spanish Literature," "he stood for the unity of the kingdom, for the supremacy of Castile over Leon, and his example proved that, against almost any odds, the Spaniards could hold their own against the Moors. In the long night between the disaster of Alarcos and the crowning triumph of Navas de Tolosa the Cid's figure grew glorious as that of a man who had never despaired of his country, and in the hour of victory the legend of his inspiration was not forgotten."

The inner spirit of chivalry reaches its highest exponence in Edmund Spencer's "The Faerie Queene" (1585). It is its loftiest note, its apotheosis, beatified by a consummate artist and poet of transcendent genius, who in his heart inhabited the magical shadowy land from which men were daily drawing further and further away. For him magicians work manifold charms; enchanted palaces display their most wonderful festivities; tilt-yards provide interminable tournaments, sea-gods, nymphs, fairies, kings intermingle in these feasts, surprises, dangers. If it be a fantasmagoria, Spenser finds himself so thoroly at home in this world that the reader is there too. There is no note of astonishment at any supernal event. The gods and goddesses of Pagan Olympus are framed to seem akin to Christian chivalry, and discrepancies and anachronisms disappear as such under the witchery of the incomparable beauty of the glamor of his world of Faerie.

"The delicate fancies of the old Welsh poetry," says H. A. Taine in his "History of English Literature," whose keen Gallic intuition has grasped Spenser more clearly than any English writer, "the grand ruins of the German epics, the marvellous splendors of the conquered East, all the recollections which four centuries of adventure had scattered among the minds of men had been gathered into one great dream; and giants, dwarfs, monsters, the whole medley of imaginary creatures, of superhuman exploits and splendid follies, were grouped around a unique conception, exalted and sublime love, like courtiers prostrated at the feet of a king. It was an ample and buoyant subject-matter from which the great artists of the age—Ariosto, Tasso, Cervantes, Rabelais—had hewn their poems. Spenser alone takes it seriously and naturally. He is on the level of so much nobleness, dignity, reverie. He is not yet settled and shut in by that species of exact common sense which was to found and cramp the whole modern civilization."

But it would be unjust to the poet to present it merely as an effort of literary beauty. It is designed to "present the image of a brave knight perfected in the twelve private morall vertues, as Aristotle hath devised." Only six of the twelve books were written, portraying respectively the adventures of the Knights of Holiness, of Temperance, of Chastity, of Friendship, of Justice and of Courtesy. The adventures of these, of course, are with personified temptations and sins, and one of the most gripping passages in the entire work is his description of the "seven deadly sins."

> But this (her coach) was drawne of six unequall beasts
>   On which her six sage Counsellors did ryde,
>   Taught to obey their bestiall beheasts,
>   With like conditions to their kinds applyde.
>   Of which the first, that all the rest did guyde,
>   Was sluggish Idlenesse, the nourse of Sin;
>   Upon a slouthful Asse he chose to ryde,
>   Arayd in habit black, and amis thin,
> Like to a holy Monck, the seruice to begin.
>
> And greedye Auarice by him did ryde
>   Upon a Camell loaden all with gold,
>   Two iron coffers hong on either syde,
>   With precious metall full as they might hold,
>   And in his lap an heape of coine he told,
>   For of his wicked pelfe his God he made,
>   And unto hell himselfe for money sold.
>   Accursed usurie was all his trade,
> And right and wrong ylike in equall ballaunce waide.
>
> And next to him malicious Enuie rode (Envy)
>   Upon a rauenous Wolf, and still did chaw
>   Betweene his cankred teeth a venemous tode (toad)
>   That all the poison ran about his chaw;
>   But inwardly he chawen his own maw

> At neighbour's wealth, that made him ever sad;
> For death it was when any good he saw,
> And wept, that cause of weeping none he had,
> But when he heard of harme, he wexed wondrous glad.

The allegorical nature of the work should be touched on that the reader may gleam an idea of the motive of the author. "In the First Book," says Henry Coppee in his interpretative "English Literature," "we are at once struck with the fine portraiture of the Red Crosse Knight, the Patron of Holinesse, St. George of England, whose red-cross banner distinguishes her among the nations of the earth. Then follows the adventure—that of St. George and the Dragon. By slaying this monster he will give aid to a fair lady, Una, who riding upon a lowly ass, shrouded by a veil, covered with a black stole 'as one that inly mourned' and leading a milk-white lamb, is the Church." Then follows a battle with a loathsome serpent in the "Wood of Error."

"On leaving the Wood of Error, the knight and Lady Una encounter a venerable hermit, and are led into his hermitage. This is Archimago, a vile magician thus disguised, and is designed to present the monastic system, the disfavor into which the monasteries had fallen and the black arts secretly studied among the better arts in the cloisters. In this Archimago's retreat foul spirits impersonate both knight and lady and present these false doubles to each. Each sees what seems to be the other's fall from virtue, and, horrified by the sight, the real persons leave the hermitage by separate ways and wander, in inextricable mazes lost, until fortune and faery bring them together again and disclose the truth."

The union of the religious and the chivalric in Spenser leads naturally to the Epic of the Crusades, the "Jerusalem Delivered" of Torquato Tasso (1544), which ranks as one of the finest artificial epics in literature. "Altho an artificial, it is in a sense a national epic," says Richard Garnett in his "Italian Literature." "Catholicism was putting forth in its utmost strength to drive back the Ottoman and the heretic, and altho, when Tasso began his 'Jerusalem,' he could have foreseen neither Lepanto nor the Massacre of St. Bartholomew, it is a remarkable instance of the harmony which pervades all human affairs that both should have happened ere he had completed it. Had either been the subject of his poem, the result would have been failure, but the great theme of the Crusades exhibits the dominant thought of his own day exalted to a commanding elevation, purged of all contemporary littleness, transfigured in the radiance of piety and history."

Of a later date, but belonging here because it was not affected by

THE EPICS OF CHIVALRY

the lowering of the standard of chivalry too far, is "The Lusiads" of Luis Vas de Camoens (1524-1580). While the epic deals mainly with the discovery of the way to the East Indies by Vasco de Gama, it has as its hero the whole Portuguese nation.

The "Morgante Maggiore" of Luigi Pulci (1432-1487) occupies a curious place in the epic literature of Europe. Its inexplicable mixture of religion and buffoonery, of noble aspiration and mocking frivolity, leads to the supposition that it was designed to be the beginning of burlesque. It has a noble theme. Orlando (Roland), standing alone on the battle ground at Roncesvalles, with all his friends slain, is visited by the Angel Gabriel, who promises to make him captain of an invincible host, a boon refused, as Orlando does not wish to live with his companions gone.

Almost in the same year as the publication of the "Morgante Maggiore" appeared part of a much greater work, the "Orlando Innamorato" of Matteo Maria Boiardo (1434-1494). The story seems original, tho the heroes are Orlando and Rinaldo, but while there is a great deal of movement, a maze of adventures, magic piled upon magic and surprises galore, a purposeful central theme is lacking.

Lodovico Ariosto (1474-1533), who wrote the famous "Orlando Furioso" as a sequel to Boiardo's poem, produced a finer but more complex work. With the "Morgante Maggiore" not far in the background, the hint of the burlesque could not be omitted, and it appears in the madness of Orlando, in Astolfo's flight to the moon in search of Orlando's brains, in the abode of discord among the monks and such passages which are, none the less, among the most characteristic of Ariosto's work.

The burlesque of chivalry thus begun had its death-knell sounded by Cervantes. Thereafter epics might be contrived, but they would be archaisms, and heroic deeds could not be told of characters who had been associated with ridicule; besides greater and deeper notes were in vibration and Italy and England became athrob with the writing of the two supernal matters of Epic Song.

CHAPTER IX

DANTE AND MILTON

Two GREAT figures stand apart, singularly alike in many ways, the crowned emperors of Religious Epic Poetry—Dante and Milton. The vague and shadowy form of Homer may appear beside them, but others there are none; poets and prophets, singers and seers, so high they stand that the finitude of all others makes them appear—one had almost said—divine. The Holy Spirit of Pure Greatness had descended upon each of them, and it is scarce conceivable that a time will ever come when the Divina Commedia and the Paradise Lost can fail to inspire the minds of this world's noblest souls. Milton records history, while Dante sets forth a revelation; the Puritan submerges his personality, the Florentine emphasizes it. Dante is the only one of the great poets who has dared to make himself the hero of his poem, and he has done so with a magnificent unconsciousness because of his ability to lose himself in his love for Beatrice.

This love for Beatrice, a purely spiritual love, tho Beatrice de Portinari lived in flesh and blood, is not the least amazing of the characteristics of the man. Dante and his beloved were mere children when he first saw her, each nine years old, and there is no reason to suppose that his devotion ever had any effect upon her. The Vita Nuova, which is the record of his attachment to Beatrice, is a dithyrambic of purely platonic adoration which stands alone in the world's literature.

The Divina Commedia originally was intended to be a further glorification of Beatrice. After she was in Paradise he writes, "After this sonnet there appeared to me a wondrous vision, wherein I beheld things which made me resolve to say no more concerning my Blest One until I could treat of her more worthily." Thus the great poet intended to depict Heaven as a setting for his beloved Beatrice. It is typical, however, of the man that he would not feel himself worthy to approach even in mind the Paradise wherein she dwelt until he himself had passed through the two intervening worlds of the Inferno and the Purgatorio, and while it cannot truly be said that Beatrice is the heroine of the Divina Commedia, she is its inspiration. To her gracious presence and her early death, therefore, are due one of the greatest epics of the world.

DANTE AND MILTON

This marvellous work describes, in one hundred cantos, a vision of the three Catholic worlds of the dead—Hell, Purgatory and Heaven—allotting, besides an introductory canto, thirty-three cantos to each. In politics Dante is at once a worshipper of freedom and a Ghibelline or enemy of the popedom; in religion he is by turns a scholastic disputer, an adoring mystic, a stern reproacher of ecclesiastical vices. Its ruling poetical character is that of stern sublimity; abrupt, concentrated; never vague, tho often wild; sometimes melting into overflowing tenderness and everywhere seen through a cloud of imagery, whose shapes are sketched with astonishing brevity, yet with unexcelled picturesqueness.

The first canto, introductory to the whole work, describes the circumstances in which the supposed vision presented itself. The poet, in the year 1300 loses his way by night in a gloomy, mountainous wood. At daybreak his path is obstructed by three beasts of prey, from which he is rescued by the figure of a man who is hoarse as if by reason of long silence. The protector, declaring himself to be Virgil, offers to guide his pupil through the world of shadows.

In the second canto, which is properly the opening of the Inferno, or first division, the two pilgrims commence their mysterious journey. Virgil informs Dante that, in the limbo where he, with other virtuous heathens, reposed, he had been accosted by a beautiful maiden, descending from the bowers of the blest, who had ordered him to succor the friend who loved her. The third canto opens abruptly with the terrible words of the celebrated inscription. The poet's eye is caught by it as he looks up to a gate which faces him, the entrance to the place of punishment. Virgil stretches out his hand to him, and they enter the unblest abode. They are in the region appropriated to those, both men and angels, who have lived without infamy, yet without praise; those who have neither stood nor fallen. The adventurers next reach a gloomy river, which shuts in the everlasting prison, where, while the grim ferryman refuses to convey them across, the ground shakes and a wind rises from its bosom, through which flash a red light. Dante falls in a swoon, and, awakened by a clap of thunder, finds himself transported to the other side of the flood, and gazing down into the dark abyss, from which ascend cries of agony.

The poet figures his hell as consisting of nine concentric circles, one below another, converging like the steps of an amphitheater or the interior of a hollow cone, and terminating in the center of the earth. The poets are already in the first or uppermost circle, in which, not tormented, but grieving with eternal sighs, are the souls of the heathen, of infants and the rest of the unbaptized. From a bright illumination shining through the gloomy crowd there approach to salute Virgil four honored shades, Homer, Horace, Ovid and Lucan, who admit Dante as a sixth into "that famous company." In a fresh green meadow, surrounded by a sevenfold fortification and a moat, are the souls of antique heroes and sages.

From the quiet of this circle Virgil and his pupil descend into the second, where the actual torments of hell commence. Minos, transformed by the Florentine poet, like the other pagan deities, into a strange and grisly shape, sits at the entrance of the circle and assigns to the condemned spirits their places according to the measure of their guilt, the worst crimes being sunk deepest. This region, deprived of light, is agitated like a sea by winds incessantly crossing each other and wafting with them shrieks and sobs. It is the place of eternal sinners, among whom the pilgrim first beholds, hurried backward and forward by the tempest, Semiramis, Dido, Cleopatra, Helen, Achilles, Paris and the knight Tristram. After these comes the group in which the poet's pathos has been so justly admired, that of Francesca da Polenta (the daughter of his protector Guido) and her lover, Paolo di Malatesta of Rimini. Neither description nor translation can convey the broken-hearted tenderness which breathes through this tale of guilty love more guiltily avenged, of love stronger than death and lasting as its own eternal punishment. While the two condemned shades weep before him, Dante faints with compassion.

On recovering, he finds himself in the third circle, where the gluttonous, tormented by a demon named Cerberus, lie amid icy mud, while incessant hail and rain pour down on them. In the fourth circle the avaricious and prodigal, doomed to the same punishment, are violently driven against each other by incessant gusts of wind. On the edge of this region there boils up a black fountain, discharging its waters into the fifth circle, where it forms the River Styx, amid the mud of which lie, naked and struggling, the souls of those whose master-sin was anger.

A bark, rowed by a demon, conveys the voyagers across the stagnant expanse, beyond which rise iron walls and fiery towers, like the minarets of mosques, from which battlements, numberless fiends, headed by the furies, oppose the entrance of any living man. These fortifications shut in the city of Dis, which includes the four remaining circles of punishment, forming a deeper hell within hell itself. The sixth circle, the first of these inner ones, is an immense plain covered with tombs, around each of which flicker raging flames and from beneath the lifted covers issue loud lamentations, being the place of punishment for the great leaders of heresy.

Within this field of graves yawns a horrible and pestilential gulf, containing the last three circles, respectively appropriated to those who have sinned by violence, by fraud and by treachery. The seventh circle, guarded by the Minotaur and by Centaurs, is fenced with a river of blood. In the gory stream are punished those who were guilty of outrage against mankind by practising tyranny or cruelty, and among them are named Alexander the Great, Dionysius, Eccelino and Attila. In the second division of this region, beyond the river, those who have been, by suicide, guilty of violence toward themselves, are converted into trees with knotty trunks and dark leaves, bearing, instead of fruit, prickles and poison, and perched on by the hideous harpies. Within a ring formed by this spectral forest is a sandy plain, on which are scattered naked shadows of men and women rebellious against God, tormented by flakes of fire which rain slowly on them.

The rocks which bound the seventh circle descend in tremendous precipices to the next one, and the river falls in an awful cataract. A huge fiend, poising himself in the thick and lurid air, sinks with Dante and Virgil along the face of the cataract and deposits them at the foot of the cliff, amid the cries and fiery glare of the eighth circle. Here are the deceivers of women, who are constantly chased and lashed by devils, and flatterers, whose punishment is truly medieval. Those who have committed simony or ecclesiastical fraud are plunged head foremost into burning apertures, next to the wizards, who have their heads twisted round to their backs. Those who have committed malversation in office are plunged into a lake of boiling pitch, beside which the hypocrites walk without ceasing in slow procession, clothed in ponderous leaden capotes, gilded outside. Thieves are continually pursued and devoured by serpents, which, themselves condemned souls, no sooner destroy their victims than they change bodies with them.

The pilgrims move on in silence through a thick darkness and a giant, Antæus, lifts both travelers with one hand, stoops with them and sets them down at his feet. They are now in the ninth and lowest circle of hell, a wintry lake, where, in four divisions, traitors are entombed in ice up to the neck, shedding tears which freeze on their faces as they fall. In the first division, called Caïna, are treacherous assassins, among them Charlemagne's betrayer, Ganelon, and Mordred, King Arthur's parricidal son or nephew; the second sphere, called Antenora, imprisons those who have betrayed their country. In Ptolomea, the third icy region, are those who have betrayed their benefactors, and a similar class of sinners is found in the fourth, called Giudecca from its chief culprit, Judas Iscariot. In this last sphere the condemned lie beneath the ice, silent and motionless like images, while over them wave the six wings of Lucifer, a terrific giant, buried up to the middle in the frozen mass that fills the central chasm of the earth.

The first nine cantos of the Purgatorio are the most attractive. The scene of the action is a lofty mountain, and around its base, which the wanderers first reach on issuing from the gulf, lie valleys, waters and plains, among which linger the souls of the indolent and other spirits not yet permitted to commence their course of purification. On approaching this spot, and at the very opening of the poem, Dante breaks out into a burst of rapturous delight, which clothes every object around him with celestial love-lines. Cato of Utica conducts the travelers through this first region. An angel guides across the sea a bark filled with human souls, who are on their way to the place of expiation, and chant the psalm of the Israelites released from bondage. After several other scenes and apparitions, the gates which enclose the mountain open like thunder; the two pilgrims enter.

The sides of the mountain, which have been now reached, compose Purgatory proper. They are divided into seven successive terraces, on each of which one of the seven deadly sins is expiated by a symbolical but corporeal punishment. The sufferers are sad, but sad with hope, and ever and anon the top of the sacred hill trembles, and thence resounds the hymn of the Gloria in excelsis Deo, sung by the guardian spirits of the place when they dismiss a purified soul to the bliss of heaven. On the summit, to which the adventurers issue through a wall of flame, is the earthly Paradise; and upon this verge Dante lies a whole night, gazing at the stars and beholding a vision of the young Leah, the symbol, in the Middle Ages, of the active life, as Rachel was of the contemplative. In the last six cantos, amid the sylvan scenery of Eden, allegorical spectacles illustrate the glory of the Church, and, from a cloud of flowers scattered by angels, Beatrice, the minstrel's early idol, the inspirer of his song and identified in his soul with religion, his highest study, descends to conduct her lover to the bowers of heaven.

In the Paradiso, Dante and Beatrice, mystically raised by the mere force of aspiration, are borne from planet to planet, contemplating the happiness of the elect, discussing points of faith, and at last, in the sun, witnessing a disclosure of the divine glory, in the midst of which the poet breaks off, unable to bear, far less to describe, the entrancing majesty of the revelation.

Since the famous paraphrase of Scripture by Caedmon was familiar to Milton, it requires at least a mention before passing on the work of the greatest English poet. Caedmon (680) was a monk of Whitby, who was unable to improvise stories from the Bible and the legends of the saints as his brothers in the monastery could do, until an angel touched him upon the lips and bade him sing, and when he asked whereon he should give voice was bidden sing "The Creation," at which he found himself dowered with a gift of song and made a paraphrase of the Scripture. It is truly a paraphrase, for the old Saxon poet injects enough of himself and of his times into the song to give it original worth. He has been called "The Milton of our forefathers."

But, in verity, there is but the one John Milton (1688-1774), the

DANTE AND MILTON

author of what—if not the most original—is one of the most sublime and complete poems ever written. Its truest measure is the manner in which certain of its conceptions have usurped those of the Scripture. The modern idea of Adam and Eve is not the primal pair of Genesis, but the lovers in gentle dalliance of Paradise Lost; and since the days of the great Puritan poet the grotesque malignant spirit of the Bible has vanished and the modern idea of the devil is the magnificent fallen Lucifer, who not only dared rebellion against God, but even after his fall set himself in opposition to Omnipotence with the phrase, "Better to rule in Hell than serve in Heaven."

Paradise Lost begins with the picture of Satan and his angels having fallen from Heaven, lying in a place of utter darkness fitly called Chaos. After a period of utter consternation Satan arose, addressed himself to his colleagues lying prone on the burning lake, and as one by one the chiefs of the fallen angels answered to his call, he consulted them as to their future course. The angel legions were then aroused from the stupor of their defeat, and rank by rank, in all their thousands, the hosts fell into array. Satan, in stinging phrase, pointed out to these that all was not lost because Heaven was denied and sought to awake their vengeance. At his command a mighty palace called Pandemonium reared its towering walls and there the infernal peers held council.

Whether the battle was to be resumed immediately was broached and much debate ensued, the various fiends advising for or against warfare as their characters preferred, but to forestall ignoble peace Satan informed them of the report that God had made another world and set in it beings inferior to themselves who afterward were to be raised to a plane more eminent. The Chief of Hell himself announced his determination to learn the truth of this, and tho stopped at the mouth of the infernal pit by Sin and Death, he caused the horrid gates to gape asunder.

The Father then, speaking to the Son, pointed out Satan, who was seen flying toward the world, told him that the Tempter would succeed in his perverting quest and foreshadowed the methods of redemption. Satan meanwhile landed on the earth, observed Adam and Eve, then after flew to the Sun. He changed himself to appear as one of the lesser angels and asked the Archangel Uriel, the guardian of the Sun, the purpose of God with regard to the new beings on the earth. This learned, he flew to earth again.

Not little time lost Satan in seeking Paradise, and arrived there, he leapt the bounds that had been placed and perched himself as a cormorant in the Tree of Life overlooking the garden. When night came, changed to a toad, he squatted in the primal bower, whispering foul thoughts into the ear of Eve; but Uriel, who had noted his flight and had observed from the passions that distorted his visage that his mission could not be righteous, sent two angels to search him out. They touched the toad with a heavenly spear and forthwith up started, in his grisly shape, the Fiend. The divine messengers threatened to give battle, altho they feared the one time great archangel, but a sign from Heaven interposed and the fallen Lucifer fled in dismay.

The while that Satan, as a toad, had perched at Eve's side, she dreamed of disobedience, that the fruit of the forbidden tree was sweet and that she had but smelt the savor of a fruit an angel plucked and gave her and happiness accrued. In order to give man no excuse, God sent Raphael to warn them of Satan, told of the war in Heaven and how the issue remained undecided for two whole days, until the Son with his chariot and thunder driving in the midst of his enemies shattered them, pursued them, unable to resist, to the wall of Heaven and forced them to hurl themselves into the unknown Deep.

That night Satan entered into the body of the sleeping serpent and endued him with all his evil powers. In the morning Adam and Eve went forth to perform their various tasks and Eve suggested their laboring a little apart, altho Adam warned her that a foe was abroad and did not deem it safe. But the thought that he should think her unable to repel such a foe made her all the more determined to go apart and await the issue. The serpent approached her, not long after she was left alone, and began to speak. Eve, astonished at his power of speech and reason, asked him how it came about that he alone of the creatures of the field was thus dowered. The wily serpent replied that it was not always so, but that he had partaken of the fruit of a certain tree and it had given him wisdom above all other creatures. The tempter implied that if it had done so much for him, the result might be even more marvellous for Eve. When they reached the tree, however, the serpent leading the way, Eve drew back and refused to touch it, but with wiles and arguments the serpent overbore her protests and she tasted. The fruit seemed so pleasing that she ate largely, then sought Adam, told him of the trespass and carried some of the fruit. He was horror-stricken, but rather than allow her to suffer alone, took the fruit himself to share with her whatever fate should come.

No sooner was the transgression accomplished than the guardian angels flew to Heaven, but the Almighty declared that the entrance of Satan could not have been prevented by them. The Son was sent to adjudge Adam and Eve and to give the doom and Satan flew back to Hell. He met Sin and Death building a bridge from Hell to earth, and arriving in Pandemonium, began to boast of his success, when he and all his hosts were turned into hissing serpents.

Repentant in every degree, the first parents of mankind sent up

DANTE AND MILTON

prayers for forgiveness and for aid. Michael was sent down with Cherubim to drive them forth from the garden they had forfeited, but to break the harsh decree by a renewal of the promise. The twelfth and last book of the poem is a prophecy by Michael. He showed the future until the coming of Christ, His birth, His death, His resurrection and the state of the Church until His second coming. Greatly comforted by these words, Adam and Eve prepared to leave the garden. Michael then led them forth from Paradise, leaving the Cherubim behind. So "hand in hand, with wandering steps and slow, through Eden took their solitary way."

Almost it had been better had Milton not written a "Paradise Regained." Beauties it does contain, but it is false in conception and inadequate in treatment. The execution is superb, the mechanism unfortunate. Dante is narrow in a thousand ways, but he was at least as broad as his age. Milton's "Paradise Regained" is narrow with the narrowest of his time.

Since "Paradise Lost" no great epic has arisen, tho much has been written in the epic style. In Poland's cry for freedom occurred an opportunity, but the man, Sigismund Krasinski (1812-1859), was not great enough. Even his "Iridion" fails to arouse more than a passing interest, and his lesser work is as naught. A great theme unwritten is the Shogunate of Japan, and Samoa and Tahiti yet of their legends may educe a Polynesian Homer. The Great European War may bring to light some genius who will enshrine it in imperishable verse, but probably not until it has fallen back to history's perspective.

CHAPTER X

THE DEVELOPMENT OF THE DRAMA

The dramatic sense differs in many ways from that of the epic. Some great poets, of whom Goethe is the greatest, wrote dramas without being dramatists, and their works live in spite of them; but save a few such exceptions, the drama is not dependent upon poesy but upon action, and—to use a modern phrase—"to put over the footlights" some subtle conception is an art as different from the epic as is painting from poesy.

The theater is vastly more embracing than any other of the literary arts. All others appeal but to one sense, the eye or the ear; the drama appeals to both. It is this, more than any other one thing, which explains the intense pleasure the stage has given in all ages, from the dawn of history to the present time, and among all peoples, from the pantomime dances of the North American Indian to sprightly comedies beloved by the gay worldling of the Parisian boulevards.

"The play's the thing;" but in analysis it is seen that it is the thing because it grips the fancy and carries along the enthusiasm of the spectator in the proportion of the will-power involved. The primitive instinct of the battle-lust is not far from every man, and the drama which has enduring qualities is invariably one which presents one of the chief characters striving for some definite end, either good or bad, with all the forces of his being.

It is because of this that the drama languishes in indolent nations and decadent periods. Brander Matthews in his excellent book, "The Development of the Drama," points out that "the drama had no place in the existence of the weak-willed Egyptians, but it is likely to have a place of honor among the more determined nations, more particularly in the years that follow hard upon the most abundant expression of their vitality. And this is why we find the golden days of the drama in Greece just after Salamis; in Spain not long after the conquest of Peru and Mexico; in England about the time of the defeat of the Armada (in Germany during the awakening incident upon the French revolution), and in France when Louis XIV was the greatest king in Europe."

The origin of the drama probably is coeval with Language. Rude

DEVELOPMENT OF THE DRAMA

dances and pantomime gesturing would be within the reach of people whose vocabulary was extremely small, and it is not at all improbable that the first story-tellers were pantomimists. The festival dance, usually of a religious nature, moreover, has usually been the first step upward dramaward. It has not always reached the desired height—*e.g.*, the Jewish development stopped far short of the drama, but the Greek tragedy, despite its wonderful development, never entirely escaped the older conception of the ritual and its chorus.

It was but natural that the dramatic sense should find its first advance among the Greeks with reference to the rites of Dionysios, the god of wine and enemy to all that would cause unhappiness. Moreover, these same ceremonies would partake of the nature of harvest festivals, adducing another claim to popularity. The chorus singing laudatory hymns would soon feel that more ought to be told of the exploits of the god and one of the singers would recite some legendary incident, to which the rest would join in chorus. The musician and poet Arion (600 B.C.) was the first to give this dithyramb or chorus poem a regular lyric form.

The next step possible was due to the influence of the tyrant Pisistratus, one of the most enlightened despots of early times, who desired to make Athens the center of the arts. One of the ablest of these leaders of choruses, an Icarian named Thespis (536 B.C.), was ordered stationed in the city and the expenses of the "company" were borne by the state. Thespis was not content with the solo reciter, who was called the "corypheus," but he also established an answerer, a "hypocrites" (afterward the Greek word for actor). This enabled a dialog, and by donning of masks to typify various characters, consistent dramatic action could be produced.

Such was the form when Æschylus (525 B.C.), the real founder of Tragedy, appeared. Subject only to the disadvantage that not more than two characters could appear on the platform at one time, there was latitude enough in the sense that the two opposing forces always could be represented. This had caused a wonderful change from the Dionysios rite, enabling the chorus to be but as interludes to the true action, instead of the action being interpretative of the choral songs.

A great Greek tragedy could bring before a vast Greek audience, in a grandly simple form harmonized by choral music and dance, the great figures of their religious and civil history; the god Apollo in his temple at Delphi, the goddess Athene in the act of founding the Areopagus, the Furies passing on to their shrine beneath the hill, the hero orestes on his trial. The picture had at once ideal beauty of the highest kind and for the Greeks a deep reality. They seemed to be looking at an actual beginning of these rites and usages which were most dear and sacred in their daily life.

As Æschylus was the first of the great Greek dramatists, so was Sophocles (495 B.C.) the greatest. Aristotle states that Sophocles first made use of the third actor, thus setting an example for all later writers, who did not dare intrude a greater number than that which had sufficed their great master.

His "Œdipus the King" is perhaps the finest of the Greek plays now extant. Œdipus has delivered the Thebans from the Sphinx by guessing the riddle, but pestilence comes upon the city and in tracing the cause of the crime which has caused the vengeance of the gods, Œdipus finds out that—all unwittingly—he has slain his own father and that his wife was the mother he lost in babehood. In self-punishment Œdipus puts out his own eyes. "Œdipus at Colonus" and the "Antigone" are later chapters of the story of the same house. The "Tranhiniae," tells of the death of Hercules; the "Ajax" of the madness and self-destruction of the great hero; the "Electra" is the same story as the "Choephori" of Æschylus, and the "Philoctetes" tells of the means whereby that wounded and marooned hero was induced to return to the siege of Troy.

The third of the great Greek dramatists of the early period, Euripides (480 B.C.), was the most popular, but as a genius he falls far below his two predecessors. "On the serene heights of dramatic poesy," says Matthews, "where Sophocles breathed freely, as tho there only could he find his native air, the third of the great Greek dramatists was ill at ease, and in the plays of Euripides we can perceive at least the beginning of a decline. If we admit that Æschylus dealt with demigods and that Sophocles honored heroes, while Euripides is interested rather in men as they are, we must acknowledge also that man as Euripides represents him is often a pitiful creature, involved in sensational adventures far less significant than those to be found in the earlier tragedies. Indeed, it is a woman rather than man whom Euripides likes to take as the chief figure of his pathetic story—a woman often of unbridled passions and swift to act on the primary impulses of her sex."

The finest of his works is the "Iphigenia Among the Tauri," which treats with the manner in which a priestess of Artemis, called upon to sacrifice two human victims, finds them to be her brother (Orestes) and a friend, and of the manner of their escape.

Greek Comedy contains but one great name, that of Aristophanes (448 B.C.). He was a many-sided writer, one of the finest lyricists of Greece, a satirist of unsparing and searing invective and a humorist almost to the point of buffoonery. He is perhaps preëminently the personal satirist with a poet's sense of beauty and a good, full-blooded man's desire for a hearty laugh. The political turmoils of Athens afforded him much material, and he did not spare moral and social evils when the need arose.

DEVELOPMENT OF THE DRAMA

Roman Comedy was a failure. This was scarcely due to the writers, for Plautus was a thoro dramatist and Terence a most painstaking workman, but the Latin language did not lend itself to quips of speech, and a populace clamoring for gladiatorial shows found little sustenance in the lighter atmosphere of comedy. It was foredoomed to fall, in that it was imported Greek drama, and as an importation lacked healthy national life of its own.

Roman tragedy did not exist. Tragedy requires a dramatic sense on the part of the audience and presupposes culture. But the Latins never possessed true culture and "The Games" were real tragedies, combat was to the death, and to tier upon tier of men and women with down-turned thumbs, clamoring in their glut for blood, the tamer pleasures of the theater would pall. It was this that caused the opposition of the early Christians to the theater, not that they disapproved the drama, but that the "theater" meant the place where their friends and relatives had been "butchered to make a Roman Holiday."

Ensued a long pause wherein dramatic art stood still. The Christian Church, compounded of many non-unified nations, loosely linked by a half-understood and always disputatious theology, was baneful to culture and repressive of the dramatic instinct. Yet, paradoxically, it was the Church which caused the resuscitation of the drama, tho it may be admitted frankly that the theater grew away from its ecclesiastical swaddling-clothes in a manner most unexpected to the cleric. The new dramatic movement began in the Festival-Cycles.

These Festival-Cycles claimed to be nothing more than memory aids to the congregations of the meaning of the Festivals and at first were mere decorations, such as the Cradle at Christmas-tide. Then, in order to teach why the Cradle was in the Church during the service on Christmas morning, three priests, dressed as the Three Wise Men, would carry incense and adore the Figure in the Cradle. Later the Shepherds were added as a prolog. The next development was that of Herod and the conversations with the Three Wise Men, and so on, until all the various incidents connected with the Nativity story were grouped into a dramatic presentation known as the Nativity-Cycle. The same thing at Easter gave rise to the Passion-Cycle, and these were extended to include all the incidents of the Scripture and of the Apochrypha, grouped under their later name "mystery." The mystery extended rapidly and widely, and becoming too large for presentation in the church, was given outside the church door. Later it covered so wide a field that it developed into the "pageant," consisting of different groups of players presenting different scenes. The miracle-play differed mainly from the mystery in that its incidents were taken from Lives of the Saints instead of from Holy Scripture.

But a step forward of a far-reaching character was made in the "morality." This was a dramatized sermon, as the "mystery" had been a dramatized text, and the difference lay in the fact that the "morality" depended upon a plot devised by the writer, not upon a plot worn thin from the Scripture. Thus the Church dramatized fiction, requiring only that the characters be personified virtues and vices, Patience, Piety, Constancy and the like as opposed to Pride, Wrath and Sloth. But the transition from a personification of Pride to a prideful man was irresistible, and the allegory of the "morality" speedily evolved into a warmer human social satire, in which, however, the "morality" ideals" were kept up by the mouth of hell always being handy for the devils to pop out of and bear away the villain, shrieking.

From the comedies of Aristophanes, 400 B.C., to Lope de Vega (1562-1635 A.D.), over two thousand years, the stage was silent. No development of thought in the entire history of the world possesses so absolute and so lengthy an eclipse. It seems almost incredible. Some little credit may be given to Lope de Rueda, a few years the great dramatist's senior, and to the unlucky and ill-starred Cervantes —mighty novelist but puny playwright—but aside from these names Lope de Vega shines out upon the medieval night as the first star of the brilliant seventeenth century galaxy. Tales of his output seem almost fabulous. It is certain that he wrote one thousand five hundred plays, and three hundred more beside are ascribed to him.

It might be misleading to call Lope de Vega greater than Shakespeare, but more Napoleonic he really was. His imagination was upon a Gargantuan scale. He contrived incident with such ease and fertility of expedience, wrote with such force and persuasiveness as to make most of his followers seem poor indeed, and his ingenuity of diversion is marvelously fresh to-day. It is often forgotten that to him is due the honor of according the woman her due place. "Hitherto the woman had been allotted a secondary and incidental part, ludicrous in the comedies and skits, sentimental in the set piece. Lope, the expert in gallantry, in manners, in observation, placed her in her true setting as an ideal, as the mainspring of dramatic motive and chivalrous conduct." And, besides, being dramatist, he was master of the epic—*e.g.*, his "Dragontea," wherein Francis Drake is the devil. His lyrics are unsurpassed and his novels pleasing. Besides all this, he was a gallant soldier who sailed with the Armada, a courtier, a duellist of note, a gallant of the finest water, and last, an ascetic priest and flagellant.

It is worthy of noting, as did Archbishop Trench, that less than a century covered the four great dramatists each of Greece, of England, and of France and the same period the Spanish school. Tirzo de Molina (1571-1648) has a deep sense of conception and his immortality lies in the play "Burlador de Sevilla y Convidado de Piedra." He was also the creator of "Don Juan." The third of the great Spanish dramatists was Ruiz de Alarcon (1581-1639), who was born in Mexico. His deformity (he was a hunchback) went far to embitter his life. His "Verdad Sospechosa" as an ethical study is surpassed in no language and every line is polished.

Calderon, or to give him his full name, Pedro Calderon de la Barca Henao de la Barreda (1600-1681), is perhaps the best-known name in Spanish drama, but his greatness does not compare with Lope de Vega. He reveals more clearly than any of his school the close affiliation which the Spanish drama had to the mystery. Perhaps his best-known work is the "El Magico Prodigioso," but it possesses the weakness of all work which has not been able to shake off the medieval trammels, viz., that it makes the character subordinate to the incidents, instead of making the incidents revelative of character.

The drama in France owed all to Spain. The attempts at pure translated classicism during the time of the beginnings of French drama, the work of men such as Jodelle, Bezo, Garnier and de Larivey all were sadly at fault. The genius of France, with its air of decorous reserve (no matter how intimate the plot) and its keenness of psychological analysis, was not and could not be satisfied with Greek tragedy or Roman so-called comedy. It was not until Alexandre Hardy (1560-1630) appeared upon the scene that the French school found itself.

His contemporary, Pierre Corneille (1606-1684), is a master. He possessed, above all, the faculty for expunging what was not immediately relative to the plot, and from the cumbrous story of "The Cid" he made a tragedy which set all France ablaze and which draws big audiences in Paris to this very day. It was followed by two other great dramas, "Horace" and "Cinna," which not only revealed a dramatist but a poet who could not make his characters speak otherwise than loftily. The transition from this style to "Le Menteur" is amazing, for the latter is a comedy, and, moreover, a comedy of a new cast. It is not so much funny as gay. As Edward Dowden remarks, "It was something to replace the old nurse of classic tragedy with the soubrette."

Jean Racine (1639-1699) is later in time than Moliere, the greatest figure in the French drama, but is earlier in type. He was a reactionist, partly because of the unhappy influence of Philippe Quinault (1635-1688), who had made a weak school of sentimental gallantry. Racine, in order to overcome this, schooled himself to classic models. "Phedre" and "Iphiginie" both were written from Euripides and are the finest works of the modern classical school, but their power and force caused Racine to fear that he was fomenting barbarous modes of action and led to his withdrawal from dramatic work. A Biblical drama, arranged for a group of school-girls, was the only writing of his later life.

Far other was the great Moliere, a figure to stand with Sophocles, Lope de Vega, Shakespeare and Goethe. Jean-Baptiste Poquelin (1622-1673), whose stage name was Moliere, was, as Shakespeare had been, a strolling player, whose early training as a dramatist was the writing of comedies and tragedies wherein he took a leading part. He never left the stage and was playing "Le Malade Imaginaire" when he fell dying, almost his last act being to raise a laugh that it might be thought he was still feigning.

All his work is good, but "Tartuffe," "Le Malade Imaginaire" and "Le Misanthrope" stand out as do the great comedies of Shakespeare. It is small wonder that "The Misanthrope" should be written, for naught but inconstant royal favor saved Moliere from the vindictiveness of the Church. "No one of Moliere's comedies," says Brander Matthews, "is more characteristic than 'Tartuffe,' more liberal in its treatment of our common humanity, braver in its assault upon hypocrisy or more masterly in its technique. Bringing before us a man who uses the language of religion as a cloak for the basest self-seeking, Moliere devised his situations so artfully that the spectators can discount the villain's fair words, and that they know him for what he is, even before he makes his first appearance.

"Two acts are employed to set before us the family relations of the credulous Orgon, into whose confidence the unscrupulous Tartuffe has wormed himself. Tartuffe does not appear until the third of the five acts. His projects are plain, even if they are somewhat contradictory. He is seeking to capture Orgon's wealth for himself, to marry Orgon's daughter and at the same time seduce Orgon's young wife." The hypocrite appears to triumph all through until at the very last the peremptory power of the king, Louis XIV himself, is called into play to help the foolish Orgon and to send Tartuffe to prison. But to know Moliere means to know several of his works, and it would be as unfair to judge him by "Tartuffe" alone, great as it is, as it would be to form an estimate of Shakespeare by the "Taming of the Shrew."

English comedy begins with two broad farces, "Ralph Roister Doister" and "Gammer Gurton's Needle," both by clerics, and the first tragedy is "Gorboduc," by Sackville and Norton. But England's first great name is Christopher Marlowe (1564-1593). Three of his dramas especially are but little inferior to Shakespeare: "Tamburlaine the Great," which is based on the exploits of the great Timur conqueror; "The Rich Jew of Malta," wherein is to be found the original of Shylock, and "The Tragicall Life and Death of Doctor Faustus," which is not unworthy of comparison with Goethe's philosophical creation on the same subject. The Doctor Faustus of Mar-

DEVELOPMENT OF THE DRAMA

lowe "is the living, struggling natural man," says Taine; "not the philosophic type which Goethe has created, but a primitive and genuine man, hot-headed, fiery, the slave of his passions, the sports of his dreams, wholly engrossed by the present, molded by his lusts, contradictions and follies, who amidst noise and starts, cries of pleasure and anguish, rolls, knowing it and willing it, down the slope and crags of his precipice."

Of William Shakespeare (1564-1616) eulogy is unnecessary. To English readers his works are the most familiar heritage to Literature, and to add praise to his fame would be, in his own words, "to paint the lily and gild refined gold." In creation of character he stands unsurpassed and in adaptability of expression he has known no equal. Not as fertile in invention as Lope de Vega, not as heroic as Sophocles, not as keen-trained a philosopher as Goethe, not as poignant as Moliere, in other ways he transcends them all, not the less because he was clean-minded beyond all the playwrights of his day and in his outlook upon life was a gentleman to the core.

Three of his contemporaries are deserving of mention. Ben Jonson (1573-1637), "rare Ben" as he was known, had a stately wit, but it was real, and "Every Man in His Humor" and "Every Man Out of His Humor" are masterpieces of comedy; Philip Massinger (1548-1640) is remembered for his "A New Way to Pay Old Debts," while Francis Beaumont (1586-1615) and John Fletcher (1576-1625) wrote many plays, now almost forgotten. Perhaps "The Maid's Tragedy" is the most familiar.

The next period may well be forgotten. Following the restraint of the Puritans, the wild licentiousness of the Restoration found its expression in the drama. Nothing more clearly shows its essential vileness than the fact that the two names most clearly associated with this period are those of the coarse William Wycherley (1640-1715) and the lascivious William Congreve (1666-1729).

English drama was purified by the work of great actors such as David Garrick and Samuel Foote, but two dramatists, usually coupled together, can by no means be forgotten. These are Oliver Goldsmith (1728-1774), poet and writer, whose two plays, "The Good-Natured Man" and "She Stoops to Conquer," still are produced and always with pleasure, and a greater dramatist, tho less brilliant literary genius, Richard Brinsley Sheridan (1751-1836), the typical courtier of the Regency, whose plays, "The Rivals" and "The School for Scandal," will be played as long as the English stage exists. Since that time the theater has been amply supplied, but the work has been ephemeral tho clever.

It is a matter of some surprise that a nation so dramatically gifted as the Italian should have no dramatic literature, or, to speak more truly, no literature of a great dramatist. The reason seems to be mainly that those who had the dramatic instinct, Boiardo, Ariosto, Tasso, devoted it to the epic rather than to the drama. Machiavelli's "Mandragola" and Guarani's "Pastor Fido" are very poor representatives for the brilliant intellectuality of early Italy.

For the next great group of names in the dramatic world, thought turns naturally to Germany, which so long had done nothing worthy of itself. It required but the three masters—Lessing, Schiller and Goethe—to reveal not only that Germany and the Germans possessed the true fire, but that they owned besides a greater depth of thought and a certain scholarliness.

German Literature was almost at its feeblest period, being divided between a host of minor men, who vainly tried to copy the models of Greece or England, when Gotthold Ephraim Lessing (1729-1781) appeared. As the friend of Winckelmann, he made the classic dry bones live by combining them with French models and raised the German theater to an unprecedented height. "His native language, in which he always wrote," as Wolfgang Menzel in his "History of Germany" says, "breathes even in its most trifling works a free and lofty spirit, which, fascinating in every age, was more peculiarly so in that emasculated period." In at least three plays, "Minna von Barnhelm," "Emilia Galotti" and "Nathan," he showed himself not only a poet, but—to use a German word—a "theater-poet." The "Minna von Barnhelm" probably acts better than any work of Goethe and Schiller.

As a dramatic poet Schiller (1759-1805) is the one shining light of the eighteenth century, and this, not because of the excellence of his work, but because he spoke for the people, an oppressed people, with a prophet's voice. Lessing, with all his scholarliness, failed to touch the hearts of the mass, but Schiller struck the true note. The "Robbers" is somewhat amateurish in its technique of stage-craft, but determinedly strong in the reading, while "William Tell" and "Mary Stuart" represent the German dramatist at his best. The fame of Schiller, great as it is, would have been greater had it not been for the magnitude of Wolfgang von Goethe (1749-1832), who was his contemporary.

It is hard to find a class for Goethe, for he belonged to no special type. Epic poet he was not, dramatist he was not, that much is clear, and still less was he the spokesman of his age and time. No Roi Faineant could have been more outwardly contemptuous of the people than Goethe, and his statement, "The public must be controlled," was not calculated to add to the popularity of the theater at Weimar. It is true that in his earlier plays, in especial in "Goetz von Berchlingen," there is plenty of action, but stage-craft is wholly lacking. "Clavigo," "Iphigenia" and "Egmont" are not dramas, but various other forms of literature in a pseudo-dramatic disguise, and "Romeo and Juliet" need but to be read to see how Goethe has succeeded in spoiling utterly the whole dramatic purpose of the story.

His "Faust," especially the better known first part, is unquestionably the greatest work since Shakespeare, or at least since Moliere. But it is in reality a reversion to type. It is the apotheosis of the "morality." But, at the same time, it does not claim to instill hope and faith and courage; on the other hand, it is tainted deeply with the poison of pessimism and presents a picture which cannot be called fair to see. Goethe's surpassing genius is everywhere acknowledged, his searching interrogation of life, his power of self-expression in almost every department of literature; but philosophic profundity of a morbidly introspective order could not even be classed as a "morality." Almost it might be said that "Faust" is an "antimorality." To tell its history would serve no purpose, for the story has little to do with the parable.

The work of Victor Hugo and Alexandre Dumas—neither of them dramatists but primarily novelists—showed the trend of literature, and for the first three-quarters of the nineteenth century there was no real thought expended on the drama save in France, and there only of the most meager character.

Modern drama begins with Henrik Ibsen, perhaps the only modern to take rank with Sophocles and Shakespeare. It has been carried on by a number of lesser names, such as Sudermann, Rostand, d'Annunzio, Hauptmann, Maeterlinck, Synge, Shaw and Brieux, each of whom had a message to deliver and by a number of clever dramatists such as Barrie, Arnold Bennett, Clyde Fitch, Galsworthy, Henry Arthur Jones, Knoblauch, Parker, Pinero and Thomas.

It may, perhaps, be asked pertinently why Ibsen is so great, and to this query the answer is simple: He has vision. Remember that when Ibsen began writing, such banalities as "The Lady of Lyons" were considered worthy plays, and even "Rosedale," twenty-five years later, was a huge success. Against such maudlin rot was set such a masterpiece as "Ghosts," a technical and artistic marvel; against the fripperies and smug respectability of the Victorian epoch was set "The Doll's House," which may be construed as the first great voice in dramatic art admitting the individuality of woman as a human being, apart from woman as a slave or a lure. But—and this is a large but—Ibsen is far less than Sophocles or Shakespeare because of his lack of universality. "The Doll's House" heroine might be any woman, but in nearly all his other plays the characters are pathological studies.

Edmond Rostand loses greatness by the sad fact that he is not great inwardly. He is not sincere. He is a riot of exquisite fancy, brilliant facility and a supernal gift of phrase. He is too clever. His simplest work is "La Samaritaine." In "Cyrano de Bergerac" the fantasy peeps forth boldly in the rhodomontades of the large-nosed hero. In "L'Aiglon" the issue is becoming confused with details. Finally, in "Chantecler," Rostand lost hold of the ground altogether and swamped his theme in a medley of satirical under- and over-tones. Even then, a good actor, one with perception and personal power, might have made the character of "Chantecler" stand out, but given, as it was in America, to a charming actress (it is an appallingly *male* part), every bit of its emphasis was lost. That "Chantecler," none the less, is a part of the small treasury of immortal works is sure. Some time it will be revived with Reinhardt scenery, and a master actor.

There are many names to conjure with in Europe that America knows mainly as names, d'Annunzio, Hauptmann, Sudermann and the rest, but those dramatists whose greatness is known well in the United States demand more than a passing notice.

In fancifulness, Maeterlinck is at one with Rostand, and, "The Blue Bird" and "Chantecler" have a family likeness. But Maeterlinck is a mystic poet, while Rostand is a man of the world, and the inner content of their work is widely variant. "Sister Beatrice" is open to many criticisms as a work of recognized canons of dramatic art, but there is more than a suspicion that it is great enough to make rules for itself. It is further to be remembered that Maeterlinck understands the conventions of the theater, and is well aware of the value of the modern machinery of the stage as a medium for the conveyance of illusion. The demands upon imagination made by the pictorial drama of to-day have been dodged by the English playwrights, and turned into mere spectacle by the American producers, but in that atmosphere, Maeterlinck is at home.

Synge—in spite of his kink towards sordidness in minor matters—possesses Celtic idealism, and is well aware of the poetry of the stage. Clayton Hamilton has caught Synge's spirit better than many of his compatriots and tho he overpraises, still the following is pertinent: "He deeply felt the poetry, the pathos, the tragedy, the humor of the incongruity between the littleness of human actuality and the immensity of human dreams. He writes of illusions and disillusionments. Illusions are beautiful and funny [sometimes!]; disillusionments are beautiful and sad." Now that the typical use of "The Playboy of the Western World" as a traitorous political move has passed into oblivion, the sketch may take its place among the great genre dramatic interpretations of the world. "Riders of the Sea" is no more a drama than Byron's "Cain." "In the Shadows of the Glen" is very Irish, but many will prefer the wandering away of Pierrette in Housman's "Prunella" to Synge's presentation of Nora Burke's departure with her undesired tramp.

Synge gave his message unconsciously, but Brieux is a preacher, and his dramas are as absolutely preachments as were the "moralities" of the Middle Ages. "Damaged Goods" (Les Avariés) is less a drama than an anatomical lecture delivered at a clinic of social diseases by a professor with a scathing tongue. "The Affinity" (Les Hannetons) and "The Three Daughters of M. Dupont" are also marvelous works, but, lacking the advertisable character of "Damaged Goods," they could not hold their public. Not even the talent of a Brieux can substitute the classroom parable for the drama, when designed for presentation on the stage. Thus Pinero escapes because he is a master craftsman, and "The Second Mrs. Tanqueray" will abide.

The last of these writers "with a message" is George Bernard Shaw. As Irish as Synge, he is his opposite in many ways. There is a little spring in Shaw, which, when touched, startled him into full-voiced protest. This word is "respectability." It is anathema to Shaw. It connotes to him that smug hypocrisy that florid veneer, that conventional platitudinizing which is the special bane of the middle class. Whether it be a gutter-snipe taught to speak English well and thereby queening over society, or a girl held down by middle-class parents and rejoicing in a prison sentence that followed a spree, his theme is the laying bare of sham. Dean Swift and Shaw have much in common, as anyone can observe who takes the trouble to compare "Man and Superman" and the Voyage to the Land of the Houhynyms in "Gulliver's Travels." Shaw may be—often is—a mountebank, but like the Jongleur de Notre Dame he lays bare his talents as a mountebank before the shrine of Truth. If, at times, he raves, he feels himself justified by the more than horror of respectability.

Barrie is a link between the dramatic prophets of modern times who have been mentioned and the excellent craftsmen who have attacked the stage in a new manner and developed the microscopic drama. "Peter Pan" might, for a second, be thought of with "Chantecler" and "The Blue Bird," only for a second, for the thought would instantly arise that "Peter Pan" means nothing. "What Every Woman Knows" (only she doesn't) is far more revelative of the author's fertility of fancy. At times he is an execrable dramatist, as in "Little Mary," but almost always the Barrie shines through, and one enjoys the playwright's enjoyment in his own play.

A group of dramatists may be named, such as Galsworthy, Masefield, Houghton and Bennett, who seem to have set before themselves the stern mandate that under no circumstances shall their dramas be dramatic; on the contrary, they shall be real. Both in Galsworthy's "The Pigeon" and Ibsen's "The Wild Duck," the antagonism between freedom and domestication shines out, but how differently! "Strife" is not a play. Githa Sowerby's "Rutherford and Son" is a good example of the undramatic play. Not only does nothing happen, but the dramatist takes pains to show that nothing could happen. Masefield's "Nan" is a cruder example of the same order. Henry Arthur Jones is an eavesdropper and in his own words, expects his audience "to pay half a crown or half a guinea to have a wall removed and see the lives of other people as they really are."

Of the dramatists most familiar to America one must add that they have learned the craft of the visual drama better than any other. Augustus Thomas's "The Witching Hour" and "The Harvest Moon" take a high rank in this regard. Parker did the same in "Pomander Walk." Knoblauch's "Kismet," in parts, carried this to a point of genius, especially the opening and closing scenes, and even in "The Faun" the deftness did not leave him, though he made puppets in his minor characters. Belasco—though he struts a good deal in literary borrowed plumes—is the acknowledged master of making the theater fit the play. The handling of "The Return of Peter Grimm" was the apex of efficiency along this line. Whether its future holds further development along this line, or whether it will follow Reinhardt and Gordon Craig remains to be seen. Both are wildly revolutionary, but the Englishman is the least sane. The development of this note is unquestionably the most interesting feature of modern drama.

Of moving pictures, the photo-drama, there is, as yet, little to be said. Perhaps three points of interest may be noted. The first of these is that it is cheap. The second is that the photo-drama is melodramatic. The third is that it gives an opportunity for visualization more extended than is possible on any stage. There are, as yet, no writers of scenarios worthy of personal mention. There is, as yet, no photo-drama of importance. "Cabiria" was no more a single work than a performance at the Hippodrome is a single work; it was a mere framework on which was constructed a vast array of spectacular scenes. One is tempted to say of "Cabiria" as was truly said of "The Garden of Allah," that "the principals were the camels." Truth compels the statement that the credit for the "Cabiria" scenario was assigned to d'Annunzio, but the great author of "Trionfo della Morte" would be humiliated to be known only as a scenario writer.

All the great moving picture dramas are of three types: photo-dramatizations of books, of plays, or of historic pageants. To say that Rex Beach is a scenario writer is to do his novels a gross injustice; to hail Booth Tarkington likewise is to minimize his short story art.

The effort of moving picture companies of late has been the presentation on the screen of well-known novels and plays. This, in itself, is a terrible confession of weakness, for it proclaims that so far photo-drama does not inhere as an art upon its own basis. A novel is written for its literary style, for its presentation of character, as much as for its incident. Give Zola the incidents of Pickwick—how

DEVELOPMENT OF THE DRAMA

different a book it would be from that of Dickens! The purely romanticist historical writers, such as Dumas, could be photo-dramatized, but novels are an art in themselves, and to pick out incidents from novels, fit them to the movie and then proclaim that the public is being "educated" in the classics is a gross misuse of terms. The photo-drama is yet to be born, but at almost any moment, the great film may be produced. It may be said that it cannot be an old novel or an old play, but must be the first and original work of a new art.

In brief, the mechancial end of the motion picture—which is marvelous—has outrun its imaginative creators, and, more's the pity, as a result it has become associated with paucity of theme and mediocrity of treatment. No one is more aware of this than motion picture companies themselves, and they clamor for scenarios that shall be worthy. A really great motion picture has not yet been made, though parts of "The Birth of a Nation" distinctly herald the coming of a new era in photo-drama. But the picture genius in this art, whoever he may be, must be a director, not a mere scenario writer. It is in the studio, not in the library, that the great photo-drama will be created. There is more than a possibility that American dramatic art may step into the limelight through some great photo-dramatist now receiving his training in these infancy-years of a new art.

CHAPTER XI

ESSAYISTS AND HISTORIANS

The first essayist, the first historian, who were they? Truth suggests some barbarian cutting notches on a tally-stick, but common sense proposes a more modern reply. The modern essay and the modern history are truly modern. Both begin in the eighteenth century, flourish in the nineteenth century and decline in the twentieth century. In "The Tatler" (1709-1711) and in "The Spectator" (1711-1714) the periodical essay took shape, and Addison and Steele are the names which recur in connection with them. The Sir Roger de Coverley papers are undoubtedly the best known types of this period, but they are as yet unshaped, too rich in imaginative content, too full of the play of fancy to fit entirely into the frame of the modern essay.

The ponderosity of England's literary czar, Dr. Samuel Johnson, determined the character of the essay during the latter part of the century and gave to it a sententiousness from which, happily, it has been delivered. The uncompromising position of the dictator was only partly excused by his mastery of his stiff diction, but Johnson's work possesses an influence that proved of inestimable value—he dignified the essay into a power of polemic.

The founder of modern history—and one of the greatest English historians—was Gibbon, and his "Decline and Fall of the Roman Empire" stands alone as a masterpiece of the eighteenth century. Gibbon is the English voice of the great world-movement that found its volcanic vent in the French Revolution and he died (1794) in the very crux of its throes. Free from ecclesiasticism and not overbalanced by rationalism, "The Decline and Fall" is an imperishable monument to Gibbon's greatness.

Just as Lamb is foretold by Addison, so are Cobbett and Sydney Smith heralded by Dean Swift, though Cobbett's bludgeon and Sydney Smith's walking sword were poor weapons of satire compared with the rapier of the terrible Irish divine. It is with Charles Lamb that the modern essay links to the eighteenth century writers, in which he is steeped, and the quaint, almost elfin, "Essays of Elia" are immortal. Who, that has read it, can forget "A Dissertation on Roast Pig"? Dickens, in his novels, sometimes breaks into the form. A coach ride in "Pickwick," a sea scene in "Martin Chuzzlewit" are kin, and indeed, are more closely akin than the essays of Leigh Hunt, who was Lamb's co-worker and friend. Far greater than Hunt, but more purely a critic than essayist was William Hazlitt. Of the same period was De Quincy, whose "Confessions of an English Opium Eater" are marvels of imaginery in words.

Macaulay's Essays are incomparable as a high standard of classical English; they are vivid and stimulating, direct and telling. But it cannot be said that they are ever fair. Macaulay was first, last and all the time a politician, and he could not discuss the poetry of a poet without turning his criticism into a Whig pamphlet.

One of the greatest names in English literature during the nineteenth century then appeared, that of Thomas Carlyle, whose "Sartor Resartus" is the wildest great work in English, and whose "History of the French Revolution" is the most marvelous unhistorical history ever penned. Every page is worth reading—but for Carlyle's style, not because of his subject. He was as divergent as Macaulay was direct, as enthusiastic as Macaulay was composed, and when Carlyle undertook to use the sledge-hammer savagely, the result was more crushing than even Macaulay's determined assaults.

Matthew Arnold, poet as well as literary critic and essayist and greater as the first than the second, was a contemporary of the great art student, who, with Macaulay and Carlyle, gives to the century three English essayists. This was John Ruskin, primarily an æsthetic, but still more a master of prose style. Such prose as Ruskin's had never been seen before, it has not been seen since. He has no sense of debate, as Macaulay; you shall search in vain for the pungency of Carlyle; but only, perhaps, in some of the prose of Shelley is there a suggestion of what the English language may be in the hands of a master. Some of the smaller works, especially "Sesame and Lilies," are better known, but the style is at its finest in "Modern Painters." Nevertheless he is as unsafe a guide in his subjects as he is a leader in his literary technique.

Walter Pater and John Addington Symonds close the century. Pater's prose style is faultless, a most annoying and precious perfection. "Marius the Epicurean" is scarcely a book so much as an architectural production of prose-paragraphs of exquisite craftsmanship. A few pages of Pater is like a long-closed but beautiful room, and one reaches for Carlyle to blow the preciosity away. Symonds was of the same school, but with far less care and greater verbosity. His "History of the Renaissance in Italy" is admirable reading—for anyone with little else to do. It is full of information and insight, told in the longest way possible.

The American essay found its richest fruit in Ralph Waldo Emerson, a name to rank with Ruskin and Carlyle. Holding a strong severity of philosophy, he knew his prose thoroughly and made it sonorous. Such essays as "The Poet" are absolutely as fine as anything that has ever been penned in Europe. In the literary essay, William Dean Howells can never be forgotten, and in the field which is now beginning to be known as nature-study comes an array of writers beginning from Thoreau, who are incomparably the superiors in this domain.

In French Literature the essay first flowers under the pen of Montaigne (1533-1592), and the "Essais" belongs to that rare group of books wherein each volume is a companion rather than a book. The style is so carefully wrought that its light facility shows no trace of the polishing process; it is essentially playful, well bred and versatile.

The eighteenth century in France was too full of the preparations for the national cataclysm that closed it to give much time or care to the lighter essay. Montesquieu, Voltaire, Diderot and Rousseau became social reformers. At the same time it would be unfair to omit mention of the letter-writing of the wits of the salons which were closed by the revolution, closed, alas! by the guillotining of many fair ladies and gallant gentlemen for whose death there was no reason other than that they were ladies and gentlemen. Unlike the blossoming of the essay in England, the nineteenth century in France was too conscious of itself, too analytical, and men who would have been essayists in England became critical historians of literature. Such were Villemain, Nisard, Saint Beuve, and Taine.

It seems unkind to reiterate the point so frequently, but the German literature is lamentably weak. Just as there is no great German novelist, with the possible exception of Richter, and only one good German short story writer, Paul Heyse, so there is no German essayist of the first rank. There is hardly any of the second rank. Germany's gift lay in philosophy and in science, and the lighter forms of literature she has never possessed.

Spanish Literature also lacks the light essay, though Alberto Lista's work resembles Lamb's "Specimens of English Dramatic Poets." The most brilliant master of Spanish prose, Mariano Jose de Larra (1809-1837), may be compared to Dean Swift in his ferocious and bitter satire. Controversy holds high rank in Spain and the slashing pen, such as those of Antonio de Valbuena and Leopoldo Alas is greatly admired.

In Italy, the "Dialogues" of Leopardi are essay-like in form and perfect so far as their range goes, but the range is narrow. In prose he is an Italian Walter Pater. A finer mind, but a sterner writer, was Mazzini (d. 1872), who played so large a part in the Liberation of Italy. Tommasseo (1802-1874) was essentially a lexicographer, but he enriched Italian letters with many essays of considerable worth,

ESSAYISTS AND HISTORIANS

leaving a place as yet unfilled, saving for the too brilliant superficiality of Angelo de Gubernatis.

Before bidding farewell to the nineteenth century, its leading historians should be mentioned. Many of these are of the highest eminence. In England, following Gibbon and Hume, came Hallam, with a "View of the State of Europe During the Middle Ages," and "Constitutional History of England"; Milman, "History of Latin Christianity"; Grote, "History of Greece"; Macaulay and Carlyle, previously noted; Buckle, "A History of Civilization"; Freeman and Green, stimulating and popular, and Froude, whose "History of England" is a standard. Italy holds high rank in historians. One has but to name Ferrari, Botta, Colletta, Cantu and, more recently, Bonghi and Ferrero, to perceive her leadership in this line. Germany has no historians of eminence, confining her great work to drama; Spain has given little heed to history, her modern writers making fuller use of the novel.

The twentieth century opened with the closing work of George K. Chesterton, one of the few to take a niche among the half-dozen essayists of all time. Chesterton—far more Irish than English—makes an effort to be national, appears as the defender of the State Church and as the apologist of the England of his time, but like Dickens, his localization is but the thinnest veil over his universality. He is not profound, but scintillating, and his humor is of the finest. Of a very different sort is A. C. Benson, a meditative essayist. Hillaire Belloc, especially in his "On Anything, on Everything and on Something," commands attention, but he is more a journalist than a master of belles-lettres. With G. Lowes Dickinson, culminates the mood of quiet introspection into the life of the twentieth century as it appears at its opening.

America's chief essayist during the first two decades of the century is John Burroughs, who is beginning to be regarded among the great prose stylists of the United States. Kindlier than Emerson and far more perceptive, Burroughs's influence over this generation has been exceedingly great. Almost alone of all essayists of modern time, he has found in modern thought, in science, in progress, even in the nervous excitement of America, a message of peace and charm. In the pages of John Burroughs is to be found an American philosophy of life, which is both optimistic and truthful. No serener note could be struck for a happier prophecy of America's future.

CHAPTER XII

THE NOVEL AND THE SHORT STORY

THE novel truly begins where the drama fails, in the same sense that the drama begins with the close of the epic. It is clear, of course, that each overlaps the other and that in a minor sense during each period some literary work which might be classed under either of these three heads has continued, but it can be stated as a most important and illuminating fact that the great writers of the one form of literary style rarely synchronized with those of other schools.

Thus Homer and the cyclic poets were well out of the way before the four great figures of the Greek stage appeared, and these again had passed by the time the "Nimrod" fragment was written or "The Marvelous Things Beyond Thule" set forth. The two "Greek Novels," Heliodorus' "Theagenes and Charicles" and Longus' (?) "Daphnis and Cloe," are still later. In the same manner the period of the Epic of Chivalry contained no writers of "novels" and no dramatists, and the Elizabethan period in England was past before the novelists began. It is seldom realized that the modern novel is not an independent growth which has always been in existence as a form of literary art and has grown together with others, but that it is a late product in every age, taking into itself that which has gone before. The usual sequence is the saga, then the epic, then the drama and last the novel. The lyric, of course, bears no relation to the development of literature. The work of Sappho is as clear as the verse of Mrs. Barrett Browning, and the modern who would esteem himself greater than Pindar (522 B.C.) would find few in agreement with him. Great lyric poets there have been and will ever be, writers whose burning words inspire those who are their associates, men and women who have made the world fairer for their presence; but unfailing as is their place in a History of Literature, their part is small in the History of the Development of Literature.

It is common in literary criticism to confine the novel to a very small class of prose fiction, a class of indefinite boundaries and vague characteristics, but such is not the idea of the novel in the popular mind. Almost any kind of story is a "novel" in modern popular acceptance, and it is undoubtedly true that a novel is a compound of many. Therefore it seems an injustice to treat of the development of

THE NOVEL AND THE SHORT STORY

the novel and leave out such upstanding works as "Æsop's Fables," "The Arabian Nights' Entertainments," the "Gesta Romanorum" and the "Decameron" of Boccaccio when each of these went far to make the story of to-day.

Perhaps no work is so widely known or so often quoted as the collection of fables which goes under the name of Æsop. This famous slave, who lived in the days of Crœsus, was possessed of much adroitness and not a little wit, and he seems to have followed a double road in his recital of fables. Thus he collected whatever old fables and legends were current among the people and retold them in the phrase and manner of the philosophies of the schools of his time. This produced the happy result of pleasing the philosophers by advancing their arguments without their having recourse to the childish means of fables, and he pleased the court by enabling them to understand the philosophies without undergoing the confusion of fine-spun argument and dialectic. Being based on deep truth and expressed in simple forms, they possessed an intrinsic permanence. Thus such phrases as "sour grapes," a "wolf in sheep's clothing" and "dog in the manger" have become current in the language, and the literary style is a part of the heritage of modern times.

Similar in many ways are the groups of fairy tales, which, as Andrew Lang has pointed out, are even earlier than the great epic poems, often being the very first myths of primeval times. To give a well-known example, the fairy tale of the Sleeping Beauty is but the return of the seasons. The Princess Summer, getting tired of play, goes up to the dreary room of Autumn, where an old crone, Winter, causes her to prick her finger with the icy needle of Frost. Thereon she falls into a heavy sleep, being frost-bound, from which she can only be aroused by the fairy prince of Spring, who after the appointed time has elapsed is able to break through the barriers that have surrounded her, and kissing her, leads her back to her own Summer land again. These fairy tales, many of them nature stories of the most primitive character and others legends which have developed from a later time, also have had a decided impress upon the storyteller's art. Thus "The Goose That Laid the Golden Eggs" and the "Ugly Duckling" are thoroly familiar.

Scarcely less influential has been the Oriental tale, more especially in that collection known as the "Arabian Nights' Entertainments." The exact origin of these is unknown, but there seems little reason to doubt that they took final form during the Caliphates, altho certain of the stories included in the earlier portion of the work may have a Persian or even a Hindu source. There are really two different groups of stories. The first contains wonderful and impossible adventures and extravagant absurdities, in which the invention leaps from fancy to fancy and has no other aim than to entertain the imagination by the most grotesque, impossible and strange occurrences. These deal with the wonders of magic and have as their chief machinery the invention of Fairies, Genies and Peris, acting upon Mohammedan customs and interpretative of stories depicting the beliefs of the Koran. The second part consists of Arabian tales and anecdotes gathered from the story-tellers who were to the Caliphs what the trouveres were to the age of chivalry, and they are so intimately transcribed that the manners of that otherwise little-known period of history stand clear to modern vision. The stories of "Ali Baba and the Forty Thieves" and of "Sindbad the Sailor," for example, are not likely ever to be forgotten.

The one outstanding figure prior to the birth of the English novel is Giovanni Boccaccio (1313-1375), whose first novel, the "Filocopo," marks the transition from the semi-metrical romance of the character of "C'est d'Aucassin et Nicolette" to the true novel. His next work, the "Ameto," also was epoch-making, being the first of the true pastoral romances carried to their height by Sannazaro and Montemayor, and his "Fiametta" is quite distinctly the precursor of the modern novel. But Boccaccio's name as the first great novelist of the world rests upon the "Decameron," a group of stories rewritten from the "Gesta Romanorum," from the ballads of the country and from the folk-lore of the country.

"Among many lights in which this epoch-making book may be regarded," says F. M. Warren in his "History of the Novel Previous to the Sixteenth Century," "is that of an alliance between the elegant and superfine literature of courts and the vigorous but homely literature of the people. Nobles and ladies, accustomed to far-fetched and ornate compositions like the 'Filocopo,' were made able by the 'Decameron' to hear the same stories which amused the common people, told in a style which, too, the uneducated could appreciate and enjoy, but purged of much roughness and vulgarity and told in the only clear, forcible prose that had yet been produced.

"This is Boccaccio's best defense against the charge of licentiousness which has been so misconstruingly laid against him. He markedly did not write for the purpose of stimulating the passions, but reproduced the ordinary talk of moments of relaxation, giving it the attraction of a pure and classic style. How vastly more refined, indeed, is the 'Decameron' than were the manners of the time in which it was written may be well estimated by a comparison with such a collection as the 'Facetiæ of Poggio.'"

All these were rather factors that entered into the novel than its direct antecedents. "As is well understood to-day," says F. M. Warren again, "the Arthurian prose romances are the fountain head of the modern novel. They supplied its substance as well as set it a model of prose composition. They did not, however, furnish it with the vital spirit, without which it would never have been created. This shaping force came from another kind of medieval literature and is more directly due to the honest minstrels of France." It is almost superfluous to add that the plot of these "romans," often cleverly constructed, was the mutual affection of knight and lady. Their heroes and heroines comported themselves like lovers of the present day and set a worthy, if useless, example of fidelity to the forgetful swains of Arthur's household. From the prose stories of the Round Table then and from these poetical accounts of the "romans d'adventure" of refined life in the Middle Ages came the first novel of modern times.

One work, indeed, was a sort of universal legatee to the tales and romances of the Middle Ages. This was the Amadis of Gaul, which made its bow to the public in the last half of the fifteenth century. It possesses a distinct plot, and while it is filled with adventures-at-arms, all the exploits are done by the knight for love of his mistress, and when she receives his homage unwillingly, deeds of valor are but empty and the applause of Christendom unheeded. This work was imitated by the Palmerin romances, but they contain little that is new.

The beginning of the sixteenth century witnessed the "Arcadia" of Japoco Sannarzaro (1458-1530). It is excessively Latinized and stilted, but it presented the sixteenth century with a prose pastoral which formed a rule for those who came after. Jorge de Montemayor (1522-1651) wrote perhaps the best example of this forced school in his "Diana," which made a great furore through Spain. This being a story with definite coherence, it supplanted the "Arcadia" and had a wonderful effect on all romantic literature to come. It is to Spain also that the credit is due for the Picaresco school and its correlative author, Cervantes, the writer of "Don Quixote."

The inner meaning of the Picaresco attitude was a protest against the prevailing style of literature, which, in the romances of chivalry, showed an utter disregard for the real condition of the Spanish nation by celebrating only the deeds of one class in feudal society, the nobility. In the career of the picaro, instead of a hero urged on by his love and loyalty to win fame, the Spanish public was invited to compare his career with the actual adventures of any rascal taken from the common herd.

"In carrying out his hostility to the romances of chivalry, however, the insurgent went to the other extreme and made the heroes of realism from the very start the embodiment of all that is mean and crafty. Thus in the most distinctive of this school, the 'Laxarillo de Tormes,' the story is merely the scoundrelly adventure of a rascally beggar boy, who in turn is the guide of a blind man whom he shamefully abuses, of a priest who starves him because of avarice, of a noble who starves him because he spends all he has on keeping up an outward show, and after many other masters, gets in touch with the arch-priest, and the book closes with the blasphemous beggar turned hypocrite and succeeding admirably therein."

The "Don Quixote" of Miguel de Cervantes Saavedra (1547-1616) is the second great novel of literature, and its greatness is immortal. But, curiously enough, the author never believed in "Don Quixote" and always esteemed himself a dramatist. Almost, it would seem, in his own life, he passed through the processes through which a literature has to pass. He began with lyrics and sonnets, passed into the epic, developed the epic dramatic such as the "Numantia," tried his hand at the pastoral and then devoted himself to pure drama. But worldly failure had marked Cervantes for her own, and not until he was sick at heart and neglected, exasperated at the continuing popularity of impossible tales of chivalry, did he direct his magnificent powers to revealing the folly of knight-errantry. The picaresco tale had partly opened the eyes of the public, but after the Sorrowful Knight of La Mancha and his proverb-ridden squire had played their part, the tale of chivalry never again dared to try and raise its head.

Strictly speaking, Spain has since produced no great novelists, but contemporary literature has several names not to be ignored. Thus Valera, Pereda and Galdoz form a mighty triad, Valdes has a large following and the "La Regenta" of Alas is one of the finest of modern works, ranking as historically great.

The first great Italian novelist after Bocaccio is Allessandro Mansoni (1785-1873), whose "I Promessa Sposi" is probably better known than any book since the "Divina Commedia." It remains to this day the greatest Italian romance, and as a picture of human nature in Milan under the dreary Spanish rule of the seventeenth century it is unsurpassed. "It satisfies us," says Goethe, "like perfectly ripe fruit." Tomasso Grossi, Massimo d'Azeglio and Cæsare Cantu are disciples of this school, but none reach the heights of their master.

It is not until Gabrielle d'Annunzio that another great novelist appears in Italy, and d'Annunzio is far more poet than novelist. It is not to be expected that d'Annunzio could shake himself entirely free from the pessimism of that sublime lyrist, Giacomo Leopardi (1798-1837), but this is his chief weakness. The friendship of Giosue Carducci, patriot and clear-minded thinker as well as master of passion and beautiful language, has been a wise prevision for d'Annunzio, and the author of "Il Trionfo della Morte" and "La Vergine della Rocce" will go down to posterity wearing the laurel crown.

The first novel of France is "Meliador" by the great historian, Jean Froissart (1338-1404). It is in every sense typical of the writer of the immortal "Chronicles," lacking the inner life in spite of its construction of external marvels and splendors. Froissart was more than a mere historian. Like his successor, Philip de Commines (1445-

THE NOVEL AND THE SHORT STORY

1511), he was a word-painter of most uncommon force and a novelist with a genius for throwing life upon the page.

But even "Meliador" is dry reading beside the unctuous humor of "Pantagruel," the literary offspring of the famous Francois Rabelais (1490-1552). Rabelais' fun is most infectious. Life in him was so full and abounding that it could not be restrained, and as the first physician of his time he taught that few things in this world are wholesomer than laughter. Grandgousier, Gargantua, Pantagruel are not mere characters; they are sharp and distinct types, and the endless complexity of the adventures—such as that to consult the oracle of La Dive Bouteille—is for the purpose of touching with a keen shaft of ridicule some social and ecclesiastical abuse.

Literary anarchy followed. It was the time of the Huguenot controversy and all writing was embittered. Nevertheless this period, with all its vicissitudes, introduced one of the most charming of literary gentleman-adventurers, Jean de la Fontaine (1621-1693). He was irreclaimably wayward, utterly without comprehension of responsibility, but he was born to write perfect verses and he fulfilled his mission. He knew well the old cycle of Renard the Fox and the Fabliaux of the twelfth century. He hung upon the words of Boccaccio and the Tales of the Saints, and indeed sent his keen wit and happy faculty for phrasing over all literatures, calling from them whatsoever was suitable for a "Conte" and making all live anew by the touch of his life-filled pen.

The novel in a more confined sense begins anew with Alain-Rene LeSage (1668-1747) in his realistic work, "Gil Blas." The picaresco story was a determinative factor, but LeSage added more thereto and gave prophetic insight to the future historical novel. With Pierre Carlet de Chamblain de Marivaux (1688-1763) the novel becomes an analysis of passions and the incidents are subordinated, a distinction seen with especial force in his successor, A. F. Prevost d'Exiles (1697-1763), who is remembered especially for his famous novel, "Manon Lescaut."

The social analyst, Baron de Montesquieu (1689-1755), author of the "De L'Esprit de Lois"; the irrepressible and erratic genius, Francois Marie Arouet, commonly called Voltaire (1694-1778); the encyclopedic talent of Denis Diderot (1713-1783); the supernal idealist, Jean Jacques Rousseau (1712-1778), followed by the Revolution, left France in mental uncertainty, not less remarkable than the political turmoil for which the early part of the century was noted. Saint Simon, Fourier, Comte, Proudhon, all great names, as is that of Lamartine in poesy, led the way to the nation's chiefest boast, Victor Hugo (1802-1885). "Les Miserables" undoubtedly will be accounted one of the great novels of the world, but it will also be admitted to be prolix and discursive. We could ill spare the description of

Waterloo, but it forms no part of the narrative. "The Toilers of the Sea" is less marred in this fashion, but all of Hugo's novels, like his plays, consist largely of a stringing together of incidents. The Preface to Hugo's "Cromwell" and his "Hunchback of Notre Dame" together give the clue to Hugo's conception of the working purposes of the novel. To him the provocation of startling propinquities between the grotesque and the sublime is a large part of the novelist's art.

The historical novel found its apotheosis in Alexandre Dumas (1803-1870). No one can deny the dash, the brilliancy, the animation and the fanfarronade of "Les Trois Mousquetaires," and if d'Artagnan were expunged from letters, many would pine for his daring and his exploits with Athos, Porthos and Aramis. But Dumas possessed the vice of a too prolific imagination, and his later work was commercial output, not literature.

Far other was the work of Lucile Aurore Dupin (George Sand) (1804-1876). In proportion as Dumas is dashing, she is calm, where he is mercurial she is lethargic, and the absolute placidity of "La Petite Fadette" is the truest style of the writer. Her meteoric and passionate life with De Musset, Chopin and others in her long list of lovers, finds reflection in her letters rather than her novels.

It is impossible to avoid comparing the peasant types of George Sand with those of Honore de Balzac (1799-1850), the realist. He was not a man but a book, and his life is in the pages of the "Human Comedy." The steadiness with which he worked and his voracity for vastness of purview coupled to detail is wonderful, but there seems a distinct sense of smallness in his very desire for fame. It is the genius of a gross rather than that of a fine soul. Balzac suffered from the desire to do too much. The novelist is swallowed up in the desire to be a super-reporter, to journalize all of life by himself. He is a bourgeois squirrel in a cage of his own making, the cage, as Henry James phrases it, being "the complicated but dreadfully definite French word that built itself so solidly in and roofed itself so impenetrably over him." In this Flaubert's "Madame Bovary" is singularly similar. Greater almost than Balzac is the great French realist Emile Zola, the most Russian of all Frenchmen. But alas, unlike the Russian, he would not take the trouble to master his subject. Germany, especially modern Germany, has followed the lines of technical science too closely to pay much attention to the novel. The vogue of Ernst von Wolzogen in itself shows how utterly lacking is Germany in any great novelists.

The German novel is on a different plane. No great names rise to mind like those of Rabelais, La Fontaine, Victor Hugo, Balzac, Dumas and Zola. In the first place, there is no German literature worthy the name between Wolfram von Eschenbach and Lessing, and

THE NOVEL AND THE SHORT STORY

neither Klopstok, Lessing, Herder, Goethe, Schiller, Jean Paul Richter or Heine contributed aught of importance to the development of the novel. Paul Heyse, perhaps, will stand out with Sudermann as of chief importance among later German writers; George Ebers has written well and largely of Egypt; Frederick Spielhagen possesses power in revealing the weaknesses of the present social order, and Theodor Storm is one of the masters of the short story.

In Russia, on the other hand, the novel has had a distinguished career. Turgeniev, Tolstoi and Dostoievsky take rank with Hugo and Dumas, with Dickens and Thackeray, and modern thought is beginning to place Russian literature upon an exceedingly high plane, superior to any contemporary nation's output. It may seem at first a little strange to think of supposedly backward Russia as leading the van, but Tolstoi's "War and Peace" and Turgeniev's "Crime and Punishment" are so far in advance of their times as to be prophetic. Dostoievsky's work is more typically national, but even there the realism that is the most characteristic note of all Russian writing shines out in unabated force.

The greatness of the French novelists is only rivalled by the English school. Altho foreshadowed by Geoffrey Chaucer (1328-1340), the English novel never truly came to its own until the great revival after the close of the artificial period headed by Alexander Pope. The essayists, Addison and Steele, lead up to England's first great satirist, Jonathan Swift (1667-1745), whose "Gulliver's Travels" is entirely forgotten as a political lampoon, but is perennial as a tale. Conscious of the impending insanity which at last fell upon him, embittered by neglect and failure, he looms upon the horizon of English men of letters as the unhappiest of them all. With the "Robinson Crusoe" of Daniel Defoe (1661-1731) and the famous "Pilgrim's Progress" of John Bunyan (1628-1688), the path was made straight for Samuel Richardson (1689-1761), the "Father of Modern Prose Fiction," his first book, "Pamela," being a masterpiece.

There is at once a curious likeness and unlikeness between Richardson and his successor, Henry Fielding (1707-1754), the first a plebeian, the second a patrician; the first stilted in description of noble life, but at home in his own class, the other presenting a wonderful picture of the court, but most unfair to the dependent populace. Yet both had an aggressive influence on the third of the school, Tobias George Smollet (1721-1771), whose "Roderick Random," "Peregrine Pickle" and "Humphrey Clinker," despite a good deal of indecency, bear comparison with other great novels in delineation of character.

Contemporaneous with this must be noted the sentimental school of Lawrence Sterne (1713-1771) with "Tristram Sandy" and "The Sentimental Journey," the former famous for its portraitures of Uncle Toby and Corporal Trim, and Oliver Goldsmith (1728-1774), whose best prose work was the "Vicar of Wakefield," and a much lesser light, Henry Mackenzie (1745-1831), who is barely remembered by his first novel, "The Man of Feeling." The literary forgeries of Ossian and the Rowlie poems (McPherson and Chatterton) being passed by, the quiet morality of Maria Edgeworth, and the painstaking accuracy of Jane Austen being duly noted, the greatest romanticist of the world appears, Sir Walter Scott (1771-1832), poet as well as novelist.

The Waverly Novels are world-books, and while they are curiously uneven, all bear stamp of emperishability. Scott was poet as well as novelist, and the "Lay of the Last Minstrel," "Marmion" and "The Lady of the Lake" have an honored place, but it is especially for his novels that Scott was great, "Woodstock," "Ivanhoe," "The Talisman," "Quentin Durward" and "Kenilworth" being the most popular. He very wrongly allowed the romanticists like the curiously influential Lord Byron (1788-1324), and even small men, to overshadow his verse.

The founder of a new school in the novel was Lytton Bulwer (1806-?) (often called Bulwer Lytton). He reflects curiously the development since Scott. The idiosyncrasies of the two national poets of Ireland and Scotland, Thomas Moore (1779-1852) and Robert Burns (1759-1796), can be noted in his work, and the two lyric geniuses, Percy Bysshe Shelley (1792-1822) and John Keats (1795-1821), left their mark upon him, tho he seems quietly to have passed by the convenient ballads of William Wordsworth (1770-1850) and the monotony of Robert Southey (1774-1843). The early works of Bulwer, "Pelham" and "Eugene Aram," are especially influenced by contemporaneous and earlier verse. But after his entrance to Parliament Bulwer gave his genius a wider scope and wrote "Rienzi" and "Last Days of Pompeii." Later he wrote "My Novel," which is perhaps his masterpiece, which, while not the most popular, best reveals his finished style.

Bulwer was a voluminous writer, but his genius was far inferior to that of the two great English modern novelists, Charles Dickens (1812-1870), and William Makepeace Thackeray (1811-1863). Dickens' first book, "Pickwick Papers," belongs to every man. No person with pretensions to information but is familiar with its characters, and the vogue of Dickens has been so great that not to have read all his works is a blot upon literary reputation.

Thackeray was a social philosopher who never wrote about people but about representatives of classes. Colonel Newcome is perhaps Thackeray's only living character, for even Becky Sharp in "Vanity Fair" is a group of characticstics rather than a person possessing those characteristics. The names of Charles Kingsley and George Eliot carry on the period of contemporaneous literature.

THE NOVEL AND THE SHORT STORY

The contemporary novel in England has a few names that carry weight, and of these the chiefest is H. G. Wells. One has an equal privilege of hating Mr. Wells as of liking him, but there can be no doubt as to his size. Arnold Bennett's world is tiny, but he knows it thoroughly; Wells' world is Gargantuan and he knows it passably well. That he cannot avoid preaching—and preaches more as he grows older—is unfortunate, but a great novelist often is measured by his influence, and it will be as impossible to forget Wells in the novel hereafter as it would be for a modern dramatist to ignore Ibsen. That Wells nearly always endeavors to handle more than the limits allow—as the hopelessly poor ending of "The World Set Free," shines out clearly by his success in smaller things such as "Mr. Polly." The realistic school, to which Mr. Wells thinks he belongs (in spite of his earlier works), is more truly carried out by Compton Mackenzie, Gissing and Bennett.

In every period, however, Romanticism will claim its rightful heritage, and the reader who does not know his William J. Locke and his Joseph Conrad is as sadly to lack as the adventure lover who is ignorant of Rider Haggard, the swashbuckler disciple who has failed to know his Anthony Hope, his Stanley Weyman or his Mac Cutcheon, or the lover of fantasy who has passed by George MacDonald, George K. Chesterton and William Stephens.

The American novel of the twentieth century falls far below the English novel, just as the American short story is immeasurably the superior. Good novels are written by Richard Harding Davis, Mary Johnston, Winston Churchill, Owen Johnson, Theodore Dreiser, Rex Beach, Thomas Dixon, even to a hundred names. Only in one field does the American novel rise (and that is short story in its character) viz., the sunshine optimism form, the deliberate intention to be pleasing. This form is artificial sentimental, overdone, pseudo-religious yet very joyous withal. To this school belong Alice Hegan Rice, Kathleen Norris, Gene Stratton Porter, Frances Hodgson Burnett, and many others. The "best seller" note in these is no detriment to them, they are frankly written as books to please, not as works of art; the eye is to the market, not to the laurel wreath. The awful thought occurs: Is the market, then, a more powerful stimulus to American novelists than the laurel wreath? At least the short story is our work.

Historically, the short story begins not with the "Fables" of Æsop, for they are parables, nor with the "Decameron" of Boccaccio, for the stories therein are rather condensed romances, but rather with the "Gesta Romanorum" of unknown authorship, Gower's "Confessio Amantis," and Chaucer's "Canterbury Tales." The first two collections named contain the larger number of all the good fourteenth century short stories in typical forms, Chaucer's work shows examples carried to the highest point of artistry.

The earliest forms were the "contes dévots" or "devout tales," which were a French manner of telling miracle-stories. The best example in readable English is Chaucer's "Prioress Tale," which tells of a murdered lad who was miraculously able to reveal his whereabouts and to bring justice upon his murderers by continuing to sing to the Virgin Mary after his throat was cut.

Equally naive, and posssessing even more charm, was the "lai." Like the "conte dévot," the "lai" was Celtic, had its origin in Ireland, and carried the fairy tale glamour into mediæval Europe. In Chaucer, the "Wife of Bath's Tale" is a true "lai," where the fairy hag takes on a form of beauty for the knight who gives her power over him.

The third factor in the development of the short story, as exemplified by this first and greatest master, was the "fablau," a realistic "good story," often gross and sometimes frankly indecent, as may be seen in Chaucer's "The Miller's Tale" and "The Reeve's Tale." The importance of this factor lay in the motivation usually taking its root in a sataric comment upon character and upon life.

Typically medieval and probably Teutonic was the beast-fable of which "The Fox and the Wolf" is the most famous. Henryson is even more a master of this form than Chaucer, and he possesses a mint of humor, but his English is crabbed and exceedingly hard to read.

A fifth type takes its place in the development of the short story, and this is the "novella," the precursor of the renaissance form. One of the modes of this was the "exempla" or illustrations which could be used in sermons. Of these there were vast collections. In Chaucer "The Pardoner's Tale" is such an "'exempla," teaching its moral of the deathful sin of avarice.

With Chaucer to show what could be done, the short story should have advanced steadily, but instead, a century of silence followed, and then the "novella" was developed to the exclusion of the other type. This, however, lent itself to drama so readily that the Elizabethans seized it for this purpose, and what the dramatists did not use fell into the hands of the Euphuists who dressed and decorated it to death. In one example only—Aphra Behn's "Orvonoks" (1688)—the seventeenth century saw a worthy English short story.

The eighteenth century harked back to the "exempla" and Addison and Johnson brought in the short story again, mainly as an illustration to a more or less didactic and often dull essay. Hannah More, with more religion and less wit, showed how this form could be spoiled and her "Cheap Repositary Tracts" were as effective a means of slaughtering the eighteenth century type of short story as had been Lyly's "Euphues." Maria Edgeworth, indeed, tried to revive the

THE NOVEL AND THE SHORT STORY

"exemplum" in her "Moral Tales" in the first decade of the nineteenth century.

America can proudly boast of being the founder of the modern short story. In the decade between 1820 and 1830 Washington Irving took the romantic material of his age, infused it with humor, treated it with a measure of classical style, and became the father of the modern form. "Rip Van Winkle" and the "Romance of Sleepy Hollow" may fairly be classed as the best of the work that inaugurated a new age. Still, his work was too classic for his public, he established no school, and stands alone, a solitary figure in America's literary history.

There is a curious belief abroad that Poe was a meteor in the world of letters, that he devised the matter as well as the form of his tales of horror. Nothing could be further from truth. Poe's materials were not only not new, they were the hackneyed themes of an age of decadent romanticism, but Poe was a marvelous master of the craft of suspense and spared no pains to make every incident, every word, indeed, lead to the climax.

The detective story owes its origin to Poe. "The Murders in the Rue Morgue" is the forerunner of Gaboriau, of Sherlock Holmes, of Arsene Lupin. Even Robert Louis Stevenson owes more to "The Gold Bug" than he would have cared to own. Modern writers have improved upon Poe, but his is the foundation on which they build.

Contemporaneous with Poe in point of time but far in advance in point of development was Nathaniel Hawthorne. "Rappaccini's Daughter" and "Ethan Brand" still show the love of the horrible that Poe had carried to its utmost height, but they also show a perception of romantic narrative and instead of a pictured horrible or an allegory, he chose the story, though even there, he could not quite avoid preachments. Each of these two masters had but one worthy disciple, Fitz-James O'Brien, whose "What Was It?" is worthy of Poe; and Edward Everett Hale, whose "The Man Without a Country" is as Hawthornesque in its moral note as it is ill-constructed in its emotional unbalance.

By contrast, some of the work of Dickens approaches the short story, and "The Cricket on the Hearth" may take rank among the best. Mrs. Gaskell's "Cousin Phillis" is perhaps the only other short story in England worthy of mention until the effulgence of Rudyard Kipling appears on the horizon.

The flood of the short story belongs to America. Three tales have made one man great. These are "The Luck of Roaring Camp," "The Outcasts of Poker Flat" and "Tennessee's Partner," and the name of Bret Harte is imperishably blazoned in literature. They are sentimental, they are over-colored, they are Victorian—that worst of opprobrious terms—but they are none the less great. Bret Harte once and for all made his local color the *deus ex machina* of his story. Any one of the three mentioned is not only American, it is blaringly Californian.

This discovery led to the utilization by writers of every nook and corner where geographic isolation had perpetuated local characteristics. The French and racial tangles of Lousiana produced Geo. W. Cable's "Old Creole Days." Thomas Nelson Page used "In Ole Virginia," Sarah Orne Jewett exploits the Maine coast, Mary Wilkins-Freeman in her "A Humble Romance" reveals New England, and Margaret Deland has made "Old Chester Tales" redolent of western Pennsylvania. The short story of local color in the twentieth century has scarcely degenerated, but it has become swamped with mediocrity. It would be invidious to give names.

In Henry James is a different branching of the short story, the psychological variety. "The Madonna of the Future" is an early example of a style which, in "The Turn of the Screw," became an unpleasant pathological exhibition. Almost as great a figure as Henry James, one of the most compelling writers of the day is Edith Wharton, also a psychologist in type.

The late nineteenth century developed two masters of the short story worthy of rank with Poe and Hawthorne, and coming later in the development, better craftsmen. The first of these is Robert Louis Stevenson, and his best known short story is "Dr. Jekyll and Mr. Hyde." "A Lodging for the Night," though less well known, is greater. Stevenson's is the work of the finished artist and the reader of slap-dash is apt to miss the flavor.

Rudyard Kipling was the second of the great masters. He ran riot with local color, but showed himself in control of his vivid splashes; he emphasized and re-emphasized and then underscored some more, but there was always something worth emphasizing. Some of his short stories will be classed among the greatest. For local color nothing can rival "The Hunting of Kaa," for psychology and charm "The Brushwood Boy" is perennial, for adventure and grip "The Man Who Would Be King" is likely to be long without a peer. He has a host of imitators, some occasionally good, such as Jack London in his earlier work, but most of his is machine-made for the ten and fifteen cent magazines. Only Ambrose Bierce stands fiercely apart.

America's latest master was O. Henry, but it is scarcely fair to class him as a short-story writer, he was rather a sketch-writer. Class characteristics are his plane, and like many another writer of to-day—Montagu Glass may be named as an example—he depends on the extrinsic interest rather than the intrinsic interest of the subject. In England the delightful W. W. Jacobs still writes of coastwise life. Of good shipshape shore stories the magazines are full—

a list might easily include a hundred names, but none of these are great. If it be asked why, the answer is easy. The reading public wants journalism and will read Gouverneur Morris or George Randolph Chester rather than such gems as Booth Tarkington's "Monsieur Beaucaire," or an occasional "best" of Richard Harding Davis.

To discriminate and evaluate among the short stories of to-day is as impossible as it would be foolish. The dust must settle first. There is no denying that the second decade of the twentieth century has given fewer good short stories than the first decade, and this again fewer than the last decade of the nineteenth century. The novel is steadily advancing, and the short story declining. From Washington Irving to O. Henry is almost a century during which that American has led the world in the art of the short story. Who can tell where the oriflamme of the United States may lead the world in the century to come?

ENGLISH POETRY

ENGLISH POETRY

GEOFFREY CHAUCER

THE PROLOGUE TO THE CANTERBURY TALES

1
Whan that Aprille with his shoures soote
The droghte of Marche hath perced to the roote
And bathed every veyne in swich licour,
Of which vertu engendred is the flour;
Whan Zephirus eek with his swete breeth
Inspired hath in every holt and heeth
The tendre croppes, and the yonge sonne
Hath in the Ram his halfe cours y-ronne,
And samale fowles maken melodye,
That slepen al the night with open yë,
(So priketh hem nature in hir corages
Than longen folk to goon on pilgrimages,
And palmers for to seken straunge strondes,
To ferne halwes, couthe in sondry lones;
And specially, from every shires ende
Of Engelond, to Caunterbury they wende,
The hole blisful martir for to seke,
That hem hath holpen, whan that they were seke.

Bifel that, in that sesoun on a day,
In Southwerk at the Tabard as I lay
Redy to wenden on my pilgrimage
To Caunterbury with ful devout corage,
At night was come in-to that hostelrye
Wel nyne and twenty in a compaignye,
Of sondry folk, by aventure y-falle
In felawshipe, and pilgrims were they alle,
That toward Caunterbury wolden ryde;
The chambres and the stables weren wyde,
And wel we weren esed atte beste,
And shortly, whan the sonne was to reste,
So hadde I spoken with hem everichon,

That I was of hir felawshipe anon,
And made forward erly for to ryse,
To take our wey, ther as I yow devyse.

  But natheles, whyl I have tyme and space,
Er that I ferther in this tale pace,
Me thinketh it acordaunt to resoun,
To telle yew al the condicioun
Of ech of hem, so as it semed me,
And whiche they weren, and of what degree;
And eek in what array that they were inne:
And at a knight than wol I first biginne.

  A Knight ther was, and that a worthy man,
That fro the tyme that he first bigan
To ryden out, he loved chivalrye,
Trouthe and honour, fredom and curteisye.
Ful worthy was he in his lordes werre,
And thereto hadde he riden (no man ferre)
As wel in cristendom as in hethenesse,
And evere honoured for his worthinesse.
At Alisaundre he was, whan it was wonne;
Ful ofte tyme hadde the bord bigonne
Aboven alle naciouns in Pruce.
In Lettow hadde he reysed and in Ruce,
No cristen man so ofte of his degree.
In Gernade at the sege eek hadde he be
Of Algezir, and riden in Belmarye.
At Lyeys was he, and at Satalye,
Whan they were wonne; and in the Grete See
At many a noble armee hadde he be,
At mortal batailles hadde he been fiftene,
And foughten for our feith at Tramissene
In listes thryes, and ay slayn his foo.
This ilke worthy knight hadde been also
Somtyme with the lord of Palatye,
Ageyn another hethen in Turkye:
And evermore he hadde a sovereyn prys.
And though that he were worthy, he was wys,
And of his port as meek as is a mayde.
He nevere yet no vileynye ne sayde
In al his lyf, un-to no maner wight.
He was a verray parfit gentil knight.
But for to tellen yow of his array,
His hors were goode, but he was nat gay.
Of fustian he wered a gipoun
Al bismotered with his habergeoun.

For he was late y-come from his viage,
And wente for to doon his pilgrimage.
  With him ther was his sone, a yong Squyer,
A lovyer, and a lusty bacheler,
With lokkes crulle, as they were leyd in presse.
Of twenty yeer of age he was, I gesse.
Of his stature he was of evene lengthe,
And wonderly delivere, and greet of strengthe.
And he hadde been somtyme in chivachye,
In Flaundres, in Artoys, and Picardye,
And born him wel, as of so litel space,
In hope to stonden in his lady grace.
Embrouded was he, as it were a mede
Al ful of fresshe floures, whyte and rede.
Singinge he was, or floytinge, al the day;
He was as fresh as in the month of May.
Short was his goune, with sleves longe and wyde.
Wel coude he sitte on hors, and faire ryde.
He coude songes make and wel endyte,
Iuste and eek daunce, and wel purtreye and wryte.
So hote he lovede, that by nightertale
He sleep namore than doth a nightingale.
Curteys he was, lowly, and servisable,
And carf biforn his fader at the table.

  A Yeman hadde he, and servaunts namo
At that tyme, for him liste ryde so;
And he was clad in cote and hood of grene;
A sheef of pecok arwes brighte and kene
Under his belt he bar ful thriftily,
(Wel coude he dresse his takel yemanly:
His arwes drouped noght with fetheres lowe),
And in his hand he bar a mighty bowe.
A not-heed hadde he, with a broun visage.
Of wode-craft wel coude he al the usage.
Upon his arm he bar a gay bracer,
And by that syde a swerd and a bokeler,
And on that other syde a gay daggere,
Harneised wel, and sharp as point of spere;
A Cristofre on his brest of silver shene
An horn he bar, the bawdrik was of grene;
A forster was he, soothly, as I gesse.

  Ther was also a Nonne, a Prioresse,
That of hir smyling was ful simple and coy;
Hir gretteste ooth was but by seynt Loy;
And she was cleped madame Eglentyne.

Ful wel she song the service divyne,
Entuned in hir nose ful semely;
And Frensh she spak ful faire and fetisly,
After the scole of Stratford atte Bowe,
For Frensh of Paris was to hir unknowe.
At mete wel y-taught was she with-alle;
She leet no morsel from hir lippes falle,
Ne wette hir fingeres in hir sauce depe.
Wel coude she carie a morsel, and wel kepe,
That no drope ne fille up-on hir brest.
In curteisye was set ful moche hir lest.
Hir over lippe wyped she so clene,
That in hir coppe was no ferthing sene
Of grece, whan she dronken hadde hir draughte.
Ful semely after hir mete she raughte,
And sikerly she was of greet disport,
And ful plesaunt, and amiable of port,
And peyned hir to countrefete chere
Of court, and been estatlich of manere,
And to ben holden digne of reverence.
But, for to speken of hir conscience,
She was so charitable and so pitous,
She wolde wepe, if that she sawe a mous
Caught in a trappe, if it were deed or bledde.
Of smale houndes had she, that she fedde
With rosted flesh, or milk and wastel breed.
But sore weep she if oon of hem were deed,
Or if men smoot it with a yerde smerte:
And al was conscience and tendre herte.
Ful semely hir wimpel pinched was;
Hir nose tretys; hir eyen greye as glas;
Hir mouth ful smal, and ther-to softe and reed;
But sikerly she hadde a fair forheed.
It was almost a spanne brood, I trowe;
For, hardily, she was nat undergrowe.
Ful fetis was hir cloke, as I was war.
Of smal coral aboute hir arm she bar
A peire of bedes, gauded al with grene;
And ther-on heng a broche of gold ful shene,
On which ther was first write a crowned A,
And after, *Amor vincit omnia*.

Another Nonne with hir hadde she,
That was hir chapeleyne, and Preestes thre.

A Monk ther was, a fair for the maistrye,
An out-rydere, that lovede venerye;

GEOFFREY CHAUCER

A manly man, to been an abbot able.
Ful many a deyntee hors hadde he in stable:
And, whan he rood, men mighte his brydel here
Ginglen in a whistling wynd as clere,
And eek as loude as doth the chapel-belle,
Ther-as this lord was keper of the celle.
The reule of seint Maure or of seint Beneit,
By-cause that it was old and som-del streit,
This ilke monk leet olde thinges pace
And held after the newe world the space.
He yaf nat of that text a pulled hen,
That seith, that hunters been nat holy men;
Ne that a monk, whan he is reechelees
Is likned til a fish that is waterlees;
This is to seyn, a monk out of his cloistre.
But thilke text held he nat worth an oistre.
And I seyde his opinioun was good.
What sholde he studie, and make him-selven wood,
Upon a book in cloistre alwey to poure,
Or swinken with his handes, and laboure,
As Austin bit? How shal the world be served?
Lat Austin have his swink to him reserved.
Therfor he was a pricasour aright;
Grehoundes he hadde, as swifte as fowel in flight;
Of priking and of hunting for the hare
Was al his lust, for no cost wolde he spare.
I seigh his sleves purfiled at the hond
With grys, and that the fyneste of a lond;
And, for to festne his hood under his chin,
He hadde of gold y-wroght a curious pin:
A love-knot in the gretter ende ther was.
His heed was balled, that shoon as any glas,
And eek his face, as he hadde been anoint.
He was a lord ful fat and in good point;
His eyen stepe, and rollinge in his heed,
That stemed as a forneys of a leed;
His botes souple, his hors in greet estaat.
Now certeinly he was a fair prelaat;
He was nat pale as a for-pyned goost.
A fat swan loved he best of any roost
His palfrey was as broun as is a berye.

A frere ther was, a wantown and a merye,
A limitour, a ful solempne man.
In alle the ordres foure is noon that can
So moche of daliaunce and fair langage.

He hadde maad full many a mariage
Of yonge wommen, at his owne cost.
Un-to his ordre he was a noble post.
Ful wel biloved and famulier was he
With frankeleyns over-al in his contree,
And eek with worthy wommen of the toun:
For he had power of confessioun,
As seyde him-self, more than a curat,
For of his ordre he was licentiat.
Ful swetely herde he confessioun,
And plesaunt was his absolucion;
He was an esy man to yeve penaunce
Ther as he wiste to han a good pitaunce;
For unto a povre ordre for to yive
Is signe that a man is wel y-shrive.
For if he yaf, he dorste make avaunt,
He wiste that a man was repentaunt.
For many a man so hard is of his herte,
He may not wepe al-thogh him sore smerte.
Therfore, in stede of weping and preyeres,
Men moot yeve silver to the povre freres.
His tipet was ay farsed ful of knyves
And pinnes, for to yeven faire wyves.
And certeinly he hadde a mery note;
Wel coude he singe and pleyen on a rote.
Of yeddinges he bar utterly the prys.
His nekke whyt was as the flour-de-lys.
Ther-to he strong was as a champioun
He knew the tavernes wel in every toun,
And everich hostiler and tappestere
Bet than a lazar or a beggestere;
For un-to swich a worthy man as he
Acorded nat, as by his facultee,
To have with seke lazars aqueyntaunce.
It is nat honest, it may nat avaunce
For to delen with no swich poraille,
But all with riche and sellers of vitaille.
And over-al, ther-as profit sholde aryse,
Curteys he was, and lowly of servyse.
Ther nas no man nowhere so vertuous.
He was the beste beggere in his hous;
For thogh a widwe hadde noght a sho,
So plesaunt was his *In principio,*
Yet wolde he have a ferthing, er he wente.
His purchas was well bettre than his rente.

And rage he coude as it were right a whelpe.
In love-dayes ther coude he mochel helpe.
For ther he was nat lyk a cloisterer,
With thredbare cope, as is a povre scoler,
But he was lyk a maister or a pope,
Of double worsted was his semi-cope,
That rounded as a belle out of the presse.
Somwhat he lipsed, for his wantownesse,
To make his English swete up-on his tongue;
And in his harping, whan that he had songe,
His eyen twinkled in his heed aright,
As doon the sterres in the frosty night.
This worthy limitour was cleped Huberd.

A Marchant was ther with a forked berd,
In mottelee, and hye on horse he sat,
Up-on his heed a Flaundrish bever hat;
His botes clasped faire and fetisly.
His resons he spak ful solempnely,
Sowninge always thencrees of his winning.
He wolde the see were kept for any thing
Bitwixe Middleburgh and Orewelle.
Wel coude he in eschaunge sheeldes selle.
This worthy man ful well his wit bisette;
Ther wiste no wight that he was in dette,
So estatly was he of his governaunce,
With his bargaynes, and with his chevisaunce.
For sothe he was a worthy man with-alle,
But sooth to seyn, I noot how men him calle.

A Clerk ther was of Oxenford also,
That un-to logik hadde longe y-go.
As lene was his hors as is a rake,
And he nas nat right fat, I undertake;
But loked holwe, and ther-to soberly.
Ful thredbar was his overest courtepy;
For he had geten him yet no benefice,
Ne was so worldly for to have office.
For him was levere have at his beddes heed
Twenty bokes, clad in blak or reed
Of Aristotle and his philosophye,
Than robes riche, or fithele, or gay sautrye.
But al be that he was a philosophre,
Yet hadde he but litel gold in cofre;
But al that he mighte of his frendes hente,
On bokes and on lerninge he it spente
And bisily gan for the soules preye

Of hem that yaf him wher-with to scoleye.
Of studie took he most cure and most hede.
Noght o word spak he more than was nede,
And that was seyd in forme and reverence,
And short and quik, and ful of hy sentence.
Sowninge in moral vertu was his speche,
And gladly wolde he lerne, and gladly teche.

  A Sergeant of the Lawe, war and wys,
That often hadde been at the parvys,
Ther was also, ful riche of excellence.
Discreet he was, and of greet reverence:
He seemed swich, his wordes weren so wyse,
Iustice he was ful often in assyse,
By patente, and by pleyn commissioun;
For his science, and for his heigh renoun
Of fees and robes hadde he many oon.
So greet a purchasour was nowhere noon.
Al was fee simple to him in effect,
His purchasing mighte nat been infect.
Nowhere so bisy a man as he ther nas,
And yet he semed bisier than he was.
In termes hadde he caas and domes alle,
That from the tyme of king William were falle.
Therto he oude endyte, and make a thing,
Ther coude no wight pinche at his wryting;
And every statut coude he pleyn by rote.
He rood but hoomly in a medlee cote
Girt with a ceint of silk, with barres smale;
Of his arraye telle I no lenger tale.

  A Frankeleyn was in his compaignye;
Why was his berd as is the dayesye.
Of his complexioun he was sangwyn.
Wel loved he by the morwe a sop in wyn.
To liven in delyt was evere his wone,
For he was Epicurus owne sone,
That heeld opinioun that pleyn delyt
Was verraily felicitee parfyt.
An householdere, and that a greet, was he;
Seynt Iulian he was in his contree.
His breed, his ale, was alwey after oon;
A bettre envyned man was nevere noon.
With-oute bake mete was nevere his hous,
Of fish and flesh, and that so plentevous,
It snewed in his hous of mete and drinke,
Of all deyntees that men coude thinke.

After the sondry sesons of the yeer,
So chaunged he his mete and his soper.
Ful many a fat partrich hadde he in mewe,
And many a breem and many a luce in stewe.
Wo was his cook, but-if his sauce were
Poynaunt and sharp, and redy al his gere.
His table dormant in his halle alway
Stood redy covered al the longe day.
At sessiouns ther was he lord and sire.
Fu ofte tyme he was knight of the shire.
An anlas and a gipser al of silk
Heng at his girdel, whyt as morne milk
A shirreve hadde he been, and a countour;
Was nowhere such a worthy vavasour.

  An Haberdassher and a Carpenter,
A Webbe, a Dyere, and a Tapicer,
And they were clothed alle in o liveree,
Of a solempne and greet fraternitee.
Ful fresh and newe hir gere apyked was;
Hir knyves were y-chaped noght with bras,
But al with silver wroght ful clene and weel,
Hir girdles and hir pouches everydeel.
Wel semed ech of hem a fair burgeys,
To sitten in a yeldhalle on a deys.
Everich, for the wisdom that he can,
Was shaply for to been an alderman.
For catel hadde they ynogh and rente,
And eek his wyves wolde it wel assente;
And elles certein were they to blame.
It is full fair to been y-clept *ma dame*,
And goon to vigilyës al bifore,
And have a mantel roialliche y-bore.

  A Cook they hadde with hem for the nones,
To boille chiknes with the mary-bones,
And poudre-marchant tart, and galingale.
Wel coude he knowe a draughte of London ale.
He coude roste, and sethe, and broile, and frye,
Maken mortreux, and wel bake a pye.
But greet harm was it, as it thoughte me,
That on his shine a mormal hadde he;
For blankmanger, that made he with the beste.

  A Shipman was ther, woning fer by weste:
For aught I woot, he was of Dertemouthe.
He rood up-on a rouncy, as he couthe,
In a gowne of falding to the knee.

A daggere hanging on a laas hadde he
Aboute his nekke under his arm adoun.
The hote somer had maad his hewe al broun;
And, certeinly, he was a good felawe.
Ful many a draughte of wyn had he y-drawe
From Burdeux-ward, whyl that the chapman sleep.
Of nyce conscience took he no keep.
If that he faught, and hadde the hyer hond,
By water he sente him hoom to every lond.
But of his craft he rekene wel his tydes,
His stremes and his daungers him bisydes,
His herberwe and his mone, his lodemenage,
Ther nas noon swich from Hulle to Cartage.
Hardy he was, and wys to undertake;
With many a tempest hadde his berd been shake.
He knew wel alle the havenes, as they were,
From Gootlond to the cape of Finistere,
And every cryke in Britayne and in Spayne;
His barge y-cleped was the Maudelayne.

With us there was a Doctour of Phisyk,
In all this world ne was ther noon him lyk
To speke of phisik and of surgerye;
For he was grounded in astronomye.
He kepte his pacient a ful greet del
In houres, by his magic naturel.
Wel coude he fortunen the ascendent
Of his images for his pacient.
He knew the cause of everich maladye,
Were it of hoot or cold, or moiste, or drye,
And where engendred, and of what humour;
He was a verrey parfit practisour.
The cause y-knowe, and of his harm the rote,
Anon he yaf the seke man his bote.
Ful redy hadde he his apothecaries,
To sende him drogges, and his letuaries,
For ech of hem made other for to winne;
Hir frendschipe nas nat newe to biginne.
Wel knew he the olde Esculapius,
And Deiscorides, and eek Rufus;
Old Ypocras, Haly, and Galien;
Serapion, Razis, and Avicen;
Averrois, Damascien, and Constantyn;
Bernard, and Gatesden, and Gilbertyn.
Of his diete mesurable was he,
For it was of no superfluitee,

But of greet norissing ad digestible.
His studie was but litel on the Bible.
In sangwin and in pers he clad was al,
Lyned with taffata and with sendal;
And yet he was but esy of dispence;
He kepte that he wan in pestilence.
For gold in phisik is a cordial,
Therfor he lovede gold in special.

A good Wyf was ther of bisyde Bathe,
But she was som-del deef, and that was scathe.
Of cloth-making she hadde swiche an haunt,
She passed hem of Ypres and of Gaunt.
In al the parisshe wyf ne was ther noon
That to the offring bifore hir sholde goon;
And if ther dide, certeyn, so wrooth was she,
That she was out of alle charitee.
Hir coverchiefs ful fyne were of ground;
I dorste swere they weyeden ten pound
That on a Sonday were upon hir heed.
Hir hosen were of fyn scarlet reed,
Ful streite y-teyd, and shoos ful moiste and newe.
Bold was hir face, and fair, and reed of hewe.
She was a worthy womman al hir lyve,
Housbondes at chirche-dore she hadde fyve,
Withouten other compaignye in youthe;
But therof nedeth nat to speke as nouthe.
And thryes hadde she been at Ierusalem;
But hadde passed many a straunge streem;
At Rome she hadde been, and at Boloigne,
In Galice at seint Iame, and at Coloigne.
She coude moche of wandring by the weye.
Gat-tothed was she, soothly for to seye.
Up-on an amblere esily she sat,
Y-wimpled wel, and on hir heed an hat
As brood as is a bokeler on a targe;
A foot-mantel aboute hir hipes large,
And on hir feet a paire of spores sharpe.
In felaweschip wel coude she laughe and carpe.
Of remedies of love she knew per-chaunce,
For she coude of that art the olde daunce.

A good man was ther of religioun,
And was a povre Persoun of a toun;
But riche he was of holy thoght and werk.
He was also a lerned man, a clerk,
That Cristes gospel trewely wolde preche;

His parisshens devoutly wolde he teche.
Benigne he was, and wonder diligent,
And in adversitee ful pacient;
And swich he was y-preved ofte sythes.
Ful looth were him to cursen for his tythes,
But rather wolde he yeven, out of doute,
Un-to his povre parisshens aboute
Of his offring, and eek of his substaunce.
He coude in litel thing han suffisaunce.
Wyd was his parisshe, and houses fer a-sonder,
But he ne lafte nat, for reyn ne thonder,
In siknes nor in meschief to visyte
The ferreste in his parisshe, moche and lyte,
Up-on his feet, and in his hand a staf.
This noble ensample to his sheep he yaf,
That first he wroghte, and afterward he taughte;
Out of the gospel he tho wordes caughte;
And this figure he added eek ther-to,
That if gold ruste, what shal yren do?
For if a preest be foul, on whom we truste,
No wonder is a lewed man to ruste;
And shame it is, if a preest take keep,
A shiten shepherde and a clene sheep.
Wel oghte a preest ensample for to yive,
By his clennesse, how that his sheep shold live.
He sette nat his benefice to hyre,
And leet his sheep encombred in the myre,
And ran to London, un-to seynt Poules,
To seken him a chaunterie for soules,
Or with a bretherhed to been withholde;
But dwelte at hoom, and kepte wel his folde,
So that the wolf ne made it nat miscarie;
He was a shepherde and no mercenarie.
And though he holy were, and vertuous,
He was to sinful man nat despitous,
Ne of his speche daungerous ne digne,
But in his teching discreet and benigne.
To drawen folk to heven by fairnesse
By good ensample, this was his bisynesse:
But it were any persone obstinat,
What so he were, of heigh or lowe estat,
Him would he snibben sharply for the nones.
A bettre preest, I trowe that nowher non is.
He wayted after no pompe and reverence,
Ne maked him a spyced conscience,

But Cristes lore, and his apostles twelve,
He taughte, but first he folwed it him-selve.

With him ther was a Plowman, was his brother,
That hadde y-lad of dong ful many a fother,
A trewe swinkere and a good man was he,
Livinge in pees and parfit charitee.
God loved he best with al his hole herte
At all tymes, thogh him gamed or smerte,
And thanne his neighebour right as him-selve,
He wolde thresshe, and ther-to dyke and delve,
For Cristes sake, for every povre wight,
Withouten hyre, if it lay in his might.
His tythes payed he ful faire and wel,
Bothe of his propre swink and his catel.
In a tabard he rood upon a mere.

Ther was also a Reve and a Millere,
A Somnour and a Pardoner also,
A Maunciple, and my-self; ther wer namo.

The Miller was a stout carl, for the nones,
Ful big he was of braun, and eek of bones;
That proved wel, for over-al ther he cam,
At wrastling he wolde have alwey the ram.
He was short-sholdred, brood, a thikke knarre,
Ther nas no dore that he nolde heve of harre,
Or breke it, at a renning, with his heed.
His berd as any sowe or fox was reed,
And ther-to brood, as though it were a spade.
Up-on the cop right of his nose he hade
A werte, and ther-on stood a tuft of heres,
Reed as the bristles of a sowes eres,
His nose-thirles blake were and wyde.
A swerd and bokeler bar he by his syde;
His mouth as greet was as a greet forneys.
He was a janglere and a goliardeys,
And that was most of sinne and harlotryes.
Wel coude he stelen corn, and tollen thryes;
And yet he hadde a thombe of gold pardee.
A whyt cote and a blew hood wered he.
A baggepype wel coude he blowe and sowne,
And therewithal he broghte us out of towne.

A gentil Maunciple was ther of a temple,
Of which achatours might take exemple
For to be wyse in bying of vitaille.
For whether that he payde, or took by taille,
Algate he wayted so in his achat,

That he was ay biforn and in good stat.
Now is nat that of God a ful fair grace,
That swich a lewed mannes wit shal pace
The wisdom of an heep of lerned men?
Of maistres hadde he mo than thryes ten
They were of lawe expert and curious;
Of which ther were a doseyn in that hous,
Worthy to be stiwardes of rent and lond
Of any lord that is in Engelond,
To make him live by his propre good,
In honour dettelees, but he were wood,
Or live as scarsly as him list desire;
And able for to helpen al a shire
In any cas that mighte falle or happe;
And yit this maunciple sette hir aller cappe.

The Reve was a sclendre colerik man,
His berd was shave as ny as ever he can.
His heer was by his eres round y-shorn.
His top was dokked lyk a preest biforn.
Ful longe were his legges, and ful lene,
Y-lyk a staf, ther was no calf y-sene.
Wel coude he kepe a gerner and a binne;
Ther was noon auditour coude on him winne.
Wel wiste he, by the droghte, and by the reyn,
The yeldyng of his seed, and of his greyn.
His lordes sheep, his neet, his dayerge,
His swyn, his hors, his stoor, and his pultrye,
Was hoolly in this reves governing,
And by his covenaunt yaf the rekening,
Sin that his lord was twenty yeer of age;
Ther coude no man bring him in arrerage.
Ther nas baillif, ne herde, ne other hyne,
That he knew his sleighte and his covyne;
They were adrad of him, as of the deeth.
His woning was ful fair up-on an heeth,
With grene trees shadwed was his place.
He coude bettre than his lord purchace.
Ful riche he was astored prively,
His lord wel coude he plesen subtilly,
To yeve and lene him of his owne good,
And have a thank, and yet a cote, and hood.
In youthe he lerned hadde a good mister;
He was a well good wrighte, a carpenter.
This reve sat up-on a ful good stot,
That was al pomely grey, and highte Scot.

GEOFFREY CHAUCER

A long surcote of pers up-on he hade,
And by his syde he bar a rusty blade.
Of Northfolk was this reve, of which I telle,
Bisyde a toun men clepen Baldeswelle.
Tukked he was, as is a frere, aboute,
And evere he rood the hindreste of our route.

A Somnour was ther with us in that place,
That hadde a fyr-reed cherubinnes face,
For sauceflem he was, with eyen narwe.
As hoot he was, and lecherous as a sparwe,
With scalled browes blake, and piled berd;
Of his visage children were aferd.
Ther nas quik-silver, litarge, ne brimstoon,
Boras, ceruce, ne oille of tartre noon,
Ne oynement that wolde clense and byte,
That him mighte helpen of his whelkes whyte,
Ne of the knobbes sittinge on his chekes.
Wel loved he garleek, oynons, and eek lekes,
And for to drinken strong wyn, reed as blood.
Thanne wolde he speke, and crye as he were wood.
And whan that he wel dronken hadde the wyn,
Than wolde he speke no word but Latyn.
A fewe termes hadde he, two or thre,
That he had lerned out of som decree;
No wonder is, he herde it al the day;
And eey ke knowen wel, how that a jay
Can clepen "Watte," as well as can the pope.
But who-so coude in other thing him grope,
Thanne hadde he spent all his philosophye;
Ay *"Questio quid iuris"* wolde he crye.
He was a gentil harlot and a kynde;
A bettre felawe sholde men noght fynde.
He wolde suffre for a quart of wyn
A good felawe to have his concubyn
A twelf-month, and excuse him atte fulle:
And prively a finch eek coude he pulle.
And if he fond owher a good felawe,
He wolde techen him to have non awe,
In swich cas, of the erchedeknes curs,
But-if a mannes soule were in his purs;
For in his purs he sholde y-punissed be.
"Purs is the erchedeknes helle," seyde he.
But wel I woot he lyed right in dede;
Of cursing oghte ech gulty man him drede—
For curs wol slee right as assoilling saveth—

And also war him of a *significavit*
In daunger hadde he at his owne gyse
The yonger girles of the diocyse,
And knew hir counseil, and was al hir reed.
A gerland hadde he set up-on his heed,
As greet as it were for an ale-stake;
A bokeler hadde he maad him of a cake.

With him ther rood a gentil Pardoner
Of Rouncivale, his frend and his compeer,
That streight was comen fro the court of Rome.
Ful loude he song, "Com hider, love, to me."
This somnour bar to him a stiff burdoun,
Was nevere trompe of half so greet a soun.
This pardoner hadde heer as yelow as wex,
But smothe it heng, as doth a strike of flex;
By ounces henge his lokkes that he hadde,
And ther-with he his shuldres overspradde;
But thinne it lay, by colpons oon and oon;
But hood, for jolitee, ne wered he noon,
For it was trussed up in his walet.
Him thoughte, he rood al of the newe jet;
Dischevele, save his cappe, he rood al bare.
Swiche glaringe eyen hadde he as an hare.
A vernicle hadde he sowed on his cappe.
His walet lay biforn hi min his lappe,
Bret-ful of pardoun come from Rome al hoot.
A voys he hadde as smal as hath a goot.
No berd hadde he, ne nevere sholde have,
As smothe it was as it were late y-shave;
I trowe he was a gelding or a mare.
But of his craft, fro Berwik into Ware,
Ne was ther swich another pardoner.
For in his male he hadde a pilwe-beer,
Which that, he seyde, was our lady veyl:
He seyde, he hadde a gobet of the seyl
That sëynt Peter hadde, whan that he wente
Up-on the see, til Iesu Crist him hente.
He hadde a croys of latoun, ful of stones,
And in a glas he had pigges bones.
But with thise relikes, whan that he fond
A povre person dwelling up-on lond,
Up-on a day he gat him more moneye
Than that the person gat in monthes tweye.
And thus with feyned flaterye and japes,
He made the person and the peple his apes.

GEOFFREY CHAUCER

But trewely to tellen, atte laste,
He was in chirche a noble ecclesiaste.
Wel coude he rede a lessoun or a storie,
But alderbest he song an offertorie;
For wel he wiste, whan that song was songe,
He moste preche, and wel affyle his tonge,
To winne silver, as he ful wel coude;
Therefore he song so meriely and loude.

Now have I told you shortly, in a clause,
Thestat, tharray, the nombre, and eek the cause
Why that assembled was this compaignye
In Southwerk, at this gentil hostelrye,
That highte the Tabard, faste by the Belle.
But now is tyme to yow for to telle
How that we baren us that ilke night,
Whan we were in that hostelrye alight.
And after wol I telle of our viage,
And al the remenaunt of our pilgrimage.
But first I pray yow of your curteisye,
That ye narette it nat my vileinye,
Thogh that I pleynly speke in this matere,
To telle yow hir wordes and hir chere;
Ne thogh I speke hir wordes proprely.
For this ye knowen al-so wel as I,
Who-so shal telle a tale after a man,
He moot reherce, as ny as evere he can,
Everich a word, if it be in his charge,
Al speke he never so rudeliche and large;
Or elles he moot telle his tale untrewe,
Or feyne thing, or fynde wordes newe
He may nat spare, al-thogh he were his brother;
He moot as wel seye o word as another.
Crist spak him-self ful brode in holy writ,
And wel ye woot, no vileinye is it.
Eek Plato seith, who-so that can him rede,
"The wordes mote be cosin to the dede."
Also I prey yow to foryeve it me,
Al have I nat set folk in hir degree
Here in this tale, as that they sholde stonde;
My wit is short, ye may wel understonde.

Greet chere made our hoste us everichon,
And to the soper sette he us anon;
And served us with vitaille at the beste.
Strong was the wyn, and well to drinke us leste.
A semely man our hoste was with-alle

For to han been a marshall in an halle;
A large man he was with eyen stepe,
A fairer burgeys was ther noon in Chepe:
Bold of his speche, and wys, and wel y-taught,
And of manhod him lakkede right naught.
Eek therto he was right a mery man,
And after soper pleyen he bigan,
And spak of mirthe amonges othere thinges,
Whan that we hadde maad our rekeninges;
And seyde thus: "Now, lordinges, trewely
Ye ben to me right welcome hertely:
For by my trouthe, if that I shal nat lye,
I ne saugh this yeer so mery a compaignye
At ones in this herberwe as is now.
Fayn wolde I doon yow mirthe, wiste I how.
And of a mirthe I am right now bithoght,
To doon yow ese, and it shall coste noght.

Ye goon to Caunterbury; God yow spede,
The blisful martir quyte yow your mede.
And wel I woot, as ye goon by the weye,
Ye shapen yow to talen and to pleye;
For trewely, comfort ne mirthe is noon
To ryde by the weye doumb as a stoon;
And therefore wol I maken yow disport,
As I seyde erst, and doon yow some confort.
And if yow lyketh alle, by oon assent,
Now for to stonden at my jugement,
And for to werken as I shal yow seye,
To-morwe, whan ye ryden by the weye,
Now, by my fader soule, that is deed,
But ye be merye, I wol yeve yow myn heed.
Hold up your hond, withoute more speche."
Our counseil was nat longe for to seche;
Us thoughte it was noght worth to make it wys,
And graunted him with-outen more avys,
And bad him seye his verdit, as him leste.

"Lordinges," quod he, "now herkneth for the beste;
But tak it not, I prey yow, in desdeyn;
This is the poynt, to speken short and pleyn,
That ech of yow, to shorte with our weye,
In this viage, shal telle tales tweye,
To Caunterbury-ward, I mene it so,
And hom-ward he shal tellen othere two,
Of aventures that whylom han bifalle.
And which of yow that bereth him best of alle,

That is to seyn, that telleth in this cas
Tales of best sentence and most solas,
Shal han a soper at our aller cost
Here in this place, sitting by this post,
Whan that we come agayn fro Caunterbury.
And for to make yow the more mery,
I wol my-selven gladly with yow ryde,
Right at myn owne cost, and be your gyde.
And who-so wol my jugement withseye
Shal paye al that we spenden by the weye.
And if ye vouche-sauf that it be so,
Tel me anon, with-outen wordes mo,
And I wol erly shape me therfore."
    This thing was graunted, and our othes swore
With ful glad herte, and preyden him also
That he wold vouche-sauf for to do so,
And that he wolde been our govenour,
And of our tales juge and reportour,
And sette a soper at a certeyn prys;
And we wold reuled been at his devys,
In heigh and lowe; and thus, by oon assent,
We been acorded to his jugement.
And ther-up-on the wyn was fet anoon;
We dronken, and to reste wente echoon,
With-outen any lenger taryinge.
A-morwe, whan that day bigan to springe,
Up roos our host, and was our aller cok,
And gadrede us togidre, alle in a flok,
And forth we riden, a litel more than pas,
Unto the watering of seint Thomas.
And there our host bigan his hors areste,
And seyde; "Lordinges, herkneth if yow leste.
Ye woot your forward, and I it yow recorde.
If even-song and morwe-song acorde,
Lat se now who shal telle the firste tale.
As evere mote I drinke wyn or ale,
Who-so be rebel to my jugement
Shal paye for al that by the weye is spent.
Now draweth cut, er that we ferrer twinne;
He which that hath the shortest shal biginne."
"Sire knight," quod he, "my maister and my lord,
Now draweth cut, for that is myn acord.
Cometh neer," quod he, "my lady prioresse;
And ye, sir clerk, lat be your shamfastnesse,
Ne studieth noght; ley hond to, every man."

Anon to drawen every wight bigan,
And shortly for to tellen, as it was,
Were it by aventure, or sort, or cas,
The sothe is this, the cut fil to the knight,
Of which ful blythe and glad was every wight;
And telle he moste his tale, as was resoun,
By forward and by composicioun,
As ye han herd; what nedeth wordes mo?
And whan this goode man saugh it was so,
As he that wys was and obedient
To kepe his forward by his free assent,
He seyde: "Sin I shal biginne the game,
What, welcome be the cut, a Goddes name!
Now lat us ryde, and herkneth what I say."

And with that word we riden forth our weye;
And he bigan with right a mery chere
His tale anon, and seyde in this manere.

THE NUN'S PRIEST'S TALE

2

A POVRE widye somdel stope in age,
Was whylom dwelling in a narwe cotage,
Bisyde a grove, stondyng in a dale.
This widde, of which I telle yow my tale,
Sin thilke day that she was last a wyf,
In pacience ladde a ful simple lyf,
For litel was hir catel and hir rente;
By housbondrye, of such as God hir sente,
She fond hir-self, and eek hir doghtren two.
Three large sowes hadde she, and namo,
Three kyn, and eek a sheep that highte Malle.
Foul sooty was hir bour, and eek hir halle
In which she eet ful many a sclendre meel.
Of poynaunt sauce hir neded never a deel.
No deyntee morsel passed thurgh hir throte;
Hir dyete was accordant to hir cote.
Repleccioun ne made hir nevere syk;
Attempree dyete was al hir phisyk,
And exercyse, and hertes suffisaunce.
The goute lette hir no-thing for to daunce,
Ne poplexye shente nat hir heed;
No wyn ne drank she, neither whyt ne reed;
Hir bord was served most with whyt and blak,
Milk and broun breed, in which she fond no lak,
Seynd bacoun, and somtyme an ey or tweye,

For she was as it were a maner deye.
  A yerd she hadde, enclosed al aboute
With stikkes, and a drye dich with-oute,
In which she hadde a cok, hight Chauntecleer,
In all the land of crowing nas his peer.
His vois was merier than the merye orgon
On messe-dayes that in the chirche gon;
Wel sikerer was his crowing in his logge,
Than is a clokke, or an abbey orlogge.
By nature knew he ech ascencioun
Of equinoxial in thilke toun;
For whan degrees fiftene were ascended,
Thanne crew he, that it might nat ben amended.
His comb was redder than the fyn coral,
And batailed, as it were a castel-wal.
His bile was blak, and as the yeet it shoon;
Lyk asur were his legges, and his toon;
His nayles whytter than the lilie flour,
And lyk the burned gold was his colour.
This gentil cok hadde in his governaunce
Sevene hennes, for to doon al his plesaunce,
Which were his sustres and his paramours,
And wonder lyk to him, as of colours.
Of whiche the faireste hewed on hir throte
Was cleped faire damoysele Pertelote.
Curteys she was, discreet, and debonaire,
And compaignable, and bar hir-self so faire,
Sin thilke day that she was seven night old,
That trewely she hath the herte in hold
Of Chauntecleer loken in every lith;
He loved hir so, that wel him was therwith.
But such a joye was it to here hem singe,
Whan that the brighte sonne gan to springe,
In sweet accord, "My lief is faren in londe."
For thilke tyme, as I have understonde,
Bestes and briddes coude speke and singe.
  And so bifel, that in a dawenynge,
As Chauntecleer among his wyves alle
Sat on his perche, that was in the halle,
And next him sat this faire Pertelote,
This Chauntecleer gan gronen in his throte,
As man that in his dreem is drecched sore.
And whan that Pertelote thus herde him rore,
She was agast, and seyde, "O herte deere,
What eyleth yow, to grone in this manere?

Ye ben a verray sleper, fy for shame!"
And he answerde and seyde thus, "Madame,
I pray yow, that ye take it nat agrief:
By God, me mette I was in swich meschief
Right now, that yet myn herte is sore afright.
Now God," quod he, "my swevene rede aright,
And keep my body out of foul prisoun!
Me mette, how that I romed up and doun
Withinne our yerde, wher as I saugh a beste,
Was lyk an hound, and wolde han maad areste
Upon my body, and wolde han had me deed.
His colour was bitwixe yelwe and reed;
And tipped was his tail, and bothe his eres
With blak, unlyk the remenant of his heres;
His snowte smal with glowinge eyen tweye.
Yet of his look for fere almost I deye;
This caused my my groning, douteless."

"Avoy!" quod she, "fy on yow, herteles!
Allas!" quod she, "for, by that God above,
Now han ye lost myn herte and al my love;
I can nat love a coward, by my feith.
For certes, what, so any womman seith,
We alle desyren, if it might be,
To han housebondes hardy, wyse, and free,
And secree, and no nigard, ne no fool,
Ne him that is agast of every tool,
Ne noon avauntour, by that God above!
How dorste ye sayn for shame unto youre love,
That any thing mighte make yow aferd?
Have ye no mannes herte, and han a berd?
Allas! and conne ye been agast of swevenis?"
No-thing, God wot, but vanitee, is sweven is.
Swevenes engendren of repleccciouns,
And ofte of fume, and of complecciouns,
Whan humours been to habundant in a wight.
Certes this dreem, which ye han met to-night,
Cometh of the grete superfluitee
Of youre rede *colera,* pardee,
Which causeth folk to dremen in here dremes
Of arwes, and of fyr with rede lemes,
Of grete bestes, that they wol hem byte,
Of contek, and of whelpes grete and lyte;
Right as the humour of malencolye
Causeth ful many a man, in sleep, to crye,
For fere of blake beres, or boles blake,

Or elles, blake develes wole him take.
Of others humours coude I telle also,
That werken many a man in sleep ful wo;
But I wol passe as lightly as I can.

Lo Catoun, which that was so wys a man,
Seyde he nat thus, ne do no fors of dremes?
Now, sire," quod she, "whan we flee fro the bemes,
For Goddes love, as take some laxatyf;
Up peril of my soule, and of my lyf,
I counseille yow the beste, I wol nat lye,
That bothe of colere, and of malencolye
Ye purge yow; and for ye shul nat tarie,
Though in this toun is noon apotecarie,
I shal my-self to herbes techen yow,
That shul ben for your hele, and for your prow;
And in our yerd tho herbes shal I fynde,
The whiche han of here propretee, by kynde,
To purgen yow binethe, and eek above.
Forget not this, for Goddes owene love!
Ye been full colerik of compleccioun.
Ware the sonne in his ascencioun
Ne fynde yow nat repleet of humours hote;
And if it do, I dar wel leye a grote,
That ye shul have a fevere terciane,
Or an agu, that may be youre bane.
A day or two ye shul have digestyves
Of wormes, or ye take your laxatyves,
Of lauriol, centaure, and fumetere,
Or elles of ellebor, that groweth there,
Of catapuce, or of gaytres beryis,
Of erbe yve, growing in our yerd, that mery is;
Pekke hem up right as they growe, and ete hem in.
Be mery, housbond, for your fader kyn!
Dredeth no dream; I can say yow namore."

"Madame," quod he, *"graunt mercy* of your lore.
But natheles, as touching daun Catoun,
That hath of wisdom such a gret renoun,
Though that he bad no dremes for to drede,
By God, men may in olde bokes rede
Of many a man, more of auctoritee
Than evere Caunton was, so moot I thee,
That al the revers seyn of this sentence,
And han wel founden by experience,
That dremes ben significaciouns,
As wel of joye as tribulaciouns

That folk enduren in this lyf present.
Ther nedeth make of this noon argument;
The verray preve sheweth it in dede.
Oon of the gretteste auctours that men rede
Seith thus, that whylom two felawes wente
On pilgrimage, in a ful good entente;
And happed so, thay come into a toun,
Wher as ther was swich congregacioun
Of peple, and eek so streit of herbergage,
That they ne founde as muche as o cotage,
In which they bothe might y-logged be.
Wherfor thay mosten, of necessitee,
As for that night, departen compaignye;
And each of hem goth to his hostelrye,
And took his logging as it wolde falle.
That oon of hem was logged in a stalle,
Fer in a yerd, with oxen of the plough;
That other man was logged wel y-nough,
As was his aventure, or his fortune,
That us governeth all as in commune.
And so bifel, that, long er it were day,
This man mette in his bed, ther as he lay,
How that his felawe gan up-on him calle,
And seyde, 'allas! for in an oxes stalle
This night I shall be mordered ther I lye.
Now help me, dere brother, or I dye;
In all haste come to me,' he sayde.
This man out of his sleep for fere abrayde;
But whan that he was wakned of his sleep,
He turned him, and took of this no keep;
Him thoughte his dream nas but a vanitee.
Thus twyes in his sleping dremed he.
And atte thridde tyme yet his felawe
Com, as him thoughte, and seide, 'I am now slawe;
Bihold my bloody woundes, depe and wyde!
Arys up erly in the morwe-tyde,
And at the west gate of the toun,' quod he,
'A carte ful of donge ther shaltow see,
In which my body is hid ful prively;
Do thilke carte arresten boldely.
My gold caused my mordre, sooth to sayn;'
And tolde him every poynt how he was slayn,
With a ful pitous face, pale of hewe.
And truste wel, his dreem he fond ful trewe;
For on the morwe, as sone as it was day,

To his felawes in he took the way;
And whan that he came to this oxes stalle,
After his felawe he bigan to calle.
The hostiler answerde him anon,
And seyde, 'sire, your felawe is agon,
As sone as day he wente out of the town.'
This man gan fallen in suspecioun,
Remembring on his dremes that he mette,
And forth he goth, no lenger wolde he lette,
Unto the west gate of the toun, and fond
A dong-carte, as it were to donge lond,
That was arrayed in that same wyse
As he han herd the dede man devyse;
And with an hardy herte he gan to crye
Vengeaunce and justice of this felonye:—
'My felawe mordered is this same night,
And in this carte he lyth gapinge upright.
I crye out on the ministres,' quod he,
'That sholden kepe and reulen this citee;
Harrow! allas! her lyth my felawe slayn!'
What sholde I more un-to this tale sayn?
The peple out-strete, and caste the carte to grounde,
And in the middel of the dong they founde
The dede man, that mordred was al newe.

O blisful God, that are so just and trewe!
Lo, how that thou biwreyest mordre alway!
Mordre wol out, that se we day by day.
Mordre is so wlatsom and abhominable
To God, that is so just and resonable,
That he ne wol not suffre it heled be;
Though it abyde a yeer, or two, or three,
Mordre wol out, this my conclusioun.
And right anoon, ministres of that toun
Han hent the carter, and so sore him pyned,
And eek the hostiler so sore engyned,
That thay biknewe hir wikkednesse anoon,
And were an-hanged by the nekke-boon.

"Here may men seen that dremes been to drede.
And certes, in the same book I rede,
Right in the nexte chapitre after this,
(I gabbe nat, so have I joye or blis,)
Two men that wolde han passed over see,
For certeyn cause, in-to a fer contree,
If that the winde ne hadde been contrarie,
That made hem in a citee for to tarie,

That stood ful mery upon an haven-syde.
But on a day, agayn the even-tyde,
The wind gan chaunge, and blew right as hem leste.
Jolif and glad they went un-to hir reste,
And casten hem ful erly for to saille;
But to that oo man fel a greet mervaille.
That oon of hem, in sleping as he lay,
Him mette a wonder dreem, agayn the day;
Him thoughte a man stood by his beddes syde,
And him comaunded, that he sholde abyde,
And seyde him thus, 'If thou to-morwe wende,
Thou shalt be dreynt; my tale is at an ende.'
He wook, and tolde his felawe what he mette,
And preyde him his viage for to lette;
As for that day, he preyde him to abyde.
His felawe, that lay by his beddes syde,
Gan for to laughe, and scorned him ful faste.
'No dreem,' quod he, 'may so myn herte agaste,
That I wol lette for to do my thinges.
I sette not a straw by thy dreminges,
For swevenes been but vanitees and japes.
Men dreme al-day of owles or of apes,
And eek of many a mase therwithal;
Men dreme of thing that nevere was ne shal.
But sith I see that thou wolt heer abyde,
And thus for-sleuthen wilfully thy tyde,
Got wot it reweth me; and have good day.'
And thus he took his leve, and wente his way.
But er that he hadde halfe his cours y-seyled,
Noot I nat why, ne what mischaunce it eyled,
But casuelly the shippes botme rente,
And ship and man under the water wente
In sighte of othere shippes it byside,
That with hem seyled at the same tyde.
And therfor, faire Pertelote so dere,
By swiche ensamples olde maistow lere,
That no man sholde been to recchelees
Of dremes, for I sey thee, douteless,
That many a dreem ful sore is for to drede.

"Lo, in the lyf of seint Kenelm, I rede,
That was Kenulpus sone, the noble king
Of Mercenrike, how Kenelm mette a thing;
A lyte er he was mordred, on a day.
His mordre in his avisioun he say.
His norice him expouned every del

His swevene, and bad him for to kepe him wel
For traisoun; but he nas but seven yeer old,
And therfore litel tale hath he told
Of any dreem, so holy was his herte.
By God, I hadde levere than my sherte
That ye had rad his legende, as have I.
Dame Pertelote, I say yow trewely,
Macrobeus, that writ the avisioun
In Affrike of the worthy Cipioun,
Affermeth dremes, and seith that they been
Warning of thinges that men after seen.
And forther-more, I pray yow loketh wel
In the olde testament, of Daniel,
If he held dremes any vanitee.
Reed eek of Joseph, and ther shul ye see
Wher dremes ben somtyme (I sey nat alle)
Warnings of thinges that shul after falle.
Loke of Egipt the king, daun Pharao,
His bakere and his boteler also,
Wher they ne felte noon effect in dremes.
Who so wol seken actes of sondry remes,
May rede of dremes many a wonder thing.
  "Lo Cresus, which that was of Lyde king,
Mette he nat that he sat upon a tree,
Which signified he sholde anhanged be?
Lo heer Andromacha, Ectores wyf,
That day that Ector sholde lese his lyf,
She dremed on the same night biforn,
How that the lyf of Ector sholde be lorn,
If thilke day he wente in-to bataille;
She warned him, buit it mighte nat availle;
He wente for to fighte natheless,
But he was slayn anoon of Achilles.
But thilke tale is al to long to telle,
And eek it is ny day, I may nat dwelle.
Shortly I seye, as for conclusioun,
That I shal han of this avisioun
Adversitee; and I seye forther-more,
Then I ne telle of laxatyves no store,
For they ben venimous, I woot it well;
I hem defye, I love hem nevere a del.
  "Now let us speke of mirthe, and stinte al this;
Madame Pertelote, so have I blis,
Of o thing God hath sent me large grace;
For whan I see the beautee of your face,

Ye ben so scarlet-reed about youre yĕn,
It maketh al my drede for you to dyen;
For, also siker as *In principio,
Mulier est hominis confusio;*
Madame, the sentence of this Latin is—
Womman is mannes joye and al his blis.
For whan I fele a-night your softe syde,
I am so ful of joye and of solas
That I defyye bothe sweven and dreem."
And with that word fley doun fro the beem,
For it was day, and eek his hennes alle;
And with a chuk he gan hem for to calle,
For he had founde a corn, lay in the yerd.
Roial he was, he was namore aferd; . . .
He loketh as it were a grim leoun;
And on his toos he rometh up and doun,
Him deyned not to sette his foot to grounde.
He chukketh, whan he hath a corn y-founde,
And to him rennen thanne his wyves alle.
Thus roial, as a prince is in his halle,
Leve I this Chauntecleer in his pasture;
And after wol I telle his aventure.

 Whan that the month in which the world bigan,
That highte March, whan God first maked man,
Was complet, and y-passed were also,
Sin March bigan, thritty dayes and two,
Bifel that Chauntecleer, in all his pryde,
His seven wyves walking by his syde,
Caste up his eyen to the brighte sonne,
That in the signe of Taurus hadde y-ronne
Twenty degrees and oon, and somwhat more;
And knew by kynde, and by noon other lore,
That it was pryme, and crew with blisful stevene.
"The sonne," he sayde, "is clomben up on hevene
Fourty degrees and oon, and more, y-wis.
Madame Pertelote, my worldes blis,
Herkneth thise blisful briddes how they singe,
And see the fresshe floures how they springe;
Ful is myn hert of revel and solas."
But sodienly him fil a sorweful cas;
For evere the latter ende of joye is wo.
Got woot that worldly joye is sone ago;
And if a rethor coude faire endyte,
He in a chronique saufly mighte it write,
As for a sovereyn notabilitee.

GEOFFREY CHAUCER

Now every wys man, lat him herkne me;
This storie is al-so trewe, I undertake,
As is the book of Launcelot de Lake,
That wommen holde in ful gret reverence.
Now wol I torne agayn to my sentence.

A col-fox, ful of sly iniquitee,
That in the grove hadde woned yeres three,
By heigh imaginacioun forn-cast,
The same night thurgh-out the hegges brast
Into the yerd, ther Chauntecleer the faire
Was wont, and eek his wyves, to repaire;
And in a bed of wortes still he lay,
Til it was passed undern of the day,
Wayting his tyme on Chauntecleer to falle
As gladly doon thise homicydes alle,
That in awayt liggen to mordre men.
O false mordrer, lurking in thy den!
O newe Scariot, newe Genilon!
False dissimilour, O Greek Sinon,
That broghtest Troye al outrely to sorwe!
O Chauntecleer, acursed be that morwe,
That thou into that yerd flough fro the bemes!
Thou were ful wel y-warned by thy dremes,
That thilke day was perilous to thee.
But what that God forwot mot nedes be,
After the opinioun of certeyn clerkis.
Witnesse on him, that any perfit clerk is,
That in scole is gret altercacioun
In this matere, and greet disputisoun,
And hath ben of an hundred thousand men.
But I ne can not bulte it to the bren,
As can the holy doctour Augustyn,
Or Boece, or the bishop Bradwardyn,
Whether that Goddes worthy forwiting
Streyneth me nedely for to doon a thing,
(Nedely clepe I simple necessitee);
Or elles, if free choys be graunted me
To do that same thing, or do it noght,
Though God forwot it, er that it was wroght;
Or if his writing streyneth nevere a del
But by necessitee condicionel.
I wol not han to do of swich matere;
My tale is of a cok, as ye may here,
That took his counseil of his wyf, with sorwe,
To walken in the verd upon that morwe

That he had met the dreem, that I of tolde.
Wommennes counseils been ful ofte colde;
Wommannes counseil broghte us first to wo,
And made Adam fro paradys to go,
Ther as he was ful mery, and wel at ese.
But for I noot, to whom it mighte displese,
If I counseil of wommen wolde blame,
Passe over, for I seyde it in my game.
Rede auctours, wher they trete of swich matere,
And what thay seyn of wommen ye may here.
Thise been the cokkes wordes, and nat myne;
I can noon harme of no womman divyne.

    Faire in the sond, to bathe hire merily,
Lyth Pertelote, and alle hir sustres by,
Agayn the sonne; and Chauntecleer so free
Song merier than the mermayde in the see;
For Phisiologus seith sikerly,
How that they singen wel and merily.
And so bifel, that as he caste his yë,
Among the wortes, on a boterflye,
He was war of this fox that lay ful lowe.
No-thing ne liste him thanne for to crowe,
But cryde anon, "cok, cok," and up he sterte,
As man that was affrayed in his herte.
For naturelly a beest desyreth flee
Fro his contrarie, if he may it see,
Though he never erst had seyn it with his yë.

    This Chauntecleer, whan he gan him espye
He wolde han fled, but that the fox anon
Seyde, "Gentil sire, allas! wher wol ye gon?
Be ye affrayed of me that am your freend?
Now certes, I were worse than a feend,
If I to yow wolde harm or vileinye.
I am nat come your counseil for tespye;
But trewely, the cause of my cominge
Was only for to herkne how that ye singe.
For trewely ye have as mery a stevene,
As eny aungel hath, that is in hevene;
Therwith ye han in musik more felinge
Than hadde Boece, or any that can singe,
My lord your fader (God his soule blesse!)
And eek your moder, of hir gentilesse,
Han in myn hous y-been, to my gret ese;
And certes, sire, ful fayn wolde I yow plese.
But for men speke of singing, I wol saye,

GEOFFREY CHAUCER

So mote I brouke wel myn eyen tweye,
Save yow, I herde nevere man so singe,
As dide your fader in the morweninge;
Certes, it was of herte, al that he song.
And for to make his voys the more strong,
He wolde so peyne him, that with both his yën
He moste winke, so loude he wolde cryen,
And stonden on his tiptoon therwithal,
And strecche forth his nekke long and smal.
And eek he was of swich discrecioun,
That there nas no man in no regioun
That him in song or wisdom mighte passe.
I have weel rad in daun Burnel the Asse,
Among his vers, how that ther was a cok,
For that a prestes sone yaf him a knok
Upon his leg, whyl he was yong and nyce,
He made him for to lese his benefyce.
But certeyn, ther nis no comparisoun
Bitwix the wisdom and discrecioun
Of your fader, and of his subtiltee.
Now singeth, sire, for seinte charitee,
Let se, conne ye your fader countrefete?"
This Chauntecleer his winges gan to bete,
As man that coude his tresoun nat espye,
So was he ravisshed with his flaterye.

Allas! ye lordes, many a fals flatour
Is in your courtes, and many a losengeour,
That plesen yow wel more, by my feith,
Than he that soothfastnesse unto yow seith.
Redeth Ecclesiaste of flaterye;
Beth war, ye lordes, of hir trecherye.

This Chauntecleer stood hye up-on his toos,
Strecching his nekke, and held his eyen cloos,
And gan to crowe loude for the nones;
And daun Russel the fox sterte up at ones,
And by the gargat hente Chauntecleer,
And on his bak toward the wode him beer,
For yet ne was ther no man that him sewed.
O destinee, that mayst nat been eschewed!
Allas, that Chauntecleer fleigh fro the bemes!
Allas, his wyf ne roghte nat of dremes!
And on a Friday fil al this meschaunce.
O Venus, that art goddesse of plesaunce,
Sin that thy servant was this Chauntecleer,
And in thy service dide al his poweer,

More for delyt, than world to multiplye,
Why woldestow suffre him on thy day to dye?
O Gaufred, dere mayster soverayn,
That, whan thy worthy king Richard was slayn
With shot, compleynedest his deth so sore,
Why ne hadde I now thy sentence and thy lore,
The Friday for to chide, as diden ye?
(For on a Friday soothly slayne was he.)
Than wolde I shewe you how that I coude pleyne
For Chauntecleres drede, and for his peyne.

  Certes, swich crye ne lamentacioun
Was nevere of ladies maad, whan Ilioun
Was wonne, and Pirrus with his streite swerd,
Whan he hadde hent king Priam by the berd,
And slayn him (as saith us *Eneydos*),
As maden alle the hennes in the clos,
Whan they had seyn of Chauntecleer the sighte.
But sovereynly dame Pertelote shrighte,
Ful louder than dide Hasdrubales wyf,
Whan that hir housbond hadde lost his lyf,
And that the Romayns hadde brend Cartage,
She was so ful of torment and of rage,
That wilfully into the fyr she sterte,
And brende hir-selven with a stedfast herte.
O woful hennes, right so cryden ye,
As, whan that Nero brende the citee
Of Rome, cryden senatoures wyves,
For that hir housbondes losten all hir lyves;
Withouten gilt this Nero hath hem slayn.
Now wol I torne to my tale agayn:
This sely widwe, and eek hir doghtres two,
Herden thise hennes crye and maken wo,
And out at dores sterten thay anoon,
And syen the fox toward the grove goon,
And bar upon his bak the cok away;
And cryden, "Out! harrow! and weylaway!
Ha, ha, the fox!" and after him they ran,
And eek with staves many another man;
Ran Colle our dogge, and Talbot, and Gerland,
And Malkin, with a distaf in hir hand;
Ran cow and calf, and eek the verray hogges
So were they fered for berking of the dogges
And shouting of the men and wimmen eke,
They ronne so, hem thoughte hir herte breke.
They yelleden as feendes doon in helle;

The dokes cryden as men wolde hem quelle;
The gees for fere flowen over the trees;
Out of the hyve cam the swarm of bees;
So hidous was the noyse, a! *benedicite!*
Certes, he Jakke Straw, and his meynee,
No maden nevere shoutes half so shrille,
Whan that they wolden any Fleming kille,
As thilke day was maad upon the fox.
Of bras thay broghten bemes, and of box,
Of horn, of boon, in whiche they blewe and pouped,
And therwithal thay shryked and they houped;
It semed as that hevene sholde falle.
Now, gode men, I pray yow herneth alle!

 Lo, how fortune turneth sodeinly
The hope and pryde eek of hir enemy.
This cok, that lay upon the foxes bak,
In al his drede, un-to the fox he spak,
And seyde, "sire, if that I were as ye,
Yet sholde I seyn (as wis God helpe me),
Turneth agayn, ye proude cherles alle!
A verray pestilence up-on yow falle!
Now am I come un-to this wodes syde;
Maugree your heed, the cok shal heer abyde;
I wol him ete in feith, and that anon."—
The fox answered, "In feith, it shal be don,"—
And as he spak that word, al sodeinly
This cok brak from his mouth deliverly,
And heighe up-on a tree he fleigh anon.
And whan the fox saugh that he was y-gon,
"Allas!" quod he, "O Chauntecleer, allas!
I have to yow," quod he, "y-doon trespas.
In-as-muche as I mawed yow aferd,
Whan I yow hente, and broghte out of the yerd;
But, sire, I dide it in no wikke entente;
Com doun, and I shal telle yow what I mente.
I shal seye sooth to yow, God help me so.'
"Nay than,' quod he, "I shrewe us bothe two,
And first I shrewe my-self, bothe blood and bones,
If thou bigle me ofter than ones.
Thou shalt namore, thurgh thy flaterye
Do me to singe and winke with myn yë.
For he that winketh, whan he sholde see,
Al wilfully, God lat him never thee!"
"Nay," quod the fox, "but God yive him meschaunce,
That is so undiscreet of governaunce,

That iangleth whan he sholde holde his pees."
  Lo, swich it is for to be recchelees,
And necligent, and truste on flaterye.
But ye that holden this tale a foyle,
  As of a fox, or of a cok and hen,
Taketh the moralitee, good men.
For seint Paul seith, that al that writen is,
  To our doctryne it is y-write, y-wis.
Taketh the fruyt, and lat the chaf be stille.
  Now, gode God, if that it be thy wille,
As seith my lord, so make us alle good men;
And bring us to his heighe blisse. Amen.

* * *

TRADITIONAL BALLADS

A GEST OF ROBYN HODE

Lythe and lishtin, gentilmen,
  That be of frebore blode;
I shall you tel of a gode yeman,
  His name was Robyn Hode.

Robyn was a prude outlaw,
  Whyles he walked on grounde;
So curteyse an outlaw as he was one
  Was never non yfounde.

Robyn stode in Bernesdale,
  And lenyd hym to a tre;
And bi him stode Litell Johnn,
  A gode yeman was he.

And alsoo dyd gode Scarlok,
  And Much, the miller's son;
There was none ynch of his bodi
  But it was worth a grome.

Than bespake Lytell Johnn
  All untoo Robyn Hode:
Maister, and ye wolde dyne betyme
  It wolde doo you moche gode.

Than bespake hym gode Robyn:
  To dyne have I noo lust;

TRADITIONAL BALLADS

Till that I have som bolde baron,
  Or som unkouth gest.

. . . .

That may pay for the best,
  Or some knyght or som squyer
That dwelleth here bi west.

A gode maner than had Robyn;
  In londe where that he were,
Every day or he wold dyne
  Thre messis wolde he here.

The one in the worship of the Fader,
  And another of the Holy Gost,
The thirde was of Our dere Lady
  That he loved allther moste.

Robyn loved Oure dere Lady;
  For dout of dydly synne,
Wolde he never do compani harme
  That any woman was in.

"Maistar," than sayde Lytil Johnn,
  "And we our borde shal sprede,
Tell us wheder that we shall go
  And what life that we shall lede.

"Where we shall take, where we shall leve,
  Where we shall abide behynde;
Where we shall robbe, where we shall reve,
  Where we shall bete and bynde."

"Thereof no force," than sayde Robyn;
  "We shall do well inowe;
But loke ye do no husbonde harme
  That tilleth with his ploughe.

"No more ye shall no gode yeman
  That walketh by grene-wode shawe;
Ne no knyght ne no squyer
  That wol be a gode felawe.

"These bisshoppes and these archebishoppes,
  Ye shall them bete and bynde;

The hye sherif of Notyngham,
  Hym hold ye in your mynde."

"This worde shalbe holde," sayde Lytell Johnn,
  "And this lesson we shall lere;
It it fer dayes; God sende us a gest,
  That we were at our dynere."

"Take thy gode bowe in thy honde," sayde Robyn;
  "Late Much wende with the;
And so shal Willyam Scarlok,
  And no man abyde with me.

"And walke up to the Saylis
  And so to Watlinge Strete,
And wayte after some unkuth gest,
  Up chaunce ye may them mete.

"Be he erle, or ani baron,
  Abbot, or ani knyght,
Bringhe hym to lodge to me;
  His dyner shall be dight."

They werte up to the Saylis,
  These yemen all three;
They loked est, they loked weest,
  They myght no man see.

But as they loked in to Bernysdale,
  Bi a derne strete,
Than came a knyght ridinghe;
  Full sone they gan hym mete.

All dreri was his semblaunce,
  And lytell was his pryde;
His one fote in the styrop stode,
  That othere wavyd beside.

His hode hanged in his iyn two;
  He rode in symple aray;
A soriar man than he was one
  Rode never in somer day.

Lytell Johnn was full curteyes,
  And sette hym on his kne:

TRADITIONAL BALLADS

"Welcom be ye, gentyll knyght,
  Welcom ar ye to me.

"Welcom be thou to grene wode,
  Hendë knyght and fre;
My maister hath abiden you fastinge,
  Syr, al these oures thre."

"Who is thy maister?" sayde the knyght;
  John sayde, "Robyn Hode";
"He is a gode yoman," sayde the knyght,
  "Of hym I have herde moche gode.

"I graunte," he sayde, "with you to wende,
  My bretherne, all in fere;
My purpos was to have dyned to day
  At Blith or Dancastere."

Furth than went this gentyl knight,
  With a careful chere;
The teris oute of his iyen ran,
  And fell downe by his lere.

They brought him to the lodgë-dore;
  Whan Robyn gan hym see,
Full curtesly dyd of his hode
  And sette hym on his knee.

"Welcome, sir knight," than sayde Robyn,
  "Welcome art thou to me;
I have abyden you fastinge, sir,
  All these ouris thre."

Than answered the gentyll knight,
  With wordes fayre and fre:
"God the save, goode Robyn,
  And all thy fayre meyne."

They wasshed togeder and wyped bothe,
  And sette to theyr dynere;
Brede and wyne they had right ynoughe,
  And noumbles of the dere.

Swannes and fessauntes they had full gode,
  And foules of the ryvere;

There fayled none so litell a birde
    That ever was bred on bryre.

"Do gladly, sir knight," sayde Robyn;
    "Gramarcy, sir," sayde he;
"Suche a dinere had I nat
    Of all these wekys thre.

"If I come ageyne, Robyn,
    Here by thys contrē,
As gode a dyner I shall the make
    As thou haest made to me."

"Gramarcy, knyght," sayde Robyn;
    "My dyner whan I have,
I was never so gredy, by dere worthi God,
    My dyner for to crave.

"But pay or ye wende," sayde Robyn;
    "Me thynketh it is gode ryght;
It was never the maner, by dere worthi God,
    A yoman to pay for a knyght."

"I have nought in my coffer," saide the knyght,
    "That I may profer for shame":
"Litell John, go loke," sayde Robyn,
    "Ne lat not for no blame.

"Tel me truth," than saide Robyn,
    "So God have parte of the":
"I have no more but ten shelynges," sayde the knight
    "So God have parte of me."

"If thou have no more," sayde Robyn,
    "I woll nat one peny;
And yf thou have nede of any more,
    More shall I lend the.

"Go nowe furth, Litell Johnn,
    The truth tell thou me;
If there be no more but ten shelinges,
    No peny that I se."

TRADITIONAL BALLADS

Lytell Johnn sprede downe hys mantell
  Full fayre upon the grounde,
And there he fonde in the knyghts cofer
  But even halfe a pounde.

Litell John let it lye full styll,
  And went to hys maysteer full lowe;
"What tydynges, Johnn?" sayde Robyn;
  "Sir, the knyght is true inowe."

"Fyll of the best wine," sayde Robyn,
  "The knyght shall begynee;
Moche wonder thinketh me
  Thy clothynge is so thinne.

"Tell me one worde," sayde Robyn,
  "And counsel shal it be;
I trowe thou wert made a knyght of force,
  Or ellys of yemanry.

"Or ellys thou hast been a sori husbande,
  And lyved in stroke and strife;
An okerer, or ellis a lechoure," sayde Roybn,
  "Wyth wronge has led thy lyfe."

"I am none of those," sayde the knyght,
"By God that madë me;
And hundred wynter here before
  Myn auncetres knyghtes have be.

"But oft it hath befal, Robyn,
  A man hath be disgrate;
But God that sitteth in heven above
  May amende his state.

"Withyn this two yere, Robyne," he sayde,
  "My neighbors well it knowe,
Foure hundred pounde of gode money
  Ful well than myght I spende.

"Nowe have I no gode," saide the knyght,
  "God hath shapen such an ende,
But my chyldren and my wyfe,
  Tyll God yt may amende."

"In what maner," than sayde Robyn,
  "Hast thou lorne thy rychesse?"
"For my greate foly," he sayde,
  "And for my kyndenesse.

"I had a sone, forsoth, Robyn,
  That shulde have been myn ayre,
Whanne he was twenty wynter olde,
  In felde wolde just full fayre.

"He slewe a knyght of Lancashire,
  And a squyer bolde;
For to save him in his rhyght
  My godes beth sette and solde.

"My londes beth sette to wedde, Robyn,
  Untyll a certayn day,
To a ryche abbot here besyde
  Of Seynt Mari Abbey."

"What is the som?" sayde Robyn;
  "Trouth than tell thou me";
"Sir," he sayde, "foure hundred pounde;
  The abbot told it to me."

"Nowe and thou lese thy lond," sayde Robyn,
  "What shall fall of the?"
"Hastely I wol me buske [sayd the knyght]
  Over the saltë see,

"And se where Criste was quyke and dede,
  On the mount of Calverë;
Fare wel, frende, and have gode day;
  It may not better be."

Teris fell out of hys eyen two;
  He wolde have gone hys way;
"Farewel, frendes, and have gode day,
  I have no more to pay."

"Where be thy frendes?" sayde Robyn:
  "Syr, never one wol me knowe;
While I was ryche ynowe at home
  Great boste than wolde they blowe.

TRADITIONAL BALLADS

"And nowe they renne away fro me,
  As bestis on a rowe;
They take no more hede of me
  Thanne they me never sawe."

For ruthe thanne wept Litell Johnn,
  Scarlok and Much in fere;
"Fyl of the best wyne," sayde Robyn,
  "For here is a symple chere.

"Hast thou any frends," sayde Robyn,
  "Thy borowes that wyll be?"
"I have none," than sayde the knyght,
  "But God that dyed on tree."

"Do away thy japis," sayde Robyn,
  "Thereof wol I right none;
Wenest thou I wolde have God to borowe,
  Peter, Poule, or Johnn?

"Nay, by hym that made me,
  And shope both sonne and mone,
Fynde me a better borowe," sayde Robyn,
  "Or money getest thou none."

"I have none other," sayde the knyght,
  "The sothe for to say,
But yf yt be Our dere Lady;
  She fayled me never or thys day."

"By dere worthy God," sayde Robyn,
  "To seche all Englonde thorowe,
Yet fonde I never to my pay
  A moche better borowe.

"Come nowe furth, Litell Johnn,
  And go to my tresourē,
And bringe me foure hundred pound,
  And loke well tolde it be."

Furth than went Litell Johnn,
  And Scarlok went before;
He tolde oute four hundred pounde
  By eight and twenty score.

"Is thys well tolde?" sayde litell Much;
  Johnn sayde: "What greveth the?
It is almus to helpe a gentyll knyght
  Thal is fal in povertë.

"Master," than sayde Lityll John,
  "His clothinge is full thynne;
Ye must gyve the knight a lyveray,
  To lappe his body therein.

"For ye have scarlet and grene, mayster,
  And many a riche aray;
Ther is no marchaunt in mery Englond
  So ryche, I dare well say."

"Take hym thre yerdes of every colour,
  And loke well mete that it be";
Lytell Johnn toke none other mesure
  But his bowë-tree.

And at every handfull that he met
  He lept over fotes three;
"What devylles drapar," sayd litell Much,
  "Thynkest thou for to be?"

Scarlock stode full stil and loughe,
  And sayd, "By God Almyght,
Johnn may gyve hym gode mesure,
  For it costeth hym but lyght."

"Mayster," than said Litell Johnn
  All unto Robyn Hode,
"Ye must give the knight a hors
  To lede home al this gode."

"Take him a gray coursar," sayde Robyn,
  "And a saydle newe;
He is Oure Ladye's messangere;
  God graunt that he be true."

"And a gode palfray," sayde lytell Much,
  "To mayentene hym in his right";
"And a peyre of botes," sayde Scarlock,
  "For he is a gentyll knight."

TRADITIONAL BALLADS

"What shalt thou gyve hym, Litell John?" [said Robyn;]
"Sir, a peyre of gilt sporis clene,
To pray for all this company;
God bringe hym oute of tene."

"Whan shal mi day be," said the knyght,
"Sir, and your wyll be?"
"This day twelve moneth," saide Robyn,
"Under this grene-wode tre.

"'It were greate shame," sayde Robyn,
"A knight alone to ryde,
Withoutë squyre, yoman, or page,
To walkë by his syde.

"I shall lende Litell Johann, my man,
For he shalbe thy knave;
In a yeman's stede he may the stande,
If thou greate nedë have."

The Second Fytte

Now is the knight gone on his way;
This game hym thought full gode;
Whanne he loked on Bernesdale
He blessyd Robyn Hode.

And whanne he thought on Bernysdale,
On Scarlok, Much and Johnn,
He blessyd them for the best company
That ever he in come.

Than spake that gentyll knyght,
To Lytell Johan gan he saye,
"To-morrowe I must to Yorke toune
To Saynt Mary abbay.

"And to the abbot that place
Foure hundred pounde I must pay;
And but I be there upon this nyght
My londe is lost for ay."

The abbot sayd to his covent,
There he stode on grounde,

"This day twelfe moneth came a knyght
  And borowed foure mondred pounde.

["He borowed four hondred pounde]
  Upon his londe and fee;
But he come this ylkë day
  Disherited shall he be."

"It is full erely," sayed the pryoure,
  The day is not yet ferre gone;
I had lever to pay an hondred pounde,
  And lay it downe anone.

"The knyght is ferre beyonde the see,
  In Englonde is his ryght,
And suffreth honger and colde
  And many a sory nyght.

"It were grete pytë," said the pryoure,
  "So to have his londe;
And ye be so lyght of your consyence,
  Ye do to hym moch wronge."

"Thou arte ever in my berde," sayd the abbot,
  "By God and Saynt Rycharde";
With that cam in a fat-heded monke,
  The heygh selerer.

"He is dede or hanged," sayed the monke,
  "By God that bought me dere,
And we shall have to spende in this place
  Foure hondred pounde by yere."

The abbot and the hy selerer
  Stertë forthe full bolde,
The highe justyce of Englonde
  The abbot there dyde holde.

The hye justyce and many mo
  Had taken into theyr honde
Holy all the knyghtes det,
  To put that knyght to wronge.

They demed the knyght wonder sore,
  The abbot and his meynë

TRADITIONAL BALLADS

"But he come this ylkĕ day
  Disherited shall he be."

"He wyll not come yet," sayd the justyce,
  "I dare well undertake";
But in sorowe tymë for them all
  The knyght came to the gate.

Than bespake that gentyll knyght
  Untyll his meynë:
"Now put on your symple wedes
  That ye brought fro the see."

[They put on their symple wedes,]
  They came to the gates anone;
The porter was redy hymselfe
  And welcomed them everychone.

"Welcome, syr knyght," sayd the porter,
  "My lorde to mete is he,
And so is many a gentyll man,
  For the love of the."

The porter swore a full grete othe:
  "By God that madĕ me,
Here be the best coresed hors
  That ever yet sawe I me.

"Lede them in to the stable," he sayd,
  "That eased myght they be";
"They shall not come thein," sayd the knyght,
  "By God that dyed on a tre."

Lordĕs were to mete isette
  In that abbotes hall;
The knyght went forth and kneled downe,
  And salued them grete and small.

"Do gladly, syr abbot," sayd the knyght,
  "I am come to holde my day":
The fyrst word that the abbot spake,
  "Hast thou brought my pay?"

"Not one peny," sayd the knight,
  "By God that maked me";

"Thou art a shrewed dettour," sayd the abbot;
    "Syr justyce, drynke to me.

"What doost thou here," sayd the abbot,
    "But thou haddest brought thy pay?"
"For God," than sayed the knight,
    "To pray of a lenger daye."

"Thy daye is broke," sayd the justyce,
    "Londe gettest thou none":
"Now, good syr justyce, be my frende
    And fende me of my fone!"

"I am holde with the abbot," sayd the justyce,
    "Both with cloth and fee":
"Now, good syr sheryf, be my frende!"
    "Nay, for God," sayd he.

"Now, good syr abbot, be my frende,
    For thy curteysë,
And holde my londës in thy honde
    Tyll I have made the gree!

"And I wyll be thy true servaunte,
    And trewely serve the,
Tyll ye have foure hondred pounde
    Of money good and free."

The abbot sware a full grete othe,
    "By God that dyed on a tree,
Get thy londe where thou may,
    For thou getest none of me."

"By dere worthy God," then sayd the knyght,
    "That all this worldë wrought,
But I have my londe agayne,
    Full dere it shall be bought.

"God that was of a mayden borne,
    Leve us well to spede!
For it is good to assay a frende
    Or that a man have nede."

The abbot lothely on hym gan loke,
    And vylaynesly hym gan call;

"Out," he sayd, "thou false knyght,
  Spede the out of my hall!"

"Thou lyest," then sayd the gentyll knyght,
  "Abbot, in thy hal;
False knyght was I never,
  By God that made us all."

Up then stode that gentyll knyght,
  To the abbot sayd he,
"To suffre a knyght to knele so longe,
  Thou canst no curteysye.

"In joustes and in tournaments
  Full ferre than have I be,
And put myself as ferre in prees
  As ony that ever I see."

"What wyll ye gyve more," sayd the justyce,
  "And the knyght shall make a releyse?
And elles dare I safly swere
  Ye holde never your londe in pees."

"An hondred pounde," sayd the abbot;
  The justice sayd, "Gyve hym two";
"Nay, be God," sayd the knyght,
  "Ye get not my land so.

"Though ye wolde gyve a thousand more,
  Yet were ye never the nere;
Shal there never be myn heyre
  Abbot, justice ne frere."

He stert hym to a borde anone,
  Tyll a table rounde,
And there he shoke oute of a bagge
  Even four hundred pound.

"Have here thi golde, sir abbot," saide the knight,
  "Which that thou lentest me;
Had thou ben curtes at my comynge,
  I would have rewarded thee."

The abbot sat styll, and ete no more,
  For all his ryall fare;

He cast his hede on his shulder,
  And fast began to stare.

"Take me my golde agayne," saide the abbot,
  "Sir justice, that I toke the"
"Not a peni," said the justice,
  "Bi God, that dyed on tree."

"Sir abbot, and ye men of lawe,
  Now have I holde my daye;
Now shall I have my londe agayne,
  For ought that you can saye."

The knyght stert out of the dore,
  Awaye was all his care,
And on he put his good clothynge
  The other he lefte there.

He wente hym forth full mery syngynge,
  As men have told in tale;
His lady met hym at the gate,
  At home in Verysdale.

"Welcome, my lorde," sayd his lady;
  "Syr, lost is all your good?"
"Be mery, dame," sayd the knyght,
  "And pray for Robyn Hode,

"That ever his soule be in blysse:
  He holpe me out of tene;
Ne had be his kyndenesse,
  Beggers had we bene.

"The abbot and I accorded ben,
  He is served of his pay;
The god yoman lent it me
  As I cam by the way."

This knight than dwelled fayre at home,
  The sothe for to saye,
Tyll he had got four hundred pound,
  Al redy for to pay.

He purveyed him an hundred bowes,
  The strynges well ydyght,

An hundred shefe of arowes gode,
  The hedys burneshed full bryght;

And every arowe an ellë longe,
  With pecok well idyght,
Inocked all with whyte silver;
  It was a semely syght.

He purveyed him an hondreth men.
  Well harnessed in that stede,
And hym selfe in that same suite,
  And clothed in whyte and rede.

He bare a launsgay in his honde,
  And a man ledde his male,
And reden with a lyght songe
  Unto Bernysdale.

[But at Wentbrydge] there was a wrastelyng,
  And there taryed was he,
And there was all the best yemen
  Of all the west countree.

A full fayre game there was up set,
  A whyte bulle up i-pyght,
A grete courser, with sadle and brydil,
  With golde burnyssht full bryght.

A payre of gloves, a rede golde rynge,
  A pype of wyne, in fay;
What man that bereth hym best i-wys
  The pryce shall bere away.

There was a yoman in that place,
  And best worthy was he,
And for he ferre and frembde bested,
  Slayne he shulde have be.

The knight had ruthe of this yoman,
  In place where that he stode;
He sayde that yoman shulde have no harme,
  For love of Robyn Hode.

The knyght pressed in to the place,
  An hurdreth folowed hym free,

With bowes bent and arowes sharpe,
  For to shende that companye.

They shulderd all and made hym rome,
  To wete what he wolde say;
He toke the yeman bi the hande,
  And gave hym al the play.

He gave hym five marke for his wyne,
  There it lay on the molde,
And bad it shulde be set a broche,
  Drynkë who so wolde.

Thus longe taried this gentyll knyght,
  Tyll that play was done;
So longe abode Robyn fastinge
  Thre houres after the none.

The Thirde Fytte

Lyth and lystyn, gentilmen,
  All that nowe be here;
Of Litell Johnn, that was the knightes man,
  Goode myrth ye shall here.

It was upon a mery day
  That yonge men wolde go shete;
Lytell Johnn fet his bowe anone,
  And sayde he wolde them mete.

Thre tymes Litell Johnn shet aboute,
  And alway cleft the wande;
The proude sherif of Notingham
  By the markes gan stande.

The sherif swore a full greate othe:
  By hym that dyede on a tre,
This man is the best arschere
  That ever I dyd see.

"Say me nowe, wight yonge man,
  What is nowe thy name?
In what countre were thou borne,
  And where is thy wonynge wane?"

TRADITIONAL BALLADS

"In Holdernes, sir, I was borne,
   I-wys al of my dame;
Men cal me Reynolde Grenelef
   Whan I am at home."

"Sey me, Reynolde Grenelefe,
   Wolde thou dwell with me?
And every yere I woll the gyve
   Twenty marke to thy fee."

I have a maister," sayde Litell Johnn,
   "A curteys knight is he;
May ye levë gete of hym,
   The better may it be."

The sherif gate Litell John
   Twelve moneths of the knight;
Therefore he gave him right anone
   A gode hors and a wight.

Nowe is Litell John the sherifes man,
   God lende us well to spede!
But alwey thought Lytell John
   To quyte hym wele his mede.

"Nowe so God me helpe," sayde Litell John,
   "And by my true leutye,
I shall be the worst servaunt to hym
   That ever yet had he."

It fell upon a Wednesday
   The sherif on huntynge was gone,
And Litel John lay in his bed,
   And was foriete at home.

Therfore he was fastinge
   Til it was past the none;
"Gode sir stuarde, I pray to the,
   Gyve me my dynere," saide Litell John.

"It is to longe for Grenelefe
   Fastinge thus for to be;
Therfor I pray the, sir stuarde,
   Mi dyner gif thou me."

"Shalt thou never ete ne drynke," saide the stuarde,
　"Tyll my lorde be come to towne":
"I make myn avowe to God," saide Litell John,
　I had lever to crake thy crowne."

The boteler was full uncurteys,
　There he stode on flore;
He start to the botery
　And shet fast the dore.

Lytell Johnn gave the boteler suche a tap
　His back went nere in two;
Though he liveth an hundred wynter,
　The wors he still shall goe.

He sporned the dore with his fote;
　It went open wel and fyne;
And there he made large lyveray,
　Bothe of ale and of wyne.

"Sith ye wol nat dyne," sayde Litell John,
　"I shall gyve you to drinke;
And though ye lyve an hundred wynter,
　On Lytel Johnn ye shall thinke."

Litell John ete, and Litel John drank,
　The while that he wolde;
The sherife had in his kechyn a coke,
　A stoute man and a bolde.

"I make myn avowe to God," saide the coke,
　"Thou arte a shrewde hyne
In ani householde for to dwel,
　For to aske thus to dyne."

And there he lent Litell John
　Godë strokis thre;
"I make myn avowe," sayde Lytell John,
　"These strokis lyked well me.

"Thou arte a bolde man and a hardy,
　And so thinketh me;
And or I pas fro this place
　Assayed better shalt thou be."

Lytell Johnn drew a ful gode sworde,
  The coke toke another in hande;
They thought no thynge for to fle,
  But stifly for to stande.

There they faught sore togedere
  Two mylë way and more;
Myght neyther other harme done,
  The mountnaunce of an owre.

"I make myn avowe to God" sayde Litel Johnn,
  "And by my true lewtë;
Thou art one of the best sworde-men
  That ever yit sawe I me.

"Cowdest thou shote as well in a bowe,
  To grene wode thou shuldest with me,
And two times in the yere thy clothinge
  Chaunged shuldë be;

"Are every yere of Robyn Hode
  Twenty merke to thy fe;"
"Put up thy swerde," saide the coke,
  "And felowes woll we be."

Thanne he fet to Lytell Johnn
  The nowmbles of a do,
Gode brede and full gode wyne;
  They ete and drank theretoo.

And when they had dronkyn well,
  Theyre trouthes togeder they plight
That they wolde by with Robyn
  That ylkë samë nyght.

They dyd them to the tresoure-hows,
  As fast as they myght gone;
The lokkes, that were of full gode stele,
  They brake them everichone.

They toke away the silver vessell,
  As all that thei might get;
Pecis, masars, ne sponis,
  Wolde thei not forget.

Also they toke the gode pens,
  Thre hundred pounde and more,
And did them streyte to Robyn Hode,
  Under the grene wode hore.

"God the save, my dere mayster,
  And Criste the save and se!"
And thanne sayde Robyn to Litell Johnn,
  "Welcome myght thou be.

"Also be that fayre yeman
  Thou bryngest there with the;
What tydynges fro Notyngham?
  Lytill Johnn, tell thou me."

"Well the gretith the proude sheryf,
  And sendeth the here by me
His cok and his silver vessell,
  And thre hundred pounde and thre."

"I make myne avowe to God," sayde Robyn,
  "And to the Trenytë,
It was never by his gode wyll
  This gode is come to me."

Lytyll Johnn there hym bethought
  On a shrewde wyle;
Fyve myle in the forest he ran,
  Hym happed all his wyll.

Than he met the proude sheref,
  Huntynge with houndes and horne;
Lytell Johnn coude of curtesye,
  And knelyd hym beforne.

"God the save, my dere mayster,
  And Criste the save and se!"
"Reynolde Grenelefe," sayde the shyref,
  "Where hast thou nowe be?"

"I have be in this forest;
  A fayre syght can I se;
It was one of the fayrest syghtes
  That ever yet sawe I me.

"Yonder I sawe a ryght fayre harte,
   His coloure is of grene;
Seven score of dere upon a herde
   Be with hym all bydene."

"Their tyndes are so sharp, maister,
   Of sexty, and well mo,
That I durst not shote for drede,
   Lest they wolde me slo.

"I make myn avowe to God," sayde the shyref,
   "That syght wolde I fayne se":
"Buske you thyderwarde, mi dere mayster,
   Anone, and wende with me."

The sherif rode, and Litell Johnn
   Of fote he was full smerte,
And whane they came before Robyn,
   "Lo, here is the mayster-herte."

Still stode the proude sherif,
   A sory man was he;
"Wo the worthe, Raynolde Grenelefe,
   Thou hast betrayed me."

"I make myn avowe to God," sayde Litell Johnn,
   "Mayster, ye be to blame;
I was mysserved of my dynere
   When I was with you at home."

Sone he was to souper sette,
   And served with silver white,
And when the sherif sawe his vessell,
   For sorowe he myght nat ete.

"Make glad chere," sayde Robyn Hode,
   "Sherif, for charitē,
And for the love of Litill Johnn
   Thy lyfe I graunt to the."

Whan they had souped well,
   The day was al gone;
Robyn commaunded Litell Johnn
   To drawe of his hose and shone;

His kirtell, and his cote a pye,
  That was fured well and fine
And toke hym a grene mantel.
  To lap his body therein.

Robyn commaunded his wight yonge men,
  Under the grene wode tree,
They shulde lye in that same sute
  That the sherif myght them see.

All nyght lay the proude sherif
  In his breche and in his schert;
No wonder it was, in grene wode;
  Though his sydes gan to smerte.

"Make glad chere," sayde Robyn Hode,
  "Sheref, for charitë;
For this is our ordre i-wys
  Under the grene-wode tree"

"This is harder order," sayde the sherief,
  "Than any ankir or frere;
For all the golde in mery Englonde
  I wolde nat longe dwell her."

"All this twelve monthes," sayde Robin,
  "Thou shalt dwell with me;
I shall the teche, proude sherif,
  An outlawe for to be."

"Or I here another nyght lye," sayde the sherif,
  "Robyn, nowe pray I the,
Smyte of mijn hede rather to-morowe,
  And I forgyve it the.

"Lat me go," than sayde the sherif
  "For sayntë charitë,
And I woll be the best frende
  That ever yet had ye."

"Thou shalt swere me an othe," sayde Robyn,
  "On my bright bronde;
Shalt thou never awayte me scathe
  By water ne by lande.

"And if thou fynde any of my men,
  By nyght or by day,
Upon thyn othe thou shalt swere
  To helpe them that thou may."

Nowe hathe the sherif sworne his othe,
  And home he began to gone;
He was as full of grene wode
  As ever was hepe of stone.

The Fourth Fytte

The sherif dwelled in Notingham;
  He was fayne he was agone;
And Robyn and his mery men
  Went to wode anone.

"Go we to dyner," sayde Littell Johnn;
  Robyn Hode sayde, "Nay;
For I drede Our Lady be wroth with me,
  For she sent me nat my pay."

"Have no doute, maister," sayde Litell Johnn;
  "Yet is not the sonne at rest;
For I dare say, and savely swere,
  The knight is true and truste."

"Take thy bowe in thy hande," sayde Robyn,
  "Late Much wende with the,
And so shal Wyllyam Scarlok,
  And no man abyde with me.

"And walke up under the Sayles,
  And to Watlynge-strete,
And wayte after some unketh gest;
  Up-chaunce ye may them mete.

"Whether he be messengere,
  Or a man that myrthës can,
Of my good he shall have some,
  Yf he be a pore man."

Forth then stert Lytel Johan,
  Half in tray and tene,

And gyrde hym with a full good swerde,
  Under a mantel of grene.

They went up to the Sayles,
  These yemen all thre;
They loked est, they loked west,
  They myght no man se.

But as they loked in Bernysdale,
  By the hye waye,
Than were they ware of two blacke monkes,
  Eche on a good palferay.

Then bespake Lytell Johan,
  To Much he gan say,
"I dare lay my lyfe to wedde,
  These monkes have brought our pay.

"Make glad chere," sayd Lytell Johan,
  "And frese our bowes of ewe,
And loke your hertes be seker and sad,
  Your strynges trusty and trewe.

"The monke hath two and fifty men,
  And seven somers full stronge;
There rydeth no bysshop in this londe
  So ryally, I understond.

"Brethren," sayd Lytell Johan,
  "Here are no more but we thre;
But we brynge them to dyner,
  Our mayster dare we not se.

"Bende your bowes," sayd Lytell Johan,
  "Make all yon prese to stonde;
The formost monke, his lyfe and his deth
  Is closed in my honde.

"Abyde, cherle monke,' sayd Lyttel Johan,
  "No ferther that thou gone;
Yf thou docst, by dere worthy God,
  Thy deth is in my honde.

"And evyll thryfte on thy hede," sayd Lytell Johan,
  "Ryght under thy hattes bonde,

For thou hast made our mayster wroth,
  He is fastynge so longe."

"Who is your mayster?" sayd the monke;
  Lytell Johan sayd, Robyn Hode;
"He is a stronge thefe," sayd the monke,
  "Of hym herd I never good."

"Thou lyest," than sayd Lytell Johan,
  "And that shall rewé the;
He is a yeman of the forest,
  To dyne he hath bodë the."

Much was redy with a bolte,
  Redly and anone,
He set the monke to-fore the brest,
  To the grounde that he can gone.

Of two and fyfty wyght yonge yemen
  There abode not one,
Saf a lytell page and a grome,
  To lede the somers with Lytel Johan.

They brought the monke to the lodge-dore,
  Whether he were loth or lefe,
For to speke with Robyn Hode,
  Maugre in theyr tethe.

Robyn dyde a downe his hode,
  The monke whan that he se;
The monke was not so curteyse,
  His hode then let he be.

"He is a chorle, mayster, by dere worthy God,"
  Than sayd Lytell Johan:
"Thereof no force," sayd Robyn,
  "For curteysy can he none.

"How many men," sayd Robyn,
  "Had this monke, Johan?"
"Fyfty and two whan that we met,
  But many of them be gone."

"Let blowe a horne," sayd Robyn,
  "That felaushyp may us knowe";

Seven score of wyght yemen,
  Came pryckynge on a rowe.

And everych of them a good mantell
  Of scarlet and of raye;
All they came to good Robyn,
  To wyte what he wolde say.

They made the monke to wasshe and wype,
  And syt at his denere,
Robyn Hode and Lytell Johan
  They served him both in-fere.

"Do gladly, monke," sayd Robyn.
  "Gramercy, syr," sayd he.
"Where is your abbay, whan ye are at home,
  And who is your avowē?"

"Saynt Mary abbay," sayd the monke,
  "Though I be symple here."
"In what offyce?" said Robyn:
  "Syr, the hye selerer."

"Ye be the more welcome," sayd Robyn,
  "So ever mote I the:
Fyll of the best wyne," sayd Robyn,
  "This monke shall drynke to me.

"But I have grete mervayle," sayd Robyn,
  "Of all this longē day;
I drede Our Lady be wroth with me,
  She sent me not my pay."

"Have no doute, mayster," sayd Lytell Johan,
  "Ye have no nede, I saye;
This monke hath brought it, I dare well swere,
  For he is of her abbay."

"And she was a borowe," sayd Robyn,
  "Betwene a knyght and me,
Of a lytell money that I hym lent,
  Under the grene-wode tree.

"And yf thou hast that sylver ibrought,
  I pray the let me se;

And I shall helpë the eftsones,
  Yf thou have nede to me."

The monke swore a full grete othe,
  With a sory chere,
"Of the borrowehode thou spekest to me,
  Herde I never ere."

"I make myn avowe to God," sayd Robyn,
  "Monke, thou art to blame;
For God is holde a ryghtwys man,
  And so is his dame.

"Thou toldest with thyn own tonge,
  Thou may not say nay,
How thou arte her servaunt,
  And servest her every day.

"And thou art made her messengere.
  My money for to pay;
Therefore I cun the morë thanke
  Thou arte come at thy day..

"What is in your cofers?" sayd Robyn,
  "Trewe than tell thou me":
"Syr," he sayd, "twenty marke,
  Al so mote I the."

"Yf there be no more," sayd Robyn,
  "I wyll not one peny;
Yf thou hast myster of ony more,
  Syr, more I shall lende to the."

"And yf I fynde more," sayd Robyn,
  "I-wys thou shalte it for gone;
For of thy spendynge-sylver, monke,
  Thereof wyll I ryght none.

"Go nowe forthe, Lytell Johan,
  And the trouth tell thou me;
If there be no more but twenty marke,
  No peny that I se."

Lytell Johan spred his mantell downe,
  As he had done before,

And he tolde out of the monkes male
  Eyght hondred pounde and more.

Lytell Johan let it lye full styll,
  And went to his mayster in hast;
"Syr," he sayd, "the monke is trewe ynowe,
  Our Lady hath doubled your cast."

"I make myn avowe to God," sayd Robyn—
  "Monke, what tolde I the?—
Our Lady is the trewest woman
  That ever yet founde I me.

"By dere worthy God," sayd Robyn,
  "The seche all Englond thorowe,
Yet founde I never to my pay
  A moche better borowe.

"Fyll of the best wyne, and do hym drynke," sayd Robyn,
  "And grete well thy lady hende,
And yf she have nede to Robyn Hode,
  A frende she shall hym fynde.

"And yf she nedeth any more sylver,
  Come thou agayne to me,
And, by this token she hath me sent,
  She shall have such thre."

The monke was goynge to London ward,
  There to hold grete mote,
The knyght that rode so hye on hors,
  To brynge hym under fote.

"Whether be ye away?" sayd Robyn:
  "Syr, to maners in this londe,
Too reken with our reves,
  That have done moch wronge."

"Come now forth, Lytell Johan,
  And harken to my tale;
A better yemen I knowe none,
  To seke a monkes male."

TRADITIONAL BALLADS

"How moch is in yonder other corser?" sayd Robyn,
  "The soth must we see";
By Our Lady," than sayd the monke,
  "That were no curteysye,

"To byde a man to dyner,
  And syth hym bete and bynde."
"It is our olde maner," sayd Robyn,
  "To leve but lytell behynde."

The monke toke the hors with spore,
  No lenger wolde he abyde:
"Aske to drynke," than sayd Robyn,
  "Or that ye forther ryde."

"Nay, for God," than sayd the monke,
  "Me reweth I cam so nere;
For better chepe I myght have dyned
  In Blythe or in Dankestere."

"Grete well your abbot," sayd Robyn,
  "And your pryour, I you pray,
And byd hum send me such a monke
  To dyner every day."

Now lete we that monke be styll,
  And speke we of that knyght:
Yet he came to holde his day,
  Whyle that it was lyght.

He dyde him streyt to Bernysdale,
  Under the grene-wode tre,
And he founde there Robyn Hode,
  And all his mery meynë.

The knyght lyght doune of his good palfray;
  Robyn whan he gan see,
So curteysly he dyde adoune his hode,
  And set hym on his knee.

"God the save, Robyn Hode,
  And all this company":
"Welcome be thou, gentyll knyght,
  And ryght welcome to me."

Than bespake hym Robyn Hode,
  To that knyght so fre:
What nede dryveth the to grene-wode?
  I praye the, syr knyght, tell me.

"And welcome be thou, gentyll knyght,
  Why hast thou be so longe?"
"For the abbot and the hye iustyce
  Wolde have had my londe."

"Hast thou thy londe agayne?" sayd Robyn;
  "Treuth than tell thou me":
"Ye, for God," sayd the knyght,,
  "And that thanke I God and the.

"But take no grefe, that I have be so longe;
  I came by a wrastelynge,
And there I holpe a pore yeman,
  With wronge was put behynde."

"Nay, for God," sayd Robyn,
  "Syr knyght, that thanke I the;
What man that helpeth a good yeman,
  His frende than wyll I be."

"Have here foure hondred pounde," sayd the knyght,
  "The whiche ye lent to me;
And here is also twenty marke
  For your curteysy."

"Nay, for God," sayd Robyn,
  "Thou broke it well for ay;
For Our Lady, by her hye selerer,
  Hath sent to me my pay.

"And yf I toke it i-twyse,
  A shame it were to me;
But trewely, gentyll knyght,
  Welcome arte thou to me."

Whan Robyn had tolde his tale,
  He leugh and made good chere:
"By my trouthe," then sayd the knyght,
  "Your money is redy here."

TRADITIONAL BALLADS

"Broke it well," said Robyn,
  "Thou gentyll knyght so fre;
And welcome be thou gentyll knyght,
  Under my trystell-tre.

"But what shall these bowes do?" sayd Robyn,
  "And these arowes ifedred fre?"
"By God," than sayd the knyght,
  "A pore present to the."

"Come now forth, Lytell Johan,
  And go to my treasurë,
And brynge me there foure hondred pounde;
  The monke over-tolde it me.

"Have here foure hondred pounde,
  Thou gentyll knyght and trewe,
And bye thee hors and harnes good,
  And gylte thy pores all newe.

"And yf thou fayle on spendynge,
  Com to Robyn Hode,
And by my trouth thou shalt none fayle,
  The whyles I have any good.

"And broke well thy foure hondred pound,
  Which I lent to the,
And make thy selfe no more so bare,
  By the counsell of me."

Thus than holpe hym good Robyn,
  The knyght all of his care:
God, that syt in heven hye,
  Graunte us well to fare!

The Fyfth Fytte

Now hath the knyght his leve i-take,
  And wente hym on his way;
Robyn Hode and his mery men
  Dwelled styll full many a day.

Lyth and lysten, gentil men,
  And herken what I shall say,

How the proud sheryfe of Notyngham
  Dyde crye a full fayre play;

That all the best archers of the north
  Sholde come upon a day,
And he that shoteth allther best
  The game shall bere away.

He that shoteth allther best,
  Furthest fayre and lowe,
At a payre of fynly buttes,
  Under the grene wode shawe,

A ryght arowe he shall have,
  The shafe of sylver whyte,
The hede and feders of ryche rede golde,
  In Englond is none lyke.

This than herde good Robyn,
  Under his trystell-tre:
"Make you redy, ye might yonge men;
  That shotynge wyll I se.

"Buske you, my mery yonge men;
  Ye shall go with me;
And I wyll wete the shryvës fayth,
  Trewe and yf he be."

Whan they had theyr bowes i-bent,
  Theyr takles fedred fre,
Seven score of wyght yonge men
  Stode by Robyns kne.

Whan they cam to Notyngham,
  The buttes were fayre and longe;
Many was the bolde archere
  That shot with bowës stronge.

"There shall but syx shote with me;
  The other shal kepe my he[ve]de,
And stande with good bowes bent,
  That I be not desceyved."

The fourth outlawe his bowe gan bende,
  And that was Robyn Hode,

TRADITIONAL BALLADS

And that behelde the proud sheryfe,
    All by the but he stode.

Thryës Robyn shot about,
    And alway he slist the wand,
And so dyde good Gylberte
    With the whytë hande.

Lytell Johan and good Scatheloke
    Were archers good and fre;
Lytell Much and good Reynolde,
    The worste wolde they not be.

Whan they had shot aboute,
    These archours fayre and good,
Evermore was the best,
    For soth, Robyn Hode.

Hym was delyvered the good arowe,
    For best worthy was he;
He toke the yeft so curteysly,
    To grene-wode wolde he.

They cryed out on Robyn Hode,
    And grete hornes gan they blowe:
"Wo worth the, treason!" sayd Robyn,
    "Ful evyl thou art to knowe.

"And wo be thou! thou proude sheryf,
    Thus gladdynge thy gest;
Otherwyse thou behote me
    In yonder wylde forest.

"But had I the in grene-wode,
    Under my trystell-tre,
Thou sholdest leve me a better wedde
    Than thy trewe lewtë.

Full many a bowë there was bent,
    And arowes let they glyde;
Many a kyrtell there was rent,
    And hurt many a syde.

The outlawes shot was so stronge
    That no man myght them dryve,

'And the proud sheryfes men,
  They fled away full blyve.

Robyn sawe the busshement to-broke,
  In grene wode he wolde have be;
Many an arowe there was shot
  Amonge that company.

Lytell Johan was hurte full sore,
  With an arowe in his kne,
That he myght neyther go nor ryde;
  It was full grete pytë.

"Mayster," then sayd Lytell Johan,
  "If ever thou lovedst me,
And for that ylkë lordës love
  That dyed upon a tre,

"And for the medes of my servyce,
  That I have served the,
Lete never the proud sheryf
  Alyve now fyndë me.

"But take out thy browne swerde,
  And smyte all of my hede,
And gyve me woundës depe and wyde;
  No lyfe on me be lefte."

"I wolde not that," sayd Robyn,
  "Johan, that thou were slawe,
For all the golde in merry Englonde,
  Though it lay now on a rawe."

"God forbede," sayd Lytell Much,
  "That dyed on a tre,
That thou sholdest, Lytell Johan,
  Parte our company."

Up he toke hym on his backe,
  And bare hym well a myle;
Many a tyme he layd him downe,
  And shot another whyle.

Then was there a fayre castell,
  A lytell within the wode;

TRADITIONAL BALLADS

Double-dyched it was about,
  And walled, by the rode.

And there dwelled that gentyll knyght,
  Syr Rychard at the Lee,
That Robyn had lent his good,
  Under the grene-wode tre.

In he toke good Robyn,
  And all his company:
"Welcome be thou, Robyn Hode,
  Welcome art thou to me;

"And moche I thanke the of thy comfort,
  And of thy curteysye,
And of thy grete kyndnesse,
  Under the grene-wode tre.

"I love no man in all this worlde
  So much as I do the;
For all the proud sheryf of Notyngham,
  Ryght here shalt thou be.

"Shute the gates, and drawe the brydge,
  And let no man come in,
And arme you well, and make you redy,
  And to the walles ye wynne.

"For one thynge, Robyn, I the behote;
  I swere by Saynt Quyntyne,
These forty dayes thou wonnest with me,
  To soupe, ete, and dyne."

Bordes were layde, and clothes were spredde,
  Redely and anone;
Robyn Hode and his merry men
  To metë can they gone.

The Sixth Fytte

Lythe and lysten, gentylmen,
  And herkyn to your songe;
Howe the proude shyref of Notyngham,
  And men of armys stronge,

Full fast cam to the hye shyref,
    The contrë up to route,
And they besette the knyghtes castell,
    The wallës all aboute.

The proude shyref loude gan crye,
    And sayde, "Thou traytour knight,
Thou kepest here the kynges enemys,
    Agaynst the lawe and right."

"Sir, I wyll avow that I have done,
    The dedys that here be dyght,
Upon all the landës that I have,
    As I am a trewe knyght.

"Wende furth, sirs, on your way,
    And do no more to me
Tyll ye wyt oure kyngës wille,
    What he wyll say to the."

The shyref thus had his answere,
    Without any lesynge;
Forth he yede to London towne,
    All to tel our kinge.

Ther he telde him of that knight,
    And eke of Robyn Hode,
And also of the bolde archars,
    That were soo noble and gode.

"He wyll avowe that he hath done,
    To mayntene the outlawes stronge;
He wyll be lorde, and set you at nought,
    In all the northe londe."

"I wil be at Notyngham," saide our kynge,
    "Within this fourteenyght,
And take I wyll Robyn Hode
    And so I wyll that knight.

"Go nowe home, shyref," sayde our kynge,
    "And do as I byd the;
And ordeyn gode archers ynowe,
    Of all the wyde contrë."

The shyref had his leve i-take,
  And went hym on his way,
And Robyn Hode to grene wode,
  Upon a certen day.

And Lytel John was hole of the arowe
  That shot was in his kne,
And dyd hym streyght to Robyn Hode,
  Under the grene wode tree.

Robyn Hode walked in the forest,
  Under the levys grene;
The proude shyref of Notyngham
  Thereof he had grete tene.

The shyref there fayled of Robyn Hode,
  He myght not have his pray;
Than he awayted this gentyll knyght,
  Bothe by nyght and day.

Ever he wayted the gentyll knyght,
  Syr Richarde at the Lee,
As he went on haukynge by the ryver-syde,
  And lete his haukës flee.

Toke he there this gentyll knight,
  With men of armys stronge,
And led hym to Notynghamwarde,
  Bound bothe fote and hande.

The shyref sware a full grete othe,
  Bi him that dyed on rode,
He had lever than an hundred pound
  That he had Robyn Hode.

This harde the knyghtës wyfe,
  A fayr lady and a free;
She set hir on a gode palfrey,
  To grene wode anone rode she.

Whanne she cam in the forest,
  Under the grene wode tree,
Founde she there Robyn Hode,
  And al his fayre menë.

"God the save, gode Robyn,
   And all thy company;
For Our der Ladyes sake,
   A bone graunte thou me.

"Late never my wedded lorde
   Shamefully slayne be;
He is fast bound to Notinghamwarde,
   For the love of the."

Anone than saide goode Robyn
   To that lady so fre,
"What man hath your lorde ytake?"
   "The proude shirife," than sayd she.

. . . .

"For soth as I the say;
He is nat yet thre mylës
   Passed on his way."

Up than sterte gode Robyn,
   As man that had ben wode:
"Buske you, my mery men,
   For hym that dyed on rode.

"And he that this sorowe forsaketh
   By hym that dyed on tre,
Shall he never in grene wode
   No lenger dwel with me."

Sone there were gode bowës bent,
   Mo than seven score;
Hedge ne dyche spared they none
   That was them before.

"I make myn avowe to God," sayde Robyn
   "The sherif wolde I fayne see;
And if I may him take,
   I-quyt then shall he be."

And when they came to Notingham,
   They walked in the strete;
And with the proude sherif i-wys
   Sonë can they mete.

TRADITIONAL BALLADS

"Abyde, thou proude sherif," he sayde,
  "Abyde, and speke with me;
Of some tidinges of oure kinge
  I wolde fayne here of the.

"This seven yere, by dere worthy God,
  Ne yede I this fast on fote;
I make myn avowe to God, thou proude sherif,
  It is not for thy gode."

Robyn bent a full goode bowe,
  An arrowe he drowe at wyll;
He hit so the proude sherife
  Upon the grounde he lay full still.

And or he myght up aryse,
  On his fete to stonde,
He smote of the sherifs hede
  With his bright bronde.

"Lye thou there, thou proude sherife;
  Evyll mote thou thryve:
There myght no man to the truste
  The whyles thou were a lyve."

His men drewe out theyr bryght swerdes,
  That were so sharpe and kene,
And layde on the sheryves men,
  And dryved them downe bydene.

Robyn stert to that knyght,
  And cut a two his bonde,
And toke hym in his hand a bowe,
  And bad hym by hym stonde.

"Leve thy hors the behynde,
  And lerne for to renne;
Thou shalt with me to grene wode,
  Through myre, mosse, and fenne.

"Thou shalt with me to grene wode,
  Without ony leasynge,
Tyll that I have gete us grace
  Of Edwarde, our comly kynge."

The Seventh Fytte

The kynge came to Notynghame,
  With knyghtes in grete araye,
For to take that gentyll knyght
  And Robyn Hode, and yf he may.

He asked men of that countrē,
  After Robyn Hode,
And after that gentyll knyght,
  That was so bolde and stout.

Whan they had tolde hym the case
  Our kynge understode ther tale,
And seased in his honde
  The knyghtēs londēs all.

All the passe of Lancasshyre
  He went both ferre and nere,
Tyll he came to Plomton Parke;
  He faylyd many of his dere.

There our kynge was wont to se
  Herdēs many one,
He coud unneth fynde one dere,
  That bare ony good horne.

The kynge was wonder wroth with all,
  And swore by the Tryntē,
"I wolde I had Robyn Hode,
  With eyen I myght hym se.

"And he that wolde smyte of the knyghtēs hede,
  And brynge it to me,
He shall have the knyghtēs londes,
  Syr Rycharde at the Le.

"I gyve it hym with my charter,
  And sele it with my honde,
To have and holde for ever more,
  In all mery Englonde."

Than bespake a fayre olde knyght,
  That was treue in his fay:

"A, my leegë lorde the kynge,
　One worde I shall you say.

"There is no man in this countrë
　May have the knyghtës londes,
Whyle Robyn Hode may ryde or gone,
　And bere a bowe in his hondes,

"That he ne shall lese his hede,
　That is the best ball in his hode:
Give it no man, my lorde the kynge,
　That ye wyll any good."

Half a yere dwelled our comly kynge
　In Notyngham, and well more;
Coude he not here of Robyn Hode,
　In what countrë that he were.

But alway went good Robyn
　By halke and eke by hyll,
And alway slewe the kyngës dere,
　And welt them at his wyll.

Than bespake a proude fostere,
　That stode by our kyngës kne:
"Yf ye wyll see good Robyn,
　Ye must do after me.

"Take fyve of the best knyghtes
　That be in your lede,
And walke downe by yon abbay,
　And gete you monkës wede.

"And I wyll be your ledes-man,
　And lede you the way,
And or ye come to Notyngham,
　Myn here then dare I lay,

"That ye shall mete with good Robyn,
　On lyve yf that he be;
Or ye come to Notyngham,
　With even ye shall hym se."

Full hastely our kynge was dyght,
　So were his knyghtës fyve,

Everych of them in monkës wede,
　And hasted them thyder blyve.

Our kynge was grete above his cole,
　A brode hat on his crowne,
Ryght as he were abbot-lyke,
　They rode up into the towne.

Styf botes our kynge had on,
　Forsoth as I you say;
He rode syngynge to grene wode,
　The covent was clothed in graye.

His male-hors and his grete somers
　Folowed our kynge behynde,
Tyll they came to grene wode,
　A myle under the lynde.

There they met with good Robyn,
　Stondynge on the waye,
And so dyde many a bolde archere,
　For soth as I you say.

Robyn toke the kyngës hors,
　Hastely in that stede,
And sayd, "Syr abbot, by your leve,
　A whyle ye must abyde.

"We be yemen of this foreste,
　Under the grene-wode tre;
We lyve by our kyngës dere,
　Other shift have not wee.

"And ye have chyrches and rentës both,
　And gold full grete plentë;
Gyve us some of your spendynge,
　For saynt charytë."

Than bespake our cumly kynge,
　Anone than sayd he;
"I brought nomore to grene-wode
　But forty younde with me.

"I have layne at Notyngham,
　This fourtynyght with our kynge,

And spent I have full moche good
  On many a grete lordynge.

"And I have but forty pounde,
  No more than have I me;
But if I had an hondred pounde,
  I would give it to thee."

Robyn toke the forty pounde
  And departed it in two partye;
Halfendell he gave his mery men,
  And bad them mery to be.

Full curteysly Robyn gan say;
  "Syr, have this for your spendyng;
We shall mete another day;"
  "Gramercy," than sayd our kynge.

"But well the greteth Edwarde, our kynge
  And sent to the his seale,
And byddeth the com to Notyngham,
  Both to mete and mele."

He toke out the brode targe,
  And sone he lete hym se;
Robyn coud his courteysy,
  And set hym on his kne.

"I love no man in all the worlde
  So well as I do my kynge;
Welcome is my lordës seale;
  And, monke, for thy tydynge,

"Syr abbot, for thy tydynges,
  To day thou shalt dyne with me,
For the love of my kynge,
  Under my trystell-tre."

Forth he lad our comly kynge,
  Full fayre by the honde;
Many a dere there was slayne,
  And full fast dyghtande.

Robyn toke a full grete horne,

And loude he gan blowe;
Seven score of wyght yonge men
   Came redy on a rowe.

All they kneled on theyr kne,
   Full fayre before Robyn:
The kynge sayd hym selfe untyll,
   And swore by Saynt Austyn,

"Here is a wonder semely sight;
   Me thynketh, by Goddës pyne,
His men are more at his byddynge
   Then my men be at myn."

Full hastely was theyr dyner idyght,
   And therto gan they gone;
They served our kynge with all theyr myght,
   Both Robyn and Lytell Johan.

Anone before our kynge was set
   The fattë venyson,
The good whyte brede, the good rede wyne,
   And therto the fyne ale and browne.

"Make good chere," said Robyn,
   "Abbot, for charytë;
And for this ylkë tydynge,
   Blyssed mote thou be.

"Now shalte thou se what lyfe we lede,
   Or thou hens wende;
Than thou may enfourme our kynge,
   Whan ye togyder lende."

Up they sterte all in hast,
   Theyr bowes were smartly bent;
Our kynge was never so sore agast,
   He wende to have be shente.

Two yerdes there we up set,
   Thereto gan they gange;
By fyfty pase, our kynge sayd,
   The merkës were to longe.

TRADITIONAL BALLADS

On every syde a rose-garlonde,
   They shot under the lyne:
"Who so fayleth of the rose-garlonde," sayd Robyn,
   "His takyll he shall tyne.

"And yelde it to his mayster,
   Be it never so fyne;
For no man wyll I spare,
   So drynge I ale or wyne;

"And bere a buffet on his hede,
   I-wys ryght all bare":
And all that fell in Robyns lote,
   He smote them wonder sare.

Twyse Robyn shot aboute,
   And ever he cleved the wande,
And so dyde good Gylberte
   With the whytë hande.

Lytell Johan and good Scathelocke,
   For nothynge wolde they spare;
When they fayled of the garlonde,
   Robyn smote them full sore.

At the last shot that Robyn shot,
   For all his frendës fare,
Yet he fayled of the garlonde
   Thre fyngers and mare.

Than bespake good Gylberte,
   And thus he gan say;
"Mayster," he sayd, "your takyll is lost,
   Stande forth and take your pay."

"If it be so," sayd Robyn,
   "That may no better be,
Syr abbot, I delyver the myn arowe,
   I pray the, syr, serve thou me."

"It falleth not for myn ordre," sayd our kynge,
   "Robyn, by thy leve,
For to smyte no good yeman,
   For doute I sholde hym greve."

"Smyte on boldely," sayd Robyn,
  "I give the large leve":
Anone our kynge, with that worde,
  He folde up his sleve,

And sych a buffet he gave Robyn,
  To grounde he yede full nere:
"I make myn avowe to God," sayd Robyn,
  "Thou arte a stalworthe frere.

"There is pith in thyn arme," sayd Robyn,
  "I trowe thou canst well shete";
Thus our kynge and Robyn Hode
  Togeder gan they mete.

Robyn behelde our comly kynge
  Wystly in the face,
So dyde Syr Rycharde at the Le,
  And kneled downe in that place.

And so dyde all the wylde outlawes,
  Whan they se them knele:
"My lorde the kynge of Englonde,
  Now I knowe you well."

"Mercy then, Robyn," sayd our kynge,
  "Under your trystyll-tree,
Of thy goodnesse and thy grace,
  For my men and me!"

"Yes, for God," sayd Robyn,
  "And also God me save,
I aske mercy, my lorde the kynge,
  And for my men I crave."

"Yes, for God," than sayd our kynge,
  "And therto sent I me,
With that thou leve the grene-wode,
  And all thy company;

"And come home, syr, to my courte,
  And there dwell with me."
"I make myn avowe to God," sayd Robyn
  "And ryght so shall it be.

"I wyll come to your courte,
  Your servyse for to se,
And brynge with me of my men
  Seven score and thre.

"But me lyke well your servyse,
  I wyll come agayne full soone,
And shote at the donnë dere,
  As I am wonte to done.'

The Eighth Fytte

"Haste thou ony grene cloth," sayd our kynge,
  "That thou wylte sell nowe to me?"
"Ye, for God," sayd Robyn,
  "Thyrty yerdes and thre."

"Robyn," sayd our kynge,
  "Now pray I the,
Sell me some of that cloth,
  To me and my meynë."

"Yes, for God," then sayd Robyn,
  "Or elles I were a fole;
Another day we wyll me clothe,
  I trowe, ayenst the Yole."

The kynge kest of his cole then,
  A grene garment he dyde on,
And every knyght also, iwys,
  Another hal full sone.

Whan they were clothed in Lyncolne grene,
  They keste away theyr graye;
"Now we shall to Notyngham,"
  All thus our kynge gan say.

They bente theyr bowes and forth they went,
  Shotynge all in-fere,
Towarde the towne of Notyngham,
  Outlawes as they were.

Our kynge and Robyn rode togyder,
  For soth as I you say,

And they shote plucke-buffet,
  As they went by the way.

And many a buffet our kynge wan
  Of Robyn Hode that day,
And nothynge spared good Robyn
  Our kynge when he did pay.

"So god me helpē," sayd our kynge,
  "Thy game is nought to lere;
I sholde not get a shote of the,
  Though I shote all this yere."

All the people of Notyngham
  They stode and behelde;
They sawe nothynge but mantels of grene
  That covered all the felde.

Than every man to other gan say,
  "I drede our kynge be slone;
Come Robyn Hode to the towne, i-wys
  On lyve he lefte never one."

Full hastely they began to fle,
  Both yemen and knaves,
And old wyves that myght evyll goo,
  They hypped on theyr staves.

The kynge loughe full fast,
  And commaunded theym agayne;
When they se our comly kynge,
  I-wys they were full fayne.

They ete and dranke, and made them glad,
  And sange with notës hye;
Than bespake our comly kynge
  To Syr Richarde at the Lee.

He gave hym there his londe agayne,
  A good man he bad hym be;
Robyn thanked our comly kynge,
  And set hym on his kne.

Had Robyn dwelled in the kynges courte
  But twelve monethes and thre,

That he had spent an hondred pounde,
   And all his mennes fe.

In every place where Robyn came
   Ever more he layde downe,
Both for knyghtës and for squyres,
   To gete hym grete renowne.

By than the yere was all agone
   He had no man by twayne,
Lytell Johann and good Scathelocke,
   With hym all for to gone.

Robyn sawye yonge men shote
   Full faire upon a day;
"Alas!" than sayd good Robyn,
   "My welthe is went away.

"Somtyme I was an archere good,
   A styffe and eke a stronge;
I was compted the best archere
   That was in mery Englonde.

"Alas!" then sayd good Robyn,
   "Alas and well a woo!
Yf I dwele lenger with the kynge,
   Sorowe wyll me sloo"

Forth than went Robyn Hode
   Tyll he came to our kynge:
"My lorde the kynge of Englonde,
   Graunte me myn askynge.

"I made a chapell in Bernsydale,
   That semely is to se,
It is of Mary Magdaleyne,
   And thereto wolde I be.

"I myght never in this seven nyght
   No tyme to slepe ne wynke,
Nother all these seven dayes
   Nother ete ne drynke.

"Me longeth sore to Bernysdale,
   I may not be therfro:

Barefote and wolwarde I have hyght
  Thyder for to go."

"Yf it be so," than sayd our kynge,
  "It may no better be;
Seven nyght I gyve the leve,
  No lengre, to dwell fro me."

"Gramercy, lorde," then sayd Robyn,
  And set hym on his kne;
He toke his leve full courteysly,
  To grene wode then went he.

Whan he came to grene wode,
  In a mery mornynge,
There he herde the notës small
  Of byrdës mery syngynge.

"It is ferre gone," sayd Robyn,
  "That I was last here;
Me lyste a lytell for to shote
  At the donnë dere."

Robyn slewe a full grete harte;
  His horne than gan he blow,
That all the outlawes of that forest
  That horne coud they knowe,

And gadred them togyder,
  In a lytell throwe.
Seven score of wyght yonge men
  Came redy on a rowe,

And fayre dyde of theyr hodes,
  And set them on theyr kne:
"Welcome," they sayd, "our mayster.
  Under this grene-wode tre."

Robyn dwelled in grene wode
  Twenty yere and two;
For all drede of Edwarde our kynge,
  Agayne wolde he not goo.

Yet he was begyled, i-wys,
  Through a wycked woman,

The pyroresse of Kyrkësly,
  That nye was of hys kynne:

For the love of a knyght,
  Syr Roger of Donkesly,
That was her ownë speciall;
  Full evyll mote they the!

They toke togyder theyr counsell
  Robyn Hode for to sle,
And how they myght best do that dede,
  His banis for to be.

Than bespake good Robyn,
  In place where as he stode,
"To morrow I muste to Kyrke[s]ly,
  Craftely to be leten blode.

Syr Roger of Donkestere,
  By the pryoresse he lay,
And there they betrayed good Robyn Hode,
  Though theyr falsë playe.

Cryst have mercy on his soule,
  That dyed on the rode!
For he was a good outlawe,
  And dyde pore men moch god.

* * *

RICHARD ROWLANDS

OUR BLESSED LADY'S LULLABY

Upon my lap, my Sovereign sits,
  And sucks upon my breast;
Meanwhile his love sustains my life,
  And gives my body rest.
    Sing, lullaby, my little boy,
    Sing, lullaby, my livës joy.

When thou hast taken thy repast,
  Repose, my babe, on me,
So may thy mother and thy nurse,

Thy cradle also be.
    Sing, lullaby, my little boy,
    Sing, lullaby, my livës joy.

I grieve that duty doth not work
  All that my wishing would,
Because I would not be to thee
  But in the best I should.
    Sing, lullaby, my little boy,
    Sing, lullaby, my livës joy.

Yet as I am and as I may,
  I must and will be thine,
Though all too little for thyself
  Vouchsafing to be mine.
    Sing, lullaby, my little boy,
    Sing, lullaby, my livës joy.

My wits, my words, my deeds, my thoughts,
  And else what is in me,
I rather will not wish to use,
  If not in serving thee.
    Sing, lullaby, my little boy,
    Sing, lullaby, my livës joy.

My babe, my bliss, my child, my choice,
  My fruit, my flower, and bud,
My Jesus, and my only joy,
  The sum of all my good.
    Sing, lullaby, my little boy,
    Sing, lullaby, my livës joy.

My sweetness, and the sweetest most
  That heaven could earth deliver,
Soul of my love, spirit of my life,
  Abide with me for ever.
    Sing, lullaby, my little boy,
    Sing, lullaby, my livës joy.

Live still with me, and be my love,
  And death will me refrain,
Unless thou let me die with thee,
  To live with thee again.
    Sing, lullaby, my little boy,
    Sing, lullaby, my livës joy.

Leave now to wail, thou luckless wight
  That wrought'st thy race's woe,
Redress is found and foilèd is
  Thy fruit-alluring foe.
    Sing, lullaby, my little boy,
    Sing, lullaby, my livës joy.

The fruit of death from Paradise
  Made the exiled mourn;
My fruit of life to Paradise
  Makes joyful thy return.
    Sing, lullaby, my little boy,
    Sing, lullaby, my livës joy.

Grow up, good fruit be nourished by
  These fountains two of me,
That only flow with maiden's milk,
  The only meat for thee.
    Sing, lullaby, my little boy,
    Sing, lullaby, my livës joy.

The earth has now a heaven become,
  And this base bower of mine,
A princely palace unto me,
  My son doth make to shine.
    Sing, lullaby, my little boy,
    Sing, lullaby, my livës joy.

His sight gives clearness to my sight,
  When waking I him see,
And sleeping, his mild countenance
  Gives favour unto me.
    Sing, lullaby, my little boy,
    Sing, lullaby, my livës joy.

When I him in mine arms embrace,
  I feel my heart embraced,
Even by the inward grace of his,
  Which he in me hath placed.
    Sing, lullaby, my little boy,
    Sing, lullaby, my livës joy.

And when I kiss his loving lips,
  Then his sweet-smelling breath
Doth yield a savour to my soul,

That feeds love, hope, and faith.
    Sing, lullaby, my little boy,
    Sing, lullaby, my livës joy.

The shepherds left their keeping sheep,
  For joy to see my lamb;
How may I more rejoice to see
  Myself to be the dam.
    Sing, lullaby, my little boy,
    Sing, lullaby, my livës joy.

Three kings their treasures hither brought
  Of incense, myrrh, and gold;
The heaven's treasure, and the king
  That here they might behold.
    Sing, lullaby, my little boy,
    Sing, lullaby, my livës joy.

One sort an angel did direct,
  A star did guide the other,
And all the fairest son to see
  That ever had a mother.
    Sing, lullaby, my little boy,
    Sing, lullaby, my livës joy.

This sight I see, this child I have,
  This infant I embrace,
O endless comfort of the earth,
  And heaven's eternal grace.
    Sing, lullaby, my little boy,
    Sing, lullaby, my livës joy.

Thee sanctity herself doth serve,
  Thee goodness doth attend,
Thee blessedness doth wait upon,
  And virtues all commend.
    Sing, lullaby, my little boy,
    Sing, lullaby, my livës joy.

Great kings and prophets wishèd have
  To see that I possess,
Yet wish I never thee to see,
  If not in thankfulness.
    Sing, lullaby, my little boy,
    Sing, lullaby, my livës joy.

RICHARD ROWLANDS

Let heaven and earth, and saints and men,
  Assistance give to me,
That all their most concurring aid
  Augment my thanks to thee.
    Sing, lullaby, my little boy,
    Sing, lullaby, my livës joy.

And let the ensuing blessèd race,
  Thou wilt succeeding raise,
Join all their praises unto mine,
  To multiply thy praise.
    Sing, lullaby, my little boy,
    Sing, lullaby, my livës joy.

And take my service well in worth,
  And Joseph's here with me,
Who of my husband bears the name,
  Thy servant for to be.
    Sing, lullaby, my little boy,
    Sing, lullaby, my livës joy.

* * *

THOMAS NASHE

IN TIME OF PESTILENCE

Adieu, farewell earth's bliss!
This world uncertain is:
Fond are life's lustful joys,
Death proves them all but toys.
None from his darts can fly;
I am sick, I must die—
    Lord, have mercy on us!

Rich men, trust not in wealth,
Gold cannot buy you health;
Physic himself must fade;
All things to end are made;
The plague full swift goes by;
I am sick, I must die—
    Lord, have mercy on us!

Beauty is but a flower
Which wrinkles will devour;
Brightness falls from the air;
Queens have died young and fair;
Dust hath closed Helen's eye;
I am sick, I must die—
  Lord, have mercy on us!

Strength stoops unto the grave,
Worms feed on Hector brave;
Swords may not fight with fate;
Earth still holds ope her gate;
Come, come! the bells do cry;
I am sick, I must die—
  Lord, have mercy on us!

Wit with his wantonness
Tasteth death's bitterness;
Hell's executioner
Hath no ears for to hear
What vain art can reply;
I am sick, I must die—
  Lord, have mercy on us!

Haste therefore each degree
To welcome destiny;
Heaven is our heritage,
Earth but a player's stage.
Mount we unto the sky;
I am sick, I must die—
  Lord, have mercy on us!

* * *

EDMUND SPENSER

PROTHALAMION

CALM was the day, and through the trembling air
Sweet-breathing Zephyrus did softly play—
A gentle spirit, that lightly did delay
Hot Titan's beams, which then did glister fair;
When I, (whom sullen care,
Through discontent of my long fruitless stay

EDMUND SPENSER

In princes' court, and expectation vain
Of idle hopes, which still do fly away
Like empty shadows, did afflict my brain)
Walk'd forth to ease my pain
Along the shore of silver-streaming Thames;
Whose rutty bank, the which his river hems,
Was painted all with variable flowers,
And all the meads adorn'd with dainty gems
Fit to deck maidens' bowers,
And crown their paramours
Against the bridal day, which is not long:
   Sweet Thames! run softly, till I end my song.

There is a meadow by the river's side
A flock of nymphs I chancéd to espy,
All lovely daughters of the flood thereby,
With goodly greenish locks all loose untied
As each had been a bride;
And each one had a little wicker basket
Made of fine twigs, entrailéd curiously,
In which they gather'd flowers to fill their flasket,
And with fine fingers cropt full feateously
The tender stalks on high.
Of every sort which in that meadow grew
They gather'd some; the violet, pallid blue,
The little daisy that at evening closes,
The virgin lily and the primrose true:
With store of vermeil roses,
To deck their bridegrooms' posies
Against the bridal day, which was not long:
   Sweet Thames! run softly, till I end my song.

With that I saw two swans of goodly hue
Come softly swimming down along the lee;
Two fairer birds I yet did never see;
The snow which doth the top of Pindus strow
Did never whiter show,
Nor Jove himself, when he a swan would be
For love of Leda, whiter did appear;
Yet Leda was (they say) as white as he,
Yet not so white as these, nor nothing near;
So purely white they were
That even the gentle stream, the which them bare,
Seem'd foul to them, and bade his billows spare
To wet their silken feathers, lest they might

Soil their fair plumes with water not so fair,
And mar their beauties bright
That shone as Heaven's light
Against their bridal day, which was not long:
   Sweet Thames! run softly, till I end my song.

Eftsoons the nymphs, which now had flowers their fill,
Ran all in haste to see that silver brood
As they came floating on the crystal flood;
Whom when they saw, they stood amazéd still
Their wondering eyes to fill;
Them seem'd they never saw a sight so fair
Of fowls, so lovely, that they sure did deem
Them heavenly born, or to be that same pair
Which through the sky draw Venus' silver team;
For sure they did not seem
To be begot of any earthly seed,
But rather angels, or of angels' breed;
Yet were they bred of summer's heat, they say,
In sweetest season, when each flower and weed
The earth did fresh array;
So fresh they seem'd as day,
Ev'n as their bridal day, which was not long:
   Sweet Thames! run softly, till I end my song.

Then forth they all out of their baskets drew
Great store of flowers, the honour of the field,
That to the sense did fragrant odors yield,
All which upon those goodly birds they threw
And all the waves did strew,
That like old Peneus' waters they did seem
When down along by pleasant Tempe's shore
Scatter'd with flowers, through Thessaly they stream,
That they appear, through lilies' plenteous store,
Like a bride's chamber-floor.
Two of those nymphs meanwhile two garlands bound
Of freshest flowers which in that mead they found,
The which presenting all in trim array,
Their snowy foreheads therewithal they crown'd;
Whilst one did sing this lay
Prepared against that day,
Against their bridal day, which was not long:
   Sweet Thames! run softly, till I end my song.

EDMUND SPENSER

"Ye gentle birds! the world's fair ornament,
And Heaven's glory, whom this happy hour
Doth lead unto your lover's blissful bower,
Joy may you have, and gentle heart's content
Of your love's complement;
And let fair Venus, that is queen of love,
With her heart-quelling son upon you smile,
Whose smile, they say, hath virtue to remove
All love's dislike, and friendship's faulty guile
For ever to assoil.
Let endless peace your steadfast hearts accord,
And blessed plenty wait upon your board;
And let your bed with pleasures chaste abound,
That fruitful issue may to you afford
Which may your foes confound,
And make your joys redound
Upon your bridal day, which is not long:
 Sweet Thames! run softly, till I end my song."

So ended she; and all the rest around
To her redoubled that her undersong,
Which said their bridal day should not be long:
And gentle Echo from the neighbour ground
Their accents did resound.
So forth those joyous birds did pass along
Adown the lee that to them murmur'd low,
As he would speak but that he lack'd a tongue;
Yet did by signs his glad affection show,
Making his stream run slow.
And all the fowl which in his flood did dwell
'Gan flock about these twain, that did excel
The rest, so far as Cynthia doth shend
The lesser stars. So they, enrangèd well,
Did on those two attend,
And their best service lend
Against their wedding day, which was not long:
 Sweet Thames! run softly, till I end my song.

At length they all to merry London came,
To merry London, my most kindly nurse,
That to me gave this life's first native source,
Though from another place I take my name,
An house of ancient fame:
There when they came whereas those bricky towers
The which on Thames' broad aged back do ride,

Where now the studious lawyers have their bowers,
Their whilome wont the Templar-knights to bide,
Till they decay'd through pride;
Next whereunto there stands a stately place,
Where oft I gainéd gifts and goodly grace
Of that great lord, which therein wont to dwell,
Whose want too well now feels my friendless case;
But ah! here fits not well
Old woes, but joys to tell
Against the bridal day, which is not long:
   Sweet Thames! run softly, till I end my song.

Yet therein now doth a noble peer,
Great England's glory and the world's wide wonder,
Whose dreadful name late through all Spain did thunder,
And Hercules' two pillars standing near
Did make to quake and fear:
Fair branch of honour, flower of chivalry!
That fillest England with thy triumphs' fame
Joy have thou of thy noble victory,
And endless happiness of thine own name
That promiseth the same;
That through thy prowess and victorious arms
Thy country may be freed from foreign harms,
And great Elisa's glorious name may ring
Through all the world, fill'd with thy wide alarms,
Which some brave Muse may sing
To ages following:
Upon the bridal day, which is not long:
   Sweet Thames! run softly, till I end my song.

From those high towers this noble lord issúing
Like radiant Hesper, when his golden hair
In th' ocean billows he hath bathéd fair,
Descended to the river's open viewing
With a great train ensuing.
Above the rest were goodly to be seen
Two gentle knights of lovely face and feature,
Beseeming well the bower of any queen,
With gifts of wit and ornaments of nature,
Fit for so goodly stature,
That like the twins of Jove they seem'd in sight
Which deck the baldric of the Heavens bright;
They two, forth pacing to the river's side,
Received those two fair brides, their love's delight;

Which, at th' appointed tide,
Each one did make his bride
Against their bridal day, which is not long:
    Sweet Thames! run softly, till I end my song.

FAIR IS MY LOVE

FAIR is my love, when her fair golden hairs
With the loose wind ye waving chance to mark;
Fair, when the rose in her red cheeks appears;
Or in her eyes the fire of love does spark.
Fair, when her breast, like a rich-laden bark,
With precious merchandise she forth doth lay;
Fair, when that cloud of pride, which oft doth dark
Her goodly light, with smiles she drives away.
But fairest she, when so she doth display
The gate with pearls and rubies richly dight;
Through which her words so wise do make their way
To bear the message of her gentle sprite.
    The rest be works of nature's wonderment:
    But this the work of heart's astonishment.

* * *

MICHAEL DRAYTON

TO THE VIRGINIAN VOYAGE

YOU brave heroic minds
    Worthy your country's name,
        That honour still pursue;
        Go and subdue!
    Whilst loitering hinds
        Lurk here at home with shame.

Britons, you stay too long:
    Quickly aboard bestow you,
        And with a merry gale
        Swell your stretch'd sail
    With vows as strong
        As the winds that blow you.

Your course securely steer,
    West and by south forth keep!

Rocks, lee-shores, nor shoals
  When Eolus scowls
You need not fear;
  So absolute the deep.

And cheerfully at sea
  Success you still entice
    To get the pearl and gold,
    And ours to hold
Virginia,
  Earth's only paradise.

Where nature hath in store
  Fowl, venison, and fish,
    And the fruitfull'st soil
    Without your toil
Three harvests more,
  All greater than your wish.

And the ambitious vine
  Crowns with his purple mass
    The cedar reaching high
    To kiss the sky,
The cypress, pine,
  And useful sassafras.

To whom the Golden Age
  Still nature's laws doth give,
    No other cares attend,
    But them to defend
From winter's rage,
  That long there doth not live.

When as the luscious smell
  Of that delicious land
    Above the sea that flows
    The clear wind throws,
Your hearts to swell
  Approaching the dear strand;

In kenning of the shore
  (Thanks to God first given)
    O you the happiest men,
    Be frolic then!

Let cannons roar,
　　Frighting the wide heaven.

And in regions far,
　　Such heroes bring ye forth
　　　　As those from whom we came;
　　　　And plant our name
Under that star
　　Not known unto our North.

And as there plenty grows
　　Of laurel everywhere—
　　　　Apollo's sacred tree—
　　　　You it may see
A poet's brows
　　To crown, that may sing there.

Thy *Voyages* attend,
　　Industrious Hakluyt,
　　　　Whose reading shall inflame
　　　　Men to seek fame,
And much commend
　　To after times thy wit.

LOVE'S FAREWELL

Since there's no help, come let us kiss and part,—
Nay I have done, you get no more of me;
And I am glad, yea, glad with all my heart,
That thus so cleanly I myself can free;
Shake hands for ever, cancel all our vows,
And when we meet at any time again,
Be it not seen in either of our brows
That we one jot of former love retain.
Now at the last gasp of love's latest breath,
When his pulse failing, passion speechless lies,
When faith is kneeling by his bed of death,
And innocence is closing up his eyes,
　—Now if thou would'st, when all have given him over,
From death to life thou might'st him yet recover!

JOHN LYLE

SPRING'S WELCOME

10

WHAT bird so sings, yet so does wail?
O 'tis the ravish'd nightingale.
Jug, jug, jug, jug, tereu! she cries!
And still her woes at midnight rise,
Brave prick-song! Who is't now we hear?
None but the lark so shrill and clear;
Now at heaven's gate she claps her wings,
The morn not waking till she sings.
Hark, lark, with what a pretty throat
Poor robin redbreast tunes his note!
Hark how the jolly cuckoos sing
Cuckoo! to welcome in the spring!
Cuckoo! to welcome in the spring!

* * *

SIR PHILIP SIDNEY

SONG

11

Doubt you to whom my Muse these notes intendeth,
Which now my breast o'ercharged to music lendeth!
To you! to you! all song of praise is due:
Only in you, my song begins and endeth.

Who hath the eyes which marry State with Pleasure?
Who keeps the key of Nature's chiefest treasure?
To you! to you! all song of praise is due:
Only for you, the heaven forgat all measure.

Who hath the lips, where Wit in fairness reigneth?
Who mankind at once both decks and staineth?
To you! to you! all song of praise is due:
Only by you, Cupid his crown maintaineth.

Who hath the feet, whose step all sweetness planteth?
Who else, for whom Fame worthy trumpets wanteth?

To you! to you! all song of praise is due:
Only to you, her sceptre Venus granteth.

Who hath the breast, whose milk doth passions nourish?
Whose grace is such, that when it chides does cherish?
To you! to you! all song of praise is due:
Only through you, the tree of life doth flourish.

Who hath the hand, which without stroke subdueth?
Who long-dead beauty with increase reneweth?
To you! to you! all song of praise is due:
Only at you, all envy hopeless rueth.

Who hath the hair, which loosest fastest tieth?
Who makes a man live, then glad when he dieth?
To you! to you! all song of praise is due:
Only of you, the flatterer never lieth.

Who hath the voice, which soul from senses sunders?
Whose force but yours the bolts of beauty thunders?
To you! to you! all song of praise is due:
Only with you, not miracles are wonders.

Doubt you to whom my Muse these notes intendeth,
Which now my breast o'ercharged to music lendeth?
To you! to you! all song of praise is due:
Only in you, my song begins and endeth.

LOVING IN TRUTH

12

Loving in truth, and fain in verse my love to show,
That She, dear She, might take some pleasure of my pain;
Pleasure might cause her read, reading might make her know,
Knowledge might pity win, and pity grace obtain;
I sought fit words to paint the blackest face of woe,
Studying inventions fine, her wits to entertain;
Oft turning others leaves, to see if thence would flow
Some fresh and fruitful showers upon my sunburned brain.
But words came halting forth, wanting Invention's stay;
Invention, Nature's child, fled step-dame Study's blows;
And other's feet still seemed but strangers in my way.
Thus, great with child to speak, and helpless in my throes,
Biting my truant pen, beating myself for spite.
"Fool," said my Muse to me, "look in thy heart, and write!"

THOMAS LODGE

ROSALIND'S MADRIGAL

Love in my bosom like a bee
    Doth suck his sweet:
Now with his wings he plays with me,
    Now with his feet.
Within mine eyes he makes his nest,
His bed amidst my tender breast;
My kisses are his daily feast
And yet he robs me of my rest:
    Ah! wanton, will ye?

And if I sleep, then percheth he
    With pretty flight,
And makes his pillow of my knee
    The livelong night.
Strike I my lute, he tunes the string;
He music plays if so I sing,
He lends me every lovely thing,
Yet cruel he my heart doth sting:
    Whist, wanton, still ye!

Else I with roses every day
    Will whip you hence,
And bind you, when you long to play,
    For your offence.
I'll shut mine eyes to keep you in;
I'll make you fast it for your sin;
I'll count your power not worth a pin.
—Alas! what hereby shall I win
    If he gainsay me?

What if I beat the wanton boy
    With many a rod?
He will repay me with annoy,
    Because a god.
Then sit thou safely on my knee;
Then let thy bower my bosom be;
Lurk in mine eyes, I like of thee;
O Cupid, so thou pity me,
    Spare not, but play thee!

ROSALINE

Like to the clear in highest sphere
Where all imperial glory shines,
Of selfsame colour is her hair
Whether unfolded, or in twines:
   Heigh ho, fair Rosaline!
Her eyes are sapphires set in snow
Resembling heaven by every wink;
The Gods do fear whenas they glow,
And I do tremble when I think
   Heigh ho, would she were mine!

Her cheeks are like the blushing cloud
That beautifies Aurora's face,
Or like the silver crimson shroud
That Phoebus' smiling looks doth grace;
   Heigh ho, fair Rosaline!
Her lips are like two budded roses
Whom ranks of lilies neighbour nigh,
Within which bounds she balm encloses
Apt to entice a deity:
   Heigh ho, would she were mine!

Her neck is like a stately tower
Where Love himself imprison'd lies,
To watch for glances every hour
From her divine and sacred eyes:
   Heigh ho, for Rosaline!
Her paps are centres of delight,
Her breast are orbs of heavenly frame,
Wher Nature moulds the dew of light
To feed perfection with the same:
   Heigh ho, would she were mine!

With orient pearl, with ruby red,
With marble white, with sapphire blue
Her body every way is fed,
Yet soft in touch and sweet in view:
   Heigh ho, fair Rosaline!
Nature herself her shape admires;
The Gods are wounded in her sight;
And Love forsakes his heavenly fires
And at her eyes his brand doth light:
   Heigh ho, would she were mine!

Then muse not, Nymphs, though I bemoan
The absence of fair Rosaline,
Since for a fair there's fairer none,
Nor for her virtues so divine:
    Heigh ho, fair Rosaline!
Heigh ho, my heart! would God that she were mine!

* * *

ANTHONY MUNDAY

BEAUTY BATHING

BEAUTY sat bathing by a spring
  Where fairest shades did her hide;
The winds blew calm, the birds did sing
  The cool streams ran beside her.
My wanton thoughts enticed mine eye
  To see what was forbidden:
But better memory said, fie!
  So vain desire was chidden:—
      Hey nonny nonny O!
      Hey nonny nonny!

Into a slumber then I fell,
  When fond imagination
Seeméd to see, but could not tell
  Her feature or her fashion.
But, ev'n as babes in dreams do smile,
  And sometimes fall a-weeping,
So I awaked, as wise this while
  As when I fell a-sleeping:—
      Hey nonny nonny O!
      Hey nonny nonny!

SIR WALTER RALEIGH

HIS PILGRIMAGE

16

Give me my scallop-shell of quiet,
　My staff of faith to walk upon,
My scrip of joy, immortal diet,
　My bottle of salvation,
My gown of glory, hope's true gage;
And thus I'll take my pilgrimage.

Blood must be my body's balmer;
　No other balm will there be given;
Whilst my soul, like quiet palmer,
　Travelleth towards the land of heaven;
Over the silver mountains,
Where spring the nectar fountains:
　　　There will I kiss
　　　The bowls of bliss;
And drink mine everlasting fill
Upon every milken hill.
My soul will be a-dry before;
But, after, it will thirst no more.

Then by that happy blissful day,
　More peaceful pilgrims I shall see,
That have cast off their rags of clay,
　And walk apparelled fresh like me.
　　　I'll take them first
　　　To quench their thirst
And taste of nectar suckets,
　　　At those clear wells
　　　Where sweetness dwells,
Drawn up by saints in crystal buckets.

And when our bottles and all we
Are filled with immortality,
Then the blessed paths we'll travel,
Strowed with rubies thick as gravel;
Ceilings of diamonds, sapphire floors,
High walls of coral and pearly bowers.
From thence to heaven's bribeless hall,
Where no corrupted voices brawl;
No conscience molten into gold,

No forged accuser bought or sold,
No cause deferred, no vain-spent journey,
For there Christ is the king's Attorney,
Who pleads for all without degrees,
And He hath angels, but no fees.
And when the grand twelve-million jury
Of our sins, with direful fury,
Against our souls black verdicts give,
Christ pleads His death, and then we live.

Be Thou my speaker, taintless pleader,
Unblotted lawyer, true proceeder!
Thou givest salvation even for alms;
Not with a bribed lawyer's palms.
And this is mine eternal plea
To him that made heaven, earth, and sea,
That, since my flesh must die so soon,
And want a head to dine at noon,
Just at the stroke, when my veins start and spread,
Set on my soul an everlasting head!
Then am I ready, like a palmer fit,
To tread those blest paths which before I writ.
  Of death and judgment, heaven and hell,
  Who oft doth think, must needs die well.

* * *

CHRISTOPHER MARLOWE

THE PASSIONATE SHEPHERD TO HIS LOVE

17

Come live with me and be my Love,
And we will all the pleasures prove
That hills and valleys, dale and field,
And all the craggy mountains yield.

There will we sit upon the rocks
And see the shepherds feed their flocks,
By shallow rivers, to whose falls
Melodious birds sing madrigals.

There will I make thee beds of roses
And a thousand fragrant posies,

A cap of flowers, and a kirtle
Embroider'd all with leaves of myrtle.

A gown made of the finest wool,
Which from our pretty lambs we pull,
Fair linéd slippers for the cold,
With buckles of the purest gold.

A belt of straw and ivy buds
With coral clasps and amber studs:
And if these pleasures may thee move,
Come live with me and be my Love.

Thy silver dishes for thy meat
As precious as the gods do eat,
Shall on an ivory table be
Prepared each day for thee and me.

The shepherd swains shall dance and sing
For thy delight each May-morning:
If these delights thy mind may move,
Then live with me and be my Love.

* * *

ROBERT GREENE

CONTENT

Sweet are the thoughts that savour of content,
   The quiet mind is richer than a crown,
Sweet are the nights in careless slumber spent,
   The poor estate scorns Fortune's angry frown:
Such sweet content, such minds, such sleep, such bliss,
Beggars enjoy, when princes oft do miss.
The homely house that harbours quiet rest,
   The cottage that affords no pride nor care,
The mean that 'grees with country music best,
   The sweet consort of mirth and modest fare,
Obscuréd life sets down a type of bliss:
A mind content both crown and kingdom is.

RICHARD BARNFIELD

THE NIGHTINGALE

19

As it fell upon a day
In the merry month of May,
Sitting in a pleasant shade
Which a grove of myrtles made,
Beasts did leap and birds did sing,
Trees did grow and plants did spring
Every thing did banish moan
Save the Nightingale alone.
She, poor bird, as all forlorn,
Lean'd her breast against a thorn,
And there sung the dolefull'st ditty
That to hear it was great pity.
Fie, fie, fie, now would she cry;
Tereu, tereu, by and by:
That to hear her so complain
Scarce I could from tears refrain;
For her griefs so lively shown
Made me think upon mine own.
—Ah, thought I, thou mourn'st in vain,
None takes pity on thy pain:
Senseless trees, they cannot hear thee,
Ruthless beasts, they will not cheer thee;
King Pandion, he is dead,
All thy friends are lapp'd in lead:
All thy fellow birds do sing
Careless of thy sorrowing:
Even so, poor bird, like thee
None alive will pity me.

* * *

THOMAS CAMPION

TURN ALL THY THOUGHTS TO EYES

20

Turn all thy thoughts to eyes,
Turn all thy hairs to ears,
Change all thy friends to spies

And all thy joys to fears:
　True love will yet be free
　In spite of jealousy.

Turn darkness into day,
Conjectures into truth,
Believe what th' envious say,
Let age interpret youth:
　True love will yet be free
　In spite of jealousy.

Wrest every word and look,
Rack every hidden thought,
Or fish with golden hook;
True love cannot be caught:
　For that will still be free
　In spite of jealousy.

INTEGER VITAE

THE man of life upright,
　Whose guiltless heart is free
From all dishonest deeds,
　Or thought of vanity;

The man whose silent days
　In harmless joys are spent,
Whom hopes cannot delude,
　Nor sorrow discontent;

That man needs neither towers
　Nor armour for defence,
Nor secret vaults to fly
　From thunder's violence:

He only can behold
　With unaffrighted eyes
The horrors of the deep
　And terrors of the skies.

Thus, scorning all the cares
　That fate or fortune brings,
He makes the heaven his book,
　His wisdom heavenly things;

Good thoughts his only friends,
　His wealth a well-spent age,
The earth his sober inn
　And quiet pilgrimage.

* * *

BEN JONSON

SIMPLEX MUNDITIIS

Still to be neat, still to be drest,
As you were going to a feast;
Still to be powdr'd, still perfumed:
Lady, it is to be presumed,
Though art's hid causes are not found,
All is not sweet, all is not sound.

Give me a look, give me a face
That makes simplicity a grace;
Robes loosely flowing, hair as free:
Such sweet neglect more taketh me
Than all th' adulteries of art;
They strike mine eyes, but not my heart.

TO CELIA

Drink to me only with thine eyes,
　And I will pledge with mine;
Or leave a kiss but in the cup
　And I'll not look for wine.
The thirst that from the soul doth rise
　Doth ask a drink divine;
But might I of Jove's nectar sup,
　I would not change for thine.

I sent thee late a rosy wreath,
　Not so much honouring thee
As giving it a hope that there
　It could not wither'd be;
But thou thereon didst only breathe
　And sent'st it back to me;
Since when it grows, and smells, I swear,
　Not of itself but thee!

BEN JONSON

A FAREWELL TO THE WORLD

24

FALSE world, good night! since thou hast brought
  That hour upon my morn of age;
Henceforth I quit thee from my thought,
  My part is ended on thy stage.

Yes, threaten, do. Alas! I fear
  As little as I hope from thee:
I know thou canst not show nor bear
  More hatred than thou hast to me.

My tender, first, and simple years
  Thou didst abuse and then betray;
Since stir'd'st up jealousies and fears,
  When all the causes were away.

Then in a soil hast planted me
  Where breathe the basest of thy fools;
Where envious arts professèd be,
  And pride and ignorance the schools;

Where nothing is examined, weigh'd,
  But as 'tis rumour'd, so believed;
Where every freedom is betray'd,
  And every goodness tax'd or grieved.

But what we're born for, we must bear:
  Our frail condition it is such
That what to all may happen here,
  If 't chance to me, I must not grutch.

Else I my state should much mistake
  To harbour a divided thought
From all my kind—that, for my sake,
  There should a miracle be wrought.

No, I do know that I was born
  To age, misfortune, sickness, grief:
But I will bear these with that scorn
  As shall not need thy false relief.

Nor for my peace will I go far,
  As wanderers do, that still do roam;

But make my strengths, such as they are,
Here in my bosom, and at home.

AN ODE TO HIMSELF

25

Where dost thou careless lie
  Buried in ease and sloth?
Knowledge that sleeps, doth die
And this security,
  It is the common moth
That eats on wits and arts, and that destroys them both.

Are all the Aonian springs
  Dried up? lies Thespia waste?
Doth Clarius' harp want strings,
That not a nymph now sings;
  Or droop they as disgraced,
To see their seats and bowers by chattering pies defaced?

If hence thy silence be,
  As 'tis too just a cause,
Let this thought quicken thee:
Minds that are great and free
  Should not on fortune pause;
'Tis crown enough to virtue still, her own applause.

What though the greedy fry
  Be taken with false baits
Of worded balladry,
And think it poesy?
  They die with their conceits,
And only piteous scorn upon their folly waits.

Then take in hand thy lyre;
  Strike in thy proper strain;
With Japhet's line aspire
Sol's chariot, for new fire
  To give the world again:
Who aided him, will thee, the issue of Jove's brain.

And, since our dainty age
  Cannot endure reproof,
Make not thyself a page
To that strumpet the stage;
  But sing high and aloof,
Safe from the wolf's black jaw, and the dull ass's hoof.

HYMN TO DIANA

Queen and Huntress, chaste and fair,
  Now the sun is laid to sleep,
Seated in thy silver chair
  State in wonted manner keep;
    Hesperus entreats thy light,
    Goddess excellently bright.

Earth, let not thy envious shade
  Dare itself to interpose;
Cynthia's shining orb was made
  Heaven to clear when day did close:
    Bless us then with wishèd sight,
    Goddess excellently bright.

Lay thy bow of pearl apart
  And thy crystal-shining quiver:
Give unto the flying hart
  Space to breathe, how short soever:
    Thou that mak'st a day of night,
    Goddess excellently bright!

HIS SUPPOSED MISTRESS

If I freely can discover
What would please me in my lover,
  I would have her fair and witty,
  Savouring more of court than city;
  A little proud, but full of pity;
  Light and humourous in her toying;
  Oft building hopes, and soon destroying;
  Long, but sweet in the enjoying,
Neither too easy, nor too hard:
All extremes I would have barred.

She should be allowed her passions,
So they were but used as fashions;
  Sometimes froward, and then frowning,
  Sometimes sickish, and then swowning,
  Every fit with change still crowning.
  Purely jealous I would have her;
  Then only constant when I crave her,
  'Tis a virtue should not save her.
Thus, nor her delicates would cloy me,
Neither her peevishness annoy me.

JOHN DONNE

THE FUNERAL

28

Whoever comes to shroud me, do not harm
      Nor question much
That subtle wreath of hair about mine arm;
The mystery, the sign you must not touch,
      For 'tis my outward soul,
Viceroy to that which, unto heav'n being gone,
      Will leave this to control
And keep these limbs, her provinces, from dissolution.

For if the sinewy thread my brain lets fall
      Through every part
Can tie those parts, and make me one of all;
Those hairs, which upward grew, and strength and art
      Have from a better brain,
Can better do 't: except she meant that I
      By this should know my pain,
As prisoners then are manacled, when they're condemn'd to die.

Whate'er she meant by't, bury it with me,
      For since I am
Love's martyr, it might breed idolatry
If into other hands these reliques came.
      As 'twas humility
T' afford to it all that a soul can do,
      So 'tis some bravery
That, since you would have none of me, I bury some of you.

VALEDICTION, FORBIDDING MOURNING

29

As virtuous men pass mildly away,
   And whisper to their souls to go;
While some of their sad friends do say,
   Now his breath goes, and some say, No;

So let us melt, and make no noise,
   No tear-floods, nor sigh-tempests move;
'Twere profanation of our joys
   To tell the laity our love.

Moving of th' earth brings harms and fears,
  Men reckon what it did and meant;
But trepidations of the spheres,
  Though greater far, are innocent.

Dull sublunary lovers' love,
  Whose soul is sense, cannot admit
Absence; for that it doth remove
  Those things which elemented it.

But we, by a love so far refined,
  That ourselves know not what it is,
Inter-assurèd of the mind,
  Careless, eyes, lips and hands to miss,

—Our two souls therefore, which are one,
  Though I must go, endure not yet
A breach, but an expansion,
  Like gold to airy thinness beat.

If they be two, they are two so
  As stiff twin compasses are two;
Thy soul, the fixt foot, makes no show
  To move, but doth if th' other do.

And though it in the centre sit,
  Yet when the other far doth roam,
It leans and hearkens after it,
  And grows erect as that comes home.

Such wilt thou be to me, who must,
  Like th' other foot, obliquely run;
Thy firmness makes my circles just,
  And makes me end where I begun.

DEATH

30

Death, be not proud, though some have callèd thee
Mighty and dreadful, for thou art not so:
For those whom thou think'st thou dost overthrow
Die not, poor Death; nor yet canst thou kill me.
From Rest and Sleep, which but thy picture be,
Much pleasure, then from thee much more must flow;
And soonest our best men with thee do go—
Rest of their bones and souls' delivery!

Thou'rt slave to fate, chance, kings, and desperate men,
And dost with poison, war, and sickness dwell;
And poppy or charms can make us sleep as well
And better than thy stroke. Why swell'st thou then?
  One short sleep past, we wake eternally,
    And Death shall be no more: Death, thou shalt die!

THE DREAM

Dear love, for nothing less than thee
Would I have broke this happy dream;
    It was a theme
For reason, much too strong for fantasy.
Therefore thou waked'st me wisely; yet
My dream thou brak'st not, but continued'st it:
Thou art so true that thoughts of thee suffice
To make dreams truths and fables histories.
Enter these arms, for since thou thought'st it best
Not to dream all my dream, let's act the rest.

As lightning, or a taper's light,
Thine eyes, and not thy noise, waked me;
    Yet I thought thee—
For thou lov'st truth—an angel at first sight;
But when I saw thou saw'st my heart,
And knew'st my thoughts beyond an angel's art,
When thou knew'st what I dreamt, when thou knew'st when
Excess of joy would wake me, and cam'st then,
I must confess it could not choose but be
Profane to think thee anything but thee.

Coming and staying show'd thee thee;
But rising makes me doubt that now
    Thou art not thou.
That Love is weak where Fear's as strong as he;
'Tis not all spirit pure and brave,
If mixture it of Fear, Shame, Honour have.
Perchance, as torches, which must ready be,
Men light and put out, so thou dealst with me.
Thou cam'st to kindle, goest to come: then I
Will dream that hope again, but else would die.

SWEETEST LOVE, I DO NOT GO

32

Sweetest love, I do not go
   For weariness of thee,
Nor in hope the world can show
   A fitter love for me;
     But since that I
Must die at last, 'tis best
Thus to use myself in jest,
     By feignèd death to die.

Yesternight the sun went hence,
   And yet is here to-day;
He hath no desire nor sense,
   Nor half so short a way.
     Then fear not me,
But believe that I shall make
Hastier journeys, since I take
     More wings and spurs than he.

O how feeble is man's power,
   That, if good fortune fall,
Cannot add another hour,
   Nor a lost hour recall.
     But come bad chance,
And we join to it our strength,
And we teach it art and length,
     Itself o'er us t' advance.

When thou sigh'st, thou sigh'st no wind,
   But sigh'st my soul away;
When thou weep'st, unkindly kind,
   My life's blood doth decay.
     It cannot be
That thou lov'st me as thou say'st,
If in thine my life thou waste,
     That art the best of me.

Let not thy divining heart
   Forethink me any ill.
Destiny may take thy part
   And may thy fears fulfil;
They who one another keep
     But think that we
Are but turned aside to sleep:
     Alive, ne'er parted be.

LOVER'S INFINITENESS

33

If yet I have not all thy love,
    Dear, I shall never have it all;
I cannot breathe one other sigh to move,
Nor can entreat one other tear to fall;
And all my treasure, which should purchase thee,
Sighs, tears, and oaths, and letters, I have spent;
    Yet no more can be due to me,
    Than at the bargain made was meant:
If, then, thy gift of love was partial,
That some to me, some should to others fall,
    Dear, I shall never have it all.

Of if then thou gavest me all,
    All was but all which thou hadst then;
But if in thy heart since there be, or shall
New love created be by other men,
Which have their stocks entire, and can in tears,
In sighs, in oaths, in letters outbid me,
    This new love may beget new fears;
    For this love was not vowed by thee,
And yet it was, thy gift being general:
The ground, thy heart, is mine; whatever shall
    Grow there, dear I should have it all

Yet I would not have all yet;
    He that hath all can have no more;
And since my love doth every day admit
New growth, thou shouldst have new rewards in store.
Thou canst not every day give me thy heart;
If thou canst give it, then thou never gav'st it:
Love's riddles are that, though thy heart depart,
It stays at home, and thou with losing sav'st it,
But we will love a way more liberal
Than changing hearts,—to join them; so we shall
    Be one, an one another's All.

LOVE'S DEITY

34

I long to talk with some old lover's ghost,
    Who died before the god of love was born:
I cannot think that he, that then loved most,
    Sunk so low as to love one which did scorn.

But since this god produced a destiny,
And that vice-nature, custom, lets it be,
I must love her that loves not me.

Sure they which made him god meant not so much
   Nor he in his young godhead practised it;
But when an even flame two hearts did touch,
   His office was indulgently to fit
Actives to passives; correspondency
Only his subject was; it cannot be
Love, if I love who loves not me.

But every modern god will now extend
   His vast prerogative as far as Jove;
To rage, to lust, to write too, to commend;
   All is the purlieu of the god of love.
O were we awakened by his tyranny
To ungod this child again, it could not be
I should love her that loves me not.

Rebel and atheist, too, why murmur I,
   As though I felt the worst that love could do?
Love may make me leave loving, or might try
   A deeper plague, to make her love me too,
Which, since she loves before, I am loath to see,
Falsehood is worse than hate; and that must be,
If she whom I love should love me.

STAY, O SWEET

Stay, O sweet, and do not rise!
   The light that shines comes from thine eyes;
  The day breaks not: it is my heart,
Because that you and I must part.
   Stay! or else my joys will die,
  And perish in their infancy.

'Tis true, 'tis day: what though it be?
O, wilt thou therefore rise from me?
  Why should we rise because 'tis light?
Did we lie down because 'twas night?
   Love, which in spite of darkness brought us hither,
  Should in despite of light keep us together.

Light hath no tongue, but is all eye.
If it could speak as well as spy,
  This were the worst that it could say:—
That, being well, I fain would stay,
  And that I lov'd my heart and honour so,
  That I would not from him, that had them, go.

Must business thee from hence remove?
Oh, that's the worst disease of love!
  The poor, the fool, the false, love can
Admit, but not the busied man.
  He, which hath business, and makes love, doth do
  Such wrong, as when a married man doth woo.

THE BLOSSOM

36

LITTLE think'st thou, poor flower,
Whom I have watched six or seven days,
And seen thy birth, and seen what every hour
Gave to thy growth, thee to this height to raise,
And now dost laugh and triumph on this bough,
    —Little think'st thou
That it will freeze anon, and that I shall
To-morrow find thee fall'n, or not at all.

Little think'st thou, poor heart,
That labourest yet to nestle thee,
And think'st by hovering here to get a part
In a forbidden or forbidding tree,
And hop'st her stiffness by long siege to bow,
    —Little think'st thou
That thou, to-morrow, ere the sun doth wake,
Must with the sun and me a journey take.

But thou, which lov'st to be
Subtle to plague thyself, wilt say—
"Alas! if you must go, what's that to me?
Here lies my business, and here will I stay:
You go to friends, whose love and means present
    Various content
To your eyes, ears, and taste, and every part:
If then your body goes, what need your heart?"

Well, then, stay here: but know
When thou hast said and done thy most,

A naked thinking heart, that makes no show,
Is to a woman but a kind of ghost;
How shall she know my heart? Or, having none,
    Know thee for one?
Practice may make her know some other part,
But take my word, she doth not know a heart.

Meet me in London, then,
Twenty days hence, and thou shalt see
Me fresher and more fat, by being with men,
Than if I had stay'd still with her and thee.
For God's sake, if you can, be you so too:
    I will give you
There to another friend, whom you shall find
As glad to have my body as my mind.

* * *

RICHARD CORBET

FAREWELL, REWARDS AND FAIRIES

FAREWELL, rewards and fairies,
  Good housewives now may say,
For now foul sluts in dairies
  Do fare as well as they.
And though they sweep their hearths no less
  Than maids were wont to do,
Yet who of late for cleanless
  Finds sixpence in her shoe?

Lament, lament, old Abbeys,
  The Fairies' lost command!
They did but change Priests' babies,
  But some have changed your land.
And all your children, sprung from thence,
  Are now grown Puritans,
Who live as Changelings ever since
  For love of your demains.

At morning and at evening both
  You merry were and glad,
So little care of sleep or sloth
  These pretty ladies had;

When Tom came home from labour,
  Or Cis to milking rose,
Then merrily went their tabor,
  And nimbly went their toes.

Witness those rings and roundelays
  Of theirs, which yet remain,
Were footed in Queen Mary's days
  On many a grassy plain;
But since of late, Elizabeth,
  And later, James came in,
They never danced on any heath
  As when the time hath been.

By which we note the Fairies
  Were of the old Profession.
Their songs were "Ave Mary's,"
  Their dances were Procession.
But now, alas, they all are dead;
  Or gone beyond the seas;
Or farther for Religion fled;
  Or else they take their ease.

A tell-tale in their company
  They never could endure!
And whoso kept not secretly
  Their mirth, was punished, sure;
It was a just and Christian deed
  To pinch such black and blue.
Oh how the commonwealth doth want
  Such Justices as you!

* * *

FRANCIS BEAUMONT

ON THE TOMBS IN WESTMINSTER ABBEY

Mortality, behold and fear
What a change of flesh is here!
Think how many royal bones
Sleep within these heaps of stones;
Here they lie, had realms and lands,
Who now want strength to stir their hands,

Where from their pulpits seal'd with dust
They preach, "In greatness is no trust."
Here's an acre sown indeed
With the richest royallest seed
That the earth did e'er suck in
Since the first man died for sin:
Here the bones of birth have cried
"Though gods they were, as men they died!
Here are sands, ignoble things,
Dropt from the ruin'd sides of kings:
Here's a world of pomp and state
Buried in dust, once dead by fate.

MASTER FRANCIS BEAUMONT'S LETTER TO BEN JONSON

THE sun (which doth the greatest comfort bring
To absent friends, because the self-same thing
They know they see, however absent) is
Here our best haymaker (forgive me this;
It is our country's style) : in this warm shine
I lie, and dream of your full *Mermaid* Wine.
  O, we have Winter mixed with claret lees,
Drink apt to bring in drier heresies
Than beer, good only for the sonnet's strain,
With fustian metaphors to stuff the brain;
So mixed, that, given to the thirstiest one,
'Twill not prove alms, unless he have the stone:
I think with one draught man's invention fades,
Two cups had quite spoiled Homer's *Iliads!*
'Tis liquor that will find out Sutcliff's wit,
Lie where he will, and make him write worse yet.
Filled with such moisture, in most grievous qualms,
Did Robert Wisdom write his singing *Psalms;*
And so must I do this: and yet I think
It is our potion sent us down to drink,
By special Providence, keeps us from fights,
Makes us not laugh, when we make legs to Knights:
'Tis this that keeps our minds fit for our states;
A medicine to obey our Magistrates;
For we do live more free than you; no hate,
No envy at one another's happy state,
Moves us; we are equal every whit;
Of land that God gives men, here is their wit,
If we consider fully; for our best
And gravest man will with his main-house-jest

Scarce please you: we want subtlety to do
The city-tricks; lie, Hate, and flatter too:
Here are none that can bear a painted show,
Strike, when you wince, and then lament the blow;
Who (like mills set the right way for to grind)
Can make their gains alike with every wind:
Only some fellows with the subtlest pate
Amongst us, may perchance equivocate
At selling of a horse; and that's the most.
Methinks the little wit I had is lost
Since I saw you; for wit is like a rest
Held up at tennis, which men do the best
With the best gamesters. What things have we seen
Done at the *Mermaid!* heard words that have been
So nimble, and so full of subtle flame,
As if that every one (from whence they came)
Had meant to put his whole wit in a jest,
And had resolved to live a fool the rest
Of his dull life;—then when there hath been thrown
Wit able enough to justify the town
For three days past; wit that might warrant be
For the whole city to talk foolishly
Till that were cancelled; and, when we were gone,
We left an air behind us; which alone
Was able to make the two next companies
(Right witty; though but downright fools) more wise!
   When I remember this, and see that now
The country gentlemen begin to allow
My wit for dry bobs, then I needs must cry,
"I see my days of ballating grow nigh!"
I can already riddle, and can sing
Catches, sell bargains: and I fear shall bring
Myself to speak the hardest words I find
Over as oft as any, with one wind,
That takes no medicines. But one thought of thee
Makes me remember all these things to be
The wit our young men, fellows that show
No part of good, yet utter all they know;
Who, like trees of the guard, have growing souls,
Only strong Destiny, which all controls,
I hope hath left a better fate in store
For me, thy friend, than to live ever poor,
Banished unto this home. Fate once again,
Bring me thee, who canst make smooth and plain
The way of knowledge for me, and then I

(Who have no good, but in thy company,)
Protest it will my greatest comfort be,
To acknowledge all I have, to flow from thee!
Ben, when these Scenes are perfect, we'll taste wine!
I'll drink thy Muse's health! thou shalt quaff mine!

* * *

WILLIAM DRUMMOND

SAINT JOHN BAPTIST

40

The last and greatest Herald of Heaven's King
Girt with rough skins, hies to the deserts wild,
Among that savage brood the woods forth bring,
Which he more harmless found than man, and mild.
His food was locusts, and what there doth spring,
With honey that from virgin hives distill'd;
Parch'd body, hollow eyes, some uncouth thing
Made him appear, long since from earth exiled.
There burst he forth: All ye whose hopes rely
On God, with me amidst these deserts mourn,
Repent, repent, and from old errors turn!
—Who listen'd to his voice, obey'd his cry?
Only the echoes, which he made relent,
Rung from their flinty caves, Repent! Repent!

LIFE

41

This Life, which seems so fair,
Is like a bubble blown up in the air
By sporting children's breath,
Who chase it everywhere
And strive who can most motion it bequeath.
And though it sometimes seem of its own might
Like to an eye of gold to be fix'd there,
And firm to hover in that empty height,
That only is because it is so light.
—But in that pomp it doth not long appear;
For when 'tis most admired, in a thought,
Because it erst was nought, it turns to nought.

HUMAN FOLLY

42

Of this fair volume which we World do name
If we the sheets and leaves could turn with care,
Of him who it corrects, and did it frame,
We clear might read the art and wisdom rare:
Find out his power which wildest powers doth tame,
His providence extending everywhere,
His justice which proud rebels doth not spare,
In every page, no period of the same.
But silly we, like foolish children, rest
Well pleased with colour'd vellum, leaves of gold,
Fair dangling ribbands, leaving what is best,
On the great writer's sense ne'er taking hold;
   Or if by chance we stay our minds on aught,
   It is some picture on the margin wrought.

FOR THE MAGDALENE

43

"These eyes, dear Lord, once brandons of desire,
Frail scouts betraying what they had to keep,
Which their own heart, then others set on fire,
Their trait'rous black before thee here out-weep;
These locks, of blushing deeds the gilt attire,
Waves curling, wrackful shelves to shadow deep,
Rings wedding souls to sin's lethargic sleep,
To touch thy sacred feet do now aspire.
In seas of care behold a sinking bark,
By winds of sharp remorse unto thee driven,
O let me not be Ruin's aim'd-at-mark!
My faults confessed, Lord, say they are forgiven.
   Thus sighed to Jesus the Bethanian fair,
   His tear-wet feet still drying with her hair.

* * *

GEORGE WITHER

44

I LOVED A LASS

I loved a lass, a fair one,
  As fair as e'er was seen;
She was indeed a rare one,
  Another Sheba Queen;

GEORGE WITHER

But, fool as then I was,
   I thought she loved me too:
But now, alas! she's left me,
   Falero, lero, loo!

Her hair like gold did glister,
   Each eye was like a star,
She did surpass her sister,
   Which pass'd all others far;
She would me honey call,
   She'd O she'd kiss me too!
But now, alas, she's left me,
   Falero, lero, loo!

Many a merry meeting
   My love and I have had;
She was my only sweeting,
   She made my heart full glad;
The tears stood in her eyes
   Like to the morning dew:
But now, alas, she's left me,
   Falero, lero, loo!

Her cheeks were like the cherry,
   Her skin was white as snow;
When she was blithe and merry
   She angel-like did show;
Her waist exceedingly small,
   The fives did fit her shoe:
But now, alas, she's left me,
   Falero, lero, loo!

In summer time or winter
   She had her heart's desire;
I still did scorn to stint her
   From sugar, sack or fire;
The world went round about,
   No cares we ever knew:
But now, alas, she's left me,
   Falero, lero, loo!

To maidens' vows and swearing
   Henceforth no credit give;
You may give them the hearing,
   But never them believe;

They are as false as fair,
  Unconstant, frail, untrue:
For mine, alas! hath left me,
  Falero, lero, loo!

* * *

THOMAS DEKKER

COUNTRY GLEE

45

Haymakers, rakers, reapers, and mowers,
  Wait on your Summer-Queen;
Dress up with musk-rose her eglantine bowers,
  Daffodils strew the green;
    Sing, dance, and play,
    'Tis holiday;
  The sun does bravely shine
  On our ears of corn.
      Rich as a pearl
      Comes every girl,
  This is mine, this is mine, this is mine;
Let us die, ere away they be borne.

Bow to the Sun, to our queen, and that fair one
  Come to behold our sports:
Each bonny lass here is counted a rare one
  As those in princes' courts.
    These and we
    With country glee,
  Will teach the woods to resound,
  And the hills with echoes hollow:
      Skipping lambs
      Their bleating dams,
  'Mongst kids shall trip it round;
For joy thus our wenches we follow.

Wind, jolly huntsmen, your neat bugles shrilly,
  Hounds make a lusty cry;
Spring up, you falconers, the partridges freely,
  Then let your brave hawks fly.
    Horses amain,
    Over ridge, over plain,
  The dogs have the stag in chase:

'Tis a sport to content a king.
    So ho, ho! through the skies
      How the proud bird flies,
And sousing kills with a grace!
Now the deer falls; hark, how they ring!

COLD'S THE WIND

Cold's the wind, and wet's the rain,
  Saint Hugh be our good speed!
Ill is the weather that bringeth no gain,
  Nor helps good hearts in need.

Troll the bowl, the jolly nut-brown bowl,
  And here's, kind mate, to thee!
Let's sing a dirge for Saint Hugh's soul,
  And down it merrily.

* * *

ANONYMOUS

O WALY, WALY

O waly waly up the bank,
  And waly waly down the brae,
And waly waly yon burn-side
  Where I and my Love wont to gae!
I leant my back unto an aik,
  I thought it was a trusty tree;
But first it bow'd, and syne it brak,
  Sae my true Love did lichtly me.

O waly waly, but love be bonny
  A little time while it is new;
But when 'tis auld, it waxeth cauld
  And fades awa' like morning dew.
O wherefor should I busk my head?
  Or wherefore should I kame my hair?
For my true Love has me forsook,
  And says he'll never loe me mair.

Now Arthur-seat sall be my bed;
  The sheets shall ne'er be prest by me:

Saint Anton's well sall be my drink,
  Since my true Love has forsaken me.
Marti'mas wind, when wilt thou blaw
  And shake the green leaves aff the tree?
O gentle Death, when wilt thou come?
  For of my life I am wearie.

'Tis not the frost, that freezes fell,
  Now blawing snaw's inclemencie;
'Tis not sic cauld that makes me cry,
  But my Love's heart grown cauld to me.
When we came in by Glasgow town
  We were a comely sight to see;
My Love was clad in the black velvét,
  And I mysell in cramasie.

But had I wist, before I kist,
  That love had been sae ill to win;
I had lockt my heart in a case of gowd
  And pinn'd it with a siller pin.
And, O! if my young babe were born,
  And set upon the nurse's knee,
And I myself were dead and gane,
  And the green grass growing over me!

HELEN OF KIRCONNELL

I WISH I were where Helen lies;
Night and day on me she cries;
O that I were where Helen lies
  On fair Kirconnell lea!

Curst be the heart that thought the thought,
And curst the hand that fired the shot,
When in my arms burd Helen dropt,
  And died to succour me!

O think na but my heart was sair
When my Love dropt down and spak nae mair!
I laid her down wi' meikle care
  On fair Kirconnell lea.

As I went down the water-side,
None but my foe to be my guide,

None but my foe to be my guide,
    On fair Kirconnell lea;

I lighted down my sword to draw,
I hackèd him in pieces sma',
I hackèd him in pieces sma',
    For her sake that died for me.

O Helen fair, beyond compare!
I'll make a garland of thy hair
Shall bind my heart for evermair
    Until the day I die.

O that I were where Helen lies!
Night and day on me she cries;
Out of my bed she bids me rise,
    Says, "Haste and come to me!"

O Helen fair! O Helen chaste!
If I were with thee, I were blest,
Where thou lies low and takes thy rest
    On fair Kirconnell lea.

I wish my grave were growing green,
A winding-sheet drawn ower my een,
And I in Helen's arms lying,
    On fair Kirconnell lea.

I wish I were where Helen lies;
Night and day on me she cries;
And I am weary of the skies,
    Since my Love died for me.

MY LOVE IN HER ATTIRE

My Love in her attire doth shew her wit,
  It doth so well become her:
For every season she hath dressings fit,
  For Winter, Spring, and Summer.
No beauty she doth miss
When all her robes are on:
But Beauty's self she is
When all her robes are gone.

ROBERT HERRICK

THE MAD MAID'S SONG

50

Good-morrow to the day so fair,
  Good-morning, sir, to you;
Good-morrow to mine own torn hair
  Bedabbled with the dew.

Good-morning to this primrose too,
  Good-morrow to each maid
That will with flowers the tomb bestrew
  Wherein my love is laid.

Ah! woe is me, woe, woe is me!
  Alack and well-a-day!
For pity, sir, find out that bee
  Which bore my love away.

I'll seek him in your bonnet brave,
  I'll seek him in your eyes;
Nay, now I think they've made his grave
  I' th' bed of strawberries.

I'll seek him there; I know ere this
  The cold, cold earth doth shake him;
But I will go, or send a kiss
  By you, sir, to awake him.

Pray hurt him not; though he be dead,
  He knows well who do love him,
And who with green turfs rear his head,
  And who do rudely move him.

He's soft and tender (pray take heed);
  With bands of cowslips bind him,
And bring him home—but 'tis decreed
  That I shall never find him!

TO THE VIRGINS

51

Gather ye rose-buds while ye may,
  Old Time is still a-flying:
And this same flower that smiles to-day,
  To-morrow will be dying.

The glorious Lamp of Heaven, the Sun,
  The higher he's a-getting
The sooner will his race be run,
  And nearer he's to setting.

That age is best which is the first,
  When youth and blood are warmer;
But being spent, the worse, and worst
  Times, still succeed the former.

Then be not coy, but use your time;
  And while ye may, go marry;
For having lost but once your prime,
  You may for ever tarry.

A SWEET DISORDER

52

A sweet disorder in the dress
Kindles in clothes a wantonness:—
A lawn about the shoulders thrown
Into a fine distraction,—
An erring lace, which here and there
Enthrals the crimson stomacher,—
A cuff neglectful, and thereby
Ribbands to flow confusedly,—
A winning wave, deserving note,
In the tempestuous petticoat,—
A careful shoe-string, in whose tie
I see a wild civility,—
Do more bewitch me, than when art
Is too precise in every part.

TO DAFFODILS

53

Fair Daffodils, we weep to see
  You haste away so soon:
As yet the early-rising Sun
  Has not attain'd his noon.

> Stay, stay,
> Until the hasting day
> Has run
> But to the even-song;
> And, having pray'd together, we
> Will go with you along.
>
> We have short time to stay, as you,
> We have as short a Spring!
> As quick a growth to meet decay
> As you or any thing.
> We die,
> As your hours do, and dry
> Away
> Like to the Summer's rain;
> Or as the pearls of morning's dew
> Ne'er to be found again.

TO BLOSSOMS

> FAIR pledges of a fruitful tree,
> Why do ye fall so fast?
> Your date is not so past,
> But you may stay yet here awhile
> To blush and gently smile,
> And go at last.
>
> What, were ye born to be
> An hour or half's delight,
> And so to bid good-night?
> 'Twas pity Nature brought ye forth
> Merely to show your worth,
> And lose you quite.
>
> But you are lovely leaves, where we
> May read how soon things have
> Their end, though ne'er so brave:
> And after they have shown their pride
> Like you, awhile, they glide
> Into the grave.

CORINNA'S MAYING

> GET up, get up for shame! The blooming morn
> Upon her wings presents the god unshorn.

See how Aurora throws her fair
Fresh-quilted colours through the air:
Get up, sweet slug-a-bed, and see
The dew-bespangled herb and tree!
Each flower has wept and bow'd toward the east,
Above an hour since, yet you not drest;
Nay! not so much as out of bed?
When all the birds have matins said,
And sung their thankful hymns, 'tis sin,
Nay, profanation, to keep in,
Whenas a thousand virgins on this day
Spring, sooner than the lark, to fetch in May.

Rise, and put on your foliage, and be seen
To come forth, like the spring-time, fresh and green,
And sweet as Flora. Take no care
For jewels for your gown or hair:
Fear not; the leaves will strew
Gems in abundance upon you:
Besides, the childhood of the day has kept,
Against you come, some Oriental pearls unwept.
Come, and receive them while the light
Hangs on the dew-locks of the night,
And Titan on the eastern hill
Retires himself, or else stands still
Till you come forth! Wash, dress, be brief in praying:
Few beads are best when once we go a-Maying.

Come, my Corinna, come; and coming, mark
How each field turns a street, each street a park,
Made green and trimm'd with trees! see how
Devotion gives each house a bough
Or branch! each porch, each door, ere this,
An ark, a tabernacle is,
Made up of white-thorn neatly interwove,
As if here were those cooler shades of love.
Can such delights be in the street
And open fields, and we not see 't?
Come, we'll abroad: and let's obey
The proclamation made for May,
And sin no more, as we have done, by staying,
But, my Corinna, come, let's go a-Maying.

There's not a budding boy or girl this day
But is got up and gone to bring in May.

A deal of youth, ere this, is come
Back, and with white-thorn laden home:
   Some have dispatch'd their cakes and cream,
   Before that we have left to dream:
And some have wept and woo'd, and plighted troth,
And chose their priest, ere we can cast off sloth:
   Many a green-gown has been given,
   Many a kiss, both odd and even:
   Many a glance, too has been sent
   From out the eye, love's firmament:
Many a jest told of the keys betraying
This night, and locks pick'd: yet we're not a-Maying.

Come, let us go, while we are in our prime,
And take the harmless folly of the time!
   We shall grow old apace, and die
   Before we know our liberty.
   Our life is short, and our days run
   As fast away as does the sun.
And, as a vapour or a drop of rain,
Once lost, can ne'er be found again,
   So when or you or I are made
   A fable, song, or fleeting shade,
   All love, all liking, all delight
   Lies drowned with us in endless night.
Then, while time serves, and we are but decaying,
Come, my Corinna, come, let's go a-Maying.

* * *

JOSHUA SYLVESTER

LOVE'S OMNIPRESENCE

Were I as base as is the lowly plain,
And you, my Love, as high as heaven above,
Yet should the thoughts of me your humble swain
Ascend to heaven, in honour of my Love.

Were I as high as heaven above the plain,
And you, my Love, as humble and as low
As are the deepest bottoms of the main,
Whereso'er you were, with you my love should go.

Were you the earth, dear Love, and I the skies,
My love should shine on you like to the sun,
And look upon you with ten thousand eyes
Till heaven wax'd blind, and till the world were done.

Whereso'er I am, below, or else above you,
Whereso'er you are, my heart shall truly love you.

* * *

GEORGE HERBERT

LOVE

57

Love bade me welcome; yet my soul drew back,
  Guilty of lust and sin.
But quick-eyed Love, observing me grow slack
  From my first entrance in,
Drew nearer to me, sweetly questioning
  If I lacked anything.

"A guest," I answered, "worthy to be here:"
  Love said, "You shall be he."
"I, the unkind, ungrateful? Ah, my dear,
  I cannot look on Thee."
Love took my hand and smiling did reply,
  "Who made the eyes but I?"

"Truth, Lord; but I have marred them: let my shame
  Go where it doth deserve."
"And know you not," says Love, "Who bore the blame?"
  "My dear, then I will serve."
"You must sit down," says Love, "and taste my meat."
  So I did sit and eat.

VIRTUE

58

Sweet day, so cool, so calm, so bright!
  The bridal of the earth and sky—
  The dew shall weep thy fall to-night;
    For thou must die.

Sweet rose, whose hue angry and brave
Bids the rash gazer wipe his eye,

> Thy root is ever in its grave,
> And thou must die.
>
> Sweet spring, full of sweet days and roses,
> A box where sweets compacted lie,
> My music shows ye have your closes,
> And all must die.
>
> Only a sweet and virtuous soul,
> Like season'd timber, never gives;
> But though the whole world turn to coal,
> Then chiefly lives.

* * *

HENRY VAUGHAN

BEYOND THE VEIL

59

> They are all gone into the world of light,
> And I alone sit lingering here;
> Their very memory is fair and bright,
> And my sad thoughts doth clear.
>
> It glows and glitters in my cloudy breast,
> Like stars upon some gloomy grove,
> Or those faint beams in which this hill is dressed,
> After the sun's remove.
>
> I see them walking in an air of glory,
> Whose light doth trample on my days;
> My days, which are at best but dull and hoary,
> Mere glimmerings and decays.
>
> O holy Hope, and high Humility,
> High as the heavens above!
> These are your walks, and you have showed them to me,
> To kindle my cold love.
>
> Dear, beauteous Death, the jewel of the just,
> Shining nowhere but in the dark,
> What mysteries do lie beyond thy dust,
> Could Man outlook that mark!

He that hath found some fledged bird's nest, may know
  At first sight, if the bird be flown;
But what fair well or grove he sings in now,
    That is to him unknown.

And yet, as angels in some brighter dreams
  Call to the soul when man doth sleep,
So some strange thoughts transcend our wonted themes,
    And into glory peep.

If a star were confined into a tomb,
  Her captive flames must needs burn there;
But when the hand that locked her up, gives room,
    She'll shine through all the sphere.

O Father of Eternal Life, and all
  Created glories under Thee!
Resume Thy spirit from this world of thrall
    Into true liberty.

Either disperse these mists, which blot and fill
  My perspective still, as they pass;
Or else remove me hence unto that hill
    Where I shall need no glass.

THE RETREAT

Happy those early days, when I
Shined in my Angel-infancy!
Before I understood this place
Appointed for my second race,
Or taught my soul to fancy aught
But a white, celestial thought;
When yet I had not walk'd above
A mile or two from my first Love,
And looking back, at that short space
Could see a glimpse of his bright face;
When on some gilded cloud or flower
My gazing soul would dwell an hour,
And in those weaker glories spy
Some shadows of eternity;
Before I taught my tongue to wound
My conscience with a sinful sound,
Or had the black art to dispense
A several sin to every sense,

But felt through all this fleshly dress
Bright shoots of everlastingness.

O how I long to travel back,
And tread again that ancient track!
That I might once more reach that plain
Where first I felt my glorious train;
From whence th' enlighten'd spirit sees
That shady City of Palm trees!
But ah! my soul with too much stay
Is drunk, and staggers in the way:—
Some men a forward motion love,
But I by backward steps would move;
And when this dust falls to the urn,
In that state I came, return.

* * *

FRANCIS BACON, VISCOUNT ST. ALBAN

LIFE

The world's a bubble and the life of Man
    Less than a span;
In his conception wretched, from the womb
    So to the tomb;
Curst from his cradle, and brought up to years
    With cares and fears.
Who then to frail mortality shall trust,
But limns on water, or but writes in dust.

Yet whilst with sorrow here we live opprest,
    What life is best?
Courts are but only superficial schools
    To dandle fools:
The rural parts are turn'd into a den
    Of savage men:
And where's a city from foul vice so free,
But may be termed the worst of all the three?

Domestic cares afflict the husband's bed,
    Or pains his head:
Those that live single, take it for a curse
    Or do things worse:

Some would have children: those that have them moan
      Or wish them gone:
What is it, then, to have, or have no wife,
But single thraldom or a double strife?

But our affections still at home to please
      Is a disease:
To cross the seas to any foreign soil,
      Peril and toil:
Wars with their noise affright us: when they cease,
      We are worse in peace;—
What then remains, but that we still should cry
For being born, or being born, to die?

* * *

JAMES SHIRLEY

THE GLORIES OF OUR BLOOD AND STATE

The glories of our blood and state
      Are shadows, not substantial things;
There is no armour against fate;
      Death lays his icy hand on kings:
          Sceptre and Crown
          Must tumble down,
And in the dust be equal made
With the poor crooked scythe and spade.

Some men with swords may reap the field,
      And plant fresh laurels where they kill:
But their strong nerves at last must yield;
      They tame but one another still:
          Early or late
          They stoop to fate,
And must give up their murmuring breath
When they, pale captives, creep to death.

The garlands wither on your brow;
      Then boast no more your mighty deeds;
Upon Death's purple altar now
      See where the victor-victim bleeds:
          Your heads must come
          To the cold tomb;

Only the actions of the just
Smell sweet, and blossom in their dust.

* * *

THOMAS CAREW

ASK ME NO MORE

63

Ask me no more where Jove bestows,
When June is past, the fading rose;
For in your beauty's orient deep
These flowers, as in their causes, sleep.

Ask me no more whither do stray
The golden atoms of the day;
For in pure love heaven did prepare
Those powders to enrich your hair.

Ask me no more whither doth haste
The nightingale when May is past;
For in your sweet dividing throat
She winters and keeps warm her note.

Ask me no more where those stars 'light
That downwards fall in dead of night;
For in your eyes they sit, and there
Fixèd become as in their sphere.

Ask me no more if east or west
The Phœnix builds her spicy nest;
For unto you at last she flies,
And in your fragrant bosom dies.

* * *

SIR JOHN SUCKLING

THE CONSTANT LOVER

64

Out upon it, I have loved
  Three whole days together!
And am like to love three more,
  If it prove fair weather.

RICHARD LOVELACE

Time shall moult away his wings
  Ere he shall discover
In the whole wide world again
  Such a constant lover.

But the spite on 't is, no praise
  Is due at all to me:
Love with me had made no stays,
  Had it any been but she.

Had it any been but she,
  And that very face,
There had been at least ere this
  A dozen dozen in her place.

* * *

SIR WILLIAM D'AVENANT

DAWN SONG

65

The lark now leaves his wat'ry nest,
  And climbing shakes his dewy wings.
He takes this window for the East,
  And to implore your light he sings—
Awake, awake! the morn will never rise
Till she can dress her beauty at your eyes.

The merchant bows unto the seaman's star,
  The ploughman from the sun his season takes;
But still the lover wonders what they are
  Who look for day before his mistress wakes.
Awake, awake! break thro' your veils of lawn!
Then draw your curtains, and begin the dawn!

* * *

RICHARD LOVELACE

TO ALTHEA FROM PRISON

66

When Love with unconfinèd wings
  Hovers within my gates,
And my divine Althea brings

      To whisper at the grates;
When I lie tangled in her hair
      And fetter'd to her eye,
The birds that wanton in the air
      Know no such liberty.

When flowing cups run swiftly round
      With no allaying Thames,
Our careless heads with roses crown'd,
      Our hearts with loyal flames
When thirsty grief in wine we steep,
      When healths and draughts go free—
Fishes that tipple in the deep
      Know no such liberty.

When, linnet-like confinèd I
      With shriller throat shall sing
The sweetness, mercy, majesty
      And glories of my King;
When I shall voice aloud how good
      He is, how great should be,
Enlargèd winds, that curl the flood,
      Know no such liberty.

Stone walls do not a prison make,
      Nor iron bars a cage;
Minds innocent and quiet take
      That for an hermitage;
If I have freedom in my love
      And in my soul am free,
Angels alone, that soar above,
      Enjoy such liberty.

TO LUCASTA, GOING BEYOND THE SEAS

67

IF to be absent were to be
      Away from thee;
   Or that when I am gone
      You or I were alone;
Then, my Lucasta, might I crave
Pity from blustering wind, or swallowing wave.

   Though seas and land betwixt us both,
      Our faith and troth,
      Like separated souls,

All time and space controls:
Above the highest sphere we meet
Unseen, unknown, and greet as Angels greet.

So then we do anticipate
    Our after-fate,
    And are alive i' the skies
    If thus our lips and eyes
Can speak like spirits unconfined
In Heaven, their earthy bodies left behind.

* * *

EDMUND WALLER

GO, LOVELY ROSE!

    Go, lovely Rose!
Tell her, that wastes her time and me,
    That now she knows,
When I resemble her to thee,
How sweet and fair she seems to be.

    Tell her that's young
And shuns to have her graces spied,
    That hadst thou sprung
In deserts, where no men abide,
Thou must have uncommended died.

    Small is the worth
Of beauty from the light retired:
    Bid her come forth,
Suffer herself to be desired,
And not blush so to be admired.

    Then die! that she
The common fate of all things rare
    May read in thee:
How small a part of time they share
They are so wondrous sweet and fair!

JAMES GRAHAM, MARQUIS OF MONTROSE

MY DEAR AND ONLY LOVE

My dear and only Love, I pray
   That little world of thee
Be govern'd by no other sway
   Than purest monarchy;
For if confusion have a part
   (Which virtuous souls abhor),
And hold a synod in thine heart,
   I'll never love thee more.

Like Alexander I will reign,
   And I will reign alone;
My thoughts did evermore disdain
   A rival on my throne.
He either fears his fate too much,
   Or his deserts are small,
That dares not put it to the touch,
   To gain or lose it all.

And in the empire of thine heart,
   Where I should solely be,
If others do pretend a part
   Or dare to vie with me,
Or if *Committees* thou erect,
   And go on such a score,
I'll laugh and sing at thy neglect,
   And never love thee more.

But if thou wilt prove faithful then,
   And constant of thy word,
I'll make thee glorious by my pen
   And famous by my sword;
I'll serve thee in such noble ways
   Was never heard before;
I'll crown and deck thee all with bays,
   And love thee more and more.

RICHARD CRASHAW

WISHES FOR THE SUPPOSED MISTRESS

70

Whoe'er she be,
That not impossible She
That shall command my heart and me;

Where'er she lie,
Lock'd up from mortal eye
In shady leaves of destiny:

Till that ripe birth
Of studied Fate stand forth,
And teach her fair steps tread our earth;

Till that divine
Idea take a shrine
Of crystal flesh, through which to shine:

—Meet you her, my Wishes,
Bespeak her to my blisses,
And be ye call'd, my absent kisses.

I wish her beauty
That owes not all its duty
To gaudy tire, or glist'ring shoe-tie:

Something more than
Taffata or tissue can,
Or rampant feather, or rich fan.

A face that's blest
By its own beauty drest,
And can alone command the rest:

A face made up
Out of no other shop
Than what Nature's white hand sets ope.

Sydneian showers
Of sweet discourse, whose powers
Can crown old Winter's head with flowers.

Whate'er delight
Can make day's forehead bright
Or give down to the wings of night.

Soft silken hours,
Open suns, shady bowers;
'Bove all, nothing within that lowers.

Days, that need borrow
No part of their good morrow
From a fore-spent night of sorrow:

Days, that in spite
Of darkness, by the light
Of a clear mind are day all night.

Life, that dares send
A challenge to his end,
And when it comes, say, "Welcome, friend."

I wish her store
Of worth may leave her poor
Of wishes and I wish——no more.

—Now, if Time knows
That Her, whose radiant brows
Weave them a garland of my vows;

Her that dares be
What these lines wish to see:
I seek no further, it is She.

'Tis She, and here
Lo! I unclothe and clear
My wishes' cloudy character.

Such worth as this is
Shall fix my flying wishes,
And determine them to kisses.

Let her full glory,
My fancies, fly before ye;
By ye my fictions:—but her story.

THOMAS JORDAN

LET US DRINK AND BE MERRY

71

Let us drink and be merry, dance, joke, and rejoice,
With claret and sherry, theorbo and voice!
The changeable world to our joy is unjust,
    All treasure's uncertain,
    Then down with your dust!
In frolics dispose your pounds, shillings, and pence,
For we shall be nothing a hundred years hence.

We'll sport and be free with Moll, Betty, and Dolly,
Have oysters and lobsters to cure melancholy:
Fish-dinners will make a man spring like a flea,
    Dame Venus, love's lady,
    Was born of the sea:
With her and with Bacchus we'll tickle the sense,
For we shall be past it a hundred years hence.

Your most beautiful bride who with garlands is crown'd
And kills with each glance as she treads on the ground.
Whose lightness and brightness doth shine in such splendour
    That one but the stars
    Are thought fit to attend her,
Though now she be pleasant and sweet to the sense,
Will be damnable mouldy a hundred years hence.

Then why should we turmoil in cares and in fears,
Turn all our tranquil'ty to sighs and to tears?
Let's eat, drink, and play till the worms do corrupt us,
    'Tis certain, *Post mortem*
    Nulla voluptas.
For health, wealth and beauty, wit, learning and sense,
Must all come to nothing a hundred years hence.

ABRAHAM COWLEY

CHEER UP, MY MATES

72

Cheer up, my mates, the wind does fairly blow;
  Clap on more sail, and never spare;
  Farewell, all lands, for now we are
  In the wide sea of drink, and merrily we go.
Bless me, 'tis hot! another bowl of wine,
  And we shall cut the burning Line:
Hey, boys! she scuds away, and by my head I know
  We round the world are sailing now.
What dull men are those who tarry at home,
When abroad they might wantonly roam,
  And gain such experience, and spy, too,
  Such countries and wonders, as I do!
But pr'ythee, good pilot, take heed what you do,
  And fail not to touch at Peru!
  With gold there the vessel we'll store,
  And never, and never be poor,
  No, never be poor any more.

DRINKING

73

The thirsty earth soaks up the rain,
And drinks and gapes for drink again;
The plants suck in the earth, and are
With constant drinking fresh and fair;
The sea itself (which one would think
Should have but little need of drink)
Drinks twice ten thousand rivers up,
So fill'd that they o'erflow the cup.
The busy Sun (and one would guess
By 's drunken fiery face no less)
Drinks up the sea, and when he's done,
The Moon and Stars drink up the Sun:
They drink and dance by their own light,
They drink and revel all the night:
Nothing in Nature's sober found,
But an eternal health goes round.
Fill up the bowl, then, fill it high,
Fill all the glasses there—for why
Should every creature drink but I?
Why, man of morals, tell me why?

ANDREW MARVELL

HORATIAN ODE UPON CROMWELL'S RETURN FROM IRELAND

74

The forward youth that would appear,
Must now forsake his Muses dear,
    Nor in the shadows sing
    His numbers languishing.

'Tis time to leave the books in dust,
And oil the unused armour's rust,
    Removing from the wall
    The corslet of the hall.

So restless Cromwell could not cease
In the inglorious arts of peace,
    But through adventurous war
    Urgéd his active star:

And like the three-fork'd lightning first
Breaking the clouds where it was nurst,
    Did thorough his own side
    His fiery way divide:

For 'tis all one to courage high,
The emulous, on enemy;
    And with such, to enclose
    Is more than to oppose;

Then burning through the air he went
And palaces and temples rent;
    And Cæsar's head at last
    Did through his laurels blast.

'Tis madness to resist or blame
The face of angry heaven's flame;
    And if we would speak true,
    Much to the Man is due

Who, from his private gardens, where
He lived reservéd and austere,
    (As if his highest plot
    To plant the bergamot.)

Could by industrious valour climb
To ruin the great work of time,
    And cast the Kingdoms old
    Into another mould.

Though Justice against Fate complain,
And plead the ancient Rights in vain—
    But those do hold or break
    As men are strong or weak,

Nature, that hateth emptiness,
Allows of penetration less,
    And therefore must make room
    Where greater spirits come.

What field of all the civil war
Where his were not the deepest scar?
    And Hampton shows what part
    He had of wiser art,

Where, twining subtle fears with hope,
He wove a net of such a scope
    That Charles himself might chase
    To carisbrook's narrow case,

That thence the Royal actor borne
The tragic scaffold might adorn:
    While round the arméd bands
    Did clap their bloody hands.

He nothing common did or mean
Upon that memorable scene,
    But with his keener eye
    The axe's edge did try;

Nor call'd the Gods, with vulgar spite,
To vindicate his helpless right
    But bow'd his comely head
    Down, as upon a bed.

—This was that memorable hour
Which first assured the forcéd power:
    So when they did design
    The Capitol's first line,

A Bleeding Head, where they begun,
Did fright the architects to run;
    And yet in that the State
    Forsaw its happy fate!

And now the Irish are ashamed
To see themselves in one year tamed:
    So much one man can do
    That does both act and know.

They can affirm his praises best,
And have, though overcome, confest
    How good he is, how just
    And fit for highest trust;

Nor yet grown stiffer with command,
But still in the Republic's hand—
    How fit he is to sway
    That can so well obey!

He to the Commons' feet presents
A Kingdom for his first year's rents,
    And (what he may) forbears
    His fame, to make it theirs:

And has his sword and spoils ungirt
To lay them at the Public's skirt.
    So when the falcon high
    Falls heavy from the sky,

She, having kill'd, no more does search
But on the next green bough to perch,
    Where, when he first does lure,
    The falconer has her sure.

—What may not then our Isle presume
While victory his crest does plume?
    What may not others fear
    If thus he crowns each year?

As Cæsar he, ere long, to Gaul,
To Italy an Hannibal,
    And to all States not free
    Shall climacteric be.

The Pict no shelter now shall find
Within his parti-colour'd mind,
    But from this valour sad,
    Shrink underneath the plaid—

Happy, if in the tufted brake
The English hunter him mistake
    Nor lay his hounds in near
    The Caledonian deer.

But Thou, the War's and Fortune's son,
March indefatigably on;
    And for the last effect
    Still keep the sword erect:

Besides the force it has to fright
The spirits of the shady night,
    The same arts that did gain
    A power, must it maintain.

THOUGHTS IN A GARDEN

75

How vainly men themselves amaze
To win the palm, the oak, or bays,
And their incessant labours see
Crown'd from some single herb or tree,
Whose short and narrow-vergéd shade
Does prudently their toils upbraid;
While all the flowers and trees do close
To weave the garlands of Repose.

Fair Quiet, have I found thee here,
And Innocence thy sister dear?
Mistaken long, I sought you then
In busy companies of men:
Your sacred plants, if here below,
Only among the plants will grow:
Society is all but rude
To this delicious solitude.

No white nor red was ever seen
So amorous as this lovely green.
Fond lovers, cruel as their flame,
Cut in these trees their mistress' name:

ANDREW MARVELL

Little, alas, they know or heed
How far these beauties her exceed!
Fair trees! where'er your barks I wound,
No name shall but your own be found.

When we have run our passions' heat
Love hither makes his best retreat:
The gods, who mortal beauty chase,
Still in a tree did end their race;
Apollo hunted Daphne so
Only that she might laurel grow;
And Pan did after Syrinx speed
Not as a nymph, but for a reed.

What wondrous life is this I lead!
Ripe apples drop about my head;
The luscious clusters of the vine
Upon my mouth do crush their wine;
The nectarine and curious peach
Into my hands themselves do reach;
Stumbling on melons, as I pass,
Ensnared with flowers, I fall on grass.

Meanwhile the mind from pleasure less
Withdraws into its happiness;
The mind, that ocean where each kind
Does straight its own resemblance find;
Yet it creates, transcending these,
Far other worlds, and other seas;
Annihilating all that's made
To a green thought in a green shade.

Here at the fountain's sliding foot
Or at some fruit-tree's mossy root,
Casting the body's vest aside
My soul into the boughs does glide;
There, like a bird, it sits and sings,
Then whets and claps its silver wings,
And, till prepared for longer flight,
Waves in its plumes the various light.

Such was that happy Garden-state
While man there walk'd without a mate:
After a place so pure and sweet,
What other help could yet be meet!

But 'twas beyond a mortal's share
To wander solitary there:
Two paradises 'twere in one,
To live in Paradise alone.

How well the skilful gardener drew
Of flowers and herbs this dial new!
Where from above, the milder sun
Does through a fragrant zodiac run:
And, as it works, th' industrious bee
Computes its time as well as we.
How could such sweet and wholesome hours
Be reckon'd, but with herbs and flowers!

* * *

JOHN DRYDEN

ODE

To the Pious Memory of the accomplished young lady,
Mrs. Anne Killigrew, excellent in the two
sister arts of Poesy and Painting

THOU youngest virgin-daughter of the skies,
Made in the last promotion of the blest;
Whose palms, new pluck'd from Paradise,
In spreading branches more sublimely rise,
  Rich with immortal green above the rest:
Whether, adopted to some neighbouring star,
Thou roll'st above us, in thy wandering race,
  Or, in procession fix'd and regular,
  Moved with the heaven's majestic pace;
  Or, call'd to more superior bliss,
Thou tread'st with seraphims the vast abyss:
Whatever happy region be thy place,
Cease thy celestial song a little space;
Thou wilt have time enough for hymns divine,
  Since Heaven's eternal year is thine.
Hear, then, a mortal Muse thy praise rehearse,
    In no ignoble verse;

But such as thy own voice did practise here,
When thy first-fruits of Poesy were given,
To make thyself a welcome inmate there;
   While yet a young probationer,
        And candidate of heaven.

If by traduction came thy mind,
  Our wonder is the less, to find
A soul so charming from a stock so good;
Thy father was transfused into thy blood:
So wert thou born into a tuneful strain,
An early, rich, and inexhausted vein.
  But if thy pre-existing soul
    Was form'd at first with myriads more,
It did through all the mighty poets roll
Who Greek or Latin laurels wore,
And was that Sappho last, which once it was before.
If so, then cease thy flight, O heaven-born mind!
Thou hast no dross to purge from thy rich ore:
  Nor can thy soul a fairer mansion find,
  Than was the beauteous frame she left behind:
Return, to fill or mend the quire of thy celestial kind.

May we presume to say, that, at thy birth,
New joy was sprung in heaven as well as here on earth?
  For sure the milder planets did combine
  On thy auspicious horoscope to shine,
  And even the most malicious were in trine.
    Thy brother-angels at thy birth
    Strung each his lyre, and tuned it high,
    That all the people of the sky
  Might know a poetess was born on earth;
    And then, if ever, mortal ears
    Had heard the music of the spheres.
  And if no clustering swarm of bees
On thy sweet mouth distill'd their golden dew,
    'Twas that such vulgar miraclès
    Heaven had not leisure to renew:
For all the blest fraternity of love
Solemnized there thy birth, and kept thy holiday above.

    O gracious God! how far have we
Profaned thy heavenly gift of Poesy!
Made prostitute and profligate the Muse,
Debased to each obscene and impious use,

Whose harmony was first ordain'd above,
For tongues of angels and for hymns of love!
O wretched we! why were we hurried down
  This lubrique and adulterate age
(Nay, added fat pollutions of our own),
  To increase the streaming ordures of the stage?
What can we say to excuse our second fall?
Let this thy Vestal, Heaven, atone for all!
Her Arethusian stream remains unsoil'd,
  Unmix'd with foreign filth, and undefiled;
Her wit was more than man, her innocence a child.

  Art she had none, yet wanted none,
    For Nature did that want supply:
  So rich in treasures of her own,
    She might our boasted stores defy:
  Such noble vigour did her verse adorn,
  That it seem'd borrow'd, where 'twas only born.
  Her morals, too, were in her bosom bred,
    By good examples daily fed,
What in the best of books, her father's life, she read.
  And to be read herself she need not fear;
  Each test, and every light, her Muse will bear,
  Though Epictetus with his lamp were there.
  Even love (for love sometimes her Muse exprest)
Was but a lambent flame which play'd about her breast,
    Light as the vapours of a morning dream;
  So cold herself, whilst she such warmth exprest,
    'Twas Cupid bathing in Diana's stream. . . .

  Now all those charms, that blooming grace,
  The well-proportion'd shape, and beauteous face,
  Shall never more be seen by mortal eyes;
  In earth the much-lamented virgin lies.
  Not wit, nor piety could fate prevent;
  Nor was the cruel destiny content
  To finish all the murder at a blow,
  To sweep at once her life and beauty too;
  But, like a harden'd felon, took a pride
    To work more mischievously slow,
    And plunder'd first, and then destroy'd.
  O double sacrilege on things divine,
    To rob the relic, and deface the shrine!
      But thus Orinda died:

JOHN DRYDEN

Heaven, by the same disease did both translate;
As equal were their souls, so equal was their fate.

Meantime, her warlike brother on the seas
His waving streamers to the winds displays,
And vows for his return, with vain devotion, pays.
    Ah, generous youth! that wish forbear,
    The winds too soon will waft thee here!
    Slack all thy sails, and fear to come,
Alas! thou know'st not, thou art wreck'd at home!
No more shalt thou behold thy sister's face,
Thou hast already had her last embrace.
But look aloft, and if thou kenn'st from far,
Among the Pleiads a new kindled star,
If any sparkles than the rest more bright
'Tis she that shines in that propitious light.

When in mid-air the golden trump shall sound,
    To raise the nations under ground;
When, in the Valley of Jehoshaphat,
The judging God shall close the book of Fate,
    And there the last assizes keep
    For those who wake and those who sleep;
    When rattling bones together fly
    From the four corners of the sky;
When sinews o'er the skeletons are spread,
Those clothed with flesh, and life inspires the dead;
The sacred poets first shall hear the sound,
    And foremost from the tomb shall bound,
For they are cover'd with the lightest ground;
And straight, with inborn vigour, on the wing,
Like mountain larks, to the new morning sing.
There thou, sweet Saint, before the quire shall go,
As harbinger of Heaven, the way to show,
The way which thou so well hast learn'd below.

SONG FOR ST. CECELIA'S DAY

77

From Harmony, from heavenly Harmony
    This universal frame began:
    When Nature underneath a heap
        Of jarring atoms lay
    And could not heave her head,

The tuneful voice was heard from high,
    Arise, ye more than dead!
Then cold, and hot, and moist, and dry
In order to their stations leap,
    And Music's power obey.

From harmony, from heavenly harmony
    This universal frame began:
    From harmony to harmony
Through all the compass of the notes it ran,
The diapason closing full in Man.

What passion cannot Music raise and quell?
When Jubal struck the chorded shell
    His listening brethren stood around,
    And, wondering, on their faces fell
To worship that celestial sound.
Less than a god they thought there could not dwell
    Within the hollow of that shell
    That spoke so sweetly and so well.
What passion cannot Music raise and quell?

    The trumpet's loud clangor
        Excites us to arms,
    With shrill notes of anger
        And mortal alarms.
    The double double double beat
        Of the thundering drum
        Cries "Hark! the foes come;
Charge, charge, 'tis too late to retreat!"

    The soft complaining flute
        In dying notes discovers
    The woes of hopeless lovers,
Whise dirge is whisper'd by the warbling lute.

    Sharp violins proclaim
Their jealous pangs and desperation,
Fury, frantic indignation,
Depth of pains, and height of passion
    For the fair disdainful dame.
But oh! what art can teach,
What human voice can reach
    The sacred organ's praise?

Notes inspiring holy love,
Notes that wing their heavenly ways
  To mend the choirs above.
Orpheus could lead the savage race,
And trees unrooted left their place
  Sequacious of the lyre:
But bright Cecilia raised the wonder higher:
When to her Organ vocal breath was given
An Angel heard, and straight appear'd—
  Mistaking Earth for Heaven.

Grand Chorus

As from the power of sacred lays
  The spheres began to move,
And sung the great Creator's praise
  To all the blest above;
So when the last and dreadful hour
This crumbling pageant shall devour,
The trumpet shall be heard on high,
The dead shall live, the living die,
And Music shall untune the sky.

* * *

MATTHEW PRIOR

TO A CHILD OF QUALITY

Lords, knights, and squires, the numerous band
  That wear the fair Miss Mary's fetters,
Were summoned by her high command
  To show their passions by their letters.

My pen amongst the rest I took,
  Lest those bright eyes, that cannot read,
Should dart their kindling fires, and look
  The power they have to be obey'd.

Nor quality, nor reputation,
  Forbid me yet my flame to tell;
Dear Five-years-old befriends my passion,
  And I may write till she can spell.

For, while she makes her silkworm beds
  With all the tender things I swear;
Whilst all the house my passion reads,
  In papers round her baby's hair;

She may receive and own my flame;
  For, though the strictest prudes should know it,
She'll pass for a most virtuous dame,
  And I for an unhappy poet.

Then, too, alas! when she shall tear
  The rhymes some younger rival sends,
She'll give me leave to write, I fear,
  And we shall still continue friends.

For, as our different ages move,
  'Tis so ordain'd (would Fate but mend it!),
That I shall be past making love
  When she begins to comprehend it.

* * *

ISAAC WATTS

THE DYING ADRIAN TO HIS SOUL

Poor, little, pretty, fluttering thing,
  Must we no longer live together?
And dost thou prune thy trembling wing,
  To take thy flight thou knowst not whither?
Thy humorous vein, thy pleasing folly,
  Lies all neglected, all forgot:
And pensive, wavering, melancholy,
  Thou dread'st and hop'st thou know'st not what.

* * *

LADY GRISEL BAILLIE

WERENA MY HEART LICHT I WAD DEE

There ance was a may, and she lo'ed na men;
She biggit her bonnie bow'r doun in yon glen;

LADY GRISEL BAILLIE

But now she cries, Dool and well-a-day!
Come doun the green gait and come here away!

When bonnie young Johnnie cam owre the sea,
He said he saw naething sae lovely as me;
He hecht me baith rings and mony braw things—
And werena my heart licht, I wad dee.

He had a wee titty that lo'ed na me,
Because I was twice as bonnie as she;
She raised sic a pother 'twixt him and his mother
That werena my heart's licht, I wad dee.

The day it was set, and the bridal to be:
The wife took a dwam and lay doun to dee;
She maned and she graned out o' dolour and pain,
Till he vow'd he never wad see me again.

His kin was for ane of a higher degree,
Said—What had he do wi' the likes of me?
Appose I was bonnie, I wasna for Johnnie—
And werna my heart licht, I wad dee.

They said I had neither cow nor calf,
Nor dribbles o' drink rins thro' the draff,
Nor pickles o' meal rins thro' the mil-e'e—
And werena my heart licht, I wad dee.

His titty she was baith wylie and slee:
She spied me as I cam owre the lea;
And then she ran in and made a loud din—
Believe your ain e'en, and ye trow not me.

His bonnet stood ay fu' round on his brow,
His auld ane look'd ay as well as some's new:
But now he lets 't wear ony gait it will hing,
And casts himsel dowie upon the corn bing.

And now he gaes daund'ring about the dykes,
And a' he dow do is to hund the tykes:
The live-lang nicht he ne'er steeks his e'e—
And werena my heart licht, I wad dee.

Were I but young for thee, as I hae been,
We should hae been gallopin' doun in yon green,

'And linkin' it owre the lily-white lea—
And wow, gin I were but young for thee!

* * *

JOHN GAY

LOVE IN HER EYES SITS PLAYING

81

Love in her eyes sits playing,
    And sheds delicious death;
Love in her lips is straying,
    And warbling in her breath;
Love on her breast sits panting,
    And swells with soft desire:
Nor grace, nor charm, is wanting
    To set the heart on fire.

BLACK-EYED SUSAN

82

All in the Downs the fleet was moor'd,
    The streamers waving in the wind,
When black-eyed Susan came aboard;
    "O! where shall I my true-love find?
Tell me, ye jovial sailors, tell me true
If my sweet William sails among the crew."

William, who high upon the yard
    Rock'd with the billow to and fro,
Soon as her well-known voice he heard
    He sigh'd, and cast his eyes below:
The cord slides swiftly through his glowing hands,
And quick as lightning on the deck he stands.

So the sweet lark, high poised in air,
    Shuts close his pinions to his breast
If chance his mate's shrill call he hear,
    And drops at once into her nest:—
The noblest captain in the British fleet
Might envy William's lip those kisses sweet.

"O Susan, Susan, lovely dear,
    My vows shall ever true remain;
Let me kiss off that falling tear;

We only part to meet again.
Change as ye list, ye winds; my heart shall be
The faithful compass that still points to thee.

"Believe not what the landmen say
  Who tempt with doubts thy constant mind:
They'll tell thee, sailors, when away,
  In every port a mistress find:
Yes, yes, believe them when they tell thee so,
For Thou art present whersoe'er I go.

"If to fair India's coast we sail,
  Thy eyes are seen in diamonds bright,
Thy breath is Afric's spicy gale,
  Thy skin is ivory so white.
Thus every beauteous object that I view
Wakes in my soul some charm of lovely Sue.

"Though battle call me from thy arms
  Let not my pretty Susan mourn;
Though cannons roar, yet safe from harms
  William shall to his Dear return.
Love turns aside the balls that round me fly,
Lest precious tears should drop from Susan's eye."

The boatswain gave the dreadful word,
  The sails their swelling bosom spread,
No longer must she stay aboard;
  They kiss'd, she sigh'd, he hung his head.
Her lessening boat unwilling rows to land;
  "Adieu!" she cries; and waved her lily hand.

* * *

HENRY CAREY

SALLY IN OUR ALLEY

OF all the girls that are so smart
  There's none like pretty Sally;
She is the darling of my heart,
  And she lives in our alley.
There is no lady in the land
  Is half so sweet as Sally;

She is the darling of my heart,
  And she lives in our alley.

Her father he makes cabbage-nets
  And through the streets does cry 'em;
Her mother she sells laces long
  To such as please to buy 'em:
But sure such folks could ne'er beget
  So sweet a girl as Sally!
She is the darling of my heart,
  And she lives in our alley.

When she is by, I leave my work,
  I love her so sincerely;
My master comes like any Turk,
  And bangs me most severely—
But let him bang his bellyfull,
  I'll bear it all for Sally;
She is the darling of my heart,
  And she lives in our alley.

Of all the days that's in the week
  I dearly love but one day—
And that's the day that comes betwixt
  A Saturday and Monday;
For then I'm drest all in my best
  To walk abroad with Sally;
She is the darling of my heart,
  And she lives in our alley.

My master carries me to church
  And often am I blamed
Because I leave him in the lurch
  As soon as text is named;
I leave the church in sermon-time
  And slink away to Sally;
She is the darling of my heart,
  And she lives in our alley.

When Christmas comes about again
  O then I shall have money;
I'll hoard it up, and box it all,
  I'll give it to my honey;
I would it were ten thousand pound,
  I'd give it all to Sally;

She is the darling of my heart,
    And she lives in our alley.

My master and the neighbours all
    Make game of me and Sally,
And, but for her, I'd better be
    A slave and row a galley;
But when my seven long years are out
    O then I'll marry Sally,—
O then we'll wed, and then we'll bed,
    But not in our alley!

* * *

ALEXANDER POPE

EPISTLE I—OF THE NATURE AND STATE OF MAN WITH RESPECT TO THE UNIVERSE

Awake, my St. John! leave all meaner things
To low ambition, and the pride of kings.
Let us (since life can little more supply
Than just to look about us, and to die)
Expiate free o'er all this scene of man;
A mighty maze! but not without a plan;
A wild, where weeds and flow'rs promiscuous shoot;
Or garden, tempting with forbidden fruit.
Together let us beat this ample field,
Try what the open, what the covert yield!
The latent tracts, the giddy heights, explore
Of all who blindly creep, or sightless soar;
Eye nature's walks, shoot folly as it flies,
And catch the manners living as they rise:
Laugh where we must, be candid where we can;
But vindicate the ways of God to man.
Say first, of God above, or man below,
What can we reason, but from what we know?
Of man, what see we but his station here,
From which to reason, or to which refer?
Thro' worlds unnumber'd tho' the God be known,
'Tis ours to trace him only in our own.
He, who thro' vast immensity can pierce,
See worlds on worlds compose one universe,
Observe how system into system runs,

What other planets circle other suns,
What vary'd being peoples every star,
May tell why heav'n has made us as we are.
But of this frame the bearings and the ties,
The strong connections, nice dependencies,
Gradations just, has thy pervading soul
Look'd thro'? or can a part contain the whole?

Is the great chain, that draws all to agree,
And drawn support, upheld by God, or thee?
Presumptuous man! the reason wouldst thou find,
Why formed so weak, so little, and so blind?
First, if thou canst, the harder reason guess,
Why form'd no weaker, blinder, and no less?
Ask of thy mother earth, why oaks are made
Taller or stronger than the weeds they shade?
Or ask of yonder argent fields above,
Why Jove's Satellites are less than Jove?

Of systems possible, if 'tis confest
That wisdom infinite must form the best,
Where all must full or not coherent be,
And all that rises, rise in due degree;
Then, in the scale of reas'ning life, 'tis plain,
There must be, somewhere, such a rank as man:
And all the question (wrangle e'er so long)
Is only this, if God has plac'd him wrong?

Respecting man whatever wrong we call,
May, must be right, as relative to all.
In human works, tho' labour'd on with pain,
A thousand movements scarce one purpose gain;
In God's, one single can its end produce;
Yet serves to second too some other use.
So man, who here seems principal alone,
Perhaps acts second to some sphere unknown,
Touches some wheel, or verges to some goal;
'Tis but a part we see, and not a whole.

When the proud steed shall know why man restrains
His fiery course, or drives him o'er the plains;
When the dull ox, why now he breaks the clod,
Is now a victim, and now Ægypt's god:
Then shall man's pride and dullness comprehend
His actions', passions', being's, use and end;
Why doing, suff'ring, check'd, impell'd; and why
This hour a slave, the next a deity.
Then say not man's imperfect, heav'n in fault;
Say rather, man's as perfect as he ought:

His knowledge measur'd to his state and place;
His time a moment, and a point his space.
If to be perfect in a certain sphere,
What matter, soon or late, or here or there?
The blest to-day is as completely so,
As who began a thousand years ago.

Heav'n from all creatures hides the book of fate,
All but the page prescrib'd, their present state:
From brutes what men, from men what spirits know:
Or who could suffer being here below?
The lamb thy riot dooms to bleed to-day,
Had he thy reason, would he skip and play?
Pleas'd to the last, he crops the flow'ry food,
And licks the hand just rais'd to shed his blood.
Oh blindness to the future! kindly giv'n,
That each may fill the circle mark'd by heav'n:
Who sees with equal eye, as God of all,
A hero perish, or a sparrow fall,
Atoms or systems into ruin hurl'd,
And now a bubble burst, and now a world.

Hope humbly then; with trembling pinions soar;
Wait the great teacher death, and God adore.
What future bliss, he gives not thee to know,
But gives that hope to be thy blessing now.
Hope springs eternal in the human breast:
Man never *is*, but always *to be* blest:
The soul, uneasy and confin'd from home,
Rests and expatiates in a life to come.

Lo, the poor Indian! whose untutor'd mind
Sees God in clouds, or hears him in the wind;
His soul, proud science never taught to stray
Far as the solar walk, or milky way;
Yet simple nature to his hope has giv'n,
Behind the cloud-topt hill, an humbler heav'n;
Some safer world in depth of woods embrac'd,
Some happier island in the wat'ry waste,
Where slaves once more their native land behold,
No fiends torment, no Christians thirst for gold.
To Be, contents his natural desire,
He asks no angel's wing, no seraph's fire;
But thinks admitted to that equal sky,
His faithful dog shall bear him company.

Go, wiser thou! and in thy scale of sense,
Weigh thy opinion against providence;
Call imperfection what thou fancy'st such,

Say, here he gives too little, there too much:
Destroy all creatures for thy sport or gust,
Yet cry, If man's unhappy, God's unjust;
If man alone ingross not Heav'n's high care,
Alone made perfect here, immortal there:
Snatch from his hand the balance and the rod,
Re-judge his justice, be the God of God.
In pride, in reas'ning pride, our error lies;
All quit their sphere, and rush into the skies.
Pride still is aiming at the blest abodes,
Men would be angels, angels would be gods.
Aspiring to be gods if angels fell,
Aspiring to be angels men rebel:
And who but wishes to invert the laws
Of order, sins against th' eternal cause.

As for what end the heav'nly bodies shine,
Earth for whose use? pride answers, "'Tis for mine:
For me kind nature wakes her genial pow'r,
Suckles each herb, and spreads out ev'ry flow'r;
Annual for me, the grape, the rose renew
The Juice nectareous, and the balmy dew;
For me, the mine a thousand treasures brings;
For me, health gushes from a thousand springs;
Seas roll to waft me, suns to light me rise;
My foot-stool earth, my canopy the skies."

But errs not nature from this gracious end,
From burning suns when livid deaths descend,
When earthquakes swallow, or when tempests sweep
Towns to one grave, whole nations to the deep?
"No ('tis reply'd) the first almighty cause
Acts not by partial, but by gen'ral laws;
Th' exceptions few; some change since all began:
And what created perfect?"—Why then man?
If the great end be human happiness,
Then nature deviates; and can man do less?
As much that end a constant course requires
Of show'rs and sun-shine, as of man's desires;
As much eternal springs and cloudless skies,
As men for ever temp'rate, calm, and wise.
If plagues or earthquakes break not Heav'n's design,
Why then a Borgia, or a Catiline?
Who knows but he, whose hand the light'ning forms,
Who heaves old oceans, and who wings the storms;
Pours fierce ambition in a Cæsar's mind,
Or turns young Ammon loose to scourge mankind?

ALEXANDER POPE

From pride, from pride, our very reas'ning springs;
Account for moral as for nat'ral things:
Why charge we heav'n in those, in these acquit?
In both, to reason right is to submit.

Better for us, perhaps, it might appear,
Were there all harmony, all virtue here;
That never air or ocean felt the wind,
That never passion discompos'd the mind.
But all subsists by elemental strife;
And passions are the elements of life
The gen'ral order, since the whole began,
Is kept in nature, and is kept in man.

What would this man? Now upward will he soar,
And little less than angel, would be more;
Now looking downwards, just as griev'd appears
To want the strength of bulls, the fur of bears.
Made for his use all creatures if he call,
Say what their use, had he the pow'rs of all;
Nature to these, without profusion, kind,
The proper organs, proper pow'rs assign'd;
Each seeming want compensated of course,
Here with degrees of swiftness, there of force;
All in exact proportion to the state;
Nothing to add, and nothing to abate.
Each beast, each insect, happy in its own:
Is Heav'n unkind to man, and man alone?
Shall he alone, whom rational we call,
Be pleas'd with nothing, if not blest with all?

The bliss of man (could pride that blessing find)
Is not to act or think beyond mankind;
No pow'rs of body, or of soul to share,
But what his nature and his state can bear.
Why has not man a microscopic eye?
For this plain reason, man is not a fly.
Say what the use, were finer optics giv'n,
T' inspect a mite, not comprehend the heav'n?
Or touch, if tremblingly alive all o'er,
To smart and agonize at ev'ry pore?
Or, quick effluvia darting thro' the brain,
Die of a rose in aromatic pain?
If nature thunder'd in his op'ning ears,
And stunn'd him with the music of the spheres,
How would he wish that heav'n had left him still
The whisp'ring zephyr, and the purling rill?
Who finds not Providence all good and wise,

Alike in what it gives, and what denies?
  Far as creation's ample range extends,
The scale of sensual, mental pow'rs ascends:
Mark how it mounts to man's imperial race,
From the green myriads in the peopled grass:
What modes of sight betwixt each wide extreme,
The mole's dim curtain, and the lynx's beam:
Of smell, the headlong lioness between,
And hound sagacious on the tainted green:
Of hearing, from the life that fills the flood,
To that which warbles through the vernal wood?
The spider's touch, how exquisitely fine!
Feels at each thread, and lives along the line:
In the nice bee, what sense so subtly true
From pois'nous herbs extracts the healing dew:
How instinct varies in the grov'ling swine,
Compar'd, half reas'ning elephant, with thine!
'Twixt that, and reason, what a nice barrier?
For ever sep'rate, yet for ever near!
Remembrance and reflection how ally'd;
What thin partitions sense from thought divide?
And middle natures, how they long to join,
Yet never pass th' insuperable line!
Without this just gradation, could they be
Subjected, these to those, or all to thee?
The pow'rs of all subdu'd by thee alone,
Is not thy reason all these pow'rs in one?

  See, thro' this air, this ocean, and this earth,
All matter quick, and bursting into birth.
Above, how high progressive life may go!
Around, how wide! how deep extend below!
Vast chain of being! which from God began,
Natures æthereal, human, angel, man,
Beast, bird, fish, insect, what no eye can see,
No glass can reach; from infinite to thee,
From thee to nothing. On superior pow'rs
Were we to press, inferior might on ours;
Or in the full creation leave a void,
Where, one step broken, the great scale's destroy'd.
From Nature's chain whatever link you strike,
Tenth, or ten thousandth, breaks the chain alike.

  And, if each system in gradation roll
Alike essential to th' amazing whole,
The least confusion but in one, not all
That system only, but the whole must fall.

Let earth unbalanc'd from her orbit fly,
Planets and suns run lawless thro' the sky;
Let ruling angels from their spheres be hurl'd,
Being on being wreck'd, and world on world;
Heav'n's whole foundations to their centre nod,
And nature tremble to the throne of God.
All this dread order break—for whom? for thee?
Vile worm!—oh madness! pride! impiety!

What if the foot, ordain'd the dust to tread,
Or hand, to toil, aspir'd to be the head?
What if the head, the eye, or ear repin'd
To serve mere engines to the ruling mind?
Just as absurd for any part to claim
To be another, in this gen'ral frame;
Just as absurd, to mourn the tasks or pains
The great directing Mind of all ordains.

All are but parts of one stupendous whole,
Whose body nature is, and God the soul;
That, chang'd thro' all, and yet in all the same,
Great in the earth, as in th' æthereal frame,
Warms in the sun, refreshes in the breeze,
Glows in the stars, and blossoms in the trees,
Lives thro' all life, extends thro' all extent,
Spreads undivided, operates unspent;
Breathes in our soul, informs our mortal part,
As full, as perfect, in a hair as heart;
As full, as perfect, in vile man that mourns,
As the rapt seraph that adores and burns:
To him no high, no low, no great, no small;
He fills, he bounds, connects, and equals all.

Cease then, nor order imperfection name:
Our proper bliss depends on what we blame.
Know thy own point: this kind, this due degree
Of blindness, weakness, Heav'n bestows on thee.
Submit. In this, or any other sphere,
Secure to be as blest as thou canst bear:
Safe in the hand of one disposing pow'r,
Or in the natal, or the mortal hour.
All nature is but art, unknown to thee;
All chance, direction, which thou canst not see;
All discord, harmony not understood;
All partial evil, universal good.
And, spite of pride, in erring reason's spite,
One truth is clear, "Whatever is, is right."

EPISTLE II—OF THE NATURE AND STATE OF MAN WITH RESPECT TO HIMSELF, AS AN INDIVIDUAL

85
    Know then thyself, presume not God to scan,
The proper study of mankind is man.
Plac'd on this isthmus of a middle state,
A being darkly wise, and rudely great:
With too much knowledge for the sceptic side,
With too much weakness for the Stoic's pride,
He hangs between; in doubt to act, or rest;
In doubt to deem himself a God, or beast;
In doubt his mind or body to prefer;
Born but to die, and reas'ning but to err;
Alike in ignorance, his reason such,
Whether he thinks too little or too much:
Chaos of thought and passion, all confus'd;
Still by himself abus'd or disabus'd;
Created half to rise, and half to fall;
Great lord to all things, yet a prey to all;
Sole judge of truth, in endless error hurl'd:
The glory, jest, and riddle of the world!

  Go, wondrous creature! mount where science guides,
Go, measure earth, weigh air, and state the tides;
Instruct the planets in what orbs to run,
Correct old time, and regulate the sun;
Go, soar with Plato to th' empyreal sphere,
To the first good, first perfect, and first fair;
Or tread the mazy round his follow'rs trod,
And quitting sense call imitating God;
As eastern priests in giddy circles run,
And turn their heads to imitate the sun.
Go, teach eternal wisdom how to rule—
Then drop into thyself, and be a fool!

  Superior beings, when of late they saw
A mortal man unfold all nature's law,
Admir'd such wisdom in an earthly shape,
And shew'd a Newton as we shew an ape.
Could he, whose rules the rapid comet bind,
Describe or fix one movement of his mind?
Who saw its fires here rise, and there descend,
Explain his own beginning, or his end;
Alas what wonder! man's superior part
Uncheck'd may rise, and climb from art to art;
But when his own great work is but begun,
What reason weaves, by passion is undone.

ALEXANDER POPE

Trace science then, with modesty thy guide;
First strip off all her equipage of pride;
Deduct what is but vanity or dress,
Or learning's luxury, or idleness;
Or tricks to shew the stretch of human brain,
Mere curious pleasure, or ingenious pain;
Expunge the whole, or lop th' excrescent parts
Of all our vices have created arts;
Then see how little the remaining sum,
Which serv'd the past, and must the times to come!

Two principles in human nature reign;
Self-love, to urge, and reason, to restrain;
Nor this a good, nor that a bad we call,
Each works its end, to move or govern all:
And to their proper operation still
Ascribe all Good, to their improper, Ill.

Self-love, the spring of motion, acts the soul;
Reason's comparing balance rules the whole.
Man, but for that, no action could attend,
And, but for this, were active to no end:
Fix'd like a plant on his peculiar spot,
To draw nutrition, propagate, and rot:
Or, meteor-like, flame lawless thro' the void,
Destroying others, by himself destroy'd.

Most strength the moving principle requires;
Active its task, it prompts, impels, inspires.
Sedate and quiet the comparing lies,
Form'd but to check, delib'rate, and advise.
Self-love, still stronger, as its objects nigh;
Reason's at distance, and in prospect lie:
That sees immediate good by present sense;
Reason, the future and the consequence.
Thicker than arguments, temptations throng,
At best more watchful this, but that more strong.
The action of the stronger to suspend
Reason still use, to reason still attend.
Attention habit and experience gains;
Each strengthens reason, and self-love restrains.
Let subtle schoolmen teach these friends to fight,
More studious to divide than to unite;
And grace and virtue, sense and reason split,
With all the rash dexterity of wit.
Wits, just like fools, at war about a name,
Have full as oft no meaning, or the same.
Self-love and reason to one end aspire,

Pain their aversion, pleasure their desire;
But greedy that, its object would devour,
This taste the honey, and not wound the flow'r:
Pleasure, or wrong or rightly understood,
Our greatest evil, or our greatest good.

Modes of self-love the passions we may call:
'Tis real good, or seeming, moves them all:
But since not ev'ry good we can divide,
And reason bids us for our own provide:
Passions, tho' selfish, if their means be fair,
List under Reason, and deserve her care;
Those, that imparted, court a nobler aim,
Exalt their kind, and take some virtue's name.

In lazy apathy let Stoics boast
Their virtue fix'd; 'tis fix'd as in a frost;
Contracted all, retiring to the breast;
But strength of mind is exercise, not rest:
The rising tempest puts in act the soul,
Parts it may ravage, but preserves the whole.
On life's vast ocean diversely we sail,
Reason the card, but passion is the gale;
Nor God alone in the still calm we find,
He mounts the storm, and walks upon the wind.
Passions, like elements, tho' born to fight,
Yet, mix'd and soften'd, in his work unite:
These 'tis enough to temper and employ;
But what composes man, can man destroy?
Suffice that reason keep to nature's road,
Subject, compound them, follow her and God.
Love, hope, and joy, fair pleasure's smiling train,
Hate, fear, and grief, the family of pain,
These mixt with art, and to due bounds confin'd,
Make and maintain the balance of the mind:
The lights and shades, whose well accorded strife
Gives all the strength and colour of our life.

Pleasures are ever in our hands or eyes;
And, when in act they cease, in prospect rise:
Present to grasp, and future still to find,
The whole employ of body and of mind.
All spread their charms, but charm not all alike;
On diff'rent senses diff'rent objects strike;
Hence diff'rent passions more or less inflame,
As strong or weak, the organs of the frame;
And hence one master passion in the breast,
Like Aaron's serpent, swallows up the rest.

As Man, perhaps, the moment of his breath,
Receives the lurking principle of death;
The young disease, that must subdue at length,
Grows with his growth, and strengthens with his strength
So, cast and mingled with his very frame,
The mind's disease, its ruling passion came;
Each vital humour which should feed the whole,
Soon flows to this, in body and in soul:
Whatever warms the heart, or fills the head,
As the mind opens, and its functions spread,
Imagination plies her dang'rous art,
And pours it all upon the peccant part.
Nature its mother, habit is its nurse;
Wit, spirit, faculties, but make it worse;
Reason itself but gives it edge and pow'r,
And heav'n's blest beam turns vinegar more sowr.

We, wretched subjects tho' to lawful sway,
In this weak queen some fav'rite still obey:
Ah! if she lend not arms, as well as rules,
What can she more than tell us we are fools?
Teach us to mourn our nature, not to mend,
A sharp accuser, but a helpless friend!
Or from a judge turn pleader, to persuade
The choice we make, or justify it made;
Proud of an easy conquest all along,
She but removes weak passions for the strong:
So, when small humours gather to a gout,
The doctor fancies he has driv'n them out.

Yes, nature's road must ever be preferr'd;
Reason is here no guide, but still a guard;
'Tis hers to rectify, not overthrow,
And treat this passion more as friend than foe;
A mighty pow'r the strong direction sends,
And sev'ral men impels to sev'ral ends:
Like varying winds by other passions tost,
This drives them constant to a certain coast.
Let pow'r or knowledge, gold or glory, please,
Or (oft more strong than all) the love of ease;
Thro' life 'tis followed, ev'n at life's expence;
The merchant's toil, the sage's indolence,
The monk's humility, the hero's pride,
All, all alike, find reason on their side.

Th' eternal art educing good from ill,
Grafts on this passion our best principle:
'Tis thus the mercury of man is fix'd,

Strong grows the virtue with his nature mix'd;
The dross cements what else were too refin'd,
And in one int'rest body acts with mind.

As fruits, ungrateful to the planter's care,
On savage stocks inserted, learn to bear;
The surest virtues thus from passions shoot,
Wild nature's vigor working at the root.
What crops of wit and honesty appear
From spleen, from obstinacy, hate or fear!
See anger, zeal and fortitude supply;
Ev'n av'rice, prudence; sloth, philosophy;
Lust, thro' some certain strainers well refin'd,
Is gentle love, and charms all womankind;
Envy, to which th' ignoble mind's a slave,
Is emulation in the learn'd or brave;
Nor virtue, male or female, can we name,
But what will grow on pride, or grow on shame.

Thus nature gives us (let it check our pride)
The virtue nearest to our vice ally'd:
Reason the byas turns to good from ill,
And Nero reigns a Titus, if he will.
The fiery soul abhorr'd in Catiline,
In Decius charms, in Curtius is divine:
The same ambition can destroy or save,
And makes a patriot as it makes a knave.

This light and darkness in our chaos join'd,
What shall divide? The God within the mind.

Extremes in nature equal ends produce,
In man they join to some mysterious use;
Tho' each by turns the other's bound invade,
As, in some well-wrought picture, light and shade,
And oft so mix, the diff'rence is too nice
Where ends the virtue or begins the vice.

Fools! who from hence into the notion fall,
That vice or virtue there is none at all.
If white and black blend, soften, and unite
A thousand ways, is there no black or white?
Ask your own heart, and nothing is so plain;
'Tis to mistake them, costs the time and pain.

Vice is a monster of so frightful mien,
As, to be hated, needs but to be seen;
Yet seen too oft, familiar with her face,
We first endure, then pity, then embrace.
But where th' extreme of vice, was ne'er agreed:
Ask where's the North? at York, 'tis on the Tweed;

In Scotland, at the Orcades; and there,
At Greenland, Zembla, or the Lord knows where.
No creature owns it in the first degree,
But thinks his neighbour farther gone than he:
Ev'n those who dwell beneath its very zone,
Or never feel the rage, or never own;
What happier natures shink at with affright,
The hard inhabitant contends is right.

Virtuous and vicious ev'ry man must be,
Few in th' extreme, but all in the degree;
The rogue and fool by fits is fair and wise;
And ev'n the best, by fits, what they despise.
'Tis but by parts we follow good or ill;
For, vice or virtue, self directs it still;
Each individual seeks a sev'ral goal;
But heav'n's great view is one, and that the whole.
That counter-works each folly and caprice;
That disappoints th' effect of ev'ry vice;
That happy frailties to all ranks apply'd,
Shame to the virgin, to the matron pride,
Fear to the statesman, rashness to the chief,
To kings presumption, and to crowds belief:
That, virtue's ends from vanity can raise,
Which seeks no int'rest, no reward but praise;
And builds on wants, and on defects of mind,
The joy, the peace, the glory of mankind.

Heav'n forming each on other to depend,
A master, or a servant, or a friend,
Bids each on other for assistance call,
'Till one man's weakness grows the strength of all.
Wants, frailties, passions, closer still ally
The common int'rest, or endear the tie.
To these we owe true friendship, love sincere,
Each home-felt joy that life inherits here;
Yet from the same we learn, in its decline,
Those joys, those loves, those int'rests to resign;
Taught half by reason, half by mere decay,
To welcome death, and calmly pass away.

Whate'er the passion—knowledge, fame, or pelf,
Not one will change his neighbour with himself.
The learn'd is happy nature to explore,
The fool is happy that he knows no more;
The rich is happy in the plenty giv'n,
The poor contents him with the care of heaven.
See the blind beggar dance, the cripple sing,

The sot a hero, lunatic a king;
The starving chemist in his golden views
Supremely blest, the poet in his muse.
See some strange comfort ev'ry state attend,
And pride bestow'd on all, a common friend:
See some fit passion ev'ry age supply,
Hope travels thro', nor quits us when we die.

Behold the child, by nature's kindly law,
Pleas'd with a rattle, tickled with a straw:
Some livelier play-thing gives his youth delight,
A little louder, but as empty quite:
Scarfs, garters, gold, amuse his riper stage,
And beads and pray'r-books are the toys of age:
Pleas'd with this bauble still, as that before;
'Till tir'd he sleeps, and life's poor play is o'er.

Mean-while opinion gilds with varying rays
Those painted clouds that beautify our days;
Each want of happiness by hope supply'd,
And each vacuity of sense by pride:
These build as fast as knowledge can destroy;
In folly's cup still laughs the bubble joy;
One prospect lost, another still we gain;
And not a vanity is giv'n in vain;
Ev'n mean self-love becomes, by force divine,
The scale to measure others' wants by thine.
See! and confess one comfort still must rise;
'Tis this, Tho' man's a fool, yet God is wise.

EPISTLE III—OF THE NATURE AND STATE OF MAN WITH RESPECT TO SOCIETY

86

HERE then we rest; "The universal cause
Acts to one end, but acts by various laws."
In all the madness of superfluous health,
The trim of pride, the impudence of wealth,
Let this great truth be present night and day;
But most be present, if we preach or pray.

Look round our world; behold the chain of love
Combining all below and all above.
See plastic nature working to this end,
The single atoms each to other tend,
Attract, attracted to, the next in place
Form'd and impell'd its neighbour to embrace.
See matter next, with various life endu'd,
Press to one centre still, the gen'ral good.

See dying vegetables life sustain,
See life dissolving vegetate again:
All forms that perish other forms supply,
(By turns we catch the vital breath, and die)
Like bubbles on the sea of matter born,
They rise, they break, and to that sea return.
Nothing is foreign; parts relate to whole;
One all-extending, all-preserving soul
Connects each being, greatest with the least;
Made beast in aid of man, and man of beast;
All serv'd, all serving: nothing stands alone;
The chain holds on, and where it ends, unknown.

 Has God, thou fool! work'd solely for thy good,
Thy joy, thy pastime, thy attire, thy food?
Who for thy table feeds the wanton fawn,
For him as kindly spreads the flow'ry lawn:
Is it for thee the lark ascends and sings?
Joy tunes his voice, joy elevates his wings.
Is it for thee the linnet pours his throat?
Loves of his own and raptures swell the note.
The bounding steed you pompously bestride,
Shares with his lord the pleasure and the pride.
Is thine alone the seed that strews the plain?
The birds of heav'n shall vindicate their grain.
Thine the full harvest of the golden year?
Part pays, and justly, the deserving steer:
The hog, that plows not, nor obeys thy call,
Lives on the labours of this lord of all.

 Know, nature's children all divide her care;
The fur that warms a monarch, warm'd a bear.
While man exclaims, "See all things for my use!"
"See man for mine!" replies a pamper'd goose:
And just as short of reason he must fall,
Who thinks all made for one, not one for all.

 Grant that the pow'rful still the weak controul;
Be man the wit and tyrant of the whole:
Nature that tyrant checks; he only knows,
And helps, another creature's wants and woes.
Say, will the falcon, stooping from above,
Smit with her varying plumage, spare the dove?
Admires the jay the insect's gilded wings?
Or hears the hawk when Philomela sings?
Man cares for all: to birds he gives his woods,
To beasts his pastures, and to fish his floods;
For some his int'rest prompts him to provide,

For more his pleasure, yet for more his pride:
All feed on one vain patron, and enjoy
Th' extensive blessing of his luxury,
That very life his learned hunger craves,
He saves from famine, from the savage saves;
Nay, feasts the animal he dooms his feast,
And, till he ends the being, makes it blest:
Which sees no more the stroke, or feels the pain,
Than favour'd man by touch etherial slain.
The creature had this feast of life before;
Thou too must perish, when thy feast is o'er!
To each unthinking being, heav'n a friend,
Gives not the useless knowledge of its end:
To man imparts it; but with such a view
As, while he dreads it, makes him hope it too:
The hour conceal'd, and so remote the fear,
Death still draws nearer, never seeming near.
Great standing miracle! that heav'n assign'd
Its only thinking thing this turn of mind.

    Whether with reason, or with instinct blest,
Know, all enjoy that pow'r which suits them best;
To bliss alike by that direction tend,
And find the means proportion'd to their end.
Say, where full instinct is th' unerring guide,
What Pope or Council can they need beside?
Reason, however able, cool at best,
Cares not for service, or but serves when prest,
Stay 'till we call, and then not often near;
But honest instinct comes a volunteer,
Sure never to o'er-shoot, but just to hit;
While still too wide or short is human wit;
Sure by quick nature happiness to gain,
Which heavier reason labours at in vain.
This too serves always, reason never long;
One must go right, the other may go wrong.
See then the acting and comparing pow'rs
One is their nature, which are two in ours;
And reason raise o'er instinct as you can,
In this 'tis God directs, in that 'tis man.

    Who taught the nations of the field and flood
To shun their poison, and to chuse their food?
Prescient, the tides or tempests to withstand,
Build on the wave, or arch beneath the sand?
Who made the spider parallels design,
Sure as De Moivre, without rule or line?

ALEXANDER POPE

Who bid the stork, Columbus-like, explore
Heav'ns not his own, and worlds unknown before?
Who calls the council, states the certain day,
Who forms the phalanx, and who points the way?
   God, in the nature of each being, founds
It proper bliss, and set its proper bounds:
But as he fram'd a whole the whole to bless,
On mutual wants built mutual happiness:
So from the first, eternal order ran,
And creature link'd to creature, man to man.
Whate'er of life all-quick'ning æther keeps,
Or breathes thro' air, or shoots beneath the deeps,
Or pours profuse on earth, one nature feeds
The vital flame, and swells the genial seeds.
Not man alone, but all that roam the wood,
Or wing the sky, or roll along the flood,
Each loves itself, but not itself alone,
Each sex desires alike, 'till two are one.
Nor ends the pleasure with the fierce embrace;
They love themselves, a third time, in their race.
Thus beast and bird their common charge attend,
The mothers nurse it, and the sires defend;
The young dismiss'd to wander earth or air,
There stops the instinct, and there ends the care;
The link dissolves, each seeks a fresh embrace,
Another love succeeds, another race.
A longer care man's helpless kind demands;
That longer care contracts more lasting bands:
Reflection, reason, still the ties improve,
At once extend the int'rest, and the love:
With choice we fix, with sympathy we burn;
Each virtue in each passion takes its turn;
And still new deeds, new helps, new habits rise,
That graft benevolence on charities.
Still as one brood, and as another rose,
These nat'ral love maintain'd, habitual those:
The last, scarce ripen'd into perfect man,
Saw helpless him from whom their life began:
Mem'ry and fore-cast just returns engage,
That pointed back to youth, this on to age;
While pleasure, gratitude, and hope, combin'd,
Still spread the int'rest and preserv'd the kind.
   Nor think, in nature's state they blindly trod;
The state of nature was the reign of God:
Self-love and social at her birth began,

Union the bond of all things, and of man.
Pride then was not; nor arts, that pride to aid;
Man walk'd with beast, joint tenant of the shade,
The same his table, and the same his bed;
No murder cloath'd him, and no murder fed.
In the same temple, the resounding wood,
All vocal beings hymn'd their equal God:
The shrine with gore unstain'd, with gold undrest,
Unbrib'd, unbloody, stood the blameless priest:
Heav'n's attribute was universal care,
And man's prerogative, to rule, but spare.
Ah! how unlike the man of times to come!
Of half that live the butcher and the tomb;
Who, foe to nature, hears the gen'ral groan,
Murders their species, and betrays his own.
But just disease to luxury succeeds,
And ev'ry death its own avenger breeds;
The fury-passions from that blood began,
And turn'd on man, a fiercer savage, man.

See him from nature rising slow to art!
To copy instinct then was reason's part;
Thus then to man the voice of nature spake,
"Go, from the creatures thy instructions take:
Learn from the birds what food the thickets yield;
Learn from the beasts the physic of the field;
Thy arts of building from the bee receive;
Learn of the mole to plow, the worm to weave;
Learn of the little nautilus to sail,
Spread the thin oar, and catch the driving gale.
Here too all forms of social union find,
And hence let reason, late, instruct mankind:
Here subterranean works and cities see;
There towns aërial on the waving tree.
Learn each small people's genius, policies,
The ant's republic, and the realm of bees;
How those in common all their wealth bestow,
And anarchy without confusion know;
And these for ever, tho' a monarch reign,
Their sep'rate cells and properties maintain.
Mark what unvary'd laws preserve each state,
Laws wise as nature, and as fix'd as fate.
In vain thy reason finer webs shall draw,
Entangle justice in her net of law,
And right, too rigid, harden into wrong;
Still for the strong too weak, the weak too strong.

Yet go! and thus o'er all the creatures sway,
Thus let the wiser make the rest obey;
And for those arts mere instinct could afford,
Be crown'd as monarchs, or as gods ador'd."
  Great nature spoke; observant man obey'd;
Cities were built, societies were made:
Here rose one little state; another near
Grew by like means, and join'd, thro' love or fear.
Did here the trees with ruddier burdens bend,
And there the streams in purer rills descend?
What war could ravish, commerce could bestow,
And he return'd a friend, who came a foe.
Converse and love mankind might strongly draw,
When love was liberty, and nature law.
Thus states were form'd; the name of king unknown,
'Till common int'rest plac'd the sway in one.
'Twas virtue only (or in arts or arms,
Diffusing blessings, or averting harms)
The same which in a sire the sons obey'd,
A prince the father of a people made.
  'Till then, by nature crown'd, each patriarch sate,
King, priest and parent of his growing state;
On him, their second providence, they hung,
Their law his eye, their oracle his tongue.
He from the wond'ring furrow call'd the food,
Taught to command the fire, controul the flood,
Draw forth the monsters of th' abyss profound,
Or fetch th' aërial eagle to the ground,
'Till drooping, sick'ning, dying they began
Whom they rever'd as God to mourn as man:
Then, looking up from sire to sire, explor'd
One great first father, and that first ador'd.
Or plain tradition that this All begun,
Convey'd unbroken faith from sire to son;
The worker from the work distinct was known,
And simple reason never sought but one:
Ere wit oblique had broke that steady light,
Man, like his maker, saw that all was right;
To virtue, in the paths of pleasure trod,
And own'd a father when he own'd a God.
Love all the faith, and all th' allegiance then;
For nature knew no right divine in men,
No ill could fear in God; and understood
A sov'reign being, but a sov'reign good.
True faith, true policy, united ran,

That was but love of God, and this of man.
  Who first taught souls enslav'd, and realms undone,
Th' enormous faith of many made for one;
That proud exception to all nature's laws,
T' invert the world, and counter-work its cause?
Force first made conquest, and that conquest, law;
'Till superstition taught the tyrant awe,
Then shar'd the tyranny, then lent it aid,
And gods of conqu'rors, slaves of subjects made:
She, 'midst the light'ning's blaze, and thunder's sound,
When rock'd the mountains, and when groan'd the ground,
She taught the weak to bend, the proud to pray,
To pow'r unseen, and mightier far than they:
She, from the rending earth, and bursting skies,
Saw gods descend, and fiends infernal rise:
Here fix'd the dreadful, there the blest abodes;
Fear made her devils, and weak hope her gods;
Gods partial, changeful, passionate, unjust,
Whose attributes were rage, revenge, or lust;
Such as the souls of cowards might conceive,
And, form'd like tyrants, tyrants would believe.
Zeal then, not charity, became the guide;
And hell was built on spite, and heav'n on pride.
Then sacred seem'd th' etherial vault no more;
Altars grew marble then, and reek'd with gore:
Then first the flamen tasted living food;
Next his grim idol smear'd with human blood;
With heav'n's own thunders shook the world below,
And play'd the god an engine on his foe.
  So drives self-love, thro' just, and thro' unjust,
To one man's pow'r, ambition, lucre, lust.
The same self-love, in all, becomes the cause
Of what restrains him, government and laws.
For, what one likes, if others like as well,
What serves on will, when many wills rebel?
How shall he keep, what, sleeping or awake,
A weaker may surprise, a stronger take?
His safety must his liberty restrain:
All join to guard what each desires to gain.
Forc'd into virtue thus, by self-defence,
Ev'n kings learn'd justice and benevolence:
Self-love forsook the path it first pursu'd,
And found the private in the public good.
  'Twas then the studious head or gen'rous mind,
Follow'r of God, or friend of human-kind,

Poet or patriot, rose but to restore
The faith and moral nature gave before;
Relum'd her ancient light, not kindled new,
If not God's image, yet his shadow drew:
Taught pow'r's due use to people and to kings,
Taught not to slack, nor strain its tender strings,
The less, or greater, set so justly true,
That touching one must strike the other too;
'Till jarring int'rests of themselves create
Th' according music of a well-mix'd state.
Such is the world's great harmony, that springs
From order, union, full consent of things:
Where small and great, where weak and mighty, made
To serve, not suffer, strengthen, not invade;
More pow'rful each as needful to the rest,
And in proportion as it blesses blest;
Draw to one point, and to one centre bring
Beast, man, or angel, servant, lord, or king.

  For forms of government let fools contest;
Whate'er is best administer'd is best:
For modes of faith, let graceless zealots fight;
His can't be wrong whose life is in the right:
In faith and hope the world will disagree,
But all mankind's concern is charity:
All must be false that thwart this one great end;
And all of God, that bless mankind, or mend.
Man, like the gen'rous vine, supported lives;
The strength he gains is from th' embrace he gives.
On their own axis as the planets run,
Yet make at once their circle round the sun;
So two consistent motions act the soul;
And one regards itself, and one the whole.
  Thus God and nature link'd the gen'ral frame,
And bade self-love and social be the same.

EPISTLE IV—OF THE NATURE AND STATE OF MAN WITH RESPECT TO HAPPINESS

Oh happiness! our being's end and aim!
Good, pleasure, ease, content! whate'er thy name:
That something still which prompts th' eternal sigh,
For which we bear to live, or dare to die,
Which still so near us, yet beyond us lies,
O'er-look'd, seen double, by the fool, and wise.
Plant of celestial seed! if dropt below,

Say, in what mortal soil thou deign'st to grow?
Fair op'ning to some court's propitious shine,
Or deep with di'monds in the flaming mine?
Twin'd with the wreaths Parnassian lawrels yield,
Or reap'd in iron harvests of the field?
Where grows? where grows it not? If vain our toil,
We ought to blame the culture, not the soil:
Fix'd to no spot is happiness sincere,
'Tis no where to be found, or ev'ry where:
'Tis never to be bought, but always free,
And fled from monarchs, St. John! dwells with thee.

    Ask of the learn'd the way? The learn'd are blind;
This bids to serve, and that to shun mankind;
Some place the bliss in action, some in ease,
Those call it pleasure, and contentment these;
Some sunk to beasts, find pleasure end in pain;
Some swell'd to gods, confess ev'n virtue vain;
Or indolent, to each extreme they fall,
To trust in ev'ry thing, or doubt of all.

    Who thus define it, say they more or less
Than this, that happiness is happiness?

    Take nature's path, and mad opinion's leave;
All states can reach it, and all heads conceive;
Obvious her goods, in no extreme they dwell;
There needs but thinking right, and meaning well;
And mourn our various portions as we please,
Equal is common sense, and common ease.

    Remember, man the universal cause
Acts not by partial, but by gen'ral laws;
And makes what happiness we justly call
Subsist not in the good of one, but all.
There's not a blessing individuals find,
But some way leans and hearkens to the kind:
No bandit fierce, no tyrant mad with pride,
No cavern'd hermit, rests self-satisfy'd:
Who most to shun or hate mankind pretend,
Seek an admirer, or would fix a friend:
Abstract what others feel, what others think,
All pleasures sicken, and all glories sink:
Each has his share; and who would more obtain,
Shall find the pleasure pays not half the pain.
Order is heav'n's first law; and this confest,
Some are, and must be, greater than the rest,
More rich, more wise; but who infers from hence
That such are happier, shocks all common sense.

Heav'n to mankind impartial we confess,
If all are equal in their happiness:
But mutual wants this happiness increase;
All nature's diff'rence keeps all nature's peace.
Condition, circumstance is not the thing;
Bliss is the same in subject or in king,
In who obtain defence, or who defend,
In him who is, or him who finds a friend:
Heav'n breathes thro' ev'ry member of the whole
One common blessing, as one common soul.
But fortune's gifts if each alike possest,
And each were equal, must not all contest?
If then to all men happiness was meant,
God in externals could not place content.

Fortune her gifts may variously dispose,
And these be happy call'd, unhappy those;
But heav'n's just balance equal will appear,
While those are plac'd in hope, and these in fear:
Not present good or ill, the joy or curse,
But future views of better, or of worse.

Oh sons of earth! attempt ye still to rise,
By mountains pil'd on mountains, to the skies?
Heav'n still with laughter the vain toil surveys,
And buries madmen in the heaps they raise.

Know, all the good that individuals find,
Or God and nature meant to mere mankind,
Reason's whole pleasure, all the joys of sense,
Lie in three words, health, peace, and competence.
But health consists with temperance alone;
And peace, oh virtue! peace is all thy own.
The good or bad the gifts of fortune gain;
But these less taste them, as they worse obtain.
Say, in pursuit of profit or delight,
Who risk the most, that take wrong means, or right?
Of vice or virtue, whether blest or curst,
Which meets contempt, or which compassion first?
Count all th' advantage prosp'rous vice attains,
'Tis but what virtue flies from and disdains:
And grant the bad what happiness they would,
One they must want, which is, to pass for good.

Oh blind to truth, and God's whole scheme below,
Who fancy bliss to vice, to virtue woe!
Who sees and follows that great scheme the best,
Best knows the blessing, and will most be blest.
But fools the good alone unhappy call,

For ills or accidents that chance to all.
See Falkland dies, the virtuous and the just!
See god-like Turenne prostrate on the dust!
See Sidney bleeds amid the martial strife!
Was this their virtue, or contempt of life?
Say, was it virtue, more tho' heav'n ne'er gave,
Lamented Digby! sunk thee to the grave?
Tell me, if virtue made the son expire,
Why, full of days and honours, lives the sire?
Why drew Marseilles' good bishop purer breath,
When nature sicken'd and each gale was death!
Or why so long (in life if long can be)
Lent heav'n a parent to the poor and me?

    What makes all physical or moral ill?
There deviates nature, and here wanders will.
God sends not ill; if rightly understood,
Or partial ill is universal good,
Or change admits, or nature lets it fall,
Short, and but rare, 'till man improv'd it all.
We just as wisely might of heav'n complain
That righteous Abel was destroy'd by Cain,
As that the virtuous son is ill at ease,
When his lewd father gave the dire disease.
Think we, like some weak prince, th' eternal cause
Prone for his fav'rites to reverse his laws?

    Shall burning Ætna, if a sage requires,
Forget to thunder, and recall her fires?
On air or sea new motions be imprest,
On blameless Bethel! to relieve thy breast?
When the loose mountain trembles from on high,
Shall gravitation cease, if you go by?
Or some old temple, nodding to its fall,
For Chartres' head reserve the hanging wall?

    But still this world (so fitted for the knave)
Contents us not. A better shall we have?
A kingdom of the just then let it be:
But first consider how those just agree.
The good must merit God's peculiar care;
But who, but God, can tell us who they are?
One thinks on Calvin heav'n's own spirit fell;
Another deems him instrument of hell;
If Calvin feel heav'n's blessing, or its rod,
This cries there is, and that, there is no God.
What shocks one part will edify the rest,
Nor with one system can they all be blest.

ALEXANDER POPE

The very best will variously incline,
And what rewards your virtue, punish mine.
Whatever is, is right. This world, 'tis true,
Was made for Cæsar—but for Titus too;
And which more blest, who chain'd his country, say,
Or he whose virtue sigh'd to lose a day?
  "But sometimes virtue starves, while vice is fed."
What then? is the reward of virtue bread?
That vice may merit, 'tis the price of toil;
The knave deserves it, when he tills the soil,
The knave deserves it, when he tempts the main,
Where folly fights for kings, or dives for gain.
The good man may be weak, be indolent;
Nor is his claim to plenty, but content.
But grant him riches, your demand is o'er?
"No, shall the good want health, the good want pow'r?"
Add health and pow'r, and ev'ry earthly thing,
"Why bounded pow'r? why private? why no king?
Nay, why external for internal giv'n?
Why is not man a God, and earth a heav'n?"
Who ask and reason thus, will scarce conceive
God gives enough, while he has more to give:
Immense the pow'r, immense were the demand;
Say, at what part of nature will they stand?

  What nothing earthly gives, or can destroy,
The soul's calm sun-shine, and the heart-felt joy,
Is virtue's prize: a better would you fix?
Then give humility a coach and six,
Justice a conq'ror's sword, or truth a gown,
Or public spirit its great cure, a crown.
Weak, foolish man! will heav'n reward us there
With the same trash mad mortals wish for here?
The boy and man an individual makes,
Yet sigh'st thou now for apples and for cakes?
Go, like the Indian, in another life
Expect thy dog, thy bottle, and thy wife,
As well as dream such trifles are assign'd,
As toys and empires, for a god-like mind.
Rewards, that either would to virtue bring
No joy, or be destructive of the thing:
How oft by these at sixty are undone
The virtues of a saint at twenty-one!
  To whom can riches give repute, or trust,
Content, or pleasure, but the good and just?
Judges and senates have been bought for gold,

Esteem and love were never to be sold.
Oh fool! to think God hates the worthy mind,
The lover and the love of human-kind,
Whose life is healthful, and whose conscience clear,
Because he wants a thousand pounds a year.

Honour and shame from no condition rise;
Act well your part, there all the honour lies.
Fortune in men has some small diff'rence made,
One flaunts in rags, one flutters in brocade;
The cobler apron'd, and the parson gown'd,
The frier hooded, and the monarch crown'd.
"What differ more (you cry) than crown and cowl!"
I'll tell you, friend! a wise man and a fool.
You'll find, if once the monarch acts the monk,
Or, cobler-like, the parson will be drunk,
Worth makes the man, and want of it the fellow;
The rest is all but leather or prunella.

Stuck o'er with titles and hung round with strings,
That thou may'st be by kings, or whores of kings.
Boast the pure blood of an illustrious race,
In quiet flow from Lucrece to Lucrece:
But by your fathers' worth if your's you rate,
Count me those only who were good and great.
Go! if your ancient, but ignoble blood
Has crept thro' scoundrels ever since the flood,
Go! and pretend your family is young;
Nor own your fathers have been fools so long.
What can ennoble sots, or slaves, or cowards?
Alas! not all the blood of all the Howards.

Look next on greatness; say where greatness lies.
"Where, but among the heroes and the wise?"
Heroes are much the same, the point's agreed,
From Macedonia's madman to the Swede;
The whole strange purpose of their lives, to find
Or make, an enemy of all mankind!
Not one looks backward, onward still he goes,
Yet ne'er looks forward further than his nose.
No less alike the politic and wise;
All sly slow things, with circumspective eyes:
Men in their loose unguarded hours they take,
Not that themselves are wise, but others weak.
But grant that those can conquer, these can cheat;
'Tis phrase absurd to call a villain great:
Who wickedly is wise, or madly brave,
Is but the more a fool, the more a knave.

ALEXANDER POPE

Who noble ends by noble means obtains,
Or failing, smiles in exile or in chains,
Like good Aurelius let him reign, or bleed
Like Socrates, that man is great indeed.

What 's fame? a fancy'd life in others' breath,
A thing beyond us, ev'n before our death.
Just what you hear, you have, and what's unknown
The same (my Lord) if Tully's, or your own.
All that we feel of it begins and ends
In the small circle of our foes or friends;
To all beside as much an empty shade
An Eugene living, as a Cæsar dead;
Alike or when, or where they shone, or shine,
Or on the Rubicon, or on the Rhine.
A wit 's a feather, and a chief a rod;
An honest man's the noblest work of God.
Fame but from death a villain's name can save,
As justice tears his body from the grave;
When what t' oblivion better were resign'd,
Is hung on high, to poison half mankind.
All fame is foreign, but of true desert;
Plays round the head, but comes not to the heart:
One self approving hour whole years out-weighs
Of stupid starers, and of loud huzzas;
And more true joy Marcellus exil'd feels,
Than Cæsar with a senate at his heels.

In parts superior what advantage lies?
Tell (for you can) what is it to be wise?
'Tis but to know how little can be known;
To see all others' faults, and feel our own:
Condemn'd in bus'ness or in arts to drudge,
Without a second, or without a judge:
Truths would you teach, or save a sinking land?
All fear, none aid you, and few understand.
Painful preëminence! yourself to view
Above life's weakness, and its comforts too.

Bring then these blessings to a strict account;
Make fair deductions; see to what they 'mount:
How much of other each is sure to cost;
How each for other oft is wholly lost;
How inconsistent greater goods with these;
Think, and if still the things thy envy call,
Say, would'st thou be the man to whom they fall?
To sigh for ribbands if thou art so silly,
Mark how they grace Lord Umbra, or Sir Billy.
XI

Is yellow dirt the passion of thy life;
Look but on Gripus, or on Gripus' wife,
If parts allure thee, think how Bacon shin'd,
The wisest, brightest, meanest of mankind:
Or ravish'd with the whistling of a name,
See Cromwell, damn'd to everlasting fame!
If all, united, thy ambition call,
From ancient story learn to scorn them all.
There, in the rich, the honour'd, fam'd and great,
See the false scale of happiness complete!
In hearts of kings, or arms of queens who lay,
How happy those to ruin, these betray.
Mark by what wretched steps their glory grows,
From dirt and sea-weed as proud Venice rose;
In each how guilt and greatness equal ran,
And all that rais'd the hero, sunk the man:
Now Europe's laurels on their brows behold,
But stain'd with blood, or ill exchang'd for gold:
Then see them broke with toils, or sunk in ease,
Or infamous for plunder'd provinces.
Oh wealth ill-fated! which no act of fame
E'er taught to shine, or santif'yd from shame!
What greater bliss attends their close of life?
Some greedy minion, or imperious wife,
The trophy'd arches, story'd halls invade,
And haunt their slumbers in the pompous shade.
Alas! not dazzled with their noon-tide ray,
Compute the morn and ev'ning to the day;
The whole amount of that enormous fame,
A tale, that blends their glory with their shame!
  Know then this truth, enough for man to know,
Virtue alone is happiness below.
The only point where human bliss stands still,
And tastes the good without the fall to ill;
Where only merit constant pay receives,
Is blest in what it takes, and what it gives;
The joy unequal'd, if its end it gain,
And if it lose, attended with no pain:
Without satiety, tho e'er so bless'd,
And but more relish'd as the more distress'd:
The broadest mirth unfeeling folly wears,
Less pleasing far than virtue's very tears;
Good, from each object, from each place acquir'd,
For ever exercis'd, yet never tir'd;
Never elated, while one man's oppress'd;

Never dejected, while another's bless'd;
And where no wants, no wishes can remain,
Since but to wish more virtue, is to gain.
  See the sole bliss heav'n could on all bestow!
Which who but feels can taste, but thinks can know:
Yet poor with fortune, and with learning blind,
The bad must miss, the good, untaught, will find;
Slave to no sect, who takes no private road,
But looks through nature up to nature's God:
Pursues that chain which links th' immense design,
Joins heav'n and earth, and mortal and divine;
Sees, that no being any bliss can know,
But touches some above, and some below;
Learns, from this union of the rising whole,
The first, last purpose of the human soul;
And knows where faith, law, morals, all began,
All end, in love of God, and love of man.
For him alone, hope leads from goal to goal,
And opens still, and opens on his soul;
'Till lengthen'd on to faith, and unconfin'd,
It pours the bliss that fills up all the mind.
He sees, why nature plants in man alone
Hope of known bliss, and faith in bliss unknown:
(Nature, whose dictates to no other kind
Are giv'n in vain, but what they seek they find)
Wise is her present; she connects in this
His greatest virtue with his greatest bliss;
At once his own bright prospect to be blest,
And strongest motive to assist the rest.
  Self-love thus push'd to social, to divine,
Gives thee to make thy neighbour's blessing thine.
Is this too little for the boundless heart?
Extend it, let thy enemies have part:
Grasp the whole worlds of reason, life, and sense,
In one close system of benevolence:
Happier as kinder, in whate'er degree,
And height of bliss but height of charity.
  God loves from whole to parts: but human soul
Must rise from individual to the whole.
Self-love but serves the virtuous mind to wake,
As the small pebble stirs the peaceful lake;
The centre mov'd, a circle strait succeeds,
Another still, and still another spreads;
Friend, parent, neighbour, first it will embrace;
His country next; and next all human race;

Wide and more wide, th' o'erflowings of the mind
Take ev'ry creature in, of ev'ry kind;
Earth smiles around, with boundless bounty blest,
And heav'n beholds its image in his breast.

  Come then, my friend, my genius, come along;
Oh master of the poet, and the song!
And while the muse now stoops, or now ascends,
To man's low passions, or their glorious ends,
Teach me, like thee, in various nature wise,
To fall with dignity, with temper rise;
Form'd by thy converse, happily to steer
From grave to gay, from lively to severe;
Correct with spirit, eloquent with ease,
Intent to reason, or polite to please.
Oh! while along the stream of time thy name
Expanded flies, and gathers all its fame;
Say, shall my little bark attendant sail,
Pursue the triumph, and partake the gale?
When statesmen, heroes, kings, in dust repose,
Whose sons shall blush their fathers were thy foes,
Shall then this verse to future age pretend
Thou wert my guide, philosopher, and friend?
That, urg'd by thee, I turn'd the tuneful art
From sounds to things, from fancy to the heart;
For wit's false mirror held up nature's light;
Shew'd erring pride, whatever is, is right;
That reason, passion, answer one great aim;
That true self-love and social are the same;
That virtue only makes our bliss below;
And all our knowledge is, ourselves to know.

* * *

THOMAS GRAY

ELEGY

88

THE curfew tolls the knell of parting day,
  The lowing herd winds slowly o'er the lea,
The ploughman homeward plods his weary way,
  And leaves the world to darkness and to me.

Now fades the glimmering landscape on the sight,
  And all the air a solemn stillness holds,

THOMAS GRAY

Save where the beetle wheels his droning flight,
  And drowsy tinklings lull the distant folds:

Save that from yonder ivy-mantled tower
  The moping owl does to the moon complain
Of such as, wandering near her secret bower,
  Molest her ancient solitary reign.

Beneath those rugged elms, that yew-tree's shade
  Where heaves the turf in many a mouldering heap,
Each in his narrow cell for ever laid,
  The rude Forefathers of the hamlet sleep.

The breezy call of incense-breathing morn,
  The swallow twittering from the straw-built shed,
The cock's shrill clarion, or the echoing horn,
  No more shall rouse them from their lowly bed.

For them no more the blazing hearth shall burn
  Or busy housewife ply her evening care:
No children run to lisp their sire's return,
  Or climb his knees the envied kiss to share.

Oft did the harvest to their sickle yield,
  Their furrow oft the stubborn glebe has broke;
How jocund did they drive their team afield!
  How bow'd the woods beneath their sturdy stroke!

Let not Ambition mock their useful toil,
  Their homely joys, and destiny obscure;
Nor Grandeur hear with a disdainful smile
  The short and simple annals of the Poor.

The boast of heraldry, the pomp of power,
  And all that beauty, all that wealth e'er gave
Awaits alike th' inevitable hour:—
  The paths of glory lead but to the grave.

Nor you, ye Proud, impute to these the fault
  If Memory o'er their tomb no trophies raise,
Where through the long-drawn aisle and fretted vault
  The pealing anthem swells the note of praise.

Can storied urn or animated bust
  Back to its mansion call the fleeting breath?

Can Honour's voice provoke the silent dust,
  Or Flattery soothe the dull cold ear of Death?

Perhaps in this neglected spot is laid
  Some heart once pregnant with celestial fire;
Hands, that the rod of empire might have sway'd
  Or waked to ecstasy the living lyre:

But Knowledge to their eyes her ample page,
  Rich with the spoils of time, did ne'er unroll;
Chill Penury repress'd their noble rage,
  And froze the genial current of the soul.

Full many a gem of purest ray serene
  The dark unfathom'd caves of ocean bear:
Full many a flower is born to blush unseen,
  And waste its sweetness on the desert air.

Some village-Hampden, that with dauntless breast
  The little tyrant of his fields withstood,
Some mute inglorious Milton here may rest,
  Some Cromwell, guiltless of his country's blood.

Th' applause of listening senates to command,
  The threats of pain and ruin to despise,
To scatter plenty o'er a smiling land,
  And read their history in a nation's eyes

Their lot forbad: nor circumscribed alone
  Their growing virtues, but their crimes confined;
Forbad to wade through slaughter to a throne,
  And shut the gates of mercy on mankind;

The struggling pangs of conscious truth to hide,
  To quench the blushes of ingenuous shame,
Or heap the shrine of Luxury and Pride
  With incense kindled at the Muse's flame.

Far from the madding crowd's ignoble strife
  Their sober wishes never learn'd to stray;
Along the cool sequester'd vale of life
  They kept the noiseless tenour of their way.

Yet e'en these bones from insult to protect
  Some frail memorial still erected nigh,

THOMAS GRAY

With uncouth rhymes and shapeless sculpture deck'd,
    Implores the passing tribute of a sigh.

Their name, their years, spelt by th' unletter'd Muse,
    The place of fame and elegy supply:
And many a holy text around she strews,
    That teach the rustic moralist to die.

For who, to dumb forgetfulness a prey,
    This pleasing anxious being e'er resign'd,
Left the warm precincts of the cheerful day,
    Nor cast one longing lingering look behind?

On some fond breast the parting soul relies,
    Some pious drops the closing eye requires;
E'en from the tomb the voice of Nature cries,
    E'en in our ashes live their wonted fires.

For thee, who, mindful of th' unhonour'd dead,
    Dost in these lines their artless tale relate;
If chance, by lonely Contemplation led,
    Some kindred spirit shall enquire thy fate,—

Haply some hoary-headed swain may say,
    Oft have we seen him at the peep of dawn
Brushing with hasty steps the dews away,
    To meet the sun upon the upland lawn;

There at the foot of yonder nodding beech
    That wreathes its old fantastic roots so high,
His listless length at noon-tide would he stretch,
    And pore upon the brook that babbles by.

Hard by yon wood, now smiling as in scorn,
    Muttering his wayward fancies he would rove;
Now drooping, woeful-wan, like one forlorn,
    Or crazed with care, or cross'd in hopeless love.

One morn I miss'd him on the custom'd hill,
    Along the heath, and near his favourite tree;
Another came; nor yet beside the rill,
    Nor up the lawn, nor at the wood was he;

The next with dirges due in sad array
    Slow through the church-way path we saw him borne,

Approach and read (for thou canst read) the lay
　　Graved on the stone beneath yon agèd thorn.

The Epitaph

Here rests his head upon the lap of Earth
　　A youth, to Fortune and to Fame unknown;
Fair Science frown'd not on his humble birth
　　And Melancholy mark'd him for her own.

Large was his bounty, and his soul sincere;
　　Heaven did a recompense as largely send:
He gave to Mis'ry all he had, a tear,
　　He gain'd from Heaven ('twas all he wish'd) a friend.

No farther seek his merits to disclose,
　　Or draw his frailties from their dread abode,
(There they alike in trembling hope repose,)
　　The bosom of his Father and his God.

HYMN TO ADVERSITY

DAUGHTER of Jove, relentless power,
　　Thou tamer of the human breast,
Whose iron scourge and torturing hour
　　The bad affright, afflict the best!
Bound in thy adamantine chain
The proud are taught to taste of pain,
And purple tyrants vainly groan
With pangs unfelt before, unpitied and alone.

When first thy Sire to send on earth
　　Virtue, his darling child, design'd,
To thee he gave the heavenly birth
　　And bade to form her infant mind.
Stern, rugged Nurse! thy rigid lore
With patience many a year she bore;
What sorrow was, thou bad'st her know,
And from her own she learn'd to melt at others' woe.

Scared at thy frown terrific, fly
　　Self-pleasing Folly's idle brood,
Wild Laughter, noise, and thoughtless Joy,
　　And leave us leisure to be good,
Light they disperse, and with them go

The summer Friend, the flattering Foe;
  By vain Prosperity received,
To her they vow their truth, and are again believed.

Wisdom in sable garb array'd
  Immersed in rapturous thought profound,
And Melancholy, silent maid,
  With leaden eye, that loves the ground,
Still on thy solemn steps attend:
Warm Charity, the general friend,
With Justice, to herself severe,
And Pity dropping soft the sadly-pleasing tear.

O! gently on thy suppliant's head
  Dread Goddess, lay thy chastening hand!
Not in thy Gorgon terrors clad,
  Nor circled with the vengeful band
(As by the impious thou art seen)
With thundering voice, and threatening mien,
With screaming Horror's funeral cry,
Despair, and fell Disease, and ghastly Poverty;—

Thy form benign, O Goddess, wear,
  Thy milder influence impart,
Thy philosophic train be there
  To soften, not to wound my heart.
The generous spark extinct revive,
Teach me to love and to forgive
Exact my own defects to scan,
What others are to feel, and know myself a Man.

THE BARD

Pindaric Ode

"RUIN seize thee, ruthless King!
Confusion on thy banners wait!
Tho' fann'd by Conquest's crimson wing
  They mock the air with idle state.
Helm, nor hauberk's twisted mail
Nor e'en thy virtues, tyrant, shall avail
To save thy secret soul from nightly fears,
From Cambria's curse, from Cambria's tears!"
—Such were the sounds that o'er the crested pride
  Of the first Edward scatter'd wild dismay,

As down the steep of Snowdon's shaggy side
  He wound with toilsome march his long array:
Stout Glo'ster stood aghast in speechless trance;
"To arms!" cried Mortimer, and couch'd his quivering lance.

On a rock, whose haughty brow
Frowns o'er old Conway's foaming flood,
  Robed in the sable garb of woe
With haggard eyes the Poet stood;
(Loose his beard and hoary hair
Stream'd like a meteor to the troubled air)
And with a master's hand and prophet's fire
Struck the deep sorrows of his lyre:
  "Hark, how each giant-oak and desert-cave
Sighs to the torrent's awful voice beneath!
O'er thee, O King! their hundred arms they wave
  Revenge on thee in hoarser murmurs breathe;
Vocal no more, since Cambria's fatal day,
To high-born Hoel's harp, or soft Llewellyn's lay.

"Cold is Cadwallo's tongue,
  That hush'd the stormy main:
Brave Urien sleeps upon his craggy bed:
  Mountains, ye mourn in vain
  Modred, whose magic song
Made huge Plinlimmon bow his cloud-topt head.
  On dreary Arvon's shore they lie
Smear'd with gore and ghastly pale:
Far, far aloof the affrighted ravens sail;
  The famish'd eagle screams, and passes by.
Dear lost companions of my tuneful art,
  Dear as the light that visits these sad eyes,
Dear as the ruddy drops that warm my heart,
  Ye died amidst your dying country's cries—
No more I weep; They do not sleep;
  On yonder cliffs, a griesly band,
I see them sit; They linger yet,
  Avengers of their native land:
With me in dreadful harmony they join,
And weave with bloody hands the tissue of thy line."

Weave the warp and weave the woof
  The winding sheet of Edward's race:
Give ample room and verge enough

THOMAS GRAY

   The characters of hell to trace.
Mark the year, and mark the night,
When Severn shall re-echo with affright
The shrieks of death thro' Berkley's roof that ring,
Shrieks of an agonizing king!
   She-wolf of France, with unrelenting fangs
That tear'st the bowels of thy mangled mate,
   From thee be born, who o'er thy country hangs
The scourge of Heaven! What terrors round him wait
Amazement in his van, with Flight combined,
And Sorrow's faded form, and Solitude behind.

"Mighty victor, mighty lord,
   Low on his funeral couch he lies!
No pitying heart, no eye, afford
   A tear to grace his obsequies.
Is the sable warrior fled?
Thy son is gone. He rests among the dead.
The swarm that in thy noon-tide beam were born?
—Gone to salute the rising morn.
Fair laughs the Morn, and soft the zephyr blows,
   While proudly riding o'er the azure realm
In gallant trim the gilded Vessel goes:
   Youth on the prow, and Pleasure at the helm:
Regardless of the sweeping Whirlwind's sway,
That hush'd in grim repose expects his evening prey.

"Fill high the sparkling bowl,
The rich repast prepare;
   Reft of a crown, he yet may share the feast:
Close by the regal chair
   Fell Thirst and Famine scowl
   A baleful smile upon their baffled guest.
Heard ye the din of battle bray,
   Lance to lance, and horse to horse?
   Long years of havock urge their destined course,
And thro' the kindred squadrons mow their way.
   Ye towers of Julius, London's lasting shame,
With many a foul and midnight murder fed,
   Revere his Consort's faith, his Father's fame,
And spare the meek usurper's holy head!
Above, below, the rose of snow,
   Twined with her blushing foe, we spread:
The bristled boar in infant-gore
   Wallows beneath the thorny shade.

Now, brothers, bending o'er the accursèd loom,
Stamp we our vengeance deep, and ratify his doom.

"Edward, lo! to sudden fate
  (Weave we the woof; The thread is spun;)
Half of thy heart we consecrate.
  (The web is wove; The work is done.)
—Stay, oh stay! nor thus forlorn
Leave me unbless'd, unpitied, here to mourn:
In yon bright track that fires the western skies
They melt, they vanish from my eyes.
But O! what solemn scenes on Snowdon's height
  Descending slow their glittering skirts unroll?
Visions of glory, spare my aching sight,
Ye unborn ages, crowd not on my soul!
No more our long-lost Arthur we bewail:—
All hail, ye genuine kings! Britannia's issue, hail!

"Girt with many a baron bold
Sublime their starry fronts they rear;
And gorgeous dames, and statesmen old
In bearded majesty, appear.
In the midst a form divine!
Her eye proclaims her of the Briton-Line:
Her lion-port, her awe-commanding face
Attemper'd sweet to virgin-grace.
What strings symphonious tremble in the air,
  What strains of vocal transport round her play?
Hear from the grave, great Taliessin, hear;
  They breathe a soul to animate thy clay.
Bright Rapture calls, and soaring as she sings,
Waves in the eye of Heaven her many-colour'd wings.

"The verse adorn again
  Fierce War, and faithful Love,
And Truth severe, by fairy Fiction drest.
  In buskin'd measures move
Pale Grief, and pleasing Pain,
With Horror, tyrant of the throbbing breast.
A voice as of the cherub-choir
  Gales from blooming Eden bear,
  And distant warblings lessen on my ear
That lost in long futurity expire.
Fond impious man, think'st thou yon sanguine cloud
  Raised by thy breath, has quench'd the orb of day?

THOMAS GRAY

To-morrow he repairs the golden flood
   And warms the nations with redoubled ray.
Enough for me: with joy I see
   The different doom our fates assign:
Be thine Despair and sceptred Care,
   To triumph and to die are mine."
—He spoke, and headlong from the mountain's height
Deep in the roaring tide he plunged to endless night.

ODE ON THE PLEASURE ARISING FROM VICISSITUDE

Now the golden Morn aloft
   Waves her dew-bespangled wing,
With vermeil cheek and whisper soft
   She woos the tardy Spring:
Till April starts, and calls around,
The sleeping fragrance from the ground,
And lightly o'er the living scene
Scatters his freshest, tenderest green.

New-born flocks, in rustic dance,
   Frisking ply their feeble feet;
Forgetful of their wintry trance
   The birds his presence greet:
But chief, the sky-lark warbles high
His trembling thrilling ectasy;
And lessening from the dazzled sight,
Melts into air and liquid light.

Yesterday the sullen year
   Saw the snowy whirlwind fly;
Mute was the music of the air,
   The herd stood drooping by;
Their raptures now that wildly flow
No yesterday nor morrow know;
'Tis Man alone that joy descries
With forward and reverted eyes.

Smiles on past Misfortune's brow
   Soft Reflection's hand can trace,
And o'er the cheek of Sorrow throw
   A melancholy grace;
While Hope prolongs our happier hour,
Or deepest shades, that dimly lour

And blacken round our weary way,
Gilds with a gleam of distant day.

Still, where rosy Pleasure leads,
  See a kindred Grief pursue;
Behind the steps that Misery treads
  Approaching Comfort view:
The hues of bliss more brightly glow
Chastised by sabler tints of woe,
And blended form, with artful strife,
The strength and harmony of life.

See the wretch that long has tost
  On the thorny bed of pain,
At length repair his vigour lost
  And breathe and walk again:
The meanest floweret of the vale,
The simplest note that swells the gale,
The common sun, the air, the skies,
To him are opening Paradise.

* * *

WILLIAM COLLINS

FIDELE

92

To FAIR Fidele's grassy tomb
  Soft maids and village hinds shall bring
Each opening sweet of earliest bloom,
  And rifle all the breathing Spring.

No wailing ghost shall dare appear
  To vex with shrieks this quiet grove;
But shepherd lads assemble here,
  And melting virgins own their love.

No wither'd witch shall here be seen,
  No goblins lead their nightly crew;
The female fays shall haunt the green,
  And dress thy grave with pearly dew.

The redbreast oft at evening hours
  Shall kindly lend his little aid,

With hoary moss, and gather'd flowers,
  To deck the ground where thou art laid.

When howling winds, and beating rain,
  In tempest shake thy sylvan cell;
Or 'midst the chase, on every plain,
  The tender thought on thee shall dwell;

Each lonely scene shall thee restore,
  For thee the tear be duly shed;
Beloved, till life can charm no more;
  And mourn'd, till Pity's self be dead.

THE PASSIONS

An Ode for Music

When Music, heavenly maid, was young,
While yet in early Greece she sung,
The Passions oft, to hear her shell,
Throng'd around her magic cell
Exulting, trembling, raging, fainting,
Possest beyond the Muse's painting,
By turns they felt the glowing mind
Disturb'd, delighted, raised, defined:
'Till once, 'tis said, when all were fired,
Fill'd with fury, rapt, inspired,
From the supporting myrtles round
They snatch'd her instruments of sound,
And, as they oft had heard apart
Sweet lessons of her forceful art,
Each, for Madness ruled the hour,
Would prove his own expressive power.

* * *

GEORGE SEWELL

THE DYING MAN IN HIS GARDEN

Why, Damon, with the forward day
Dost thou thy little spot survey,
From tree to tree, with doubtful cheer,
Pursue the progress of the year,

What winds arise, what rains descend,
When thou before that year shalt end?

What do thy noontide walks avail,
To clear the leaf, and pick the snail,
Then wantonly to death decree
An insect usefuller than thee?
Thou and the worm are brother-kind,
As lowly, as earthy, and as blind.

Vain wretch! canst thou expect to see
The downy peach make court to thee?
Or that thy sense shall ever meet
The bean-flower's deep-embosom'd sweet
Exhaling with an evening blast?
Thy evenings then will all be past!

Thy narrow pride, thy fancied green
(For vanity's in little seen)
All must be left when Death appears,
In spite of wishes, groans, and tears;
Not any of all thy plants that grow
But Rosemary will with thee go.

* * *

JOHN LOGAN

THE BRAES OF YARROW

Thy braes were bonny, Yarrow stream,
When first on them I met my lover;
Thy braes how dreary, Yarrow stream,
When now thy waves his body cover!
For ever now, O Yarrow stream!
Thou art to me a stream of sorrow;
For never on thy banks shall I
Behold my Love, the flower of Yarrow.

He promised me a milk-white steed
To bear me to his father's bowers;
He promised me a little page
To squire me to his father's towers;
He promised me a wedding-ring,—

The wedding-day was fix'd to-morrow;—
Now he is wedded to his grave,
Alas, his watery grave, in Yarrow!

Sweet were his words when last we met;
My passion I as freely told him;
Clasp'd in his arms, I little thought
That I should never more behold him!
Scarce was he gone, I saw his ghost;
It vanish'd with a shriek of sorrow;
Thrice did the water-wraith ascend,
And gave a doleful groan thro' Yarrow.

His mother from the window look'd
With all the longing of a mother;
His little sister weeping walk'd
The green-wood path to meet her brother;
They sought him east, they sought him west,
They sought him all the forest thorough;
They only saw the cloud of night,
They only heard the roar of Yarrow.

No longer from thy window look—
Thou hast no son, thou tender mother!
No longer walk, thou lovely maid;
Alas, thou hast no more a brother!
No longer seek him east or west
And search no more the forest thorough;
For, wandering in the night so dark,
He fell a lifeless corpse in Yarrow.

The tear shall never leave my cheek,
No other youth shall be my marrow—
I'll seek thy body in the stream,
And then with thee I'll sleep in Yarrow.
—The tear did never leave her cheek,
No other youth became her marrow;
She found his body in the stream,
And now with him she sleeps in Yarrow.

HENRY FIELDING

A HUNTING SONG

96

The dusky night rides down the sky,
   And ushers in the morning;
The hounds all join in glorious cry,
   The huntsman winds his horn,
     And a-hunting we will go.

The wife around her husband throws
   Her arms, and begs his stay;
"My dear, it rains, and hails, and snows,
   You will not hunt to-day?"
     But a-hunting we will go.

"A brushing fox in yonder wood
   Secure to find we seek:
For why? I carried, sound and good,
   A cartload there last week,
     And a-hunting we will go."

Away he goes, he flies the rout,
   Their steeds all spur and switch,
Some are thrown in, and some thrown out,
   And some thrown in the ditch;
     But a-hunting we will go.

At length his strength to faintness worn,
   Poor Reynard ceases flight;
Then, hungry, homeward we return,
   To feast away the night.
     Then a-drinking we will go.

SAMUEL JOHNSON

ON THE DEATH OF DR. ROBERT LEVET

97.

As on we toil from day to day,
CONDEMNED to Hope's delusive mine,
By sudden blasts or slow decline
  Our social comforts drop away.

Well tried through many a varying year,
  See Levet to the grave descend,
Officious, innocent, sincere,
  Of every friendless name the friend.

Yet still he fills affection's eye,
  Obscurely wise and coarsely kind;
Nor, letter'd arrogance, deny
  Thy praise to merit unrefined.

When fainting nature called for aid,
  And hovering death prepared the blow,
His vigorous remedy display'd
  The power of art without the show.

In misery's darkest cavern known,
  His useful care was ever nigh,
Where hopeless anguish pour'd his groan,
  And lonely want retired to die

No summons mock'd by chill delay,
  No petty gain disdain'd by pride;
The modest wants of every day
  The toil of every day supplied.

His virtues walked their narrow round,
  Nor made a pause, nor left a void;
And sure the eternal Master found
  The single talent well employ'd.

The busy day, the peaceful night,
  Unfelt, uncounted, glided by;
His frame was firm—his powers were bright,
  Though now his eightieth year was nigh.

Then with no fiery throbbing pain,
    No cold gradations of decay,
Death broke at once the vital chain,
    And freed his soul the nearest way.

* * *

OLIVER GOLDSMITH

THE DESERTED VILLAGE

98

Sweet Auburn! loveliest village of the plain,
Where health and plenty cheer'd the labouring swain,
Where smiling Spring its earliest visit paid,
And parting Summer's lingering blooms delay'd;
Dear lovely bowers of innocence and ease,
Seats of my youth, when every sport could please:
How often have I loiter'd o'er thy green,
Where humble happiness endear'd each scene!
How often have I paused on every charm,
The shelter'd cot, the cultivated farm,
The never-failing brook, the busy mill,
The decent church that topp'd the neighbouring hill;
The hawthorn bush, with seats beneath the shade,
For talking age and whispering lovers made!
How often have I bless'd the coming day,
When toil, remitting, lent its turn to play,
And all the village train, from labour free,
Led up their sports beneath the spreading tree!
While many a pastime circled in the shade,
The young contending as the old survey'd;
And many a gambol frolick'd o'er the ground,
And sleights of art and feats of strength went round;
And still, as each repeated pleasure tired,
Succeeding sports the mirthful band inspired—
The dancing pair that simply sought renown,
By holding out to tire each other down;
The swain mistrustless of his smutted face,
While secret laughter titter'd round the place;
The bashful virgin's side-long looks of love;
The matron's glance, that would those looks reprove.

These were thy charms, sweet village! sports like these,
With sweet succession, taught e'en toil to please;
These round thy bowers their cheerful influence shed;
These were thy charms—but all these charms are fled.

Sweet smiling village, loveliest of the lawn,
Thy sports are fled, and all thy charms withdrawn;
Amidst thy bowers thy tyrant's hand is seen,
And Desolation saddens all thy green:
One only master grasps the whole domain,
And half a tillage stints thy smiling plain.
No more thy glassy brook reflects the day,
But, choked with sedges, works its weedy way;
Along thy glades, a solitary guest,
The hollow-sounding bittern guards its nest;
Amidst thy desert walks the lapwing flies,
And tires their echoes with unvaried cries:
Sunk are thy bowers in shapeless ruin all,
And the long grass o'ertops the mouldering wall;
And, trembling, shrinking from the spoiler's hand,
Far, far away thy children leave the land.

Ill fares the land, to hastening ills a prey,
Where wealth accumulates, and men decay.
Princes and lords may flourish, or may fade;
A breath can make them, as a breath has made:
But a bold peasantry, their country's pride,
When once destroy'd, can never be supplied.

A time there was, ere England's griefs began,
When every rood of ground maintain'd its man;
For him light Labour spread her wholesome store,
Just gave what life required, but gave no more:
His best companions, Innocence and Health;
And his best riches, ignorance of wealth.

But times are alter'd; Trade's unfeeling train
Usurp the land, and dispossess the swain;
Along the lawn, where scatter'd hamlets rose,
Unwieldy wealth and cumbrous pomp repose;
And every want to luxury allied,
And every pang that folly pays to pride.
Those gentle hours that plenty bade to bloom,
Those calm desires that ask'd but little room,
Those healthful sports that graced the peaceful scene,
Lived in each look, and brighten'd all the green—
These, far departing, seek a kinder shore,
And rural mirth and manners are no more.

Sweet Auburn! parent of the blissful hour,

Thy glades forlorn confess the tyrant's power.
Here, as I take my solitary rounds,
Amidst thy tangling walks and ruin'd grounds,
And, many a year elapsed, return to view
Where once the cottage stood, the hawthorn grew—
Remembrance wakes with all her busy train,
Swells at my breast, and turns the past to pain.

In all my wanderings through this world of care,
In all my griefs—and God has given my share,—
I still had hopes, my latest hours to crown,
Amidst these humble bowers to lay me down;
To husband out life's taper at the close,
And keep the flame from wasting, by repose:
I still had hopes, for pride attends us still,
Amidst the swains to show my book-learn'd skill,
Around my fire an evening group to draw,
And tell of all I felt, and all I saw;
And, as a hare, whom hounds and horns pursue,
Pants to the place from whence at first she flew,
I still had hopes, my long vexations past,
Here to return—and die at home at last.

O blest retirement, friend to life's decline,
Retreat from care, that never must be mine,
How blest is he who crowns, in shades like these,
A youth of labour with an age of ease;
Who quits a world where strong temptations try,
And, since 'tis hard to combat, learns to fly!
For him no wretches, born to work and weep,
Explore the mine, or tempt the dangerous deep;
No surly porter stands, in guilty state,
To spurn imploring famine from the gate;
But on he moves to meet his latter end,
Angels around befriending virtue's friend;
Sinks to the grave with unperceived decay,
While resignation gently slopes the way;
And, all his prospects brightening to the last,
His heaven commences ere the world be past!

Sweet was the sound, when oft, at evening's close,
Up yonder hill the village murmur rose.
There, as I pass'd with careless steps and slow,
The mingled notes came soften'd from below;
The swain responsive as the milk-maid sung,
The sober herd that low'd to meet their young,
The noisy geese that gabbled o'er the pool,
The playful children just let loose from school;

The watch-dog's voice that bay'd the whispering wind,
And the loud laugh that spoke the vacant mind;—
These all in sweet confusion sought the shade,
And fill'd each pause the nightingale had made.
But now the sounds of population fail,
No cheerful murmurs fluctuate in the gale,
No busy steps the grass-grown footway tread,
But all the bloomy flush of life is fled—
All but yon widow'd solitary thing,
That feebly bends beside the plashy spring;
She, wretched matron,—forced, in age, for bread,
To strip the brook with mantling cresses spread,
To pick her wintry faggot from the thorn,
To seek her nightly shed, and weep till morn,—
She only left of all the harmless train,
The sad historian of the pensive plain.

    Near yonder copse, where once the garden smiled,
And still where many a garden-flower grows wild,
There, where a few torn shrubs the place disclose,
The village preacher's modest mansion rose.
A man he was to all the country dear,
And passing rich with forty pounds a year.
Remote from towns he ran his godly race,
Nor e'er had changed, nor wish'd to change, his place;
Unskilful he to fawn, or seek for power
By doctrines fashion'd to the varying hour;
Far other aims his heart had learn'd to prize,
More bent to raise the wretched than to rise.
His house was known to all the vagrant train;
He chid their wanderings, but relieved their pain;
The long-remember'd beggar was his guest,
Whose beard descending swept his aged breast;
The ruin'd spendthrift, now no longer proud,
Claim'd kindred there, and had his claims allow'd;
The broken soldier, kindly bid to stay,
Sat by his fire, and talk'd the night away;—
Wept o'er his wounds, or, tales of sorrow done,
Shoulder'd his crutch, and show'd how fields were won.
Pleased with his guests, the good man learn'd to glow,
And quite forgot their vices in their woe;
Careless their merits or their faults to scan,
His pity gave ere charity began.

    Thus to relieve the wretched was his pride,
And even his failings lean'd to virtue's side;
But in his duty prompt at every call,

He watch'd and wept, he pray'd and felt for all:
And, as a bird each fond endearment tries,
To tempt its new-fledged offspring to the skies,
He tried each art, reproved each dull delay,
Allured to brighter worlds, and led the way.

Beside the bed where parting life was laid,
And sorrow, guilt, and pain, by turns dismay'd,
The reverend champion stood. At his control,
Despair and anguish fled the struggling soul;
Comfort came down the trembling wretch to raise,
And his last faltering accents whisper'd praise.

At church, with meek and unaffected grace,
His looks adorn'd the venerable place;
Truth from his lips prevail'd with double sway,
And fools, who came to scoff, remain'd to pray.
The service past, around the pious man
With steady zeal, each honest rustic ran;
E'en children follow'd, with endearing wile,
And pluck'd his gown, to share the good man's smile;
His ready smile a parent's warmth express'd;
Their welfare pleased him, and their cares distress'd;
To them his heart, his love, his griefs were given,
But all his serious thoughts had rest in heaven.
As some tall cliff that lifts its awful form,
Swells from the vale, and midway leaves the storm,
Though round its breast the rolling clouds are spread,
Eternal sunshine settles on its head.

Beside yon straggling fence that skirts the way,
With blossom'd furze unprofitably gay,
There, in his noisy mansion, skill'd to rule,
The village master taught his little school.
A man severe he was, and stern to view;
I knew him well, and every truant knew:
Well had the boding tremblers learn'd to trace
The day's disasters in his morning face;
Full well they laugh'd with counterfeited glee
At all his jokes, for many a joke had he;
Full well the busy whisper, circling round,
Convey'd the dismal tidings when he frown'd.
Yet he was kind, or if severe in aught,
The love he bore to learning was in fault.
The village all declared how much he knew;
'Twas certain he could write, and cipher too;
Lands he could measure, terms and tides presage,
And even the story ran that he could gauge.

OLIVER GOLDSMITH

In arguing, too, the parson own'd his skill,
For even though vanquish'd, he could argue still;
While words of learned length and thundering sound
Amazed the gazing rustics ranged around;
And still they gazed, and still the wonder grew,
That one small head could carry all he knew.
But past is all his fame;—the very spot
Where many a time he triumph'd, is forgot.

   Near yonder thorn, that lifts its head on high,
Where once the sign-post caught the passing eye,
Now lies that house where nut-brown draughts inspired,
Where grey-beard mirth and smiling toil retired,
Where village statesmen talk'd with looks profound,
And news much older than their ale went round.
Imagination fondly stoops to trace
The parlour splendours of that festive place;
The whitewash'd wall, the nicely-sanded floor,
The varnish'd clock that click'd behind the door,
The chest, contrived a double debt to pay,
A bed by night, a chest of drawers by day,
The pictures placed for ornament and use,
The twelve good rules, the royal game of goose,
The hearth, except when winter chill'd the day,
With aspen boughs, and flowers, and fennel, gay;—
While broken tea-cups, wisely kept for show,
Ranged o'er the chimney, glisten'd in a row.

   Vain transitory splendours; could not all
Reprieve the tottering mansion from its fall?
Obscure it sinks, nor shall it more impart
An hour's importance to the poor man's heart.
Thither no more the peasant shall repair,
To sweet oblivion of his daily care;
No more the farmer's news, the barber's tale,
No more the woodman's ballad shall prevail;
No more the smith his dusky brow shall clear,
Relax his ponderous strength, and lean to hear;
The host himself no longer shall be found
Careful to see the mantling bliss go round;
Nor the coy maid, half willing to be prest,
Shall kiss the cup to pass it to the rest.

   Yes! let the rich deride, the proud disdain,
These simple blessings of the lowly train;
To me more dear, congenial to my heart,
One native charm, than all the gloss of art.
Spontaneous joys, where nature has its play,

The soul adopts, and owns their first-born sway;
Lightly they frolic o'er the vacant mind,
Unenvied, unmolested, unconfined:
But the long pomp, the midnight masquerade,
With all the freaks of wanton wealth array'd,
In these, ere triflers half their wish obtain,
The toiling pleasure sickens into pain;
And, even while Fashion's brightest arts decoy,
The heart distrusting asks, if this be joy?

  Ye friends to truth, ye statesmen, who survey
The rich man's joys increase, the poor's decay,
'Tis yours to judge how wide the limits stand
Between a splendid and a happy land.
Proud swells the tide with loads of freighted ore,
And shouting Folly hails them from her shore;
Hoards, even beyond the miser's wish, abound,
And rich men flock from all the world around.
Yet count our gains. This wealth is but a name
That leaves our useful products still the same.
Not so the loss. The man of wealth and pride
Takes up a space that many poor supplied;
Space for his lake, his park's extended bounds,
Space for his horses, equipage, and hounds;
The robe that wraps his limbs in silken sloth,
Has robb'd the neighbouring fields of half their growth;
His seat, where solitary sports are seen,
Indignant spurns the cottage from the green;
Around the world each needful product flies,
For all the luxuries the world supplies;
While thus the land, adorn'd for pleasure all,
In barren splendour feebly waits the fall.

  As some fair female, unadorn'd and plain,
Secure to please while youth confirms her reign,
Slights every borrow'd charm that dress supplies,
Nor shares with art the triumph of her eyes;
But when those charms are past, for charms are frail,
When time advances, and when lovers fail,
She then shines forth, solicitous to bliss,
In all the glaring impotence of dress;
Thus fares the land by luxury betray'd;
Thus nature's simplest charms at first array'd;—
But verging to decline, its splendours rise,
Its vistas strike, its palaces surprise;
While, scourged by famine, from the smiling land
The mournful peasant leads his humble band;

OLIVER GOLDSMITH

And while he sinks, without one arm to save,
The country blooms—a garden and a grave!
  Where, then, ah! where shall poverty reside,
To 'scape the pressure of contiguous pride?
If to some common's fenceless limits stray'd,
He drives his flock to pick the scanty blade,
Those fenceless fields the sons of wealth divide,
And even the bare-worn common is denied.
  If to the city sped—what waits him there?
To see profusion that he must not share;
To see ten thousand baneful arts combined
To pamper luxury and thin mankind;
To see each joy the sons of pleasure know,
Extorted from his fellow-creature's woe:
Here while the courtier glitters in brocade,
There the pale artist plies the sickly trade;
Here while the proud their long-drawn pomp display,
There the black gibbet glooms beside the way:
The dome where Pleasure holds her midnight reign,
Here, richly deck'd, admits the gorgeous train;
Tumultuous grandeur crowds the blazing square,
The rattling chariots clash, the torches glare.
Sure scenes like these no troubles e'er annoy!
Sure these denote one universal joy!—
Are these thy serious thoughts?—ah, turn thine eyes
Where the poor houseless shivering female lies:
She once, perhaps, in village plenty bless'd,
Has wept at tales of innocence distress'd;
Her modest looks the cottage might adorn,
Sweet as the primrose peeps beneath the thorn:
Now lost to all, her friends, her virtue, fled,
Near her betrayer's door she lays her head,
And, pinch'd with cold, and shrinking from the shower,
With heavy heart deplores that luckless hour,
When idly first, ambitious of the town,
She left her wheel, and robes of country brown.
  Do thine, sweet Auburn, thine, the loveliest train,
Do thy fair tribes participate her pain?
E'en now, perhaps, by cold and hunger led,
At proud men's doors they ask a little bread!
  Ah, no. To distant climes, a dreary scene,
Where half the convex world intrudes between,
Through torrid tracts with fainting steps they go,
Where wild Altama mumurs to their woe.
Far different there from all that charm'd before,

The various terrors of that horrid shore;
Those blazing suns that dart a downward ray,
And fiercely shed intolerable day;
Those matted woods where birds forget to sing,
But silent bats in drowsy clusters cling;
Those poisonous fields, with rank luxuriance crown'd,
Where the dark scorpion gathers death around;
Where at each step the stranger fears to wake
The rattling terrors of the vengeful snake;
Where crouching tigers wait their hapless prey,
And savage men more murderous still than they:
While oft in whirls the mad tornado flies,
Mingling the ravaged landscape with the skies.
For different these from every former scene,
The cooling brook, the grassy-vested green,
The breezy covert of the warbling grove,
That only shelter'd thefts of harmless love.

   Good Heaven! what sorrows gloom'd that parting day,
That call'd them from their native walks away;
When the poor exiles, every pleasure past,
Hung round the bowers, and fondly looked their last,
And took a long farewell, and wish'd in vain,
For seats like these beyond the western main;
And shuddering still to face the distant deep,
Return'd and wept, and still return'd to weep!
The good old sire the first prepared to go
To new-found worlds, and wept for others' woe;
But for himself, in conscious virtue brave,
He only wish'd for worlds beyond the grave.
His lovely daughter, lovelier in her tears,
The fond companion of his helpless years,
Silent went next, neglectful of her charms,
And left a lover's for a father's arms.
With louder plaints the mother spoke her woes,
And bless'd the cot where every pleasure rose,
And kiss'd her thoughtless babes with many a tear,
And clasp'd them close, in sorrow doubly dear;
Whilst her fond husband strove to lend relief
In all the silent manliness of grief.

   O Luxury, thou cursed by Heaven's decree,
How ill exchanged are things like these for thee!
How do thy potions, with insidious joy,
Diffuse their pleasures only to destroy!
Kingdoms by thee to sickly greatness grown,
Boast of a florid vigour not their own;

At every draught more large and large they grow,
A bloated mass of rank unwieldy woe;
Till sapp'd their strength, and every part unsound,
Down, down they sink, and spread a ruin round.
 E'en now the devastation is begun,
And half the business of destruction done;
E"en now, methinks, as pondering here I stand,
I see the rural Virtues leave the land.
Down where yon anchoring vessel spreads the sail
That idly waiting flaps with every gale,
Downward they move, a melancholy band,
Pass from the shore, and darken all the strand;
Contented Toil, and hospitable Care,
And kind connubial Tenderness are there;
And Piety with wishes placed above,
And steady Loyalty, and faithful Love.
 And thou, sweet Poetry, thou loveliest maid,
Still first to fly where sensual joys invade!
Unfit, in these degenerate times of shame,
To catch the heart, or strike for honest fame;
Dear charming nymph, neglected and decried,
My shame in crowds, my solitary pride;
Thou source of all my bliss and all my woe,
That found'st me poor at first, and keep'st me so;
Thou guide by which the nobler arts excel,
Thou nurse of every virtue, fare thee well!
Farewell! and oh! where'er thy voice be tried,
On Torno's cliffs, or Pambamarca's side,
Whether where equinoctial fervours glow,
Or winter wraps the polar world in snow,
Still let thy voice, prevailing over time,
Redress the rigours of th' inclement clime;
Aid slighted Truth with thy persuasive strain;
Teach erring man to spurn the rage of gain;
Teach him that states, of native strength possest,
Though very poor, may still be very blest;
That Trade's proud empire hastes to swift decay,
As ocean sweeps the labour'd mole away;
While self-dependent power can time defy,
As rocks resist the billows and the sky.

ADAM AUSTIN

FOR LACK OF GOLD

99

For lack of gold she's left me, O,
And of all that's dear bereft me, O;
She me forsook for Athole's duke,
   And to endless woe she has left me, O.
A star and garter have more art
Than youth, a true and faithful heart;
For empty titles we must part,
   And for glittering show she's left me, O.

No cruel fair shall ever move
My injured heart again to love;
Through distant climates I must rove,
   Since Jeanie she has left me, O.
Ye powers above, I to your care
Give up my faithless, lovely fair;
Your choicest blessings be her share,
   Though she's for ever left me, O!

* * *

WILLIAM COWPER
LOSS OF THE ROYAL GEORGE

100

Toll for the Brave!
The brave that are no more!
All sunk beneath the wave
Fast by their native shore!

Eight hundred of the brave
Whose courage well was tried,
Had made the vessel heel
And laid her on her side.

A land-breeze shook the shrouds
And she was overset;
Down went the Royal George,
With all her crew complete.

WILLIAM COWPER

Toll for the brave!
Brave Kempenfelt is gone;
His last sea-fight is fought,
His work of glory done.

It was not in the battle;
No tempest gave the shock;
She sprang no fatal leak,
She ran upon no rock.

His sword was in its sheath,
His fingers held the pen,
When Kempenfelt went down
With twice four hundred men.

Weigh the vessel up
Once dreaded by our foes!
And mingle with our cup
The tears that England owes.

Her timbers yet are sound,
And she may float again
Full charged with England's thunder,
And plough the distant main:

But Kempenfelt is gone,
His victories are o'er;
And he and his eight hundred
Shall plough the wave no more.

TO A YOUNG LADY

101

Sweet stream, that winds through yonder glade,
Apt emblem of a virtuous maid—
Silent and chaste she steals along,
Far from the world's gay busy throng:
With gentle yet prevailing force,
Intent upon her destined course;
Graceful and useful all she does,
Blessing and blest where'er she goes;
Pure-bosm'd as that watery glass,
And Heaven reflected in her face.

THE POPLAR FIELD

102

The poplars are fell'd, farewell to the shade
And the whispering sound of the cool colonnade;
The winds play no longer and sing in the leaves,
Nor Ouse on his bosom their image receives.

Twelve years have elapsed since I first took a view
Of my favourite field, and the bank where they grew:
And now in the grass behold they are laid,
And the tree is my seat that once lent me a shade.

The blackbird has fled to another retreat
Where the hazels afford him a screen from the heat;
And the scene where his melody charm'd me before
Resounds with his sweet-flowing ditty no more.

My fugitive years are all hasting away,
And I must ere long lie as lowly as they,
With a turf on my breast and a stone at my head,
Ere another such grove shall arise in its stead.

'Tis a sight to engage me, if anything can,
To muse on the perishing pleasures of man;
Short-lived as we are, our enjoyments, I see,
Have a still shorter date; and die sooner than we.

THE CASTAWAY

103

Obscurest night involved the sky,
  The Atlantic billows roared,
When such a destined wretch as I
  Washed headlong from on board,
Of friends, of hope of all bereft,
His floating home for ever left.

No braver chief could Albion boast
  Than he with whom he went,
Nor ever ship left Albion's coast
  With warmer wishes sent.
He loved them both, but both in vain,
Nor him beheld, nor her again.

Not long beneath the whelming brine,
  Expert to swim, he lay;

WILLIAM COWPER

Nor soon he felt his strength decline,
  Or courage die away;
But waged with death a lasting strife,
Supported by despair of life.

He shouted: nor his friends had failed
  To check the vessel's course,
But so the furious blast prevailed,
  That, pitiless perforce,
They left their outcast mate behind,
And scudded still before the wind.

Some succour yet they could afford;
  And such as storms allow,
The cask, the coop, the floated cord,
  Delayed not to bestow.
But he (they knew) nor ship nor shore,
Whate'er they gave, should visit more.

Nor, cruel as it seemed, could he
  Their haste himself condemn,
Aware that flight, in such a sea,
  Alone could rescue them;
Yet bitter felt it still to die
Deserted, and his friends so nigh.

He long survives, who lives an hour
  In ocean, self-upheld;
And so long he, with unspent power,
  His destiny repelled;
And ever, as the minutes flew,
Entreated help, or cried "Adieu!"

At length, his transient respite past,
  His comrades, who before
Had heard his voice in every blast,
  Could catch the sound no more:
For then, by toil subdued, he drank
The stifling wave, and then he sank.

No poet wept him; but the page
  Of narrative sincere,
That tells his name, his worth, his age,
  Is wet with Anson's tear:

And tears by bards or heroes shed
Alike immortalize the dead.

I therefore purpose not, or dream,
　Descanting on his fate,
To give the melancholy theme
　A more enduring date:
But misery still delights to trace
Its semblance in another's case.

No voice divine the storm allayed,
　No light propitious shone,
When, snatched from all effectual aid,
　We perished, each alone:
But I beneath a rougher sea,
And whelmed in deeper gulfs than he.

ON THE RECEIPT OF MY MOTHER'S PICTURE OUT OF NORFOLK

104

OH that those lips had language! Life has passed
With me but roughly since I heard thee last.
Those lips are thine—thy own sweet smile I see,
The same that oft in childhood solaced me;
Voice only fails, else how distinct they say,
"Grieve not, my child, chase all thy fears away!"
The meek intelligence of those dear eyes
(Blessed be the art that can immortalize,
The art that baffles Time's tyrannic claim
To quench it) here shines on me still the same.
　Faithful remembrancer of one so dear,
O welcome guest, though unexpected here!
Who bidst me honour with an artless song,
Affectionate, a mother lost so long,
I will obey, not willingly alone,
But gladly, as the precept were her own:
And, while that face renews my filial grief,
Fancy shall weave a charm for my relief,
Shall steep me in Elysian reverie,
A momentary dream that thou art she.
　My mother! when I learnt that thou wast dead,
Say, wast thou conscious of the tears I shed?
Hovered thy spirit o'er thy sorrowing son,
Wretch even then, life's journey just begun?
Perhaps thou gavest me, though unfelt, a kiss:

WILLIAM COWPER

Perhaps a tear, if souls can weep in bliss—
Ah, that maternal smile! It answers—Yes.
I heard the bell toll on thy burial day,
I saw the hearse that bore thee slow away,
And, turning from my nursery window, drew
A long, long sigh, and wept a last adieu!
But was it such?—It was.—Where thou art gone
Adieus and farewells are a sound unknown.
May I but meet thee on that peaceful shore,
The parting word shall pass my lips no more!
Thy maidens, grieved themselves at my concern,
Oft gave me promise of thy quick return.
What ardently I wished I long believed,
And, disappointed still, was still deceived.
By expectation every day beguiled,
Dupe of *to-morrow* even from a child.
Thus many a sad to-morrow came and went,
Till, all my stock of infant sorrow spent,
I learnt at last submission to my lot;
But, though I less deplored thee, ne'er forgot.

Where once we dwelt our name is heard no more,
Children not thine have trod my nursery floor;
And where the gardener Robin, day by day,
Drew me to school along the public way,
Delighted with my bauble coach, and wrapped
In scarlet mantle warm, and velvet capped,
'Tis now become a history little known,
That once we called the pastoral house our own.
Short-lived possession! but the record fair
That memory keeps, of all thy kindness there,
Still outlives many a storm that has effaced
A thousand other themes less deeply traced.
The nightly visits to my chamber made,
That thou mightst know me safe and warmly laid;
Thy morning bounties ere I left my home,
The biscuit, or confectionary plum;
The fragrant waters on my cheek bestowed
By thy own hand, till fresh they shone and glowed;
All this, and more endearing still than all,
Thy constant flow of love, that knew no fall,
Ne'er roughened by those cataracts and brakes
That humour interposed too often makes;
All this still legible in memory's page,
And still to be so to my latest age,
Adds joy to duty, makes me glad to pay

Such honours to thee as my numbers may;
Perhaps a frail memorial, but sincere,
Not scorned in heaven, though little noticed here.
   Could Time, his flight reversed, restore the hours,
When, playing with thy vesture's tissued flowers,
The violet, the pink, and jessamine,
I pricked them into paper with a pin
(And thou wast happier than myself the while,
Wouldst softly speak, and stroke my head and smile),
Could these few pleasant days again appear,
Might one wish bring them, would I wish them here?
I would not trust my heart—the dear delight
Seems so to be desired, perhaps I might.—
But no—what here we call our life is such
So little to be loved, and thou so much,
That I should ill requite thee to constrain
Thy unbound spirit into bonds again.
   Thou, as a gallant bark from Albion's coast
(The storms all weathered and the ocean crossed)
Shoots into port at some well-havened isle,
Where spices breathe, and brighter seasons smile,
There sits quiescent on the floods that show
Her beauteous form reflected clear below,
While airs impregnated with incense play
Around her, fanning light her streamers gay;
So thou, with sails how swift! hast reached the shore,
"Where tempests never beat nor billows roar,"
And thy loved consort on the dangerous tide
Of life long since has anchored by thy side.
But me, scarce hoping to attain that rest,
Always from port withheld, always distressed—
Me howling blasts drive devious, tempest tost,
Sails ripped, seams opening wide, and compass lost,
And day by day some current's thwarting force
Sets me more distant from a prosperous course.
Yet, oh, the thought that thou art safe, and he!
That thought is joy, arrive what may to me.
My boast is not, that I deduce my birth
From loins enthroned and rulers of the earth;
But higher far my proud pretensions rise—
The son of parents passed into the skies!
And now, farewell!—Time unrevoked has run
His wonted course, yet what I wished is done.
By contemplation's help, not sought in vain,
I seemed to have lived my childhood o'er again;

To have renewed the joys that once were mine,
Without the sin of violating thine:
And, while the wings of Fancy still are free,
And I can view this mimic show of thee,
Time has but half succeeded in his theft—
Thyself removed, thy power to soothe me left.

THE DIVERTING HISTORY OF JOHN GILPIN

105

JOHN GILPIN was a citizen
  Of credit and renown,
A train-band captain eke was he
  Of famous London town.

John Gilpin's spouse said to her dear,
  "Though wedded we have been
These twice ten tedious years, yet we
  No holiday have seen.

"To-morrow is our wedding-day,
  And we will then repair
Unto the Bell at Edmonton,
  All in a chaise and pair.

"My sister, and my sister's child,
  Myself, and children three,
Will fill the chaise; so you must ride
  On horseback after we."

He soon replied, "I do admire
  Of womankind but one,
And you are she, my dearest dear,
  Therefore it shall be done.

"I am a linen-draper bold,
  As all the world doth know,
And my good friend the calender
  Will lend his horse to go."

Quoth Mrs. Gilpin, "That's well said;
  And for that wine is dear,
We will be furnished with our own,
  Which is both bright and clear."

John Gilpin kissed his loving wife;
  O'erjoyed was he to find,
That though on pleasure she was bent,
  She had a frugal mind.

The morning came, the chaise was brought,
  But yet was not allowed
To drive up to the door, lest all
  Should say that she was proud.

So three doors off the chaise was stayed,
  Where they did all get in;
Six precious souls, and all agog
  To dash through thick and thin.

Smack went the whip, round went the wheels,
  Were never folk so glad,
The stones did rattle underneath,
  As if Cheapside were mad.

John Gilpin at his horse's side
  Seized fast the flowing mane,
And up he got, in haste to ride,
  But soon came down again;

For saddle-tree scarce reached had he,
  His journey to begin,
When, turning round his head, he saw
  Three customers come in.

So down he came; for loss of time,
  Although it grieved him sore,
Yet loss of pence, full well he knew,
  Would trouble him much more.

'Twas long before the customers
  Were suited to their mind,
When Betty screaming came down stairs,
  "The wine is left behind!"

"Good lack," quoth he—"yet bring it me,
  My leathern belt likewise,
In which I bear my trusty sword,
  When I do exercise."

WILLIAM COWPER

Now Mistress Gilpin (careful soul!)
  Had two stone bottles found,
To hold the liquor that she loved,
  And keep it safe and sound.

Each bottle had a curling ear,
  Through which the belt he drew,
And hung a bottle on each side,
  To make his balance true.

Then over all, that he might be
  Equipped from top to toe,
His long red cloak, well brushed and neat,
  He manfully did throw.

Now see him mounted once again
  Upon his nimble steed,
Full slowly pacing o'er the stones,
  With caution and good heed.

But finding soon a smoother road
  Beneath his well-shod feet,
The snorting beast began to trot,
  Which galled him in his seat.

So, "Fair and softly," John he cried,
  But John he called in vain;
That trot became a gallop soon,
  In spite of curb and rein.

So stooping down as needs he must
  Who cannot sit upright,
He grasped the mane with both his hands,
  And eke with all his might.

His horse, who never in that sort
  Had handled been before,
What thing upon his back had got
  Did wonder more and more.

Away went Gilpin, neck or nought;
  Away went hat and wig;
He little dreamt, when he set out,
  Of running such a rig.

The wind did blow, the cloak did fly,
  Like streamer long and gay,
Till, loop and button failing both,
  At last it flew away.

Then might all people well discern
  The bottles he had slung;
A bottle swinging at each side,
  As hath been said or sung.

The dogs did bark, the children screamed,
  Up flew the windows all;
And every soul cried out, "Well done!"
  As loud as he could bawl.

Away went Gilpin—who but he?
  His fame soon spread around;
"He carries weight! He rides a race!"
  "'Tis for a thousand pound!"

And still, as fast as he drew near,
  'Twas wonderful to view,
How in a trice the turnpike-men
  Their gates wide open threw.

And now, as he went bowing down
  His reeking head full low,
The bottles twain behind his back
  Were shattered at a blow.

Down ran the wine into the road,
  Most piteous to be seen,
Which made his horse's flanks to smoke
  As they had basted been.

But still he seemed to carry weight,
  With leathern girdle braced;
For all might see the bottle-necks
  Still dangling at his waist.

Thus all through merry Islington
  These gambols he did play,
Until he came unto the Wash
  Of Edmonton so gay;

WILLIAM COWPER

And there he threw the Wash about
  On both sides of the way,
Just like unto a trundling mop,
  Or a wild goose at play.

At Edmonton his loving wife
  From the balcony spied
Her tender husband, wondering much
  To see how he did ride.

"Stop, stop, John Gilpin!—Here's the house!"
  They all at once did cry;
"The dinner waits, and we are tired;"—
  Said Gilpin—"So am I!"

But yet his horse was not a whit
  Inclined to tarry there!
For why?—his owner had a house
  Full ten miles off at Ware.

So like an arrow swift he flew,
  Shot by an archer strong;
So did he fly—which brings me to
  The middle of my song.

Away went Gilpin, out of breath,
  And sore against his will,
Till at his friend the calender's
  His horse at last stood still.

The calender, amazed to see
  His neighbour in such trim,
Laid down his pipe, flew to the gate,
  And thus accosted him:

"What news? what news? your tidings tell;
  Tell me you must and shall—
Say why bareheaded you are come,
  Or why you come at all?"

Now Gilpin had a pleasant wit,
  And loved a timely joke;
And thus unto the calender
  In merry guise he spoke:

"I came because your horse would come,
  And, if I well forebode,
My hat and wig will soon be here,—
  They are upon the road."

The calender, right glad to find
  His friend in merry pin,
Returned him not a single word,
  But to the house went in;

Whence straight he came with hat and wig;
  A wig that flowed behind,
A hat not much the worse for wear,
  Each comely in its kind.

He held them up, and in his turn
  Thus showed his ready wit,
"My head is twice as big as yours,
  They therefore needs must fit.

"But let me scrape the dirt away
  That hangs upon your face;
And stop and eat, for well you may
  Be in a hungry case."

Said John, "It is my wedding day,
  And all the world would stare,
If wife should dine at Edmonton,
  And I should dine at Ware."

So turning to his horse, he said,
  "I am in haste to dine;
'Twas for your pleasure you came here,
  You shall go back for mine."

Ah, luckless speech, and bootless boast!
  For which he paid full dear;
For, while he spake, a braying ass
  Did sing most loud and clear;

Whereat his horse did snort, as he
  Had heard a lion roar,
And galloped off with all his might,
  As he had done before.

WILLIAM COWPER

Away went Gilpin, and away
  Went Gilpin's hat and wig;
He lost them sooner than at first;
  For why?—they were too big.

Now Mistress Gilpin, when she saw
  Her husband posting down
Into the country far away,
  She pulled out half a crown;

And thus unto the youth she said
  That drove them to the Bell,
"This shall be yours, when you bring back
  My husband safe and well."

The youth did ride, and soon did meet
  John coming back again:
Whom in a trice he tried to stop,
  By catching at his rein;

But not performing what he meant,
  And gladly would have done,
The frighted steed he frighted more,
  And made him faster run.

Away went Gilpin, and away
  Went postboy at his heels,
The postboy's horse right glad to miss
  The lumbering of the wheels.

Six gentlemen upon the road,
  Thus seeing Gilpin fly,
With postboy scampering in the rear,
  They raised the hue and cry:

"Stop thief! stop thief!—a highwayman!"
  Not one of them was mute;
And all and each that passed that way
  Did join in the pursuit.

And now the turnpike gates again
  Flew open in short space;
The toll-men thinking, as before,
  That Gilpin rode a race.

And so he did, and won it too,
  For he got first to town;
Nor stopped till where he had got up
  He did again get down.

Now let us sing, Long live the King!
  And Gilpin, long live he!
And when he next doth ride abroad
  May I be there to see!

* * *

RICHARD BRINSLEY SHERIDAN

DRINKING SONG

106

Here's to the maiden of bashful fifteen,
  Here's to the widow of fifty;
Here's to the flaming extravagant quean,
  And here's to the housewife that's thrifty;

Chorus.   Let the toast pass,
      Drink to the lass,
I'll warrant she'll prove an excuse for the glass.

Here's to the charmer, whose dimples we prize,
  And now to the maid who has none, sir,
Here's to the girl with a pair of blue eyes,
  And here's to the nymph with but one, sir.

Chorus.   Let the toast pass,
      Drink to the lass,
I'll warrant she'll prove an excuse for the glass.

Here's to the maid with a bosom of snow,
  And to her that's as brown as a berry;
Here's to the wife with a face ful of woe,
  And now to the girl that is merry:

Chorus.   Let the toast pass,
      Drink to the lass,
I'll warrant she'll prove an excuse for the glass.

For let 'em be clumsy, or let 'em be slim,
  Young or ancient, I care not a feather;
So fill a pint bumper quite up to the brim,
  And let us e'en toast them together.

Chorus.   *Let the toast pass,*
            Drink to the lass,
I'll warrant she'll prove an excuse for the glass.

* * *

MICHAEL BRUCE

TO THE CUCKOO

107

Hail! beauteous Stranger of the wood!
    Attendant on the Spring!
Now heav'n repairs thy rural seat,
    And woods thy welcome sing.

Soon as the daisy decks the green,
    Thy certain voice we hear:
Hast thou a star to guide thy path,
    Or mark the rolling year?

Delightful visitant! with thee
    I hail the time of flow'rs,
When heav'n is fill'd with music sweet
    Of birds among the bow'rs.

The schoolboy wand'ring in the wood
    To pull the flow'rs so gay,
Starts, thy curious voice to hear,
    And imitates thy lay.

Soon as the pea puts on the bloom,
    Thou fly'st thy vocal vale,
An annual guest, in other lands,
    Another Spring to hail.

Sweet bird! thy bow'r is ever green,
    Thy sky is ever clear;
Thou hast no sorrow in thy song,
    No winter in thy year!

Alas! sweet bird! not so my fate,
    Dark scowling skies I see
Fast gathering round, and fraught with woe
    And wintry years to me.

O could I fly, I'd fly with thee:
  We'd make, with social wing,
Our annual visit o'er the globe,
  Companions of the Spring.

* * *

GEORGE HALKET

LOGIE O' BUCHAN

108

O Logie o' Buchan, O Logie the laird,
They ha'e ta'en awa' Jamie, that delved in the yaird,
Wha played on the pipe and the viol sae sma',
They ha'e ta'en awa' Jamie, the flower o' them a'!

He said, "Think na lang, lassie, though I gang awa'!"
He said, "Think na lang, lassie, though I gang awa'!"
For simmer is coming, cauld winter's awa',
And I'll come and see thee in spite o' them a'!"

Though Sandy has ousen, has gear, and has kye,
A house and a hadden, and siller forbye;
Yet I tak' mine ain lad, wi' his staff in his hand,
Before I'd ha'e him, wi' the houses and land.

My daddy looks sulky, my minnie looks sour;
They frown upon Jamie because he is poor;
Though I lo'e them as weel as a dochter should do,
They're nae hauf sae dear to me, Jamie, as you.

I sit on my creepie, I spin at my wheel,
And think on the laddie that lo'ed me sae weel:
He had but a sixpence, he brak' it in twa,
And gi'ed me the hauf o't when he gaed awa'.

Then haste ye back, Jamie, and bide na awa'!
Then haste ye back, Jamie, and bide na awa'!
The simmer is coming, cauld winter's awa',
And ye'll come and see me in spite o' them al'.

WILLIAM HAMILTON OF BANGOUR

THE BRAES OF YARROW

109

"Busk ye, busk ye, my bonnie, bonnie bride!
  Busk ye, busk ye, my winsome marrow!
Busk ye, busy ye, my bonnie, bonnie bride!
  And think nae mair on the braes of Yarrow!"

"Where got ye that bonnie, bonnie bride?
  Where got ye that winsome marrow?"
"I got her where I durst not well be seen—
  Pu'ing the birks on the braes of Yarrow."

"Weep not, weep not, my bonnie, bonnie bride!
  Weep not, weep not, my winsome marrow!
Nor let thy heart lament to leave
  Pu'ing the birks on the braes of Yarrow."

"Why does she weep, thy bonnie, bonnie bride?
  Why does she weep, thy winsome marrow?
And why dare ye nae mair weel be seen
  Pu'ing the birks on the braes of Yarrow?"

"Lang maun she weep, lang maun she, maun she weep,
  Lang maun she weep with dule and sorrow;
And lang maun I nae weel be seen
  Pu'ing the birks on the braes of Yarrow.

"For she has tint her lover, lover dear—
  Her lover dear, the cause of sorrow;
And I have slain the comeliest swain
  That ever pu'ed birks on the braes of Yarrow.

"Why runs thy stream O Yarrow, Yarrow, reid?
  Why on thy braes is heard the voice of sorrow?
And why yon melancholious weeds
  Hung on the bonnie birks of Yarrow.

"What's yonder floats on the rueful, rueful flood?
  What's yonder floats? O dule and sorrow!
'Tis he, the comely swain I slew
  Upon the duleful braes of Yarrow.

"Wash, O wash his wounds, his wounds in tears,
  His wounds in tears of dule and sorrow;
And wrap his limbs in mourning weeds,
  And lay him on the braes of Yarrow.

"Then build, then build, ye sisters, sisters sad,
  Ye sisters sad, his tomb with sorrow:
And weep around, in woeful wise,
  His hapless fate on the braes of Yarrow.

"Curse ye, curse ye, his useless, useless shield,
  My arm that wrought the deed of sorrow,
The fatal spear that pierced his breast—
  His comely breast on the braes of Yarrow!

"Did I not warn thee not to, not to love,
  And warn from fight? But, to my sorrow,
Too rashly bold, a stronger arm
  Thou met'st, and fell on the braes of Yarrow."

"Sweet smells the birk, green grows, green grows the grass,
  Yellow on Yarrow's braes the gowan;
Fair hangs the apple frae the rock,
  Sweet the wave of Yarrow flowing!"

"Flows Yarrow sweet? As sweet, as sweet flows Tweed;
  As green its grass, its gowan as yellow;
As sweet smells on its braes the birk,
  The apple from its rocks as mellow.

"Fair was thy love, fair, fair indeed thy love;
  In flowery bands thou didst him fetter:
Though he was fair, and well beloved again
  Than me, he never loved thee better.

"Busk ye then, busk, my bonnie, bonnie bride!
  Busk, ye, busk ye, my winsome marrow!
Busk ye, and lo'e me on the banks of Tweed,
  And think nae mair on the braes of Yarrow!"

"How can I busk, a bonnie, bonnie bride?
  How can I busk, a winsome marrow?
How lo'e him on the banks of Tweed
  That slew my love on the braes of Yarrow!

"O Yarrow fields, may never, never rain
　Nor dew thy tender blossoms cover!
For there was basely slain my love—
　My love as he had not been a lover.

"The boy put on his robes, his robes of green,
　His purple vest—'twas my ain sewing:
Ah, wretched me! I little, little knew
　He was in these to meet his ruin!

"The boy took out his milk-white, milk-white steed,
　Unheedful of my dule and sorrow;
But ere the to-fall of the night
　He lay a corpse on the braes of Yarrow.

"Much I rejoiced, that woeful, woeful day;
　I sang, my voice the woods returning;
But lang ere night the spear was flown
　That slew my love and left me mourning.

"What can my barbarous, barbarous father do,
　But with his cruel rage pursue me?
My lover's blood is on thy spear;
　How canst thou, barbarous man, then woo me?

"My happy sisters may be, may be proud—
　With cruel and ungentle scoffin'
May bid me seek, on Yarrow's braes,
　My lover nailed in his coffin.

"My brother Douglas may upbraid,
　And strive with threat'ning words to move me:
My lover's blood is on thy spear,
　How canst thou ever bid me love thee?

"Yes, yes, prepare the bed, the bed of love!
　With bridal sheets my body cover!
Unbar, ye bridal maids, the door;
　Let in the expected husband lover!

"But who the expected husband, husband is?
　His hands, methinks, are bathed in slaughter.
Ah me! what ghastly spectre's yon,
　Comes in his pale shroud bleeding after?

"Pale as he is, here lay him, lay him down;
　O lay his cold head on my pillow:
Take aff, take aff these bridal weeds,
　And crown my careful head with willow.

"Pale though thou art, yet best, yet best beloved!
　Oh! could my warmth to life restore thee,
Ye'd lie all night between my breasts!
　No youth lay ever there before thee.

"Pale, pale indeed! O lovely, lovely youth!
　Forgive, forgive so foul a slaughter;
And lie all night between my breasts!
　No youth shall ever lie there after."

"Return, return, O mournful, mournful bride!
　Return, and dry thy useless sorrow!
Thy lover heeds nought of thy sighs—
　He lies a corpse on the braes of Yarrow."

* * *

SAMUEL ROGERS

A WISH

110

　Mine be a cot beside the hill;
　A bee-hive's hum shall soothe my ear;
　A willowy brook, that turns a mill,
　With many a fall shall linger near.

　The swallow, oft, beneath my thatch,
　Shall twitter from her clay-built nest;
　Oft shall the pilgrim lift the latch,
　And share my meal, a welcome guest.

　Around my ivy'd porch shall spring
　Each fragrant flower that drinks the dew;
　And Lucy, at her wheel, shall sing
　In russet gown and apron blue.

　The village-church among the trees,
　Where first our marriage-vows were given,

THE SLEEPING BEAUTY

111

Sleep on, and dream of Heaven awhile—
Tho' shut so close thy laughing eyes,
Thy rosy lips still wear a smile
And move, and breathe delicious sighs!

Ah, now soft blushes tinge her cheeks
And mantle o'er her neck of snow:
Ah, now she murmurs, now she speaks
What most I wish—and fear to know!

She starts, she trembles, and she weeps!
Her fair hands folded on her breast:
—And now, how like a saint she sleeps!
A seraph in the realms of rest!

Sleep on secure! Above controul
Thy thoughts belong to Heaven and thee:
And may the secret of thy soul
Remain within its sanctuary!

* * *

WILLIAM BLAKE

THE TIGER

112

Tiger, tiger, burning bright
In the forests of the night,
What immortal hand or eye
Could frame thy fearful symmetry?

In what distant deeps or skies
Burnt the fire of thine eyes?
On what wings dare he aspire?
What the hand dare seize the fire?

And what shoulder and what art
Could twist the sinews of thy heart?

And, when thy heart began to beat,
What dread hand and what dread feet?

What the hammer? What the chain?
In what furnace was thy brain?
What the anvil? What dread grasp
Dare its deadly terrors clasp?

When the stars threw down their spears,
And water'd heaven with their tears,
Did He smile His work to see?
Did He who made the lamb make thee?

Tiger, tiger, burning bright
In the forests of the night,
What immortal hand or eye
Dare frame thy fearful symmetry?

* * *

SUSANNA BLAMIRE

AND YE SHALL WALK IN SILK ATTIRE

And ye shall walk in silk attire,
  And siller hae to spare,
Gin ye'll consent to be his bride,
  Nor think o' Donald mair.
Oh, wha wad buy a silken goun
  Wi' a puir broken heart?
Oh what's to me a siller croun,
  Gin frae my love I part?

The mind wha's every wish is pure
  Far dearer is to me;
And ere I'm forced to break my faith,
  I'll lay me doun and dee:
For I ha'e pledged my virgin troth
  Brave Donald's fate to share;
And he has gi'en to me his heart,
  Wi' a' its virtues rare.

His gentle manners wan my heart,
  He gratefu' took the gift;

Could I but think to tak' it back,
　　It wad be waur than theft.
For langest life can ne'er repay
　　The love he bears to me;
And ere I'm forced to break my troth
　　I'll lay me doun and dee.

* * *

WILLIAM WORDSWORTH

ODE ON INTIMATIONS OF IMMORTALITY FROM RECOLLECTIONS OF EARLY CHILDHOOD

114

There was a time when meadow, grove, and stream,
　　The earth, and every common sight
　　　　To me did seem
　　　　Apparell'd in celestial light,
　　The glory and the freshness of a dream.
It is not now as it has been of yore;—
　　　　Turn wheresoe'er I may,
　　　　　　By night or day,
The things which I have seen I now can see no more!
　　　　The rainbow comes and goes,
　　　　And lovely is the rose;
　　　　The moon doth with delight
　　Look round her when the heavens are bare;
　　　　Waters on a starry night
　　　　Are beautiful and fair;
　　The sunshine is a glorious birth;
　　But yet I know, where'er I go,
That there hath pass'd away a glory from the earth.

Now, while the birds thus sing a joyous song,
　　　　And while the young lambs bound
　　　　As to the tabor's sound,
To me alone their came a thought of grief:
A timely utterance gave that thought relief,
　　　　And I again am strong.
The cataracts blow their trumpets from the steep,—
No more shall grief of mine the season wrong:
I hear the echoes through the mountains throng,

The winds come to me from the fields of sleep,
    And all the earth is gay,
      Land and sea
   Give themselves up to jollity,
    And with the heart of May
  Doth every beast keep holiday;—
      Thou child of joy
Shout round me, let me hear thy shouts, thou happy
    Shepherd-boy!

Ye blessèd creatures, I have heard the call
   Ye to each other make; I see
The heavens laugh with you in your jubilee;
    My heart is at your festival,
    My head hath its coronal,
The fulness of your bliss, I feel—I feel it all.
     O evil day! if I were sullen
      While Earth herself is adorning
        This sweet May morning;
      And the children are pulling
        On every side
     In a thousand valleys far and wide,
    Fresh flowers; while the sun shines warm,
And the babe leaps up on his mother's arm:—
    I hear, I hear, with joy I hear!
    —But there's a tree, of many, one,
A single field which I have look'd upon,

Both of them speak of something that is gone:
     The pansy at my feet
     Doth the same tale repeat:
Whither is fled the visionary gleam?
Where is it now, the glory and the dream?

Our birth is but a sleep and a forgetting;
The Soul that rises with us, our life's Star,
    Hath had elsewhere its setting
      And cometh from afar:
    Not in entire forgetfulness,
    And not in utter nakedness,
But trailing clouds of glory do we come
     From God, who is our home:
Heaven lies about us in our infancy!
Shades of the prison-house begin to close
    Upon the growing boy,

But he beholds the light, and whence it flows,
    He sees it in his joy;
The youth, who daily farther from the east
    Must travel, still is Nature's priest,
      And by the vision splendid
      Is on his way attended;
At length the man perceives it die away,
And fade into the light of common day.

Earth fills her lap with pleasures of her own;
Yearnings she hath in her own natural kind,
And, even with something of a mother's mind
      And no unworthy aim,
    The homely nurse doth all she can
To make her foster-child, her inmate, Man,
      Forget the glories he hath known
And that imperial palace whence he came.

Behold the Child among his new-born blisses,
A six years' darling of a pigmy size!
See, where 'mid work of his own hand he lies,
Fretted by sallies of his mother's kisses,
With light upon him from his father's eyes!
See, at his feet, some little plan or chart,
Some fragment from his dream of human life,
Shaped by himself with newly-learnéd art;
    A wedding or a festival,
    A mourning or a funeral;
      And this hath now his heart,
    And unto this he frames his song:
      Then will he fit his tongue
To dialogues of business, love, or strife;
      But it will not be long
      Ere this be thrown aside,
      And with new joy and pride
The little actor cons another part;
Filling from time to time his "humorous stage"
With all the Persons, down to palsied Age,
That life brings with her in her equipage;
      As if his whole vocation
      Were endless imitation.

Thou, whose exterior semblance doth belie
    Thy soul's immensity;
Thou best philosopher, who yet dost keep

Thy heritage, thou eye among the blind,
That, deaf and silent, read'st the eternal deep,
Haunted for ever by the eternal Mind,—
      Mighty Prophet! Seer blest!
      On whom those truths do rest
Which we are toiling all our lives to find;
Thou, over whom thy immortality
Broods like the day, a master o'er a slave,
A presence which is not to be put by;
Thou little child, yet glorious in the might
Of heaven-born freedom on thy being's height,
Why with such earnest pains dost thou provoke
The years to bring the inevitable yoke,
Thus blindly with thy blessedness at strife?
Full soon thy soul shall have her earthly freight,
And custom lie upon thee with a weight
Heavy as frost, and deep almost as life!

      O joy! that in our embers
      Is something that doth live,
      That Nature yet remembers
      What was so fugitive!
The thought of our past years in me doth breed
Perpetual benediction: not indeed
For that which is most worthy to be blest,
Delight and liberty, the simple creed
Of childhood, whether busy or at rest,
With new-fledged hope still fluttering in his breast:
      —Not for these I raise
      The song of thanks and praise;
    But for those obstinate questionings
    Of sense and outward things,
    Fallings from us, vanishings,
    Blank misgivings of a creature
Moving about in worlds not realized,
High instincts, before which our mortal nature
Did tremble like a guilty thing surprised:
      But for those first affections,
      Those shadowy recollections,
      Which, be they what they may,
Are yet the fountain-light of all our day,
Are yet a master-light of all our seeing;
  Uphold us—cherish—and have power to make
Our noisy years seem moments in the being
Of the eternal silence: truths that wake,

WILLIAM WORDSWORTH

            To perish never;
Which neither listlessness, nor mad endeavour,
            Nor man nor boy,
Nor all that is at enmity with joy,
Can utterly abolish or destroy!
    Hence, in a season of calm weather
        Though inland far we be,
Our souls have sight of that immortal sea
        Which brought us hither;
        Can in a moment travel thither—
And see the children sport upon the shore,
And hear the mighty waters rolling evermore.

Then sing, ye birds, sing, sing a joyous song!
        And let the young lambs bound
        As to the tabor's sound!
    We, in thought, will join your throng
        Ye that pipe and ye that play,
        Ye that through your hearts to-day
        Feel the gladness of the May!
What though the radiance which was once so bright
Be now for ever taken from my sight,
    Though nothing can bring back the hour
Of splendour in the grass, of glory in the flower;
        We will grieve not, rather find
        Strength in what remains behind,
        In the primal sympathy
        Which having been must ever be,
        In the soothing thoughts that spring
        Out of human suffering,
        In the faith that looks through death,
In years that bring the philosophic mind.

And O, ye Fountains, Meadows, Hills, and Groves,
Forbode not any severing of our loves!
Yet in my heart of hearts I feel your might;
I only have relinquish'd one delight
To live beneath your more habitual sway;
I love the brooks which down their channels fret
Even more than when I tripp'd lightly as they;
The innocent brightness of a new-born day
        Is lovely yet;
The clouds that gather round the setting sun
Do take a sober colouring from an eye
That hath kept watch o'er man's mortality;

Another race hath been, and other palms are won.
Thanks to the human heart by which we live,
Thanks to its tenderness, its joys and fears,
To me the meanest flower that blows can give
Thoughts that do often lie too deep for tears.

NATURE AND THE POET

115

I was thy neighbour once, thou rugged Pile!
Four summer weeks I dwelt in sight of thee:
I saw thee every day; and all the while
Thy form was sleeping on a glassy sea.

So pure the sky, so quiet was the air!
So like, so very like, was day to day!
Whene'er I look'd, thy image still was there;
It trembled, but it never pass'd away.

How perfect was the calm! It seem'd no sleep,
No mood, which season takes away, or brings:
I could have fancied that the mighty Deep
Was even the gentlest of all gentle things.

Ah! then if mine had been the painter's hand
To express what then I saw; and add the gleam,
The light that never was on sea or land,
The consecration, and the Poet's dream,—

I would have planted thee, thou hoary pile,
Amid a world how different from this!
Beside a sea that could not cease to smile;
On tranquil land, beneath a sky of bliss.

A picture had it been of lasting ease,
Elysian quiet, without toil or strife;
No motion but the moving tide, a breeze,
Or merely silent Nature's breathing life.

Such, in the fond illusion of my heart,
Such picture would I at that time have made;
And seen the soul of truth in every part,
A steadfast peace that might not be betray'd.

So once it would have been,—'tis so no more;
I have submitted to a new control:

A power is gone, which nothing can restore;
A deep distress hath humanized my soul.

Not for a moment could I now behold
A smiling sea, and be what I have been:
The feeling of my loss will ne'er be old;
This, which I know, I speak with mind serene.

Then, Beaumont, Friend! who would have been the friend
If he had lived, of him whom I deplore,
This work of thine I blame not, but commend;
This sea in anger, and that dismal shore.

O 'tis a passionate work!—yet wise and well,
Well chosen is the spirit that is here;
That hulk which labours in the deadly swell,
This rueful sky, this pageantry of fear!

And this huge Castle, standing here sublime,
I love to see the look with which it braves,
—Cased in the unfeeling armour of old time—
The lightning, the fierce wind, and trampling waves.

—Farewell, farewell the heart that lives alone,
Housed in a dream, at distance from the Kind!
Such happiness, wherever it be known
Is to be pitied; for 'tis surely blind.

But welcome fortitude, and patient cheer,
And frequent sights of what is to be borne!
Such sights, or worse, as are before me here:—
Not without hope we suffer and we mourn.

RUTH: OR THE INFLUENCES OF NATURE

When Ruth was left half desolate
Her father took another mate;
And Ruth, not seven years old,
A slighted child, at her own will
Went wandering over dale and hill,
In thoughtless freedom bold.

And she had made a pipe of straw,
And music from that pipe could draw

Like sounds of wind and floods;
Had built a bower upon the green,
As if she from her birth had been
An infant of the woods.

Beneath her father's roof, alone
She seem'd to live; her thoughts her own;
Herself her own delight:
Pleased with herself, nor sad nor gay,
She passed her time; and in this way
Grew up to woman's height.

There came a youth from Georgia's shore—
A military casque he wore
With splendid feathers drest;
He brought them from the Cherokees;
The feathers nodded in the breeze
And made a gallant crest.

From Indian blood you deem him sprung:
But no! he spake the English tongue
And bore a soldier's name;
And, when America was free
From battle and from jeopardy,
He 'cross the ocean came.

With hues of genius on his cheek,
In finest tones the youth could speak:
—While he was yet a boy
The moon, the glory of the sun,
And streams that murmur as they run
Had been his dearest joy.

He was a lovely youth! I guess
The panther in the wilderness
Was not so fair as he,
And when he chose to sport and play,
No dolphin ever was so gay
Upon the tropic sea.

Among the Indians he had fought;
And with him many tales he brought
Of pleasure and of fear;
Such tales as, told to any maid

By such a youth, in the green shade,
Were perilous to hear.

He told of girls, a happy rout!
Who quit their fold with dance and shout,
Their pleasant Indian town,
To gather strawberries all day long;
Returning with a choral song
When daylight is gone down.

He spake of plants that hourly change
Their blossoms, through a boundless range
Of intermingling hues;
With budding, fading, faded flowers,
They stand the wonder of the bowers
From morn to evening dews.

He told of the Magnolia, spread
High as a cloud, high over head!
The cypress and her spire;
—Of flowers that with one scarlet gleam
Cover a hundred leagues, and seem
To set the hills on fire.

The youth of green savannahs spake,
And many an endless, endless lake
With all its fairy crowds
Of islands, that together lie
As quietly as spots of sky
Among the evening clouds.

"And," then he said, "how sweet it were
A fisher or a hunter there,
In sunshine or in shade
To wander with an easy mind,
And build a household fire, and find
A home in every glade!

"What days and what bright years! Ah me!
Our life were life indeed, with Thee
So pass'd in quiet bliss;
And all the while," said he, "to know
That we were in a world of woe,
On such an earth as this!"

And then he sometimes interwove
Fond thoughts about a father's love,
"For there," said he, "are spun
Around the heart such tender ties,
That our own children to our eyes
Are dearer than the sun.

"Sweet Ruth! and could you go with me
My helpmate in the woods to be,
Our shed at night to rear;
Or run, my own adopted bride,
A sylvan huntress at my side,
And drive the flying deer!

"Beloved Ruth!"—No more he said.
The wakeful Ruth at midnight shed
A solitary tear:
She thought again—and did agree
With him to sail across the sea,
And drive the flying deer.

"And now, as fitting is and right,
We in the church our faith will plight,
A husband and a wife."
Even so they did; and I may say
That to sweet Ruth that happy day
Was more than human life.

Through dream and vision did she sink,
Delighted all the while to think
That, on those lonesome floods
And green savannahs, she should share
His board with lawful joy, and bear
His name in the wild woods.

But, as you have before been told,
This Stripling, sportive, gay, and bold,
And with his dancing crest
So beautiful, through savage lands
Had roam'd about, with vagrant bands
Of Indians in the West.

The wind, the tempest roaring high,
The tumult of a tropic sky
Might well be dangerous food

For him, a youth to whom was given
So much of earth—so much of heaven,
And such impetuous blood.

Whatever in those climes he found
Irregular in sight or sound
Did to his mind impart
A kindred impulse, seem'd allied
To his own powers, and justified
The workings of his heart.

Nor less, to feed voluptuous thought,
The beauteous forms of Nature wrought,—
Fair trees and gorgeous flowers;
The breezes their own languor lent;
The stars had feelings, which they sent
Into those favour'd bowers.

Yet, in his worst pursuits, I ween
That sometimes there did intervene
Pure hopes of high intent:
For passions link'd to forms so fair
And stately, needs must have their share
Of noble sentiment.

But ill he lived, much evil saw,
With men to whom no better law
Nor better life was known;
Deliberately and undeceived
Those wild men's vices he received,
And gave them back his own

His genius and his moral frame
Were thus impair'd, and he became
The slave of low desires;
A man who without self-control
Would seek what the degraded soul
Unworthily admires.

And yet he with no feign'd delight
Had woo'd the maiden, day and night
Had loved her, night and morn:
What could he less than love a maid
Whose heart with so much nature play'd—
So kind and so forlorn?

Sometimes most earnestly he said,
"O Ruth! I have been worse than dead;
False thoughts, thoughts bold and vain
Encompass'd me on every side
When I, in confidence and pride,
Had cross'd the Atlantic main.

Before me shone a glorious world
Fresh as a banner bright, unfurl'd
To music suddenly:
I look'd upon those hills and plains,
And seem'd as if let loose from chains
To live at liberty!

No more of this—for now, by thee,
Dear Ruth! more happily set free,
With nobler zeal I burn;
My soul from darkness is released
Like the whole sky when to the east
The morning doth return.

Full soon that better mind was gone;
No hope, no wish remain'd, not one,—
They stirr'd him now no more;
New objects did new pleasure give,
And once again he wish'd to live
As lawless as before.

Meanwhile, as thus with him it fared,
They for the voyage were prepared,
And went to the sea-shore:
But, when they thither came, the youth
Deserted his poor bride, and Ruth
Could never find him more.

God help thee, Ruth!—Such pains she had
That she in half a year was mad
And in a prison housed;
And there, exulting in her wrongs
Among the music of her songs
She fearfully caroused.

Yet sometimes milder hours she knew,
Nor wanted sun, nor rain, nor dew,
Nor pastimes of the May,

—They all were with her in her cell;
And a clear brook with cheerful knell
Did o'er the pebbles play.

When Ruth three seasons thus had lain,
There came a respite to her pain;
She from her prison fled;
But of the vagrant none took thought;
And where it liked her best she sought
Her shelter and her bread.

Among the fields she breathed again:
The master-current of her brain
Ran permanent and free;
And, coming to the banks of Tone,
There did she rest; and dwell alone
Under the greenwood tree.

The engines of her pain, the tools
That shaped her sorrow, rocks and pools,
And airs that gently stir
The vernal leaves—she loved them still,
Nor ever tax'd them with the ill
Which had been done to her.

A barn her Winter bed supplies;
But, till the warmth of Summer skies
And Summer days is gone,
(And all do in this tale agree)
She sleeps beneath the greenwood tree,
And other home hath none.

An innocent life, yet far astray!
And Ruth will, long before her day,
Be broken down and old.
Sore aches she needs must have! but less
Of mind, than body's wretchedness,
From damp, and rain, and cold.

If she is prest by want of food
She from her dwelling in the wood
Repairs to a road-side;
And there she begs at one steep place,
Where up and down with easy pace
The horsemen-travellers ride.

That oaten pipe of hers is mute
Or thrown away: but with a flute
Her loneliness she cheers;
This flute, made of a hemlock stalk,
At evening in his homeward walk
The Quantock woodman hears.

I, too, have pass'd her on the hills
Setting her little water-mills
By spouts and fountains wild—
Such small machinery as she turn'd
Ere she had wept, ere she had mourn'd,
A young and happy child!

Farewell! and when thy days are told,
Ill-fated Ruth! in hallow'd mould
Thy corpse shall buried be;
For thee a funeral bell shall ring,
And all the congregation sing
A Christian psalm for thee.

WE ARE SEVEN

A SIMPLE Child,
That lightly draws its breath,
And feels its life in every limb,
What should it know of death?

I met a little cottage Girl:
She was eight years old, she said;
Her hair was thick with many a curl
That clustered round her head.

She had a rustic, woodland air,
And she was wildly clad:
Her eyes were fair, and very fair;
—Her beauty made me glad.

"Sisters and brothers, little Maid,
"How many may you be?"
"How many? Seven in all," she said,
And wondering looked at me.

"And where are they? I pray you tell."
She answered, "Seven are we;

And two of us at Conway dwell,
And two are gone to sea.

"Two of us in the church-yard lie,
My sister and my brother;
And, in the church-yard cottage, I
Dwell near them with my mother."

"You say that two at Conway dwell,
And two are gone to sea,
Yet ye are seven!—I pray you tell,
Sweet Maid, how this may be."

Then did the little maid reply,
"Seven boys and girls are we;
Two of us in the church-yard lie,
Beneath the church-yard tree."

"You run above, my little Maid,
Your limbs they are alive;
If two are in the church-yard laid,
Then ye are only five."

"Their graves are green, they may be seen,"
The little Maid replied,
"Twelve steps or more from my mother's door,
And they are side by side.

"My stockings there I often knit,
My kerchief there I hem;
And there upon the ground I sit,
And sing a song to them.

"And often after sun-set, Sir,
When it is light and fair,
I take my little porringer,
And eat my supper there.

"The first that died was sister Jane;
In bed she moaning lay,
Till God released her of her pain;
And then she went away.

"So in the church-yard she was laid;
And, when the grass was dry,

Together round her grave we played,
My brother John and I.

"And when the ground was white with snow,
And I could run and slide,
My brother John was forced to go,
And he lies by her side."

"How many are you, then," said I,
"If they two are in heaven?"
Quick was the little Maid's reply,
"O Master! we are seven."

"But they are dead; those two are dead!
Their spirits are in heaven!"
'Twas throwing words away; for still
The little Maid would have her will,
And said, "Nay, we are seven!"

THE DAFFODILS

118

I WANDER'D lonely as a cloud
That floats on high o'er vales and hills,
When all at once I saw a crowd,
A host of golden daffodills,
Beside the lake, beneath the trees
Fluttering and dancing in the breeze.

Continuous as the stars that shine
And twinkle on the milky way,
They stretch'd in never-ending line
Along the margin of a bay:
Ten thousand saw I at a glance
Tossing their heads in sprightly dance.

The waves beside them danced, but they
Out-did the sparkling waves in glee:—
A Poet could not but be gay
In such a jocund company!
I gazed—and gazed—but little thought
What wealth the show to me had brought;

For oft, when on my couch I lie
In vacant or in pensive mood,

They flash upon that inward eye
Which is the bliss of solitude;
And then my heart with pleasure fills,
And dances with the daffodils.

TO THE DAISY

WITH little here to do or see
Of things that in the great world be,
Sweet Daisy! oft I talk to thee
    For thou art worthy,
Thou unassuming commonplace
Of Nature, with that homely face,
And yet with something of a grace
    Which love makes for thee!

Oft on the dappled turf at ease
I sit and play with similes,
Loose types of things through all degrees,
    Thoughts of thy raising;
And many a fond and idle name
I give to thee, for praise or blame
As is the humour of the game,
    While I am gazing.

A nun demure, of lowly port;
Or sprightly maiden, of Love's court,
In thy simplicity the sport
    Of all temptations;
A queen in crown of rubies drest;
A starveling in a scanty vest;
Are all, as seems to see thee best,
    Thy appellations.

A little Cyclops, with one eye
Staring to threaten and defy,
That thought comes next—and instantly
    The freak is over,
The shape will vanish, and behold!
A silver shield with boss of gold
That spreads itself, some fairy bold
    In fight to cover.

I see thee glittering from afar—
And then thou art a pretty star,

Not quite so fair as many are
 In heaven above thee!
Yet like a star, with glittering crest,
Self-poised in air thou seem'st to rest;—
May peace come never to his nest
 Who shall reprove thee!

Sweet Flower! for by that name at last
When all my reveries are past
I call thee, and to that cleave fast,
 Sweet silent Creature!
That breath'st with me in sun and air,
Do thou, as thou are wont, repair
My heart with gladness, and a share
 Of thy meek nature!

WRITTEN IN EARLY SPRING

120

I HEARD a thousand blended notes
While in a grove I sate reclined,
In that sweet mood when pleasant thoughts
Bring sad thoughts to the mind.

To her fair works did Nature link
The human soul that through me ran;
And much it grieved my heart to think
What Man has made of Man.

Through primrose tufts, in that sweet bower,
The periwinkle trail'd its wreaths;
And 'tis my faith that every flower
Enjoys the air it breathes.

The birds around me hopp'd and play'd,
Their thoughts I cannot measure,—
But the least motion which they made
It seem'd a thrill of pleasure.

The budding twigs spread out their fan
To catch the breezy air;
And I must think, do all I can,
That there was pleasure there.

If this belief from heaven be sent,
If such be Nature's holy plan,

Have I not reason to lament
What Man has made of Man?

TO THE SKYLARK

121

Ethereal minstrel! pilgrim of the sky!
Dost thou despise the earth where cares abound?
Or while the wings aspire, are heart and eye
Both with thy nest upon the dewy ground?
Thy nest which thou canst drop into at will,
Those quivering wings composed, that music still!

To the last point of vision, and beyond
Mount, daring warbler!—that love-prompted strain
—'Twixt thee and thine a never-failing bond—
Thrills not the less the bosom of the plain:
Yet might'st thou seem, proud privilege! to sing
All independent of the leafy Spring.

Leave to the nightingale her shady wood;
A privacy of glorious light is thine,
Whence thou dost pour upon the world a flood
Of harmony, with instinct more divine;
Type of the wise, who soar, but never roam—
True to the kindred points of Heaven and Home.

THE AFFLICTION OF MARGARET

122

Where art thou, my beloved Son,
Where art thou, worse to me than dead!
O find me, prosperous or undone!
Or if the grave be now thy bed,
Why am I ignorant of the same
That I may rest; and neither blame
Nor sorrow may attend thy name?

Seven years, alas! to have received
No tidings of an only child—
To have despair'd, have hoped, believed,
And been for evermore beguiled,—
Sometimes with thoughts of very bliss!
I catch at them, and then I miss;
Was ever darkness like to this?

He was among the prime in worth,
An object beauteous to behold;
Well born, well bred; I sent him forth
Ingenuous, and bold:
If things ensued that wanted grace
As hath been said, they were not base;
And never blush was on my face.

Ah! little doth the young-one dream
When full of play and childish cares,
What power is in his wildest scream
Heard by his mother unawares!
He knows it not, he cannot guess;
Years to a mother bring distress;
But do not make her love the less.

Neglect me! no, I suffer'd long
From that ill thought; and being blind
Said "Pride shall help me in my wrong:
Kind mother have I been, as kind
As ever breathed:" and that is true;
I've wet my path with tears like dew,
Weeping for him when no one knew.

My Son, if thou be humbled, poor,
Hopeless of honour and of gain,
O! do not dread thy mother's door;
Think not of me with grief and pain:
I now can see with better eyes;
And worldly grandeur I despise
And fortune with her gifts and lies.

Alas! the fowls of heaven have wings,
And blasts of heaven will aid their flight;
They mount—how short a voyage brings
The wanderers back to their delight!
Chains tie us down by land and sea;
And wishes, vain as mine, may be
All that is left to comfort thee.

Perhaps some dungeon hears thee groan
Maim'd, mangled by inhuman men;
Or thou upon a desert thrown
Inheritest the lion's den;
Or hast been summon'd to the deep

Thou, thou, and all thy mates, to keep
An incommunicable sleep.

I look for ghosts: but none will force
Their way to me; 'tis falsely said
That their was ever intercourse
Between the living and the dead;
For surely then I should have sight
Of him I wait for day and night
With love and longings infinite.

My apprehensions come in crowds;
I dread the rustling of the grass;
The very shadows of the clouds
Have power to shake me as they pass;
I question things, and do not find
One that will answer to my mind;
And all the world appears unkind.

Beyond participation lie
My troubles, and beyond relief:
If any chance to heave a sigh
They pity me, and not my grief.
Then come to me, my Son, or send
Some tidings that my woes may end!
I have no other earthly friend.

SHE WAS A PHANTOM OF DELIGHT

123

She was a phantom of delight
When first she gleam'd upon my sight;
A lovely apparition, sent
To be a moment's ornament;
Her eyes as stars of twilight fair;
Like Twilight's, too, her dusky hair;
But all things else about her drawn
From May-time and the cheerful dawn;
A dancing shape, an image gay,
To haunt, to startle, and waylay.

I saw her upon nearer view,
A spirit, yet a woman too!
Her household motions light and free,
And steps of virgin-liberty;

A countenance in which did meet
Sweet records, promises as sweet:
A creature not too bright or good
For human nature's daily food,
For transient sorrows, simple wiles,
Praise, blame, love, kisses, tears, and smiles.

And now I see with eye serene
The very pulse of the machine;
A being breathing thoughtful breath,
A traveller between life and death:
The reason firm, the temperate will,
Endurance, foresight, strength, and skill;
A perfect woman, nobly plann'd
To warn, to comfort, and command;
And yet a Spirit still, and bright
With something of angelic light.

TO THE HIGHLAND GIRL OF INVERSNEYDE

Sweet Highland Girl, a very shower
Of beauty is thy earthly dower!
Twice seven consenting years have shed
Their utmost bounty on thy head:
And these gray rocks, this household lawn,
These trees—a veil just half withdrawn,
This fall of water that doth make
A murmur near the silent lake,
This little bay, a quiet road
That holds in shelter thy abode;
In truth together ye do seem
Like something fashion'd in a dream;
Such forms as from their covert peep
When earthly cares are laid asleep!
But O fair Creature! in the light
Of common day, so heavenly bright
I bless Thee, Vision as thou art,
I bless thee with a human heart:
God shield thee to thy latest years!
I neither know thee nor thy peers:
And yet my eyes are fill'd with tears.

With earnest feeling I shall pray
For thee when I am far away;

For never saw I mien or face
In which more plainly I could trace
Benignity and home-bred sense
Ripening in perfect innocence.
Here scatter'd, like a random seed,
Remote from men, Thou dost not need
The embarrass'd look of shy distress,
And maidenly shamefacédness:
Thou wear'st upon thy forehead clear
The freedom of a mountaineer:
A face with gladness overspread,
Soft smiles, by human kindness bred;
And seemliness complete, that sways
Thy courtesies, about thee plays;
With no restraint, but such as springs
From quick and eager visitings
Of thoughts that lie beyond the reach
Of thy few words of English speech:
A bondage sweetly brook'd, a strife
That gives thy gestures grace and life!
So have I, not unmoved in mind,
Seen birds of tempest-loving kind,
Thus beating up against the wind.

What hand but would a garland cull
For thee who are so beautiful?
O happy pleasure! here to dwell
Beside thee in some healthy dell;
Adopt your homely ways, and dress,
A shepherd, thou a shepherdess!
But I could frame a wish for thee
More like a grave reality:
Thou art to me but as a wave
Of the wild sea: and I would have
Some claim upon thee, if I could,
Though but of common neighbourhood.
What joy to hear thee, and to see!
Thy elder brother I would be,
Thy father, anything to thee.
Now thanks to heaven! that of its grace
Hath led me to this lonely place:
Joy have I had; and going hence
I bear away my recompense.
In spots like these it is we prize
Our memory, feel that she hath eyes:

Then why should I be loth to stir?
I feel this place was made for her;
To give new pleasure like the past,
Continued long as life shall last.
Nor am I loth, though pleased at heart,
Sweet Highland Girl! from thee to part;
For I, methinks, till I grow old
As fair before me shall behold
As I do now, the cabin small,
The lake, the bay, the waterfall;
And Thee, the spirit of them all!

THE SOLITARY REAPER

125

BEHOLD her, single in the field,
Yon solitary Highland Lass!
Reaping and singing by herself;
Stop here, or gently pass!
Alone she cuts and binds the grain,
And sings a melancholy strain;
O listen! for the vale profound
Is overflowing with the sound.

No nightingale did ever chaunt
More welcome notes to weary bands
Of travellers in some shady haunt,
Among Arabian sands:
No sweeter voice was ever heard
In spring-time from the cuckoo-bird,
Breaking the silence of the seas
Among the farthest Hebrides.

Will no one tell me what she sings?
Perhaps the plaintive numbers flow
For old, unhappy, far-off things,
And battles long ago:
Or is it some more humble lay,
Familiar matter of to-day?
Some natural sorrow, loss, or pain,
That has been, and may be again!

Whate'er the theme, the maiden sang
As if her song could have no ending;
I saw her singing at her work,

And o'er the sickle bending;
I listen'd, till I had my fill;
And, as I mounted up the hill,
The music in my heart I bore
Long after it was heard no more.

THE REVERIE OF POOR SUSAN

126

At the corner of Wood Street, when daylight appears,
Hangs a Thrush that sings loud, it has sung for three years:
Poor Susan has pass'd by the spot, and has heard
In the silence of morning the song of the bird.

'Tis a note of enchantment; what ails her? She sees
A mountain ascending, a vision of trees;
Bright volumes of vapour through Lothbury glide,
And a river flows on through the vale of Cheapside.

Green pastures she views in the midst of the dale
Down which she so often has tripp'd with her pail;
And a single small cottage, a nest like a dove's,
The one only dwelling on earth that she loves.

She looks, and her heart is in heaven: but they fade,
The mist and the river, the hill and the shade;
The stream will not flow, and the hill will not rise,
And the colours have all pass'd away from her eyes!

* * *

SAMUEL TAYLOR COLERIDGE

KUBLA KHAN

127

In Xanadu did Kubla Khan
  A stately pleasure-dome decree:
Where Alph, the sacred river, ran
Through caverns measureless to man
  Down to a sunless sea.
So twice five miles of fertile ground
With walls and towers were girded round:
And here were gardens bright with sinuous rills,
Where blossomed many an incense-bearing tree

And here were forests ancient as the hills,
Enfolding sunny spots of greenery.

But oh! that deep romantic chasm which slanted
Down the green hill athwart a cedarn cover!
A savage place! as holy and enchanted
As e'er beneath a waning moon was haunted
By woman wailing for her demon-lover!
And from this chasm, with ceaseless turmoil seething,
As if this earth in fast thick pants were breathing,
A mighty fountain momently was forced;
Amid whose swift half-intermitted burst
Huge fragments vaulted like rebounding hail,
Or chaffy grain beneath the thresher's flail:
And 'mid these dancing rocks at once and ever
It flung up momently the sacred river.
Five miles meandering with a mazy motion
Through wood and dale the sacred river ran,
Then reached the caverns measureless to man,
And sank in tumult to a lifeless ocean:
And 'mid this tumult Kubla heard from far
Ancestral voices prophesying war!
    The shadow of the dome of pleasure
   Floated midway on the waves;
     Where was heard the mingled measure
      From the fountain and the caves.
It was a miracle of rare device,
A sunny pleasure-dome with caves of ice!

    A damsel with a dulcimer
     In a vision once I saw:
    It was an Abyssinian maid,
     And on her dulcimer she played,
    Singing of Mount Abora.
    Could I revive within me
    Her symphony and song,
To such a deep delight 'twould win me,
That with music loud and long,
I would build that dome in air,
That sunny dome! those caves of ice!
And all who heard should see them there,
And all should cry, Beware! Beware!
His flashing eyes, his floating hair!
Weave a circle round him thrice,
    And close your eyes with holy dread,

For he on honey-dew hath fed,
And drunk the milk of Paradise.

YOUTH AND AGE

128

Verse, a breeze 'mid blossoms straying,
Where Hope clung feeding, like a bee—
Both were mine! Life went a-maying
   With Nature, Hope, and Poesy,
      When I was young!
When was young?—Ah, woful when!
Ah! for the change 'twixt Now and Then!
This breathing house not built with hands,
This body that does me grievous wrong,
O'er aery cliffs and glittering sands
How lightly then it flash'd along:
Like those trim skiffs, unknown of yore,
On winding lakes and rivers wide,
That ask no aid of sail or oar,
That fear no spite of wind or tide!
Nought cared this body for wind or weather
When Youth and I lived in't together.

   Flowers are lovely; Love is flower-like;
Friendship is a sheltering tree;
O! the joys, that came down shower-like,
Of Friendship, Love, and Liberty,
      Ere I was old!
Ere I was old? Ah woful Ere,
Which tells me, Youth's no longer here.
O Youth! for years so many and sweet,
'Tis known that Thou and I were one,
I'll think it but a fond conceit—
It cannot be, that Thou art gone!
Thy vesper-bell hath not yet toll'd:—
And thou wert aye a masker bold!
What strange disguise hast now put on
To make believe that Thou art gone?
I see these locks in silvery slips,
This drooping gait, this alter'd size:
But Springtide blossoms on thy lips,
And tears take sunshine from thine eyes!
Life is but Thought: so think I will
That Youth and I are housemates still.

Dew-drops are the gems of morning,
But the tears of mournful eve!
Where no hope is, life's a warning
That only serves to make us grieve
    When we are old:
—That only serves to make us grieve
With oft and tedious taking-leave,
Like some poor nigh-related guest
That may not rudely be dismist,
Yet hath out-stay'd his welcome while,
And tells the jest without the smile.

CHRISTABEL

PART THE FIRST

'Tis the middle of night by the castle clock,
And the owls have awakened the crowing cock
Tu—whit!——Tu—whoo!
And hark, again! the crowing cock,
How drowsily it crew!

Sir Leoline, the Baron rich,
Hath a toothless mastiff bitch;
From her kennel beneath the rock
Maketh answer to the clock,
Four for the quarters, and twelve for the hour;
Ever and aye, by shine and shower,
Sixteen short howls, not over loud;

Some say, she sees my lady's shroud.
Is the night chilly and dark?
The night is chilly, but not dark.
The thin gray cloud is spread on high,
It covers but not hides the sky.
The moon is behind, and at the full;
And yet she looks both small and dull.
The night is chill, the cloud is gray:
'Tis a month before the month of May,
And the Spring comes slowly up this way.

The lovely lady, Christabel,
Whom her father loves so well,
What makes her in the wood so late,

A furlong from the castle gate?
She had dreams all yesternight—
Of her own betrothed knight;
And she in the midnight wood will pray
For the weal of her lover that's far away.

She stole along, she nothing spoke,
The sighs she heaved were soft and low,
And naught was green upon the oak
But moss and rarest mistletoe:
She kneels beneath the huge oak-tree,
And in silence prayeth she.

The lady sprang up suddenly,
The lovely lady, Christabel!
It moaned as near, as near can be,
But what it is she cannot tell.—
On the other side it seems to be,
Of the huge, broad-breasted, old oak-tree.

The night is chill; the forest bare;
Is it the wind that moaneth bleak?
There is not wind enough in the air
To move away the ringlet curl
From the lovely lady's cheek—
There is not wind enough to twirl
The one red leaf, the last of its clan,
That dances as often as dance it can,
Hanging so light, and hanging so high,
On the topmost twig that looks up at the sky.
Hush, beating heart of Christabel!
Jesu, Maria, shield her well!
She folded her arms beneath her cloak,
And stole to the other side of the oak.
  What sees she there?

There she sees a damsel bright
Drest in a silken robe of white,
That shadowy in the moonlight shone:
The neck that made that white robe wan,
Her stately neck, and arms were bare;
Her blue-veined feet unsandalled were,
And wildly glittered here and there
The gems entangled in her hair.

I guess, 'twas frightful there to see—
A lady so richly clad as she—
  Beautiful exceedingly!

Mary mother, save me now!
(Said Christabel,) And who art thou?

The lady strange made answer meet,
And her voice was faint and sweet:—
Have pity on my sore distress,
I scarce can speak for weariness:
Stretch forth thy hand, and have no fear!
Said Christabel, How camest thou here?
And the lady, whose voice was faint and sweet,
Did thus pursue her answer meet:—

My sire is of a noble line,
And my name is Geraldine:
Five warriors seized me yestermorn,
Me, even me, a maid forlorn:
They choked my cries with force and fright,
And tied me on a palfrey white.
The palfrey was as fleet as wind,
And they rode furiously behind.
They spurred amain, their steeds were white:
And once we crossed the shade of night.

As sure as Heaven shall rescue me,
I have no thought what men they be;
Nor do I know how long it is
(For I have lain entranced I wis)
Since one, the tallest of the five,
Took me from the palfrey's back,
A weary woman, scarce alive.
Some muttered words his comrades spoke:
He placed me underneath this oak;
He swore they would return with haste;
Whither they went I cannot tell—
I thought I heard, some minutes past,
Sounds as of a castle bell.
Stretch forth thy hand (thus endeth she),
And help a wretched maid to flee.

Then Christabel stretched forth her hand,
And comforted fair Geraldine:

SAMUEL TAYLOR COLERIDGE

O well, bright dame! may you command
The service of Sir Leoline;
And gladly our stout chivalry
Will he send forth and friends withal
To guide and guard you safe and free
Home to your noble father's hall.

She rose: and forth with steps they passed
That strove to be, and were not, fast.
Her gracious stars the lady blest,
And thus spake on sweet Christabel:
All our household are at rest,
The hall as silent as the cell;
Sir Leoline is weak in health,
And may not well awakened be,
But we will move as if in stealth,
And I beseech your courtesy,
This night, to share your couch with me.

They crossed the moat, and Christabel
Took the key that fitted well;
A little door she opened straight,
All in the middle of the gate,
The gate that was ironed within and without,
Where an army in battle array had marched out,
The lady sank, belike through pain,
And Christabel with might and main
Lifted her up a weary weight,
Over the threshold of the gate:
Then the lady rose again,
And moved, as she were not in pain.

So free from danger, free from fear,
They crossed the court: right glad they were.
And Christabel devoutly cried
To the lady by her side,
Praise we the Virgin all divine
Who hath rescued thee from thy distress!
Alas, alas! said Geraldine,
I cannot speak from weariness.
So free from danger, from from fear,
They crossed the court: right glad they were.
Outside her kennel, the mastiff old
Lay fast asleep, in moonshine cold.
The mastiff old did not awake,

Yet she an angry moan did make!
And what can ail the mastiff bitch
Never till now she uttered yell
Beneath the eye of Christabel.
Perhaps it is the owlet's scritch:
For what can ail the mastiff bitch?

They passed the hall, that echoes still,
Pass as lightly as you will!
The brands were flat, the brands were dying,
Amid their own white ashes lying;
But when the lady passed, there came
A tongue of light, a fit of flame;
And Christabel saw the lady's eye,
And nothing else saw she thereby,
Save the boss of the shield of Sir Leoline tall,
Which hung in a murky old niche in the wall.
O softly tread, said Christabel,
My father seldom sleepeth well.
Sweet Christabel her feet doth bare,
And jealous of the listening air
They steal their way from stair to stair,
Now in the glimmer, and now in gloom,
And now they passed the Baron's room,
As still as death, with stifled breath!
And now they reached her chamber door;
And now doth Geraldine press down
The rushes of the chamber floor.
The moon shines dim in the open air,
And not a moonbeam enters there.
But they without its light can see
The chamber carved so curiously,
Carved with figures strange and sweet,
All made out of the carver's brain,
For a lady's chamber meet:
The lamp with twofold silver chain
Is fastened to an angel's feet.
The silver lamp burns dead and dim;

But Christabel the lamp will trim.
She trimmed the lamp, and made it bright,
And left it swinging to and fro,
While Geraldine, in wretched plight,
Sank down upon the floor below.

O weary lady, Geraldine,
I pray you, drink this cordial wine!
It is a wine of virtuous powers;
My mother made it of wild flowers.

And will your mother pity me,
Who am a maiden most forlorn?
Christabel answered,—Woe is me!
She died the hour that I was born.

I have heard the gray-haired friar tell
How on her death-bed she did say,
That she should hear the castle-bell
Strike twelve upon my wedding-day.
O mother dear! that thou wert here!
I would, said Geraldine, she were!

But soon with altered voice, said she—
"Off, wandering mother! Peak and pine!
I have power to bid thee flee."
Alas! what ails poor Geraldine?
Why stares she with unsettled eye?
Can she the bodiless dead espy?
And why with hollow voice cries she,
"Off, woman, off! this hour is mine—
Though thou her guardian spirit be,
Off, woman, off! 'tis given to me."

Then Christabel knelt by the lady's side,
And raised to heaven her eyes so blue—
"Alas!" said she, "this ghastly ride—
Dear lady! it hath wildered you!
The lady wiped her moist cold brow,
And faintly said, "'Tis over now!"

Again the wild-flower wine she drank:
Her fair large eyes 'gan glitter bright,
And from the floor whereon she sank,
The lofty lady stood upright:
She was most beautiful to see,
Like a lady of a far countrée.

And thus the lofty lady spake—
"All they who live in the upper sky,
Do love you, holy Christabel!

And you love them, and for their sake
And for the good which me befel,
Even I in my degree will try,
Fair maiden, to requite you well.
But now unrobe yourself; for I
Must pray, ere yet in bed I lie."
Quoth Christabel, So let it be!
And as the lady bade, did she.
Her gentle limbs did she undress,
And lay down in her loveliness.

But through her brain of weal and woe
So many thoughts moved to and fro,
That vain it were her lids to close;
So half-way from the bed she rose,
And on her elbow did recline
To look at the lady Geraldine.

Beneath the lamp the lady bowed,
And slowly rolled her eyes around;
Then drawing in her breath aloud,
Like one that shuddered, she unbound
The cincture from beneath her breast:
Her silken robe, and inner vest,
Dropt to her feet, and full in view,
Behold! her bosom and half her side—
A sight to dream of, not to tell!
O shield her! shield sweet Christabel!

Yet Geraldine nor speaks nor stirs;
Ah! what a stricken look was hers!
Deep from within she seems half-way
To lift some weight with sick assay,
And eyes the maid and seeks delay;
Then suddenly, as one defied,
Collects herself in scorn and pride,
And lay down by the Maiden's side!—
And in her arms the maid she took,
      Ah wel-a-day!
And with low voice and doleful look
These words did say:
"In the touch of this bosom there worketh a spell,
Which is lord of thy utterance, Christabel!
Thou knowest to-night, and wilt know to-morrow,
This mark of my shame, this seal of my sorrow;

> But vainly thou warrest,
>   For this is alone in
> Thy power to declare,
>   That in the dim forest
> Thou heard'st a low moaning,
> And found'st a bright lady, surpassingly fair;
> And didst bring her home with thee in love and in charity,
> To shield and shelter her from the damp air."

THE CONCLUSION TO PART THE FIRST

It was a lovely sight to see
The lady Christabel, when she
Was praying at the old oak-tree;
>   Amid the jagged shadows
>   Of mossy leafless boughs,
>   Kneeling in the moonlight,
>   To make her gentle vows;
Her slender palms together prest,
Heaving sometimes on her breast;
Her face resigned to bliss or bale—
Her face, oh call it fair not pale,
And both blue eyes more bright than clear,
Each about to have a tear.

With open eyes (ah woe is me!)
Asleep, and dreaming fearfully,
Fearfully dreaming, yet, I wis,
Dreaming that alone, which is—
O sorrow and shame! Can this be she,
The lady, who knelt at the old oak tree?
And lo! the worker of these harms,
That holds the maiden in her arms,
Seems to slumber still and mild,
As a mother with her child.

A star hath set, a star hath risen,
O Geraldine! since arms of thine
Have been the lovely lady's prison.
O Geraldine! one hour was thine—
Thou'st had thy will! By tairn and rill,
The night-birds all that hour were still.
But now they are jubilant anew,
From cliff and tower, tu—whoo! tu—whoo!
Tu—whoo! tu—whoo! from wood and fell!

And see! the lady Christabel!
Gathers herself from out her trance;
Her limbs relax, her countenance
Grows sad and soft; the smooth thin lids
Close o'er her eyes; and tears she sheds—
Large tears that leave the lashes bright!
And oft the while she seems to smile
As infants at a sudden light!

Yea, she doth smile, and she doth weep,
Like a youthful hermitess,
Beauteous in a wilderness,
Who, praying always, prays in sleep,
And, if she move unquietly,
Perchance, 'tis but the blood so free
Comes back and tingles in her feet.
No doubt, she hath a vision sweet.
What if her guardian spirit 'twere,
What if she knew her mother near?
But this she knows, in joys and woes,
That saints will aid if men will call:
For the blue sky bends over all!

PART THE SECOND

Each matin bell, the Baron saith,
Knells us back to a world of death.
These words Sir Leoline first said,
When he rose and found his lady dead;
These words Sir Leoline will say
Many a morn to his dying day!

And hence the custom and law began
That still at dawn the sacristan,
Who duly pulls the heavy bell,
Five and forty beads must tell
Between each stroke—a warning knell,
Which not a soul can choose but hear
From Bratha Head to Wyndermere.

Saith Bracy the bard, So let it knell!
And let the drowsy sacristan
Still count as slowly as he can!
There is no lack of such, I ween,

As well fill up the space between.
In Langdale Pike and Witch's Lair,
And Dungeon-ghyll so foully rent,
With ropes of rock and bells of air
Three sinful sextons' ghosts are pent,
Who all give back, one after t'other,
The death-note to their living brother;
And oft too, by the knell offended,
Just as their one! two! three! is ended,
The devil mocks the doleful tale
With a merry peal from Borrowdale.

The air is still! through mist and cloud
That merry peal comes ringing loud;
And Geraldine shakes off her dread,
And rises lightly from the bed;
Puts on her silken vestments white,
And tricks her hair in lovely plight,
And nothing doubting of her spell
Awakens the lady Christabel.
"Sleep you, sweet lady Christabel?
I trust that you have rested well?"

And Christabel awoke and spied
The same who lay down by her side—
O rather say, the same whom she
Raised up beneath the old oak tree!
Nay, fairer yet! and yet more fair!
For she belike hath drunken deep
Of all the blessedness of sleep!
And while she spake, her looks, her air,
Such gentle thankfulness declare,
That (so it seemed) her girded vests
Grew tight beneath her heaving breasts.
"Sure I have sinn'd!" said Christabel,
"Now heaven be praised if all be well!"
And in low faltering tones, yet sweet,
Did she the lofty lady greet
With such perplexity of mind
As dreams too lively leave behind.

So quickly she rose, and quickly arrayed
Her maiden limbs, and having prayed
That He, who on the cross did groan,
Might wash away her sins unknown,

She forthwith led fair Geraldine
To meet her sire, Sir Leoline.
The lovely maid and the lady tall
Are pacing both into the hall,
And pacing on through page and groom,
Enter the Baron's presence-room.

The Baron rose, and while he prest
His gentle daughter to his breast,
With cheerful wonder in his eyes
The lady Geraldine espies,
And gave such welcome to the same,
As might beseem so bright a dame!

But when he heard the lady's tale,
And when she told her father's name,
Why waxed Sir Leoline so pale,
Murmuring o'er the name again,
Lord Roland de Vaux of Tryermaine?

Alas! they had been friends in youth
But whispering tongues can poison truth;
And constancy lives in realms above;
And life is thorny; and youth is vain;
And to be wroth with one we love
Doth work like madness in the brain.
And thus it chanced, as I divine,
With Roland and Sir Leoline.
Each spake words of high disdain
And insult to his heart's best brother:
They parted—ne'er to meet again!
But never either found another
To free the hollow heart from paining—
They stood aloof, the scars remaining,
Like cliffs which had been rent asunder;
A dreary sea now flows between.
But neither heat, nor frost, nor thunder,
Shall wholly do away, I ween,
The marks of that which once hath been.

Sir Leoline, a moment's space,
Stood gazing on the damsel's face:
And the youthful Lord of Tryermaine
Came back upon his heart again.
O then the Baron forgot his age,

His noble heart swelled high with rage;
He swore by the wounds in Jesu's side
He would proclaim it far and wide,
With trump and solemn heraldry,
That they, who thus had wronged the dame
Were base as spotted infamy!
"And if they dare deny the same,
My herald shall appoint a week,
And let the recreant traitors seek
My tourney court—that there and then
I may dislodge their reptile souls
From the bodies and forms of men!"
He spake: his eye in lightning rolls!
For the lady was ruthlessly seized; and he kenned
In the beautiful lady the child of his friend!

And now the tears were were on his face,
And fondly in his arms he took
Fair Geraldine, who met the embrace,
Prolonging it with joyous look.
Which when she viewed, a vision fell
Upon the soul of Christabel,
The vision of fear, the touch and pain!
She shrunk and shuddered, and saw again—
(Ah, woe is me! Was it for thee,
Thou gentle maid! such sights to see?)

Again she saw that bosom old,
Again she felt that bosom cold,
And drew in her breath with a hissing sound:
Whereat the Knight turned wildly round
And nothing saw but his own sweet maid
With eyes upraised, as one that prayed.
The touch, the sight, had passed away,
And in its stead that vision blest,
Which comforted her after-rest,
While in the lady's arms she lay,
Had put a rapture in her breast.
And on her lips and o'er her eyes
Spread smiles like light!
                      With new surprise,
"What ails then my beloved child?"
The Baron said—His daughter mild
Made answer, "All will yet be well!"
I ween, she had no power to tell

Aught else: so mighty was the spell.
Yet he, who saw this Geraldine,
Had deemed her sure a thing divine.
Such sorrow with such grace she blended,
As if she feared she had offended
Sweet Christabel, that gentle maid!
And with such lowly tones she prayed
She might be sent without delay
Home to her father's mansion.

                        "Nay!
Nay, by my soul!" said Leoline.
"Ho! Bracy the bard, the charge be thine!
Go thou, with music sweet and loud,
And take two steeds with trappings proud,
And take the youth whom thou lov'st best
To bear thy harp, and learn thy song,
And clothe you both in solemn vest,
And over the mountains haste along,
Lest wandering folk, that are abroad,
Detain you on the valley road.
"And when he has crossed the Irthing flood,
My merry bard! he hastes, he hastes
Up Knorren Moor, through Halegarth Wood,
And reaches soon that castle good
Which stands and threatens Scotland's wastes.

"Bard Bracy! bard Bracy! your horses are fleet,
Ye must ride up the hall, your music so sweet,
More loud than your horses' echoing feet!
And loud and loud to Lord Roland call,
Thy daughter is safe in Langdale hall!
Thy beautiful daughter is safe and free—
Sir Leoline greets thee thus through me.
He bids thee come without delay
With all thy numerous array;
And take thy lovely laughter home;
And he will meet thee on the way
With all his numerous array
White with their panting palfreys' foam:
And, by mine honour! I will say,
That I repent me of the day
When I spake words of fierce disdain
To Roland de Vaux of Tryermaine!—
—For since that evil hour hath flown,
Many a summer's sun hath shone;

Yet ne'er found I a friend again
Like Roland de Vaux of Tryermaine."

The lady fell, and clasped his knees,
Her face upraised, her eyes o'erflowing;
And Bracy replied, with faltering voice,
His gracious hail on all bestowing:
"Thy words, thou sire of Christabel,
Are sweeter than my harp can tell;
Yet might I gain a boon of thee,
This day my journey should not be,
So strange a dream hath come to me;
That I had vowed with music loud
To clear yon wood from thing unblest,
Warn'd by a vision in my rest!
For in my sleep I saw that dove,
That gentlest bird, whom thou dost love,
And call'st by thy own daughter's name—
Sir Leoline! I saw the same,
Fluttering, and uttering fearful moan,
Among the green herbs in the forest alone.
Which when I saw and when I heard,
I wonder'd what might ail the bird;
For nothing near it could I see,
Save the grass and green herbs underneath the old tree.

"And in my dream, methought, I went
To search out what might there be found;
And what the sweet bird's trouble meant,
That thus lay fluttering on the ground.
I went and peered, and could descry
No cause for her distressful cry;
But yet for her dear lady's sake
I stooped, methought, the dove to take,
When lo! I saw a bright green snake
Coiled around its wings and neck.
Green as the herbs on which it couched,
Close by the dove's its head it crouched;
And with the dove it heaves and stirs,
Swelling its neck as she swelled hers!
I woke; it was the midnight hour,
The clock was echoing in the tower;
But though my slumber was gone by,
This dream it would not pass away—
It seems to live upon my eye!

And thence I vowed this self-same day
With music strong and saintly song
To wander through the forest bare,
Lest aught unholy loiter there."

Thus Bracy said: the Baron, the while,
Half-listening heard him with a smile;
Then turn'd to Lady Geraldine,
His eyes made up of wonder and love;
And said in courtly accents fine,
"Sweet maid, Lord Roland's beauteous dove,
With arms more strong than harp or song,
Thy sire and I will crush the snake!"
He kissed her forehead as he spake,
And Geraldine in maiden wise
Casting down her large bright eyes,
With blushing cheek and courtesy fine
She turned her from Sir Leoline;
Softly gathering up her train,
That o'er her right arm fell again;
And folded her arms across her chest,
And couched her head upon her breast,
And looked askance at Christabel—
Jesu, Maria, shield her well!

A snake's small eye blinks dull and shy,
And the lady's eyes they shrunk in her head,
Each shrunk up to a serpent's eye,
And with somewhat of malice, and more of dread,
At Christabel she look'd askance!—
One moment—and the sight was fled!
But Christabel in dizzy trance
Stumbling on the unsteady ground
Shuddered aloud, with a hissing sound;
And Geraldine again turned round,
And like a thing that sought relief,
Full of wonder and full of grief,
She rolled her large bright eyes divine
Wildly on Sir Leoline.

The maid, alas! her thoughts are gone,
She nothing sees—no sight but one!
The maid, devoid of guile and sin,
I know not how, in fearful wise,
So deeply had she drunken in

That look, those shrunken serpent eyes,
That all her features were resigned
To this sole image in her mind:
And passively did imitate
That look of dull and treacherous hate!
And thus she stood, in dizzy trance,
Still picturing that look askance
With forced unconscious sympathy
Full before her father's view—
As far as such a look could be
In eyes so innocent and blue!
And when the trance was o'er, the maid
Paused awhile, and inly prayed:
Then falling at the Baron's feet,
"By my mother's soul do I entreat
That thou this woman send away!"
She said: and more she could not say:
For what she knew she could not tell,
O'er-mastered by the mighty spell.
Why is thy cheek so wan and wild,
Sir Leoline? Thy only child
Lies at thy feet, thy joy, thy pride,
So fair, so innocent, so mild;
The same, for whom thy lady died!
O, by the pangs of her dear mother
Think thou no evil of thy child!
For her, and thee, and for no other,
She prayed the moment ere she died:
Prayed that the babe for whom she died,
Might prove her dear lord's joy and pride!
   That prayer her deadly pangs beguiled,
      Sir Leoline!
   And wouldst thou wrong thy only child,
      Her child and thine?

Within the Baron's heart and brain
If thoughts, like these, had any share,
They only swelled his rage and pain,
And did but work confusion there.
His heart was cleft with pain and rage,
His cheeks they quivered, his eyes were wild,
Dishonour'd thus in his old age;
Dishonour'd by his only child,
And all his hospitality
To the insulted daughter of his friend

By more than woman's jealousy
Brought thus to a disgraceful end—
He rolled his eye with stern regard
Upon the gentle minstrel bard,
And said in tones abrupt, austere—
"Why, Bracy! dost thou loiter here?
I bade thee hence!" The bard obeyed;
And turning from his own sweet maid,
The aged knight, Sir Leoline,
Led forth the lady Geraldine!

THE CONCLUSION TO PART THE SECOND

A little child, a limber elf,
Singing, dancing, to itself,
A fairy thing with red round cheeks,
That always finds, and never seeks,
Makes such a vision to the sight
As fills a father's eyes with light;
And pleasures flow in so thick and fast
Upon his heart, that he at last
Must needs express his love's excess
With words of unmeant bitterness.
Perhaps 'tis pretty to force together
Thoughts so all unlike each other;
To mutter and mock a broken charm,
To dally with wrong that does no harm.
Perhaps 'tis tender too and pretty
At each wild word to feel within
A sweet recoil of love and pity.
And what, if in a world of sin
(O sorrow and shame should this be true!)
Such giddiness of heart and brain
Comes seldom save from rage and pain,
So talks as it's most used to do.

DEJECTION: AN ODE

Late, late yestreen I saw the new Moon,
With the old Moon in her arms;
And I fear, I fear, my master dear!
We shall have a deadly storm.
                    Ballad of Sir Patrick Spence

SAMUEL TAYLOR COLERIDGE

I

WELL! If the Bard was weather-wise, who made
  The grand old ballad of Sir Patrick Spence,
  This night, so tranquil now, will not go hence
Unroused by winds, that ply a busier trade
Than those which mould yon cloud in lazy flakes,
Or the dull sobbing draft, that moans and rakes
    Upon the strings of this Æolian lute,
    Which better far were mute.
  For lo! the New-moon winter-bright!
  And overspread with phantom light,
    (With swimming phantom light o'erspread
    But rimmed and circled by a silver thread)
I see the old Moon in her lap, foretelling
  The coming-on of rain and squally blast,
And oh! that even now the gust were swelling,
  And the slant night-shower driving loud and fast!
Those sounds which oft have raised me, whilst they awed
    And sent my soul abroad,
Might now perhaps their wonted impulse give,
Might startle this dull pain, and make it move and live!

II

A grief without a pang, void, dark, and drear,
  A stifled, drowsy, unimpassioned grief,
  Which finds no natural outlet, no relief,
    In word, or sigh, or tear—
O Lady! in this wan and heartless mood,
To other thoughts by yonder throstle woo'd,
  All this long eve, so balmy and serene,
Have I been gazing on the western sky,
  And its peculiar tint of yellow green;
And still I gaze—and with how blank an eye!
And those thin clouds above, in flakes and bars,
That give away their motion to the stars:
Those stars, that glide behind them or between,
Now sparkling, now bedimmed, but always seen;
Yon crescent Moon, as fixed as if it grew
In its own cloudless, starless lake of blue;
I see them all so excellently fair,
I see, not feel, how beautiful they are!

III

    My genial spirits fail;
    And what can these avail
To lift the smothering weight from off my breast?
      It were a vain endeavor,
      Though I should gaze for ever
On that green light that lingers in the west;
I may not hope from outward forms to win
The passion and the life, whose fountains are within.

IV

O Lady! we receive but what we give,
And in our life alone does Nature live;
Ours is her wedding-garment, ours her shroud!
    And would we aught behold, of higher worth,
Than that inanimate cold world allowed
To the poor loveless ever-anxious crowd,
    Ah! from the soul itself must issue forth
A light, a glory, a fair luminous cloud
      Enveloping the Earth—
And from the soul itself must there be sent
    A sweet and potent voice, of its own birth,
Of all sweet sounds the life and element!

V

O pure of heart! thou need'st not ask of me
What this strong music in the soul may be!
What, and wherein it doth exist,
This light, this glory, this fair luminous mist,
This beautiful and beauty-making power.
    Joy, virtuous Lady! Joy that ne'er was given,
Save to the pure, and in their purest hour,
Life, and life's effluence, cloud at once and shower,
Joy, Lady! is the spirit and the power,
Which wedding Nature to us gives in dower,
    A new Earth and new Heaven,
Undreamt of by the sensual and the proud—
Joy is the sweet voice, Joy the luminous cloud—
      We in ourselves rejoice!
And thence flows all that charms or ear or sight,
    All melodies the echoes of that voice,
All colours a suffusion from that light.

VI

There was a time when, though my path was rough,
  This joy within me dallied with distress,
And all misfortunes were but as the stuff
  Whence Fancy made me dreams of happiness:
For hope grew round me, like the twining vine,
And fruits, and foliage, not my own, seemed mine.
But now afflictions bow me down to earth:
Nor care I that they rob me of my mirth;
    But oh! each visitation
Suspends what nature gave me at my birth,
  My shaping spirit of Imagination.
For not to think of what I needs must feel
  But to be still and patient, all I can;
And haply by abstruse research to steal
  From my own nature all the natural man—
  This was my sole resource, my only plan;
Till that which suits a part infects the whole,
And now is almost grown the habit of my soul.

VII

Hence, viper thoughts, that coil around my mind,
    Reality's dark dream!
I turn from you, and listen to the wind,
  Which long has raved unnoticed. What a scream
Of agony by torture lengthened out
That lute sent forth! Thou Wind, that rav'st without,
  Bare crag, or mountain-tairn, or blasted tree,
Or pine-grove whither woodman never clomb,
Or lonely house, long held the witches' home,
  Methinks were fitter instruments for thee,
Mad Lutanist! who in this month of showers,
Of dark-brown gardens, and of peeping flowers,
Mak'st Devils' yule, with worse than wintry song,
The blossoms, buds, and timorous leaves among.
  Thou Actor, perfect in all tragic sounds!
Thou mighty Poet, even to frenzy bold!
    What tell'st thou now about?
    'Tis of the rushing of an host in rout,
With groans of trampled men, with smarting wounds—
At once they groan with pain and shudder with the cold!
But hush! there is a pause of deepest silence!
  And all that noise, as of a rushing crowd,

With groans, and tremulous shuddering—all is over—
  It tells another tale, with sounds less deep and loud!
A tale of less affright,
  And tempered with delight,
As Otway's self had framed the tender lay.
  'Tis of a little child,
  Upon a lonesome wild,
Not far from home, but she hath lost her way;
And now moans low in bitter grief and fear,
And now screams loud, and hopes to make her mother hear.

VIII

'Tis midnight, but small thoughts have I of sleep:
Full seldom may my friend such vigils keep!
Visit her, gentle Sleep! with wings of healing,
  And may this storm be but a mountain-birth,
May all the stars hang bright above her dwelling,
  Silent as though they watched the sleeping Earth!
    With light heart may she rise,
    Gay fancy, cheerful eyes.
Joy lift her spirit, joy attune her voice;
To her may all things live, from pole to pole,
Their life the eddying of her living soul!
  O simple spirit, guided from above,
Dear Lady! friend devoutest of my choice,
Thus may'st thou ever, evermore rejoice.

* * *

ROBERT SOUTHEY

130

AFTER BLENHEIM

It was a summer evening,
Old Kaspar's work was done,
And he before his cottage door
  Was sitting in the sun;
And by him sported on the green
His little grandchild Wilhelmine.

She saw her brother Peterkin
  Roll something large and round
Which he beside the rivulet
  In playing there had found;

He came to ask what he had found
That was so large and smooth and round.

Old Kaspar took it from the boy
  Who stood expectant by;
And then the old man shook his head,
  And with a natural sigh
" 'Tis some poor fellow's skull," said he,
"Who fell in the great victory.

"I find them in the garden,
  For there's many here about;
And often when I go to plough
  The ploughshare turns them out.
For many thousand men," said he,
"Were slain in that great victory."

"Now tell us what 'twas all about,"
  Young Peterkin he cries;
And little Wilhelmine looks up
  With wonder-waiting eyes;
"Now tell us all about the war,
And what they fought each other for."

"It was the English," Kaspar cried,
  "Who put the French to rout;
But what they fought each other for
  I could not well make out.
But every body said," quoth he,
"That 'twas a famous victory.

"My father lived at Blenheim then,
  Yon little stream hard by;
They burnt his dwelling to the ground,
  And he was forced to fly:
So with his wife and child he fled,
Nor had he where to rest his head.

"With fire and sword the country round
  Was wasted far and wide,
And many a childing mother then
  And newborn baby died:
But things like that, you know, must be
At every famous victory.

"They say it was a shocking sight
    After the field was won;
For many thousand bodies here
    Lay rotting in the sun:
But things like that, you know, must be
After a famous victory.

"Great praise the Duke of Marlbro' won
    And our good Prince Eugene;"
"Why 'twas a very wicked thing!"
    Said little Wilhelmine;
"Nay .. nay .. my little girl," quoth he,
"It was a famous victory.

"And every body praised the Duke
    Who this great fight did win."
"But what good came of it at last?"
    Quoth little Peterkin:—
"Why that I cannot tell," said he,
"But 'twas a famous victory."

THE SCHOLAR

131

My days among the Dead are past;
Around me I behold,
Where'er these casual eyes are cast,
The mighty minds of old:
My never-failing friends are they,
With whom I converse day by day.

With them I take delight in weal
And seek relief in woe;
And while I understand and feel
How much to them I owe,
My cheeks have often been bedew'd
With tears of thoughtful gratitude.

My thoughts are with the Dead; with them
I live in long-past years,
Their virtues love, their faults condemn,
Partake their hopes and fears,
And from their lessons seek and find
Instruction with an humble mind.

My hopes are with the Dead; anon
My place with them will be,

CHARLES LAMB

And I with them shall travel on
Through all Futurity;
Yet leaving here a name, I trust,
That will not perish in the dust.

* * *

CHARLES LAMB

THE OLD FAMILIAR FACES

132

I HAVE had playmates, I have had companions
In my days of childhood, in my joyful school-days;
All, all are gone, the old familiar faces.

I have been laughing, I have been carousing,
Drinking late, sitting late, with my bosom cronies;
All, all are gone, the old familiar faces.

I loved a Love once, fairest among women:
Closed are her doors on me, I must not see her—
All, all are gone, the old familiar faces.

I have a friend, a kinder friend has no man:
Like an ingrate, I left my friend abruptly;
Left him, to muse on the old familiar faces.

Ghost-like I paced round the haunts of my childhood,
Earth seem'd a desert I was bound to traverse,
Seeking to find the old familiar faces.

Friend of my bosom, thou more than a brother,
Why wert not thou born in my father's dwelling?
So might we talk of the old familiar faces,

How some they have died, and some they have left me,
And some are taken from me; all are departed;
All, all are gone, the old familiar faces.

133

ON AN INFANT DYING AS SOON AS BORN

I SAW where in the shroud did lurk
A curious frame of Nature's work;
A flow'ret crushéd in the bud,
A nameless piece of Babyhood,
Was in her cradle-coffin lying;
Extinct, with scarce the sense of dying:
So soon to exchange the imprisoning womb

For darker closets of the tomb!
She did but ope an eye, and put
A clear beam forth, then straight up shut
For the long dark: ne'er more to see
Through glasses of mortality,
Riddle of destiny, who can show
What thy short visit meant, or know
What thy errand here below?
Shall we say, that Nature blind
Check'd her hand, and changed her mind
Just when she had exactly wrought
A finish'd pattern without fault?
Could she flag, or could she tire,
Or lack'd she the Promethean fire
(With her nine moons' long workings sickn'd)
That should thy little limbs have quickn'd?
Limbs so firm, they seem'd to assure
Life of health, and days mature:
Woman's self in miniature!
Limbs so fair, they might supply
(Themselves now but cold imagery)
The sculptor to make Beauty by.
Or did the stern-eyed Fate descry
That babe or mother, one must die;
So in mercy left the stock
And cut the branch; to save the shock
Of young years widow'd, and the pain
When Single State comes back again
To the lone man who, reft of wife,
Thenceforward drags a maiméd life?
The economy of Heaven is dark,
And wisest clerks have miss'd the mark
Why human buds, like this should fall,
More brief than fly ephemeral
That has his day; while shrivell'd crones
Stiffen with age to stocks and stones;
And crabbed use the conscience sears
In sinners of an hundred years.
—Mother's prattle, mother's kiss,
Baby fond, thou ne'er wilt miss:
Rites, which custom does impose,
Silver bells, and baby clothes;
Coral redder than those lips
Which pale death did late eclipse;
Music framed for infant's glee,

Whistle never tuned for thee;
Though thou want'st not, thou shalt have them,
Loving hearts were they which gave them.
Let not one be missing; nurse,
See them laid upon the hearse
Of infants slain by doom perverse.
Why should kings and nobles have
Pictured trophies to their grave,
And we, churls, to thee deny
Thy pretty toys with thee to lie—
A more harmless vanity?

* * *

ELIZABETH BARRETT BROWNING

SONNETS FROM THE PORTUGUESE

I

I THOUGHT once how Theocritus had sung
Of the sweet years, the dear and wished-for years,
Who each one in a gracious hand appears
To bear a gift for mortals, old or young:
And, as I mused it in its antique tongue,
I saw, in gradual vision through my tears,
The sweet, sad years, the melancholy years,
Those of my own life, who by turns had flung
A shadow across me. Straightway I was 'ware,
So weeping, how a mystic Shape did move
Behind me, and drew me backward by the hair;
And a voice said in mastery, while I strove,—
"Guess now who holds thee?"—"Death," I said. But, there,
The silver answer rang,—"Not Death, but Love."

II

BUT only three in all God's universe
Have heard this word thou hast said,—Himself, beside
Thee speaking, and me listening! and replied
One of us . . . *that* was God, . . . and laid the curse
So darkly on my eyelids, as to amerce
My sight from seeing thee,—that if I had died,
The deathweights, placed there, would have signified
Less absolute exclusion. "Nay" is worse
From God than from all others, O my friend!

Men could not part us with their worldly jars,
Nor the seas change us, nor the tempests bend;
Our hands would touch for all the mountain-bars:
And, heaven being rolled between us at the end,
We should but vow the faster for the stars.

III

UNLIKE are we, unlike, O princely Heart!
Unlike our uses and our destinies.
Our ministering two angels look suprise
On one another, as they strike athwart
Their wings in passing. Thou, bethink thee, art
A guest for queens to social pageantries,
With gages from a hundred brighter eyes
Than tears even can make mine, to play thy part
Of chief musician. What hast *thou* to do
With looking from the lattice-lights at me,
A poor, tired, wandering singer, singing through
The dark, and leaning up a cypress tree?
The chrism is on thine head,—on mine, the dew,—
And Death must dig the level where these agree.

IV

THOU hast thy calling to some palace-floor,
Most gracious singer of high poems! where
The dancers will break footing, from the care
Of watching up thy pregnant lips for more.
And dost thou lift this house's latch too poor
For hand of thine? and canst thou think and bear
To let thy music drop here unaware
In folds of golden fulness at my door?
Look up and see the casement broken in,
The bats and owlets builders in the roof!
My cricket chirps against thy mandolin.
Hush, call no echo up in further proof
Of desolation! there's a voice within
That weeps . . . as thou must sing . . . alone, aloof.

V

I LIFT my heavy heart up solemnly,
As once Electra her sepulchral urn,
And looking in thine eyes, I overturn

ELIZABETH BARRETT BROWNING

The ashes at thy feet. Behold and see
What a great heap of grief lay hid in me,
And how the red wild sparkles dimly burn
Through the ashen grayness. If thy foot in scorn
Could tread them out to darkness utterly,
It might be well perhaps. But if instead
Thou wait beside me for the wind to blow
The gray dust up, . . . those laurels on thine head,
O my Belovèd, will not shield thee so,
That none of all the fires shall scorch and shred
The hair beneath. Stand farther off then! go.

VI

Go from me. Yet I feel that I shall stand
Henceforward in thy shadow. Nevermore
Alone upon the threshold of my door
Of individual life, I shall command
The uses of my soul, nor lift my hand
Serenely in the sunshine as before,
Without the sense of that which I forbore—
Thy touch upon the palm. The widest land
Doom takes to part us, leaves thy heart in mine
With pulses that beat double. What I do
And what I dream include thee, as the wine
Must taste of its own grapes. And when I sue
God for myself, He hears that name of thine,
And sees within my eyes the tears of two.

VII

THE face of all the world is changed, I think,
Since first I heard the footsteps of thy soul
Move still, oh, still, beside me, as they stole
Betwixt me and the dreadful outer brink
Of obvious death, where I, who thought to sink,
Was caught up into love, and taught the whole
Of life in a new rhythm. The cup of dole
God gave for baptism, I am fain to drink,
And praise its sweetness, Sweet, with thee anear.
The names of country, heaven, are changed away
For where thou art or shalt be, there or here;
And this . . . this lute and song . . . loved yesterday,
(The singing angels know) are only dear
Because thy name moves right in what they say.

VIII

What can I give thee back, O liberal
And princely giver, who hast brought the gold
And purple of thine heart, unstained, untold,
And laid them on the outside of the wall
For such as I to take or leave withal,
In unexpected largesse? am I cold,
Ungrateful, that for these most manifold
High gifts, I render nothing back at all?
Nor so; not cold,—but very poor instead.
Ask God who knows. For frequent tears have run
The colors from my life, and left so dead
And pale a stuff, it were not fitly done
To give the same as pillow to thy head.
Go farther! let it serve to trample on.

IX

Can it be right to give what I can give?
To let thee sit beneath the fall of tears
As salt as mine, and hear the sighing years
Re-sighing on my lips renunciative
Though those infrequent smiles which fail to live
For all thy adjurations? O my fears,
That this can scarce be right! We are not peers,
So to be lovers; and I own, and grieve,
That grievers of such gifts as mine are, must
Be counted with the ungenerous. Out, alas!
I will not soil thy purple with my dust,
Nor breathe my poison on thy Venice-glass,
Nor give thee any love—which were unjust.
Beloved, I only love thee! let it pass.

X

Yet, love, mere love, is beautiful indeed
And worthy of acceptation. Fire is bright,
Let temple burn, or flax; an equal light
Leaps in the flame from cedar-plank or weed:
And love is fire. And when I say at need
I love thee . . . mark! . . . *I love thee*—in thy sight
I stand transfigured, glorified aright,
With conscience of the new rays that proceed
Out of my face toward thine. There's nothing low

In love, when love the lowest: meanest creatures
Who love God, God accepts while loving so.
And what I *feel,* across the inferior features
Of what I *am,* doth flash itself, and show
How that great work of Love enhances Nature's.

XI

And therefore if to love can be desert,
I am not all unworthy. Cheeks as pale
As these you see, and trembling knees that fail
To bear the burden of a heavy heart,—
This weary minstrel-life that once was girt
To climb Aornus, and can scarce avail
To pipe now 'gainst the valley nightingale
A melancholy music,—why advert
To these things? O Belovèd, it is plain
I am not of thy worth nor for thy place!
And yet, because I love thee, I obtain
From that same love this vindicating grace,
To live on still in love, and yet in vain,—
To bless thee, yet renounce thee to thy face.

XII

Indeed this very love which is my boast,
And which, when rising up from breast to brow,
Doth crown me with a ruby large enow
To draw men's eyes and prove the inner cost,—
This love even, all my worth, to the uttermost,
I should not love withal, unless that thou
Hadst set me an example, shown me how,
When first thine earnest eyes with mine were crossed,
And love called love. And thus, I cannot speak
Of love even, as a good thing of my own:
Thy soul hath snatched up mine all faint and weak,
And placed it by thee on a golden throne,—
And that I love (O soul, we must be meek!)
Is by thee only, whom I love alone.

XIII

And wilt thou have me fashion into speech
The love I bear thee, finding words enough,
And hold the torch out, while the winds are rough,

Between our faces, to cast light on each?—
I drop it at thy feet. I cannot teach
My hand to hold my spirit so far off
From myself—me—that I should bring thee proof
In words, of love hid in me out of reach.
Nay, let the silence of my womanhood
Commend my woman-love to thy belief,—
Seeing that I stand unwon, however wooed,
And rend the garment of my life, in brief,
By a most dauntless, voiceless fortitude,
Lest one touch of this heart convey its grief.

XIV

If thou must love me, let it be for nought
Except for love's sake only. Do not say
"I love her for her smile—her look—her way
Of speaking gently,—for a trick of thought
That falls in well with mine, and certes brought
A sense of pleasant ease on such a day"—
For these things in themselves, Belovèd, may
Be changed, or change for thee,—and love, so wrought,
May be unwrought so. Neither love me for
Thine own dear pity's wiping my cheeks dry,—
A creature might forget to weep, who bore
Thy comfort long, and lose thy love thereby!
But love me for love's sake, that evermore
Thou mayst love on, through love's eternity.

XV

Accuse me not, beseech thee, that I wear
Too calm and sad a face in front of thine;
For we two look two ways, and cannot shine
With the same sunlight on our brow and hair.
On me thou lookest with no doubting care,
As on a bee shut in a crystalline;
Since sorrow hath shut me safe in love's divine,
And to spread wing and fly in the outer air
Were most impossible failure, if I strove
To fail so. But I look on thee—on thee—
Beholding, besides love, the end of love,
Hearing oblivion beyond memory;
As one who sits and gazes from above,
Over the rivers to the bitter sea.

XVI

And yet, because thou overcomest so,
Because thou art more noble and like a king,
Thou canst prevail against my fears and fling
Thy purple round me, till my heart shall grow
Too close against thine heart henceforth to know
How it shook when alone. Why, conquering
May prove as lordly and complete a thing
In lifting upward, as in crushing low!
And as a vanquished soldier yields his sword
To one who lifts him from the bloody earth,
Even so, Belovèd, I at last record,
Here ends my strife. If *thou* invite me forth,
I rise above abasement at the word.
Make thy love larger to enlarge my worth.

XVII

My poet, thou canst touch on all the notes
God set between His After and Before,
And strike up and strike off the general roar
Of the rushing worlds a melody that floats
In a serene air purely. Antidotes
Of medicated music, answering for
Mankind's forlornest uses, thou canst pour
From thence into their ears. God's will devotes
Thine to such ends, and mine to wait on thine.
How, Dearest, wilt thou have me for most use?
A hope, to sing by gladly? or a fine
Sad memory, with thy songs to interfuse?
A shade, in which to sing—of palm or pine?
A grave, on which to rest from singing? Choose.

XVIII

I never gave a lock of hair away
To a man, Dearest, except this to thee,
Which now upon my fingers thoughtfully,
I ring out to the full brown length and say
"Take it." My day of youth went yesterday:
My hair no longer bounds to my foot's glee,
Nor plant I it from rose or myrtle-tree,
As girls do, any more; it only may
Now shade on two pale cheeks the mark of tears,
Taught drooping from the head that hangs aside

Through sorrow's trick. I thought the funeral-shears
Would take this first, but love is justified,—
Take it thou, finding pure, from all those years,
The kiss my mother left here when she died.

XIX

The soul's Rialto hath its merchandise;
I barter curl for curl upon that mart,
And from my poet's forehead to my heart
Receive this lock which outweighs argosies,—
As purply black, as erst to Pindar's eyes
The dim purpureal tresses gloomed athwart
The nine white Muse-brows. For this counterpart,
The bay-crown's shade, Belovèd, I surmise,
Still lingers on thy curl, it is so black!
Thus, with a fillet of smooth-kissing breath,
I tie the shadows safe from gliding back,
And lay the gift where nothing hindereth;
Here on my heart, as on thy brow, to lack
No natural heat till mine grows cold in death.

XX

Belovèd, my Belovèd, when I think
That thou wast in the world a year ago,
What time I sat alone here in the snow
And saw no footprint, heard the silence sink
No moment at thy voice, but, link by link,
Went counting all my chains as if that so
They never could fall off at any blow
Struck by thy possible hand,—why, thus I drink
Of life's great cup of wonder! Wonderful,
Never to feel thee thrill the day or night
With personal act or speech,—nor ever cull
Some prescience of thee with the blossoms white
Thou sawest growing! Atheists are as dull,
Who cannot guess God's presence out of sight.

XXI

Say over again, and yet once over again,
That dost love me. Though the word repeated
Should seem "a cuckoo-song," as thou dost treat it,
Remember, never to the hill or plain,
Valley and wood, without her cuckoo-strain
Comes the fresh Spring in all her green completed.

Belovèd, I, amid the darkness greeted
By a doubtful spirit-voice, in that doubt's pain
Cry, "Speak once more—thou lovest!" Who can fear
Too many stars, though each in heaven shall roll,
Too many flowers, though each shall crown the year?
Say thou dost love me, love me, love me—toll
The silver iterance!—only minding, Dear,
To love me also in silence with thy soul.

XXII

When our two souls stand up erect and strong,
Face to face, silent, drawing nigh and nigher,
Until the lengthening wings break into fire
At either curvèd point,—what bitter wrong
Can the earth do to us, that we should not long
Be here contented? Think. In mounting higher,
The angels would press on us and aspire
To drop some golden orb of perfect song
Into our deep, dear silence. Let us stay
Rather on earth, Belovèd,—where the unfit
Contrarious mood of men recoil away
And isolate pure spirits, and permit
A place to stand and love in for a day,
With darkness and the death-hour rounding it.

XXIII

Is it indeed so? If I lay here dead,
Wouldst thou miss any life in losing mine?
And would the sun for thee more coldly shine
Because of grave-damps falling round my head?
I marvelled, my Belovèd, when I read
Thy thought so in the letter. I am thine—
But ... *so* much to thee? Can I pour thy wine
While my hands tremble? Then my soul, instead
Of dreams of death, resumes life's lower range.
Then, love me, Love! look on me—breathe on me!
As brighter ladies do not count it strange,
For love, to give up acres and degree,
I yield the grave for thy sake, and exchange
My near sweet view of Heaven, for earth with thee!

XXIV

Let the world's sharpness, like a clasping knife,
Shut in upon itself and do no harm.

In this close hand of Love, now soft and warm,
And let us hear no sound of human strife
After the click of the shutting. Life to life—
I lean upon thee, Dear, without alarm,
And feel as safe as guarded by a charm
Against the stab of worldlings, who if rife
Are weak to injure. Very whitely still
The lilies of our lives may reassure
Their blossoms from their roots, accessible
Alone to heavenly dews that drop not fewer,
Growing straight, out of man's reach, on the hill.
God only, who made us rich, can make us poor.

XXV

A HEAVY heart, Belovèd, have I borne
From year to year until I saw thy face,
And sorrow after sorrow took the place
Of all those natural joys as lightly worn
As the stringed pearls, each lifted in its turn
By a beating heart at dance-time. Hopes apace
Were changed to long despairs, till God's own grace
Could scarcely lift above the world forlorn
My heavy heart. Then *thou* didst bid me bring
And let it drop adown thy calmly great
Deep being! Fast it sinketh, as a thing
Which its own nature doth precipitate,
While thine doth close above it, mediating
Betwixt the stars and the unaccomplished fate.

XXVI

I LIVED with visions for my company
Instead of men and women, years ago,
And found them gentle mates, nor thought to know
A sweeter music than they played to me.
But soon their trailing purple was not free
Of this world's dust, their lutes did silent grow,
And I myself grew faint and blind below
Their vanishing eyes. Then THOU didst come—to be,
Belovèd, what they seemed. Their shining fronts,
Their songs, their splendors (better, yet the same,
As river-water hallowed into fonts),
Met in thee, and from out thee overcame
My soul with satisfaction of all wants:
Because God's gifts put man's best dreams to shame.

XXVII

My own Belovèd, who hast lifted me
From this drear flat of earth where I was thrown,
And, in betwixt the languid ringlets, blown
A life-breath, till the forehead hopefully
Shines out again, as all the angels see,
Before thy saving kiss! My own, my own,
Who camest to me when the world was gone,
And I who looked for only God, found *thee!*
I find thee; I am safe, and strong, and glad.
As one who stands in dewless asphodel
Looks backward on the tedious time he had
In the upper life,—so I, with bosom-swell,
Make witness, here, between the good and bad,
That Love, as strong as Death, retrieves as well.

XXVIII

My letters! all dead paper, mute and white!
And yet they seem alive and quivering
Against my tremulous hands which loose the string
And let them drop down on my knee to-night.
This said,—he wished to have me in his sight
Once, as a friend: this fixed a day in spring
To come and touch my hand . . . a simple thing,
Yet I wept for it!—this, . . . the paper's light . . .
Said, *Dear, I love thee;* and I sank and quailed
As if God's future thundered on my past.
This said, *I am thine*—and so its ink has paled
With lying at my heart that beat too fast.
And this . . . O Love, thy words have ill availed
If, what this said, I dared repeat at last!

XXIX

I THINK of thee!—my thoughts do twine and bud
About thee, as wild vines, about a tree,
Put out broad leaves, and soon there's nought to see
Except the straggling green which hides the wood.
Yet, O my palm-tree, be it understood
I will not have my thoughts instead of thee
Who art dearer, better! Rather, instantly
Renew thy presence; as a strong tree should,
Rustle thy boughs and set thy trunk all bare,
And let these bands of greenery which insphere thee

Drop heavily down,—burst, shattered, everywhere!
Because, in this deep joy to see and hear thee
And breathe within thy shadow a new air,
I do not think of thee—I am too near thee.

XXX

I SEE thine image through my tears to-night,
And yet to-day I saw thee smiling. How
Refer the cause?—Beloved, is it thou
Or, I who makes me sad? The acolyte
Amid the chanted joy and thankful rite
May so fall flat, with pale insensate brow,
On the altar-stair. I hear thy voice and vow,
Perplexed, uncertain, since thou art out of sight,
As he, in his swooning ears, the choir's Amen.
Beloved, dost thou love? or did I see all
The glory as I dreamed, and fainted when
Too vehement light dilated my ideal,
For my soul's eyes? Will that light come again,
As now these tears come—falling hot and real?

XXXI

THOU comest! all is said without a word.
I sit beneath thy looks as children do
In the noon-sun, with souls that tremble through
Their happy eyelids from an unaverred
Yet prodigal inward joy. Behold, I erred
In that last doubt! and yet I cannot rue
The sin most, but the occasion—that we two
Should for a moment stand unministered
By a mutual presence. Ah, keep near and close,
Thou dovelike help! and, when my fears would rise,
With thy broad heart serenely interpose:
Brood down with thy divine sufficiencies
These thoughts which tremble when bereft of those,
Like callow birds left desert to the skies.

XXXII

THE first time that the sun rose on thine oath
To love me, I looked forward to the moon
To slacken all those bonds which seemed too soon
And quickly tied to make a lasting troth.
Quick-loving hearts, I thought, may quickly loathe;

And, looking on myself, I seemed not one
For such man's love;—more like an out-of-tune
Worn viol, a good singer would be wroth
To spoil his song with, and which, snatched in haste,
Is laid down at the first ill-sounding note.
I did not wrong myself so, but I placed
A wrong on *thee*. For perfect strains may float
'Neath master-hands, from instruments defaced,—
And great souls, at one stroke, may do and doat.

XXXIII

YES, call me by my pet-name! let me hear
The name I used to run at, when a child,
From innocent play, and leave the cowslips piled,
To glance up in some face that proved me dear
With the look of its eyes. I miss the clear
Fond voices which, being drawn and reconciled
Into the music of Heaven's undefiled,
Call me no longer. Silence on the bier,
While I call God—call God!—So let thy mouth
Be heir to those who are now exanimate.
Gather the north flowers to complete the south,
And catch the early love up in the late.
Yes, call me by that name,—and I, in truth,
With the same heart, will answer and not wait.

XXXIV

WITH the same heart, I said, I'll answer thee
As those, when thou shalt call me by my name—
Lo, the vain promise! is the same, the same,
Perplexed and ruffled by life's strategy?
When called before, I told how hastily
I dropped my flowers or brake off from a game,
To run and answer with the smile that came
At play last moment, and went on with me
Through my obedience. When I answer now,
I drop a grave thought, break from solitude;
Yet still my heart goes to thee—ponder how—
Not as to a single good, but all my good!
Lay thy hand on it, best one, and allow
That no child's foot could run fast as this blood.

XXXV

If I leave all for thee, wilt thou exchange
And be all to me? Shall I never miss
Home-talk and blessing and the common kiss
That comes to each in turn, nor count it strange,
When I look up, to drop on a new range
Of walls and floors, another home than this?
Nay, wilt thou fill that place by me which is
Filled by dead eyes too tender to know change?
That's hardest. If to conquer love, has tried,
To conquer grief, tries more, as all things prove;
For grief indeed is love and grief beside.
Alas, I have grieved so I am hard to love.
Yet love me—wilt thou? Open thine heart wide,
And fold within the wet wings of thy dove.

XXXVI

When we met first and loved, I did not build
Upon the event with marble. Could it mean
To last, a love set pendulous between
Sorrow and sorrow? Nay, I rather thrilled,
Distrusting every light that seemed to gild
The onward path, and feared to overlean
A finger even. And, though I have grown serene
And strong since then, I think that God has willed
A still renewable fear . . . O love, O troth . . .
Lest these enclasped hands should never hold,
This mutual kiss drop down between us both
As an unowned thing, once the lips being cold.
And Love, be false! if *he,* to keep one oath,
Must lose one joy, by his life's star foretold.

XXXVII

Pardon, oh pardon, that my soul should make,
Of all that strong divineness which I know
For thine and thee, an image only so
Formed of the sand, and fit to shift and break.
It is that distant years which did not take
Thy sovranty, recoiling with a blow,
Have forced my swimming brain to undergo
Their doubt and dread, and blindly to forsake
Thy purity of likeness and distort
Thy worthiest love to a worthless counterfeit:

As if a shipwrecked Pagan, safe in port,
His guardian sea-god to commemorate,
Should set a sculptured porpoise, gills a-snort
And vibrant tail, within the temple-gate.

XXXVIII

First time he kissed me, he but only kissed
The fingers of this hand wherewith I write;
And ever since, it grew more clean and white,
Slow to world-greetings, quick with its "Oh, list,"
When the angels speak. A ring of amethyst
I could not wear here, plainer to my sight,
Than that first kiss. The second passed in height
The first, and sought the forehead, and half missed,
Half falling on the hair. O beyond meed!
That was the chrism of love, which love's own crown,
With sanctifying sweetness, did precede.
The third upon my lips was folded down
In perfect, purple state; since when, indeed,
I have been proud and said, "My love, my own."

XXXIX

Because thou hast the power and own'st the grace
To look through and behind this mask of me
(Against which years have beat thus blanchingly
With their rains), and behold my soul's true face,
The dim and weary witness of life's race,—
Because thou hast the faith and love to see,
Through that same soul's distracting lethargy,
The patient angel waiting for a place
In the new Heavens,—because nor sin nor woe,
Nor God's infliction, nor death's neighborhood,
Nor all which others viewing, turn to go,
Nor all which makes me tired of all, self-viewed,—
Nothing repels thee, . . . Dearest, teach me so
To pour out gratitude, as thou dost, good!

XL

Oh, yes! they love through all this world of ours!
I will not gainsay love, called love forsooth.
I have heard love talked in my early youth,
And since, not so long back but that the flowers
Then gathered, smell still. Mussulmans and Giaours
Throw kerchiefs at a smile, and have no ruth

For any weeping. Polypheme's white tooth
Slips on the nut if, after frequent showers,
The shell is over-smooth,—and not so much
Will turn the thing called love, aside to hate,
Or else to oblivion. But thou art not such
A lover, my Belovèd! thou canst wait
Through sorrow and sickness, to bring souls to touch,
And think it soon when others cry "Too late."

XLI

I THANK all who have loved me in their hearts,
With thanks and love from mine. Deep thanks to all
Who paused a little near the prison-wall
To hear my music in its louder parts
Ere they went onward, each one to the mart's
Or temple's occupation, beyond call.
But thou, who, in my voice's sink and fall
When the sob took it, thy divinest Art's
Own instrument didst drop down at thy foot
To hearken what I said between my tears, . . .
Instruct me how to thank thee! Oh, to shoot
My soul's full meaning into future years,
That *they* should lend it utterance, and salute
Love that endures, from Life that disappears!

XLII

"My future will not copy fair my past"—
I wrote that once; and thinking at my side
My ministering life-angel justified
The word by his appealing look upcast
To the white throne of God, I turned at last,
And there, instead, saw thee, not unallied
To angels in thy soul! Then I, long tried
By natural ills, received the comfort fast,
While budding, at thy sight, my pilgrim's staff
Gave out green leaves with morning dews impearled.
I seek no copy now of life's first half:
Leave here the pages with long musing curled,
And write me new my future's epigraph,
New angel mine, unhoped for in the world!

XLIII

How do I love thee? Let me count the ways.
I love thee to the depth and breadth and height

My soul can reach, when feeling out of sight
For the ends of Being an ideal Grace.
I love thee to the level of everyday's
Most quiet need, by sun and candle-light.
I love thee freely, as men strive for Right;
I love thee purely, as they turn from Praise.
I love thee with the passion put to use
In my old griefs, and with my childhood's faith.
I love thee with a love I seemed to lose
With my lost saints,—I love thee with the breath,
Smiles, tears, of all my life!—and, if God choose,
I shall but love thee better after death.

XLIV

BELOVÈD, thou hast brought me many flowers
Plucked in the garden, all the summer through
And winter, and it seemed as if they grew
In this close room, nor missed the sun and showers.
So, in the like name of that love of ours,
Take back these thoughts which here unfolded too,
And which on warm and cold days I withdrew
From my heart's ground. Indeed, those beds and bowers
Be overgrown with bitter weeds and rue,
And wait thy weeding; yet here's eglantine,
Here's ivy!—take them, as I used to do
Thy flowers, and keep them where they shall not pine.
Instruct thine eyes to keep their colors true,
And tell thy soul their roots are left in mine.

* * *

JOHN KEATS

THE REALM OF FANCY

EVER let the Fancy roam!
Pleasure never is at home:
At a touch sweet Pleasure melteth,
Like to bubbles when rain pelteth;
Then let wingèd Fancy wander
Though the thought still spread beyond her:
Open wide the mind's cage-door,
She'll dart forth, and cloudward soar.
O sweet Fancy! let her loose;

Summer's joys are spoilt by use,
And the enjoying of the Spring
Fades as does its blossoming:
Autumn's red-lipp'd fruitage too,
Blushing through the mist and dew,
Cloys with tasting: What do then?
Sit thee by the ingle, when
The sear faggot blazes bright,
Spirit of a winter's night;
When the soundless earth is muffled,
And the cakéd snow is shuffled
From the ploughboy's heavy shoon;
When the Night doth meet the Noon
In a dark conspiracy
To banish Even from her sky.
—Sit thee there, and send abroad,
With a mind self-overaw'd
Fancy, high-commission'd:—send her!
She has vassals to attend her;
She will bring, in spite of frost,
Beauties that the earth hath lost;
She will bring thee, all together,
All delights of summer weather;
All the buds and bells of May
From dewy sward or thorny spray;
All the heapéd Autumn's wealth,
With a still, mysterious stealth:
She will mix these pleasures up
Like three fit wines in a cup,
And thou shalt quaff it:—thou shalt hear
Distant harvest-carols clear;
Rustle of the reapéd corn;
Sweet birds antheming the morn:
And, in the same moment—hark!
'Tis the early April lark,
Or the rooks, with busy caw,
Foraging for sticks and straw.
Thou shalt, at one glance, behold
The daisy and the marigold;
White-plumed lilies, and the first
Hedge-grown primrose that hath burst;
Shaded hyacinth, alway
Sapphire queen of the mid-May;
And every leaf, and every flower
Pearled with the self-same shower.

Thou shalt see the field-mouse peep
Meagre from its celléd sleep;
And the snake all winter-thin
Cast on sunny bank its skin;
Freckled nest-eggs thou shalt see
Hatching in the hawthorn-tree,
When the hen-bird's wing doth rest
Quiet on her mossy nest;
Then the hurry and alarm
When the bee-hive casts its swarm;
Acorns ripe down-pattering,
While the autumn breezes sing.

Oh, sweet Fancy! let her loose;
Everything is spoilt by use:
Where's the cheek that doth not fade,
Too much gazed at? Where's the maid
Whose lip mature is ever new?
Where's the eye, however blue,
Doth not weary? Where's the face
One would meet in every place?
Where's the voice, however soft,
One would hear so very oft?
At a touch sweet Pleasure melteth
Like to bubbles when rain pelteth.
Let then wingéd Fancy find
Thee a mistress to thy mind:
Dulcet-eyed as Ceres' daughter,
Ere the God of Torment taught her
How to frown and how to chide;
With a waist and with a side
White as Hebe's, when her zone
Slipt its golden clasp, and down
Fell her kirtle to her feet,
While she held the goblet sweet,
And Jove grew languid.—Break the mesh
Of the Fancy's silken leash;
Quickly break her prison-string,
And such joys as these she'll bring:
—Let the wingéd Fancy roam!
Pleasure never is at home.

THE EVE OF ST. AGNES

136

St. Agnes' Eve!—Ah, bitter chill it was!
The owl, for all his feathers was a-cold;

The hare limp'd trembling through the frozen grass,
And silent was the flock in wooly fold:
Numb were the Beadsman's fingers, while he told
His rosary, and while his frosted breath,
Like pious incense from a censer old,
Seem'd taking flight for heaven, without a death,
Past the sweet Virgin's picture, while his prayer he saith.

His prayer he saith, this patient, holy man;
Then takes his lamp, and riseth from his knees,
And back returneth, meagre, barefoot, wan,
Along the chapel aisle by slow degrees:
The sculptur'd dead, on each side, seem to freeze,
Emprison'd in black, purgatorial rails:
Knights, ladies, praying in dumb orat'ries,
He passeth by; and his weak spirit fails
To think how they may ache in icy hoods and mails.

Northward he turneth through a little door,
And scarce three steps, ere Music's golden tongue
Flatter'd totears this aged man and poor;
But no—already had his deathbell rung;
The joys of all his life were said and sung:
His was harsh penance on St. Agnes' Eve:
Another way he went, and soon among
Rough ashes sat he for his soul's reprieve,
And all night kept awake, for sinners' sake to grieve.

That ancient Beadsman heard the prelude soft;
And so it chanc'd, for many a door was wide,
From hurry to and fro. Soon, up aloft,
The silver, snarling trumpets 'gan to chide:
The level chambers, ready with their pride,
Were glowing to receive a thousand guests:
The carved angels, ever eager-eyed,
Star'd where upon their heads the cornice rests,
With hair blown back, and wings put cross-wise on their breasts.

At length burst in the argent revelry,
With plume, tiara, and all rich array,
Numerous as shadows haunting fairily
The brain, new stuff'd, in youth, with triumphs gay
Of old romance. These let us wish away,
And turn, sole-thoughted, to one Lady there,
Whose heart had brooded, all that wintry day,
On love, and wing'd St. Agnes' saintly care,
As she had heard old dames full many times declare.

JOHN KEATS

They told her how, upon St. Agnes' Eve,
Young virgins might have visions of delight,
And soft adorings from their loves receive
Upon the honey'd middle of the night
If ceremonies due they did aright;
As, supperless to bed they must retire,
And couch supine their beauties, lily white;
Nor look behind, nor sideways, but require
Of Heaven with upward eyes for all that they desire.

Full of this whim was thoughtful Madeline;
The music, yearning like a God in pain,
She scarcely heard: her maiden eyes divine,
Fix'd on the floor, saw many a sweeping train
Pass by—she heeded not at all: in vain
Came many a tiptoe, amorous cavalier,
And back retir'd; not cool'd by high disdain,
But she saw not: her heart was otherwhere:
She sigh'd for Agnes' dreams, the sweetest of the year.

She danc'd along with vague, regardless eyes,
Anxious her lips, her breathing quick and short:
The hallow'd hour was near at hand: she sighs
Amid the timbrels, and the throng'd resort
Of whisperers in anger, or in sport;
'Mid looks of love, defiance, hate and scorn,
Hoodwink'd with fairy fancy; all amort,
Save to St. Agnes and her lambs unshorn,
And all the bliss to be before to-morrow morn.

So, purposing each moment to retire,
She linger'd still. Meantime, across the moors,
Had come young Porphyro, with heart on fire
For Madeline. Beside the portal doors,
Buttress'd from moonlight, stands he, and implores
All saints to give him sight of Madeline,
But for one moment in the tedious hours,
That he might gaze and worship all unseen;
Perchance speak, kneel, touch, kiss—in sooth such things have been.

He ventures in: let no buzz'd whisper tell:
All eyes be muffled, or a hundred swords
Will storm his heart, Love's fev'rous citadel;
For him, those chambers held barbarian hordes,
Hyena foemen, and hot-blooded lords,
Whose very dogs would execrations howl

Against his lineage: not one breast affords
Him any mercy, in that mansion foul,
Save one old beldame, weak in body and in soul.

Ah, happy chance! the aged creature came,
Shuffling along with ivory-headed wand,
To where he stood, hid from the torch's flame,
Behind a broad hall-pillar, far beyond
The sound of merriment and chorus bland:
He startled her; but soon she knew his face,
And grasp'd his fingers in her palsied hand,
Saying, "Mercy, Porphyro! hie thee from this place;
They are all here to-night, the whole blood-thirsty race!

"Get hence! get hence! there's dwarfish Hildebrand;
He had a fever late and in the fit
He cursed thee and thine, both house and land:
Then there's that old Lord Maurice, not a whit
More tame for his grey hairs—Alas me! flit!
Flit like a ghost away."—"Ah, Gossip dear,
We're safe enough; here in this arm chair sit,
And tell me how"—"Good saints! not here, not here;
Follow me, child, or else these stones will be thy bier."

He follow'd through a lowly arched way,
Brushing the cobwebs with this lofty plume;
And as she mutter'd "Well-a—well-a-day!
He found him in a little moonlight room,
Pale, lattic'd, chill, and silent as a tomb.
"Now tell me where is Madeline," said he,
"O tell me, Angela, by the holy loom
Which none but secret sisterhood may see,
When they St. Agnes' wool are weaving piously."

"St. Agnes! Ah! Ah! it is St. Agnes' Eve—
Yet men will murder upon holy days:
Thou must hold water in a witch's sieve,
And be liege-lord of all the Elves and Fays,
To venture so: it fills me with amaze
To see thee, Porphyro!—St. Agnes' Eve!
God's help! my lady fair the conjurer plays
This very night: good angels here deceive!
But let me laugh awhile, I've mickle time to grieve."

Feebly she laugheth in the languid moon,
While Porphyro upon her face doth look,
Like puzzled urchin on an aged crone

JOHN KEATS

Who keepeth clos'd a wond'rous riddle-book,
As spectacled she sits in chimney nook.
But soon his eyes grew brilliant, when she told
His lady's purpose; and he scarce could brook
Tears, at the thought of those enchantments cold,
And Madeline asleep in lap of legends old.

Sudden a thought came like a full-blown rose,
Flushing his brow, and in his pained heart
Made purple riot: then doth he propose
A stratagem, that makes the beldame start:
"A cruel man, and impious thou art:
Sweet lady, let her pray, and sleep, and dream
Alone with her good angels, far apart
From wicked men like thee. Go, go!—I deem
Thou canst not surely be the same that thou didst seem."

"I will not harm her, by all saints I swear,"
Quoth Porphyro: "O may I ne'er find grace
When my weak voice shall whisper its last prayer,
If one of her soft ringlets I displace,
Or look with ruffian passion in her face:
Good Angela, believe me by these tears;
Or I will, even in a moment's space,
Awake, with horrid shout, my foemen's ears,
And beard them, though they be more fang'd than wolves
    and bears."

"Ah! why wilt thou affright a feeble soul?
A poor, weak, palsy-striken churchyard thing,
Whose passing-bell may ere the midnight toll;
Whose prayers for thee, each morn and evening,
Were never miss'd." Thus plaining, doth she bring
A gentler speech from burning Porphyro;
So woful, and of such deep sorrowing,
That Angela gives promise she will do
Whatever he shall wish, betide her weal or woe.

Which was, to lead him, in close secrecy,
Even to Madeline's chamber, and there hide
Him in a closet, of such privacy
That he might see her beauty unespied,
And win perhaps that night a peerless bride,
While legion'd faeries pac'd the coverlet,
And pale enchantment held her sleepy-eyed.
Never on such a night have lovers met,
Since Merlin paid his Demon all the monstrous debt.

"It shall be as thou wishest," said the Dame:
"All cates and dainties shall be stored there
Quickly on this feast-night: by the tambour frame
Her own lute thou wilt see: no time to spare,
For I am slow and feeble, and scarce dare
On such a catering trust my dizzy head.
Wait here, my child, with patience; kneel in prayer
The while: Ah! thou must needs the lady wed,
Or I may never leave my grave among the dead."

So saying, she hobbled off with busy fear.
The lover's endless minutes slowly pass'd;
The dame return'd, and whisper'd in his ear
To follow her; with agèd eyes aghast
From fright of dim espial. Safe at last,
Through many a dusky gallery, they gain
The maiden's chamber, silken, hush'd, and chaste;
Where Porphyro took covert, pleas'd amain.
His poor guide hurried back with agues in her brain.

Her falt'ring hand upon the balustrade
Old Angela was feeling for the stair,
When Madeline, St. Agnes' charmèd maid,
Rose, like a mission'd spirit, unaware:
With silver taper's light, and pious care,
She turn'd, and down the agèd gossip led
To a safe level matting. Now prepare,
Young Porphyro, for gazing on that bed;
She comes, she comes again, like ring-dove fray'd and fled.

Out went the taper as she hurried in;
Its little smoke, in pallid moonshine, died;
She clos'd the door, she panted, all akin
To spirits of the air, and visions wide:
No uttered syllable, or, woe betide!
But to her heart, her heart was voluble,
Paining with eloquence her balmy side;
As though a tongueless nightingale should swell
Her throat in vain, and die, heart-stifled in her dell.

A casement high and triple-arch'd there was,
All garlanded with carven imag'ries
Of fruits, and flowers, and bunches of knot-grass,
And diamonded with panes of quaint device,
Innumerable of stains and splendid dyes.
As are the tiger-moth's deep-damask'd wings;
And in the midst, 'mong thousand heraldries,

And twilight saints, and dim emblazonings,
A shielded scutcheon blush'd with blood of queens and kings.

Full on this casement shone the wintry moon,
And threw warm gules on Madeline's fair breast,
As down she knelt for heaven's grace and boon;
Rose-bloom fell on her hands, together prest,
And on her silver cross soft amethyst,
And on her hair a glory, like a saint:
She seem'd a splendid angel, newly drest,
Save wings, for heaven: Porphyro grew faint:
She knelt, so pure a thing, so free from mortal taint.

Anon his heart revives: her vespers done,
Of all its wreathèd pearls her hair she frees;
Unclasped her warmed jewels one by one;
Loosens her fragrant bodice; by degrees
Her rich attire creeps rustling to her knees;
Half-hidden, like a mermaid in seaweed,
Pensive awhile she dreams awake, and sees
In fancy, fair St. Agnes in her bed,
But dares not look behind, or all the charm is fled.

Soon, trembling in her soft and chilly nest,
In sort of wakeful swoon, perplex'd she lay,
Until the poppied warmth of sleep oppress'd
Her soothèd limbs, and soul fatigued away;
Flown, like a thought, until the morrow-day;
Blissfully haven'd both from joy and pain;
Clasp'd like a missal where swart Paynims pray;
Blinded alike from sunshine and from rain,
As though a rose should shut, and be a bud again.

Stol'n to this paradise, and so entranced,
Porphyro gazed upon her empty dress,
And listen'd to her breathing, if it chanced
To wake into a slumberous tenderness;
Which when he heard, that minute did he bless,
And breath'd himself: then from the closet crept,
Noiseless as fear, in a wide wilderness,
And over the hush'd carpet, silent, stepped,
And 'tween the curtains peep'd, where, lo!—how fast she slept.

Then by the bed-side, where the faded moon
Made a dim, silver twilight, soft he set
XI

A table, and, half-anguish'd, threw thereon
A cloth of woven crimson, gold, and jet:—
O for some drowsy Morphean amulet!
The boisterous, midnight, festive clarion,
The kettle-drum, and far-heard clarionet,
Affray his ears, though but in dying tone:—
The hall door shuts again, and all the noise is gone.

And still she slept an azure-lidded sleep,
In blanched linen, smooth, and lavender'd,
While he from forth the closet brought a heap
Of candied apple, quince, and plum, and gourd:
With jellies soother than the creamy curd,
And lucent syrops, tinct with cinnamon;
Manna and dates, in argosy transferr'd
From Fez; and spiced dainties, every one,
From silken Samarcand to cedar'd Lebanon.

These delicates he heap'd with glowing hand
On golden dishes and in baskets bright
Of wreathèd silver: sumptuous they stand
In the retired quiet of the night,
Filling the chilly room with perfume light.—
"And now, my love, my seraph fair, awake!
Thou art my heaven, and I thine eremite:
Open thine eyes, for meek St. Agnes' sake,
Or I shall drowse beside thee, so my soul doth ache."

Thus whispering, his warm, unnerved arm
Sank in her pillow. Shaded was her dream
By the dusk curtains:— 'twas a midnight charm
Impossible to melt as icèd stream:
The lustrous salvers in the moonlight gleam:
Broad golden fringe upon the carpet lies:
It seem'd he never, never could redeem
From such a steadfast spell his lady's eyes;
She mus'd awhile, entoil'd in woofed phantasies.

Awakening up, he took her hollow lute,—
Tumultuous,—and, in chords that tenderest be,
He play'd an ancient ditty, long since mute,
In Provence call'd, "La belle dame sans merci:"
Close to her ear touching the melody;—
Wherewith disturb'd, she utter'd a soft moan:
He ceased—she panted quick—and suddenly
Her blue affrighted eyes wide open shone:
Upon his knees he sank, as smooth-sculptured stone.

JOHN KEATS

Her eyes were open, but she still beheld,
Now wide awake, the vision of her sleep:
There was a painful change, that nigh expell'd
The blisses of her dream so pure and deep
At which fair Madeline began to weep,
And moan forth witless words with many a sigh;
While still her gaze on Porphyro would keep;
Who knelt, with joined hands and piteous eye,
Fearing to move or speak, she look'd so dreamingly.

"Ah, Porphyro!" said she, "but even now
Thy voice was as sweet tremble in mine ear,
Made tuneable with every sweetest vow;
And those sad eyes were spiritual and clear:
How chang'd thou art! how pallid, chill, and drear!
Give me that voice again, my Porphyro,
Those looks immortal, those complainings dear!
Oh leave me not in this eternal woe,
For if thou diest, my Love, I know not where to go."

Beyond a mortal man impassion'd far
At these voluptuous accents, he arose,
Ethereal, flush'd, and like a throbbing star
Seen mid the sapphire heaven's deep repose;
Into her dream he melted, as the rose
Blendeth its odour with the violet,—
Solution sweet: meantime the frost-wind blows
Like Love's alarum pattering the sharp sleet
Against the window-panes; St. Agnes' moon hath set.

'Tis dark: quick pattereth the flaw-blown sleet:
"This is no dream, my bride, my Madeline!"
'Tis dark: the icèd gusts still rave and beat:
"No dream, alas! alas! and woe is mine!
Porphyro will leave me here to fade and pine.—
Cruel! what traitor could thee hither bring?
I curse not, for my heart is lost in thine,
Though thou forsakest a deceived thing:—
A dove forlorn and lost with sick unprunèd wing!"

"My Madeline! sweet dreamer! lovely bride!
Say, may I be for aye thy vassal blest?
Thy beauty's shield, heart-shap'd and vermeil dyed?
Ay, silver shrine, here will I take my rest
After so many hours of toil and quest,
A famish'd pilgrim,—saved by miracle.
Though I have found, I will not rob thy nest

Saving of thy sweet self; if thou think'st well
To trust, fair Madeline, to no rude infidel.

"Hark! 'tis an elfin-storm from faery land,
Of haggard seeming, but a boon indeed:
Arise—arise! the morning is at hand;—
The bloated wassaillers will never heed:—
Let us away, my love, with happy speed;
There are no ears to hear, or eyes to see,—
Drown'd all in Rhenish and the sleepy mead:
Awake! arise! my love, and fearless be,
For o'er the southern moors I have a home for thee."

She hurried at his words, beset with fears,
For there were sleeping dragons all around,
At glaring watch, perhaps, with ready spears—
Down the wide stairs a darkling way they found.—
In all the house was heard no human sound.
A chain-droop'd lamp was flickering by each door;
The arras, rich with horseman, hawk, and hound,
Flutter'd in the besieging wind's uproar
And the long carpets rose along the gusty floor.

They glide, like phantoms, into the wide hall;
Like phantoms, to the iron porch, they glide;
Where lay the Porter, in uneasy sprawl,
With a huge empty flagon by his side:
The wakeful bloodhound rose, and shook his hide,
But his sagacious eye an inmate owns:
By one, and one, the bolts full easy slide:—
The chains lie silent on the footworn stones;—
The key turns, and the door upon its hinges groans.

And they are gone: aye, ages ago
These lovers fled away into the storm.
That night the Baron dreamt of many a woe,
And all his warrior-guests, with shade and form
Of witch, and demon, and large coffin-worm,
Were long be-nightmar'd. Angela the old
Died palsy-twitch'd, with meagre face deform;
The Beadsman, after thousand aves told,
For aye unsought for slept among his ashes cold.

LA BELLE DAME SANS MERCI

137

"O WHAT can ail thee, knight-at-arms,
Alone and palely loitering?

JOHN KEATS

The sedge has wither'd from the lake,
  And no birds sing.

"O what can ail thee, knight-at-arms!
  So haggard and so woe-begone?
The squirrel's granary is full,
  And the harvest's done.

"I see a lily on thy brow
  With anguish moist and fever-dew,
And on thy cheeks a fading rose
  Fast withereth too.

"I met a lady in the meads,
  Full beautiful—a faery's child,
Her hair was long, her foot was light,
  And her eyes were wild.

"I made a garland for her head,
  And bracelets too, and fragrant zone;
She look'd at me as she did love,
  And made sweet moan.

"I set her on my pacing steed
  And nothing else saw all day long,
For sidelong would she bend, and sing
  A fairy's song.

"She found me roots of relish sweet,
  And honey wild and manna-dew,
And sure in language strange she said
  "I love thee true."

"She took me to her elfin grot,
  And there she wept and sigh'd full sore,
And there I shut her wild wild eyes
  With kisses four.

"And there she lullèd me asleep,
  And there I dream'd—Ah! woe betide!
The latest dream I ever dream'd
  On the cold hill's side.

"I saw pale kings and princes too,
  Pale warriors, death-pale were they all,
They cried—'La belle Dame sans Merci
  Hath thee in thrall!'

"I saw their starved lips in the gloam
  With horrid warning gapèd wide,

> And I awoke and found me here
>   On the cold hill's side.
>
> "And this is why I sojourn here
>   Alone and palely loitering,
> Though the sedge is wither'd from the lake,
>   And no birds sing."

ON THE GRASSHOPPER AND CRICKET

138

The poetry of earth is never dead;
When all the birds are faint with the hot sun,
And hide in cooling trees, a voice will run
From hedge to hedge about the new-mown mead;
That is the grasshopper's—he takes the lead
In summer luxury,—he has never done
With his delights, for when tired out with fun
He rests at ease beneath some pleasant weed.
The poetry of earth is ceasing never:
On a lone winter evening, when the frost
Has wrought a silence, from the stove there shrills
The cricket's song, in warmth increasing ever,
And seems to one in drowsiness half lost,
The grasshopper's among some grassy hills.

ON FIRST LOOKING INTO CHAPMAN'S HOMER

139

Much have I travell'd in the realms of gold
And many goodly states and kingdoms seen;
Round many western islands have I been
Which bards in fealty to Apollo hold.

Oft of one wide expanse had I been told
That deep-brow'd Homer ruled as his demesne:
Yet did I never breathe its pure serene
Till I heard Chapman speak out loud and bold:
—Then felt I like some watcher of the skies
When a new planet swims into his ken;
Or like stout Cortez—when with eagle eyes

He stared at the Pacific—and all his men
Look'd at each other with a wild surmise—
Silent, upon a peak in Darien.

JOHN KEATS

TO SLEEP

140

O soft embalmer of the still midnight!
  Shutting with careful fingers and benign
Our gloom-pleased eyes, embower'd from the light,
  Enshaded in forgetfulness divine;
O soothest Sleep! if so it please thee, close,
  In midst of this thine hymn, my willing eyes,
Or wait the amen, ere thy poppy throws
  Around my bed its lulling charities;
Then save me, or the passèd day will shine
Upon my pillow, breeding many woes;
Save me from curious conscience, that still lords
  Its strength for darkness, burrowing like a mole;
Turn the key deftly in the oilèd wards,
  And seal the hushèd casket of my soul.

141

ODE TO A NIGHTINGALE

My heart aches, and drowsy numbness pains
  My sense, as though of hemlock I had drunk,
Or emptied some dull opiate to the drains
  One minute past, and Lethe-wards had sunk:
'Tis not through envy of thy happy lot,
  But being too happy in thy happiness,—
    That thou, light-wingéd Dryad of the trees,
      In some melodious plot
Of beechen green, and shadows numberless,
  Singest of summer in full-throated ease.

O, for a draught of vintage, that hath been
  Cool'd a long age in the deep-delvéd earth,
Tasting of Flora and the country green,
  Dance, and Provençal song, and sun-burnt mirth!
O for a beaker full of the warm South,
  Full of the true, the blushful Hippocrene,
    With beaded bubbles winking at the brim,
      And purple-stainéd mouth;
That I might drink, and leave the world unseen,
  And with thee fade away into the forest dim:

Fade far away, dissolve, and quite forget
  What thou among the leaves hast never known,
The weariness, the fever, and the fret
  Here, where men sit and hear each other groan;
Where palsy shakes a few, sad, last grey hairs,

Where youth grows pale, and spectre-thin, and dies;
Where but to think is to be full of sorrow
And leaden-eyed despairs;
Where Beauty cannot keep her lustrous eyes,
Or new Love pine at them beyond to-morrow.

Away! away! for I will fly to thee,
Not charioted by Bacchus and his pards,
But on the viewless wings of Poesy,
Though the dull brain perplexes and retards:
Already with thee! tender is the night,
And haply the Queen-Moon is on her throne,
Cluster'd around by all her starry Fays;
But here there is no light
Save what from heaven is with the breezes blown
Though verdurous glooms and winding mossy ways.

I cannot see what flowers are at my feet,
Nor what soft incense hangs upon the boughs,
But, in embalmèd darkness, guess each sweet
Wherewith the seasonable month endows
The grass, the thicket, and the fruit-tree wild;
White hawthorn, and the pastoral eglantine;
Fast fading violets cover'd up in leaves;
And mid-May's eldest child,
The coming musk-rose, full of dewy wine,
The murmurous haunt of flies on summer eves.

Darkling I listen; and for many a time
I have been half in love with easeful Death,
Call'd him soft names in many a musèd rhyme,
To take into the air my quiet breath;
Now more than ever seems it rich to die,
To cease upon the midnight with no pain,
While thou art pouring forth thy soul abroad
In such an ecstasy!
Still woudst thou sing, and I have ears in vain—
To thy high requiem become a sod.

Thou wast not born for death, immortal Bird!
No hungry generations tread thee down;
The voice I hear this passing night was heard
In ancient days by emperor and clown:
Perhaps the self-same song that found a path
Through the sad heart of Ruth, when, sick for home,
She stood in tears amid the alien corn;

　　　　The same that oft-times hath
　Charm'd magic casements, opening on the foam
　　Of perilous seas, in faery lands forlorn.

Forlorn! the very word is like a bell
　To toll me back from thee to my sole self!
Adieu! the fancy cannot cheat so well
　As she is famed to do, deceiving elf.
Adieu! adieu! thy plaintive anthem fades
　Past the near meadows, over the still stream,
　　Up the hill-side; and now 'tis buried deep
　　　In the next valley-glades:
　Was it a vision, or a waking dream?
　Fled is that music:—do I wake or sleep?

* * *

PERCY BYSSHE SHELLEY

A DREAM OF THE UNKNOWN

142

I DREAM'D that as I wander'd by the way
　Bare winter suddenly was changed to Spring,
And gentle odours led my steps astray,
　Mix'd with a sound of waters murmuring
Along a shelving bank of turf, which lay
　Under a copse, and hardly dared to fling
Its green arms round the bosom of the stream,
But kiss'd it and then fled, as Thou mightest in dream.

There grew pied wind-flowers and violets,
　Daisies, those pearl'd Arcturi of the earth,
The constellated flower that never sets;
　Faint oxlips; tender blue-bells, at whose birth
The sod scarce heaved; and that tall flower that wets
Its mother's face with heaven-collected tears,
When the low wind, its playmate's voice, it hears.

And in the warm hedge grew lush eglantine,
　Green cow-bind and the moon-light-colour'd May,
And cherry-blossoms, and white cups, whose wine
　Was the bright dew yet drain'd not by the day;
And wild roses, and ivy serpentine
　With its dark buds and leaves, wandering astray;
And flowers azure, black, and streak'd with gold,
Fairer than any waken'd eyes behold.

And nearer to the river's trembling edge
  There grew broad flag-flowers, purple prank't with white,
And starry river-buds among the sedge,
  And floating water-lilies, broad and bright,
Which lit the oak that overhung the hedge
  With moonlight beams of their own watery light;
And bulrushes, and reeds of such deep green
As soothed the dazzled eye with sober sheen.

Methought that of these visionary flowers
  I made a nosegay, bound in such a way
That the same hues, which in their natural bowers
  Were mingled or opposed, the like array
Kept these imprison'd children of the Hours
  Within my hand,—and then, elate and gay,
I hasten'd to the spot whence I had come
That I might there present it—O! to Whom?

THE INVITATION

143

Best and Brightest, come away,
Fairer far than this fair day,
Which, like thee, to those in sorrow
Comes to bid a sweet good-morrow
To the rough year just awake
In its cradle on the brake.
The brightest hour of unborn Spring
Through the winter wandering,
Found, it seems, the halcyon morn
To hoar February born;
Bending from Heaven, in azure mirth,
It kiss'd the forehead of the earth,
And smiled upon the silent sea,
And bade the frozen streams be free,
And waked to music all their fountains,
And breathed upon the frozen mountains,
And like a prophetess of May
Strew'd flowers upon the barren way,
Making the wintry world appear
Like one on whom thou smilest, Dear.

Away, away from men and towns,
To the wild woods and the downs—
To the silent wilderness
Where the soul need not repress
Its music, lest it should not find

An echo in another's mind,
While the touch of Nature's art
Harmonizes heart to heart.

Radiant Sister of the Day
Awake! arise! and come away!
To the wild woods and the plains,
To the pools where winter rains
Image all their roof of leaves,
Where the pine its garland weaves
Of sapless green, and ivy dun,
Round stems that never kiss the sun,
Where the lawns and pastures be
And the sandhills of the sea,
Where the melting hoar-frost wets
The daisy-star that never sets,
And wind-flowers and violets
Which yet join not scent to hue
Crown the pale year weak and new;
When the night is left behind
In the deep east, dim and blind,
And the blue noon is over us,
And the multitudinous
Billows murmur at our feet,
Where the earth and ocean meet,
And all things seem only one
In the universal Sun.

THE RECOLLECTION

Now the last day of many days
All beautiful and bright as thou,
The loveliest and the last, is dead:
Rise, Memory, and write its praise!
Up, do thy wonted work! come, trace
The epitaph of glory fled,
For now the earth has changed its face,

A frown is on the Heaven's brow.
We wander'd to the Pine Forest
That skirts the Ocean's foam
The lightest wind was in its nest,
   The tempest in its home.
The whispering waves were half asleep,
   The clouds were gone to play,
And on the bosom of the deep

The smile of Heaven lay;
It seem'd as if the hour were one
　　Sent from beyond the skies
Which scatter'd from above the sun
　　A light of Paradise!

We paused amid the pines that stood
　　The giants of the waste,
Tortured by storms to shape as rude
　　As serpents interlaced,—
And soothed by every azure breath
　　That under heaven is blown
To harmonies and hues beneath,
　　As tender as its own:
Now all the tree-tops lay asleep,
　　Like green waves on the sea,
As still as in the silent deep
　　The ocean-woods may be.

How calm it was!—the silence there
　　But such a chain was bound,
That even the busy woodpecker
　　Made stiller by her sound
The inviolable quietness;
　　The breath of peace we drew
With its soft motion made not less
　　The calm that round us grew.

There seem'd, from the remotest seat
　　Of the wide mountain waste
To the soft flower beneath our feet
　　A magic circle traced,
A spirit interfused around,
　　A thrilling silent life;
To momentary peace it bound
　　Our mortal nature's strife;—
And still I felt the centre of
　　The magic circle there
Was one fair Form that fill'd with love
　　The lifeless atmosphere.

We paused beside the pools that lie
　　Under the forest bough;
Each seem'd as 'twere a little sky
　　Gulf'd in a world below;
A firmament of purple light
　　Which in the dark earth lay,

More boundless than the depth of night
    And purer than the day—
In which the lovely forests grew
    As in the upper air,
More perfect both in shape and hue
    Than any spreading there.
There lay the glade and neighbouring lawn,
    And through the dark-green wood
The white sun twinkling like the dawn
    Out of a speckled cloud.
Sweet views which in our world above
    Can never well be seen
Were imaged by the water's love
    Of that fair forest green:
And all was interfused beneath
    With an Elysian glow,
An atmosphere without a breath,
    A softer day below.
Like one beloved, the scene had lent
    To the dark water's breast
Its every leaf and lineament
    With more than truth exprest;
Until an envious wind crept by,
    Like an unwelcome thought
Which from the mind's too faithful eye
    Blots one dear image out.
—Though Thou art ever fair and kind,
    The forests ever green,
Less oft is peace in Shelley's mind
    Than calm in waters seen!

TO THE MOON

145

Art thou pale for weariness
Of climbing heaven, and gazing on the earth,
    Wandering companionless
Among the stars that have a different birth,—
And ever-changing, like a joyless eye
That finds no object worth its constancy?

A WIDOW BIRD

146

A widow bird sate mourning for her Love
    Upon a wintry bough;
The frozen wind crept on above
    The freezing stream below.

There was no leaf upon the forest bare,
　　No flower upon the ground,
And little motion in the air
　　Except the mill-wheel's sound.

TO A SKYLARK

147

Hail to thee, blithe Spirit!
　　Bird thou never wert,
That from heaven, or near it
　　Pourest thy full heart
In profuse strains of unpremeditated art.

Higher still and higher
　　From the earth thou springest
Like a cloud of fire;
　　The blue deep thou wingest,
And singing still dost soar, and soaring ever singest.

In the golden lightning
　　Of the sunken sun
O'er which clouds are brightening,
　　Thou dost float and run,
Like an unbodied joy whose race is just begun.

The pale purple even
　　Melts around thy flight;
Like a star of heaven
　　In the broad daylight
Thou art unseen, but yet I hear thy shrill delight:

Keen as are the arrows
　　Of that silver sphere,
Whose intense lamp narrows
　　In the white dawn clear
Until we hardly see, we feel that it is there.

All the earth and air
　　With thy voice is loud,
As, when night is bare,
　　From one lonely cloud
The moon rains out her beams, and heaven is overflow'd.

What thou art we know not;
　　What is most like thee?
From rainbow clouds there flow not

PERCY BYSSHE SHELLEY

      Drops so bright to see
As from thy presence showers a rain of melody.

    Like a poet hidden
      In the light of thought,
    Singing hymns unbidden,
      Till the world is wrought
To sympathy with hopes and fears it heeded not:

    Like a high-born maiden
      In a palace tower,
    Soothing her love-laden
      Soul in secret hour
With music sweet as love, which overflows her bower:

    Like a glow-worm golden
      In a dell of dew,
    Scattering unbeholden
      Its aerial hue
Among the flowers and grass, which screen it from the view:

    Like a rose embower'd
      In its own green leaves,
    By warm winds deflower'd,
      Till the scent it gives
Makes faint with too much sweet these heavy-winged thieves.

    Sound of vernal showers
      On the twinkling grass,
    Rain-awaken'd flowers,
      All that ever was
Joyous, and clear, and fresh, thy music doth surpass.

    Teach us, sprite or bird,
      What sweet thoughts are thine:
    I have never heard
      Praise of love or wine
That panted forth a flood of rapture so divine.

    Chorus hymeneal
      Or triumphal chaunt
    Match'd with thine, would be all
      But an empty vaunt—
A thing wherein we feel there is some hidden want.

What objects are the fountains
  Of the happy strain?
What fields, or waves, or mountains?
  What shapes of sky or plain?
What love of thine own kind? what ignorance of pain?

With thy clear keen joyance
  Languor cannot be:
Shadow of annoyance
  Never came near thee:
Thou lovest; but ne'er knew love's sad satiety.

Waking or asleep
  Thou of death must deem
Things more true and deep
  Than we mortals dream,
Or how could thy notes flow in such a crystal stream?

We look before and after,
  And pine for what is not:
Our sincerest laughter
  With some pain is fraught;
Our sweetest songs are those that tell of saddest thought.

Yet if we could scorn
  Hate, and pride, and fear;
If we were things born
  Not to shed a tear,
I know not how thy joy we ever should come near.

Better than all measures
  Of delightful sound,
Better than all treasures
  That in books are found,
Thy skill to poet were, thou scorner of the ground!

Teach me half the gladness
  That thy brain must know,
Such harmonious madness
  From my lips would flow
The world should listen then, as I am listening now!

LOVE'S PHILOSOPHY

THE fountains mingle with the river
And the rivers with the ocean,

The winds of heaven mix for ever
With a sweet emotion;
Nothing in the world is single,
All things by a law divine
In one another's being mingle—
Why not I with thine?

See the mountains kiss high heaven
And the waves clasp one another;
No sister-flower would be forgiven
If it disdain'd its brother:
And the sunlight clasps the earth,
And the moonbeams kiss the sea—
What are all these kissings worth,
If thou kiss not me?

TO THE NIGHT

149

Swiftly walk over the western wave,
    Spirit of Night!
Out of the misty eastern cave
Where, all the long and lone daylight,
Thou wovest dreams of joy and fear
Which make thee terrible and dear,—
    Swift be thy flight!

Wrap thy form in a mantle gray
    Star-inwrought!
Blind with thine hair the eyes of day,
Kiss her until she be wearied out;
Then wander o'er city and sea and land,
Touching all with thine opiate wand—
    Come, long-sought!

When I arose and saw the dawn,
    I sigh'd for thee;
When light rode high, and the dew was gone,
And noon lay heavy on flower and tree
And the weary Day turn'd to his rest
Lingering like an unloved guest,
    I sigh'd for thee.

Thy brother Death came, and cried
    Wouldst thou me?
Thy sweet child Sleep, the filmy-eyed,

Murmur'd like a noon-tide bee
Shall I nestle near thy side?
Wouldst thou me?—And I replied
 No, not thee!

Death will come when thou art dead,
 Soon, too soon—
Sleep will come when thou art fled;
Of neither would I ask the boon
I ask of thee, belovéd Night—
Swift be thine approaching flight,
 Come soon, soon!

THE CLOUD

150

I BRING fresh showers for the thirsting flowers,
 From the seas and the streams;
I bear light shade for the leaves when laid
 In the noonday dreams.
From my wings are shaken the dews that waken
 The sweet buds every one,
When rocked to rest on their mother's breast,
 As she dances about the sun.
I wield the flail of the lashing hail,
 And whiten the green plains under,
And then again I dissolve it in rain,
 And laugh as I pass in thunder.

I sift the snow on the mountains below,
 And their great pines groan aghast;
And all the night 'tis my pillow white,
 While I sleep in the arms of the blast.
Sublime on the towers of my skiey bowers,
 Lightning my pilot sits.
In a cavern under is fretted the thunder,
 It struggles and howls at fits;
Over earth and ocean, with gentle motion,
 This pilot is guiding me,
Lured by the love of the genii that move
 In the depths of the purple sea;
Over the rills, and the crags, and the hills,
 Over the lakes and the plains,
Wherever he dream, under mountain or stream
 The Spirit he loves remains;
And I all the while bask in heaven's blue smile,

Whilst he is dissolving in rains.
The sanguine sunrise, with his meteor eyes,
    And his burning plumes outspread,
Leaps on the back of my sailing rack,
    When the morning star shines dead,
As on the jag of a mountain crag,
    Which an earthquake rocks and swings,
An eagle alit one moment may sit
    In the light of the golden wings.
And when sunset may breathe from the lit sea beneath,
Its ardours of rest and of love,
And the crimson pall of eve may fall
    From the depth of heaven above,
With wings folded I rest, on mine airy nest,
    As still as a brooding dove.

That orbèd maiden with white fire laden,
    Whom mortals call the moon,
Glides glimmering o'er my fleece-like floor,
    By the midnight breezes strewn;
And wherever the beat of her unseen feet,
    Which only the angel hear,
May have broken the woof of my tent's thin roof,
    The stars peep behind her and peer;
And I laugh to see them whirl and flee,
    Like a swarm of golden bees,
When I widen the rent in my wind-built tent,
    Till the calm rivers, lakes, and seas,
Like strips of the sky fallen through me on high,
    Are each paved with the moon and these.
I bind the sun's throne with a burning zone,
    And the moon's with a girdle of pearl;
The volcanoes are dim, and the stars reel and swim,
    When the whirlwinds my banner unfurl.
From cape to cape, with a bridge-like shape,
    Over a torrent sea,
Sunbeam-proof, I hang like a roof,
    The mountains its columns be.
The triumphal arch through which I march
    With hurricane, fire, and snow,
When the powers of the air are chained to my chair,
    Is the million-coloured bow;
The sphere-fire above its soft colours wove,
    While the moist earth was laughing below.

I am the daughter of the earth and water,
    And the nursling of the sky;
I pass through the pores of the ocean and shores;
    I change, but I cannot die.
For after the rain when with never a stain,
    The pavilion of heaven is bare,
And the winds and sunbeams with their convex gleams,
    Build up the blue dome of air,
I silently laugh at my own cenotaph,
    And out of the caverns of rain,
Like a child from the womb, like a ghost from the tomb,
    I arise and unbuild it again.

MUSIC, WHEN SOFT VOICES DIE

151

Music, when soft voices die,
Vibrates in the memory—
Odours, when sweet violets sicken,
Live within the sense they quicken.

Rose leaves, when the rose is dead,
Are heap'd for the beloved's bed;
And so thy thoughts, when Thou art gone,
Love itself shall slumber on.

THE POET'S DREAM

152

On a Poet's lips I slept
Dreaming like a love-adept
In the sound his breathing kept;
Nor seeks nor finds he mortal blisses,
But feeds on the aërial kisses
Of shapes that haunt Thought's wildernesses.
He will watch from dawn to gloom
The lake-reflected sun illume
The yellow bees in the ivy-bloom,
    Nor heed nor see what things they be—
But from these create he can
Forms more real than living Man,
    Nurslings of Immortality!

THE WORLD'S WANDERERS

153

Tell me, thou Star, whose wings of light
Speed thee in thy fiery flight,

In what cavern of the night
    Will thy pinions close now?

Tell me, Moon, thou pale and gray
Pilgrim of heaven's homeless way,
In what depth of night or day
    Seekest thou repose now?

Weary Mind, who wanderest
Like the world's rejected guest,
Hast thou still some secret nest
    On the tree or billow?

* * *

THE POEMS OF JOHN MILTON

ON THE MORNING OF CHRIST'S NATIVITY

I

This is the month, and this the happy morn,
Wherein the Son of Heaven's eternal King,
Of wedded maid and Virgin Mother born,
Our great redemption from above did bring;
For so the holy sages once did sing,
  That he our deadly forfeit should release,
And with his Father work us a perpetual peace.

II

That glorious Form, that Light unsufferable,
And that far-beaming blaze of majesty,
Wherewith he wont at Heaven's high council-table
To sit the midst of Trinal Unity,
He laid aside, and, here with us to be,
  Forsook the Courts of everlasting Day,
And chose with us a darksome house of mortal clay.

III

Say, Heavenly Muse, shall not thy sacred **vein**
Afford a present to the Infant God?

Hast thou no verse, no hymn, or solemn strain,
To welcome him to this his new abode,
Now while the heaven, by the Sun's team untrod,
  Hath took no print of the approaching light,
And all the spangled host keep watch in squadron bright?

IV

See how from far upon the Eastern road
The star-led Wisards haste with odours sweet!
Oh! run; prevent them with thy humble ode,
And lay it lowly at his blessèd feet;
Have thou the honour first thy Lord to greet,
  And join thy voice unto the Angel Quire,
From out his secret altar touched with hallowed fire.

THE HYMN

I

It was the winter wild,
  While the heaven-born child
All meanly wrapt in the rude manger lies;
  Nature, in awe to him,
  Had doffed her gaudy trim,
With her great Master so to sympathize:
It was no season then for her
To wanton with the Sun, her lusty Paramour.

II

Only with speeches fair
  She woos the gentle air
To hide her guilty front with innocent snow,
  And on her naked shame,
  Pollute with sinful blame,
The saintly veil of maiden white to throw;
Confounded, that her Maker's eyes
Should look so near upon her foul deformities.

III

But he, her fears to cease,
  Sent down the meek-eyed Peace:
She, crowned with olive green, came softly sliding

    Down through the turning sphere,
      His ready Harbinger,
With turtle wing the amorous cluds dividing;
And, waving wide her myrtle wand,
She strikes a universal peace through sea and land.

IV

    No war, or battail's sound,
      Was heard the world around;
The idle spear and shield were high uphung;
    The hookèd chariot stood,
      Unstained with hostile blood;
The trumpet spake not to the armèd throng;
And Kings sat still with awful eye,
As if they surely knew their sovran Lord was by.

V

    But peaceful was the night
      Wherein the Prince of Light
His reign of peace upon the earth began.
    The winds, with wonder whist,
      Smoothly the waters kissed,
Whispering new joys to the mild Ocean,
Who now hath quite forgot to rave,
While birds of calm sit brooding on the charmèd wave.

VI

    The stars, with deep amaze,
      Stand fixed in steadfast gaze,
Bending one way their precious influence,
    And will not take their flight,
      For all the morning light,
Or Lucifer that often warned them thence;
But in their glimmering orbs did glow,
Until their Lord himself bespake, and bid them go.

VII

    And, though the shady gloom
      Had given day her room,
The Sun himself withheld his wonted speed,
    And hid his head for shame,

As his inferior flame
The new-enlightened world no more should need:
He saw a greater Sun appear
Than his bright Throne or burning axletree could bear.

VIII

The Shepherds on the lawn,
Or ere the point of dawn,
Sat simply chatting in a rustic row;
Full than little thought they than
That the mighty Pan
Was kindly come to live with them below:
Perhaps their loves, or else their sheep,
Was all that did their silly thoughts so busy keep.

IX

When such music sweet
Their hearts and ears did greet
As never was by mortal finger strook,
Divinely-warbled voice
Answering the stringèd noise,
All their souls in blissful rapture took:
The air, such pleasure loth to lose,
With thousand echoes still prolongs each heavenly close.

X

Nature, that heard such sound
Beneath the hollow round
Of Cynthia's seat the airy Region thrilling,
Now was almost won
To think her part was done,
And that her reign had here its last fulfilling:
She knew such harmony alone
Could hold all Heaven and Earth in happier union.

XI

At last surrounds their sight
A globe of circular light,
That with long beams the shamefaced Night arrayed;
The helmèd Cherubim
And sworded Seraphim
Are seen in glittering ranks with wings displayed,

Harping in loud and solemn quire,
With unexpressive notes, to Heaven's newborn Heir.

XII

    Such music (as 't is said)
    Before was never made,
But when of old the Sons of Morning sung,
    While the Creator great
    His constellations set,
And the well-balanced World on hinges hung,
And cast the dark foundations deep,
And bid the weltering waves their oozy channel keep.

XIII

    Ring out, ye crystal spheres!
    Once bless our human ears,
If ye have power to touch our senses so;
    And let your silver chime
    Move in melodious time;
And let the bass of heaven's deep organ blow
And with your ninefold harmony
Make up full consort to the angelic symphony.

XIV

    For, if such holy song
    Enwrap our fancy long,
Time will run back and fetch the Age of Gold;
    And speckled Vanity
    Will sicken soon and die,
And leprous Sin will melt from earthly mould;
And Hell itself will pass away,
And leave her dolorous mansions to the peering day.

XV

    Yea, Truth and Justice then
    Will down return to men,
The enamelled arras of the rainbow wearing;
    And Mercy set between,
    Throned in celestial sheen,
With radiant feet the tissued clouds down steering;
And Heaven, as at some festival,
Will open wide the gates of her high palace-hall.

XVI

But wisest Fate says No,
This must not yet be so;
The Babe lies yet in smiling infancy
That on the bitter cross
Must redeem our loss,
So both himself and us to glorify:
Yet first, to those ychanged in sleep,
The wakeful trump of doom must thunder through the deep,

XVII

With such a horrid clang
As on Mount Sinai rang,
While the red fire and smouldering clouds outbrake:
The aged Earth, aghast
With terror of that blast,
Shall from the surface to the centre shake,
When, at the world's last session,
The dreadful Judge in middle air shall spread his throne.

XVIII

And then at last our bliss
Full and perfect is,
But now begins; for from this happy day
The Old Dragon under ground,
In straiter limits bound,
Not half so far casts his usurpèd sway,
And, wroth to see his Kingdom fail,
Swindges the scaly horror of his folded tail.

XIX

The Oracles are dumb;
No voice or hideous hum
Runs through the archèd roof in words deceiving.
Apollo from his
Can no more divine,
With hollow shriek the steep of Delphos leaving.
No nightly trance or breathèd spell,
Inspires the pale-eyed Priest from the prophetic cell.

XX

    The lonely mountains o'er,
    And the resounding shore,
A voice of weeping heard and loud lament;
    From haunted spring, and dale
    Edgèd with poplar pale,
The parting Genius is with sighing sent;
With flower-inwoven tresses torn
The Nymphs in twilight shade of tangled thickets mourn.

XXI

    In consecrated earth,
    And on the holy hearth,
The Lars and Lemures moan with midnight plaint;
    In urns, and altars round,
    A drear and dying sound
Affrights the Flamens at their service quaint;
And the chill marble seems to sweat,
While each peculiar power forgoes his wonted seat.

XXII

    Peor and Baälim
    Forsake their temples dim,
With that twice-battered god of Palestine;
    And moonèd Ashtaroth,
    Heaven's Queen and Mother both,
Now sits not girt with tapers' holy shine:
The Libyc Hammon shrinks his horn;
In vain the Tyrian maids their wounded Thaummuz mourn.

XXIII

    And sullen Moloch, fled,
    Hath left in shadows dread
His burning idol all of blackest hue;
    In vain with cymbals' ring
    They call the grisly king,
In dismal dance about the furnace blue;
The brutish gods of Nile as fast,
Isis, and Orus, and the dog Anubis, haste.

XXIV

Nor is Osiris seen
In Memphian grove or green,
Trampling the unshowered grass with lowings loud;
Nor can he be at rest
Within his sacred chest;
Nought but profoundest Hell can be his shroud;
In vain, with timbreled anthems dark,
The sable-stolèd Sorcerers bear his worshiped ark.

XXV

He feels from Juda's land
The dreaded Infant's hand;
The rays of Bethlehem blinds his dusky eyn;
Nor all the gods beside
Longer dare abide,
Nor Typhon huge ending in snaky twine:
Our Babe, to show his Godhead true,
Can in his swaddling bands control the damnèd crew.

XXVI

So, when the Sun in bed,
Curtained with cloudy red,
Pillows his chin upon an orient wave,
The flocking shadows pale
Troop to the infernal jail,
Each fettered ghost slips to his several grave,
And the yellow-skirted Fays
Fy after the night-steeds, leaving their moon-loved maze.

XXVII

But see! the Virgin blest
Hath laid her Babe to rest,
Time is our tedious song should here have ending:
Heaven's youngest-teemèd star
Hath fixed her polished car,
Her sleeping Lord with handmaid lamp attending;
And all about the courtly stable
Bright-harnessed Angels sit in order serviceable.

SONNET TO THE NIGHTINGALE

156

O Nightingale that on yon blooming spray
Warblest at eve, when all the woods are still,
Thou with fresh hopes the Lover's heart dost fill,
While the jolly Hours lead on propitious May.
Thy liquid notes that close of the eye of Day,
First heard before the shallow cuckoo's bill,
Portend success in love. O if Jove's will
Have linked that amorous power to thy soft lay,
Now timely sing, ere the rude bird of hate
Foretell my hopeless doom, in some grove nigh;
As thou from year to year hast sung too late
For my relief, yet had'st no reason why.
Whether the Muse or Love call thee his mate,
Both them I serve, and of their train am I.

SONG ON MAY MORNING

157

Now the bright morning-star, Day's harbinger,
Comes dancing from the East, and leads with her
The flowery May, who from her green lap throws
The yellow cowslip and the pale primrose.
  Hail, bounteous May, that dost inspire
  Mirth, and youth, and warm desire!
  Woods and groves are of thy dressing;
  Hill and dale doth boast thy blessing.
Thus we salute thee with our early song,
And welcome thee, and wish thee long.

ON TIME

158

Fly, envious Time, till thou run out thy race:
Call on the lazy leaden-stepping Hours,
Whose speed is but the heavy plummet's pace;
And glut thyself with what thy womb devours,
Which is no more than what is false and vain,
And merely mortal dross;
So little is our loss,
So little is thy gain!
For, whenas each thing bad thou hast entombed,
And, last of all, thy greedy Self consumed,
Then long eternity shall greet our bliss
With an individual kiss,
And joy shall overtake us as a flood;

When everything that is sincerely good
And perfectly divine,
With Truth, and Peace, and Love shall ever shine
About the supreme Throne
Of Him, to whose happy-making sight alone
When once our heavenly-guided soul shall climb,
Then, all this earthly grossness quit,
Attired with stars we shall forever sit,
Triumphing over Death, and Chance, and thee,
  O Time!

AT A SOLEMN MUSIC

159

Blest pair of Sirens pledges of Heaven's joy,
Sphere-born harmonious Sisters, Voice and Verse,
Wed your divine sounds, and mixed power employ,
Dead things with imbreathed sense able to pierce;
And to our high-raised phantasy present
That undisturbèd Song of pure consent,
Aye sung before the sapphire-coloured Throne
To Him that sits thereon,
With saintly shout and solemn jubily;
Where the bright Seraphim in burning row
Their loud uplifted angels trumpets blow,
And the Cherubic host in thousand quires
Touch their immortal harps of golden wires,
With those just Spirits that wear victorious palms,
Hymns devout and holy psalms
Singing everlastingly:
That we on Earth, with undiscording voice,
May rightly answer that melodious noise;
As once we did, till disproportioned Sin
Jarred against Nature's chime, and with harsh din
Broke the fair music that all creatures made
To their great Lord, whose love their motions swayed
In perfect diapason, whilst they stood
In first obedience, and their state of good.
O, may we soon again renew that song,
And keep in tune with Heaven, till God ere long
To his celestial consort us unite,
To live with Him, and sing in endless morn of light!

UPON THE CIRCUMCISION

160

Ye flaming Powers, and wingèd Warriors bright,
That erst with music, and triumphant song,

First heard by happy watchful Shepherds' ear,
So sweetly sung your joy the clouds along,
Through the soft silence of the listening night,—
Now mourn; and if sad share with us to bear
Your fiery essence can distil no tear,
Burn in your sighs, and borrow
Seas wept from our deep sorrow,
He who with all Heaven's heraldry whilere
Entered the world, now bleeds to give us ease.
Alas! how soon our sin
Sore doth begin
His infancy to seize!
O more exceeding Love, or Law more just?
Just Law indeed, but more exceeding Love!
For we, by rightful doom remediless,
Were lost in death, till He, that dwelt above
High-throned in secret bliss, for us frail dust
Emptied his glory, even to nakedness;
And that great Covenant which we still transgress
Intirely satisfied,
And the full wrath beside
Of vengeful Justice bore for our excess,
And seals obedience first with wounding smart
This day; but oh! ere long,
Huge pangs and strong
Will pierce more near his heart.

TO THE LORD GENERAL CROMWELL, ON THE PROPOSALS OF CERTAIN MINISTERS AT THE COMMITTEE FOR THE PROPAGATION OF THE GOSPEL

161

CROMWELL, our chief of men, who through a cloud
  Not of war only, but detractions rude,
  Guided by faith and matchless fortitude,
  To peace and truth thy glorious way hast ploughed,
And on the neck of crowned Fortune proud
  Hast reared God's trophies, and his work pursued,
  While Darwen stream, with blood of Scots imbrued,
  And Dunbar field, resounds thy praises loud,
And Worcester's laureate wreath: yet much remains
  To conquer still; Peace hath her victories
  No less renowned than War: new foes arise,
Threatening to bind our souls with secular chains.
  Help us to save free conscience from the paw
  Of hireling wolves, whose Gospel is their maw.

TO SIR HENRY VANE THE YOUNGER

162

Vane, young in years, but in sage counsel old,
  Than whom a better senator ne'er held
  The helm of Rome, when gowns, not arms, repelled
  The fierce Epirot and the African bold,
Whether to settle peace, or to unfold
  The drift of hollow states hard to be spelled;
  Then to advise how war may best, upheld,
  Move by her two main nerves, iron and gold,
In all her equipage; besides, to know
  Both spiritual power and civil, what each means,
  What severs each, thou hast learned, which few
    have done.
The bounds of either sword to thee we owe:
  Therefore on thy firm hand Religion leans
  In peace, and reckons thee her eldest son.

ON THE LATE MASSACRE IN PIEMONT

163

Avenge, O Lord, thy slaughtered Saints, whose bones
  Lie scattered on the Alpine mountains cold;
  Even them who kept thy truth so pure of old,
When all our fathers worshiped stocks and stones,
Forget not: in thy book record their groans
  Who were thy sheep, and in their ancient fold
  Slain by the bloody Piemontese, that rolled
Mother with infant down the rocks. Their moans
The vales redoubled to the hills, and they
  To heaven. Their martyred blood and ashes sow
O'er all the Italian fields, where still doth sway
  The triple Tyrant; that from these may grow
A hundredfold, who, having learnt thy way,
  Early may fly the Babylonian woe.

ON HIS BLINDNESS

164

When I consider how my light is spent
  Ere half my days in this dark world and wide,
  And that one Talent which is death to hide
  Lodged with me useless, though my soul more bent
To serve therewith my Maker, and present
  My true account, lest He returning chide,
  "Doth God exact day-labour, light denied?"
  I fondly ask. But Patience, to prevent

That murmur, soon replies, "God doth not need
  Either man's work or his own gifts. Who best
  Bear his mild yoke, they serve him best. His state
Is kingly: thousands at his bidding speed,
  And post o'er land and ocean without rest;
  They also serve who only stand and wait."

WHEN THE ASSAULT WAS INTENDED TO THE CITY

165

Captain, or colonel, or knight in arms,
Whose chance on these defenceless doors may seize,
If deed of honour did thee ever please,
Guard them, and him within protect from harms.
He can requite thee, for he knows the charms
That call fame on such gentle acts as these,
And he can spread thy name o'er lands and seas,
Whatever clime the sun's bright circle warms.
Lift not thy spear against the Muse's bower;
The great Emathian conqueror bid spare
The house of Pindarus, when temple and tower
Went to the ground; and the repeated air
Of sad Electra's Poet had the power
To save the Athenian walls from ruin bare.

TO A VIRTUOUS YOUNG LADY

166

Lady! that in the prime of earliest youth
Wisely hast shunned the broad way and the green,
And with those few art eminently seen,
That labour up the Hill of Heavenly Truth,
The better part with Mary and with Ruth
Chosen thou hast, and they that overween,
And at thy growing virtues fret their spleen,
No anger find in thee, but pity and ruth.
Thy care is fixed, and zealously attends
To fill thy odorous Lamp with deeds of light.
And Hope that reaps not shame; therefore be sure,
Thou, when the Bridegroom with his feastful friends
Passes to bliss at the mid hour of night,
Hast gained thy entrance, Virgin wise and pure.

TO THE LADY MARGARET LEY

167

Daughter to that good Earl, once President
  Of England's Council and her Treasury,

XI

Who lived in both unstained with gold or fee,
And left them both, more in himself content,
Till the sad breaking of that Parliament
Broke him, as that dishonest victory
At Chæronea, fatal to liberty,
Killed with report that old man eloquent,
Though later born than to have known the days
Wherein your father, flourished, yet by you,
Madam, methinks I see him living yet:
So well your words his noble virtues praise
That all both judge you to relate them true
And to possess them, honoured Margaret.

ON THE DETRACTION WHICH FOLLOWED UPON MY WRITING CERTAIN TREATISES

168

A book was writ of late called *Tetrachordon*,
And woven close, both matter, form, and style;
The subject new: it walked the town a while,
Numbering good intellects; now seldom pored on.
Cries the stall-reader, "Bless us! what a word on
A title-page is this!"; and some in file
Stand spelling false, while one might walk to Mile-
End Green. Why, is it harder, sirs, than *Gordon*,
Colkitto, or *Macdonnel*, or *Galasp?*
Those rugged names to our like mouths grow sleek
That would have made Quintilian stare and gasp.
Thy age, like ours, O soul of Sir John Cheek,
Hated not learning worse than toad or asp,
When thou taught'st Cambridge and King Edward Greek.

ON THE SAME

169

I did but prompt the age to quit their clogs
By the known rules of ancient liberty,
When straight a barbarous noise environs me
Of owls and cuckoos, asses, apes, and dogs;
As when those hinds that were transformed to frogs
Railed at Latona's twin-born progeny,
Which after held the Sun and Moon in fee.
But this is got by casting pearl to hogs,
That bawl for freedom in their senseless mood,
And still revolt when Truth would set them free.
Licence they mean when thy cry Liberty;

> For who loves that must first be wise and good
> > But from that mark how far they rove we see,
> For all this waste of wealth and loss of blood.

ON THE NEW FORCERS OF CONSCIENCE UNDER THE LONG PARLIAMENT

170

> BECAUSE you have thrown off your Prelate Lord,
> > And with stiff vows renounced his Liturgy,
> > To seize the widowed whore Plurality,
> From them whose sin ye envied, not abhorred,
> Dare ye for this adjure the civil sword
> > To force our consciences that Christ set free,
> > And ride us with a Classic Hierarchy,
> > Taught ye by mere A.S. and Rutherford?
> Men whose life, learning, faith, and pure intent,
> > Would have been held in high esteem with Paul
> Must now be named and printed heretics
> > By shallow Edwards and Scotch What-d'ye-call!
> > But we do hope to find out all your tricks,
> > Your plots and packing, worse than those of Trent,
> > > That so the Parliament
> May with their wholesome and preventive shears
> Clip your phylacteries, though baulk your ears,
> > And succour our just fears,
> When they shall read this clearly in your charge:
> New *Presbyter* is but old Priest writ large.

TO MR. H. LAWES ON HIS AIRS

171

> HARRY, whose tuneful and well-measured song
> > First taught our English music how to span
> > Words with just note and accent, not to scan
> With Midas' ears, committing short and long,
> Thy worth and skill exempts thee from the throng,
> > With praise enough for Envy to look wan;
> To after age thou shalt be writ the man
> > That with smooth air couldst humour best our tongue.
> Thou honour'st Verse, and Verse, must lend her wing
> > To honour thee, the priest of Phœbus' quire,
> > That tunest their happiest lines in hym or story.
> Dante shall give Fame leave to set thee higher
> > Than his Casella, whom he wooed to sing,
> > Met in the milder shades of Purgatory.

ON THE RELIGIOUS MEMORY OF MRS. CATHERINE THOMSON, MY CHRISTIAN FRIEND, DECEASED DEC. 16, 1646

172

WHEN Faith and Love, which parted from thee never,
  Had ripened thy just soul to dwell with God
  Meekly thou didst resign this earthly load
Of death, called life, which us from life doth sever.
Thy works, and alms, and all thy good endeavour,
  Stayed not behind, nor in the grave were trod;
  But, as Faith pointed with her golden rod
Followed thee up to joy and bliss for ever.
Love led them on; and Faith, who knew them best
  Thy handmaids, clad them o'er with purple beams
  And azure wings, that up they flew so drest,
And speak the truth of thee on glorious themes
  Before the Judge; who henceforth bid thee rest,
  And drink thy fill of pure immortal streams.

ON THE LORD GENERAL FAIRFAX AT THE SIEGE OF COLCHESTER

173

FAIRFAX, whose name in arms through Europe rings,
  Filling each mouth with envy or with praise,
  And all her jealous monarchs with amaze,
  And rumours loud that daunt remotest kings,
Thy firm unshaken virtue ever brings
  Victory home, though new rebellions raise
  Their Hydra heads, and the false North displays
  Her broken league to imp their serpent wings.
O yet a nobler task awaits thy hand
  (For what can war but endless war still breed?)
  Till truth and right from violence be freed,
And public faith cleared from the shameful brand
  Of public fraud. In vain doth Valour bleed,
  While Avarice and Rapine share the land.

TO THE SAME

174

CYRIACK, this three years' day these eyes, though clear
  To outward view, of blemish or of spot,
  Bereft of light, their seeing have forgot;
Nor to their idle orbs doth sight appear
Of sun, or moon, or star, throughout the year,
  Or man, or woman. Yet I argue not
  'Against Heaven's hand or will, nor bate a jot

Of heart or hope, but still bear up and steer
Right onward. What supports me, dost thou ask?
   The conscience, friend, to have lost them overplied
   In Liberty's defence, my noble task,
Of which all Europe rings from side to side.
   This thought might lead me through the world's vain mask
Content, though blind, had I no better guide.

ON HIS DECEASED WIFE

175

METHOUGHT I saw my late espousèd saint
   Brought to me like Alcestis from the grave,
   Whom Jove's great son to her glad husband gave,
Rescued from Death by force, thought pale and faint.
Mine, as whom washed from sport of childbed taint
   Purification in the Old Law did save,
   And such as once more I trust to have
Full sight of her in Heaven without restraint,
Came vested all white, pure as her mind.
   Her face was veiled; yet to my fancied sight
   Love, sweetness, goodness, in her person shined
So clear as in no face with more delight.
   But, oh! as to embrace me she inclined,
   I waked, she fled, and day brought back my night

MR. LAWRENCE

176

LAWRENCE, of virtuous father virtuous son,
   Now that the fields are dank, and ways are mire,
   Where shall we sometimes meet, and by the fire
Help waste a sullen day, what may be won
From the hard season gaining? Time will run
   On smoother, till Favonius reinspire
   The frozen earth, and clothe in fresh attire
The lily and rose, that neither sowed nor spun.
What neat repast shall feast us, light and choice,
   Of Attic taste, with wine, whence we may rise
   To hear the lute well touched, or artful voice
Warble immortal notes and Tuscan air?
   He who of those delights can judge, and spare
   To interpose them oft, is not unwise.

TO CYRIACK SKINNER

177

CYRIACK, whose grandsire on the royal bench
   Of British Themis, with no mean applause,

Pronounced, and in his volumes taught, our laws,
Which others at their bar so often wrench,
To-day deep thoughts resolve with me to drench
In mirth that after no repenting draws;
Let Euclid rest, and Archimedes pause,
And what the Swede intend, and what the French.
To measure life learn thou betimes, and know
Toward solid good what leads the nearest way;
For other things mild Heaven a time ordains,
And disapproves that care, though wise in show,
That with superfluous burden loads the day,
And, when God sends a cheerful hour, refrains.

THE PASSION

I

Erewhile of music, and ethereal mirth,
Wherewith the stage of Air and Earth did ring,
And joyous news of heavenly Infant's birth,
My Muse with Angels did divide to sing;
But headlong joy is ever on the wing,
  In wintry solstice like the shortened light
Soon swallowed up in dark and long outliving night.

II

For now to sorrow must I tune my song,
And set my Harp to notes of saddest woe,
Which on our dearest Lord did seize ere long,
Dangers, and snares, and wrongs, and worse than so,
Which he for us did freely undergo:
  Most perfect Hero, tried in heaviest plight
Of labours huge and hard, too hard for human wight!

III

He, sovran Priest, stooping his regal head,
That dropt with odorous oil down his fair eyes,
Poor fleshly Tabernacle enterèd,
His starry front low-roofed beneath the skies:
Oh, what a mask was there, what a disguise!
  Yet more: the stroke of death he must abide;
Then lies him meekly down fast by his Brethren's side.

IV

These latest scenes confine my roving verse;
To this horizon is my Phœbus bound.
His godlike acts, and his temptations fierce,
And former sufferings, otherwhere are found;
Loud o'er the rest Cremona's trump doth sound:
   Me softer airs befit, and softer strings
Of lute, or viol still, more apt for mournful things.

V

Befriend me, Night, best Patroness of grief!
Over the pole thy thickest mantle throw,
And work my flattered fancy to belief
That Heaven and Earth are coloured with my woe;
My sorrows are too dark for day to know:
   The leaves should all be black whereon I write,
And letters, where my tears have washed, a wannish white.

VI

See, see the chariot, and those rushing wheels,
That whirled the prophet up at Chebar flood;
My spirit some transporting Cherub feels
To bear me where the Towers of Salem stood,
Once glorious towers, now sunk in guiltless blood.
   There doth my soul in holy vision sit,
In pensive trance, and anguish, and ecstatic fit.

VII

Mine eye hath found that sad sepulchral rock
That was the casket of Heaven's richest store,
And here, though grief my feeble hands up-lock,
Yet on the softened quarry would I score
My plaining verse as lively as before;
   For sure so well instructed are my tears
That they would fitly fall in ordered characters.

VIII

Or, should I thence, hurried on viewless wing,
Take up a weeping on the mountains wild,
The gentle neighbourhood of grove and spring

Would soon unbosom all their Echoes mild;
   And I (for grief is easily beguiled)
      Might think the infection of my sorrows loud
   Had got a race of mourners on some pregnant cloud.

COMUS. A MASK

179

The Persons

The Attendant Spirit, afterwards in the habit of Thyrsis.
Comus, with his Crew.

The Lady.   First Brother.   Second Brother.
                Sabrina, the Nymph.

Presented at Ludlow Castle, 1634, before the Earl of Bridgewater,
      then President of Wales

         The Chief Persons which presented were:—
The Lord Brackley;   Mr. Thomas Egerton, his Brother;
            The Lady Alice Egerton.

The first Scene discovers a wild wood.
The Attendant Spirit *descends or enters.*

   BEFORE the starry threshold of Jove's court
   My mansion is, where those immortal shapes
   Of bright aerial Spirits live insphered
   In regions mild of calm and serene air,
   Above the smoke and stir of this dim spot
   Which men call Earth, and, with low-thoughted care,
   Confined and pestered in this pinfold here,
   Strive to keep up a frail and feverish being,
   Unmindful of the crown that Virtue gives,
   After this mortal change, to her true servants
   Amongst the enthronèd gods on sainted seats.
   Yet some there be that by due steps aspire
   To lay their just hands on that golden key
   That opes the Palace of Eternity.
   To such my errand is; and, but for such,
   I would not soil these pure ambrosial weeds
   With the rank vapours of this sin-worn mould.
      But to my task. Neptune, beside the sway
   Of every salt flood and each ebbing stream,
   Took in, by lot 'twixt high and nether Jove,

Imperial rule of all the sea-girt Isles
That, like to rich and various gems, inlay
The unadornèd bosom of the Deep;
Which he, to grace his tributary gods,
By course commits to several government,
And gives them leave to wear their sapphire crowns
And wield their little tridents. But this Isle,
The greatest and the best of all the main,
He quarters to his blue-haired deities;
And all this tract that fronts the falling sun
A noble Peer of mickle trust and power
Has in his charge, with tempered awe to guide
An old and haughty Nation, proud in arms:
Where his fair offspring, nursed in princely lore,
Are coming to attend their father's state,
And new-intrusted sceptre. But their way
Lies through the perplexed paths of this drear wood,
The nodding horror of whose shady brows
Threats the forlorn and wandering passenger;
And here their tender age might suffer peril,
But that, by quick command from sovran Jove,
I was despatched for their defence and guard!
And listen why; for I will tell you now
What never yet was heard in tale or song,
From old or modern bard, in hall or bower.

   Bacchus, that first from out the purple grape
Crushed the sweet poison of misusèd wine,
After the Tuscan mariners transformed,
Coasting the Tyrrhene shore, as the winds listed,
On Circe's island fell. (Who knows not Circe,
The daughter of the Sun, whose charmèd cup
Whoever tasted lost his upright shape,
And downward fell into a grovelling swine?)
This Nymph, that gazed upon his clustering locks,
With ivy berries wreathed, and his blithe youth,
Had by him, ere he parted thence, a Son
Much like his father, but his mother more,
Whom therefore she brought up, and Comus named:
Who, ripe and frolic of his full-grown age,
Roving the Celtic and Iberian fields,
At last betakes him to this ominous wood,
And, in thick shelter of black shade imbowered,
Excels his mother at her mighty art;
Offering to every weary traveller
His orient liquor in a crystal glass,

To quench the drouth of Phœbus; which as they taste
(For most do taste through fond intemperate thirst),
Soon as the potion works, their human count'nance,
The express resemblance of the gods, is changed
Into some brutish form of wolf or bear,
Or ounce or tiger, hog, or bearded goat
All other parts remaining as they were.
And they, so perfect is their misery,
Not once perceive their foul disfigurement,
But boast themselves more comely than before,
And all their friends and native home forget,
To roll with pleasure in a sensual sty.
Therefore, when any favoured of high Jove
Chances to pass through this adventrous glade,
Swift as the sparkle of a glancing star
I shoot from heaven, to give him safe convoy,
As now I do. But first I must put off
These my sky-robes, spun out of Iris' woof,
And take the weeds and likeness of a swain
That to the service of this house belongs,
Who, with his soft pipe and smooth-dittied song,
Well knows to still the wild winds when they roar,
And hush the waving woods; nor of less faith,
And in this office of his mountain watch
Likeliest, and nearest to the present aid
Of this occasion. But I hear the tread
Of hateful steps; I must be viewless now.

Comus *enters, with a charming-rod in one hand, his glass in the other; with him a rout of Monsters, headed like sundry sorts of wild beasts, but otherwise like men and women, their apparel glistering. They come in making a riotous and unruly noise, with torches in their hands.*

    Comus. The star that bids the shepherd fold
Now the top of heaven doth hold;
And the gilded car of Day
His glowing axle doth allay
In the steep Atlantic stream:
And the slope Sun his upward beam
Shoots against the dusky pole,
Pacing toward the other goal
Of his chamber in the east.
Meanwhile, welcome joy and feast,
Midnight shout and revelry,

Tipsy dance and jollity.
Braid your locks with rosy twine,
Dropping odours, dropping wine.
Rigour now is gone to bed;
And Advice with scrupulous head,
Strict Age, and sour Severity,
With their grave saws, in slumber lie.
We, that are of purer fire,
Imitate the starry Quire,
Who, in their nightly watchful spheres,
Lead in swift round the months and years.
The sounds and seas, with all their finny drove,
Now to the Moon in wavering morrice move;
And on the tawny sands and shelves
Trip the pert Fairies and the dapper Elves.
By dimpled brook and fountain-brim,
The Wood-Nymphs, decked with daisies trim,
Their merry wakes and pastimes keep:
What hath night to do with sleep?
Night hath better sweets to prove;
Venus now wakes, and wakens Love.
Come, let us our rites begin;
'T is only daylight that makes sin,
Which these dun shades will ne'er report.
Hail, goddess of nocturnal sport,
Dark-veiled Cotytto, to whom the secret flame
Of midnight torches burns! mysterious Dame,
That ne'er art called but when the dragon womb
Of Stygian darkness spets her thickest gloom,
And makes on blot of all the air!
Stay thy cloudy ebon chair,
Wherein thou ridest with Hecat', and befriend
Us thy vowed priests, till utmost end
Of all thy dues be done, and none left out
Ere the blabbing eastern scout,
The nice Morn on the Indian steep,
From her cabined loop-hole peep,
And to the tell-tale Sun descry
Our concealed solemnity.
Come, knit hands, and beat the ground
In a light fantastic round.

The Measure

Break off, break off! I feel the different pace

Of some chaste footing near about this ground.
Run to your shrouds within these brakes and trees;
Our number may affright. Some virgin sure
(For so I can distinguish by mine art)
Benighted in these woods! Now to my charms,
And to my wily trains: I shall ere long
Be well stocked with as fair a herd as grazed
About my mother Circe. Thus I hurl
My dazzling spells into the spongy air,
Of power to cheat the eye with blear illusion,
And give it false presentments, lest the place
And my quaint habits breed astonishment,
And put the Damsel to suspicious flight;
Which must not be, for that's against my course.
I, under fair pretence of friendly ends,
And well-placed words of glozing courtesy,
Baited with reasons not unplausible,
Wind me into the easy-hearted man,
And hug him into snares. When once her eyes
Hath met the virtue of this magic dust
I shall appear some harmless villager,
Whom thrift keeps up about his country gear.
But here she comes; I fairly set aside,
And hearken, if I may her business hear.

The Lady *enters*

Lady. This way the noise was, if mine ear be true,
My best guide now. Methought it was the sound
Of riot and ill-managed merriment,
Such as the jocund flute or gamesome pipe
Stirs up among the loose unlettered hinds,
When, for their teeming flocks and granges full,
In wanton dance they praise the bounteous Pan,
And thank the gods amiss. I should be loth
To meet the rudeness and swilled insolence
Of such late wassailers; yet, oh! where else
Shall I inform my unacquainted feet
In the blind mazes of this tangled wood?
My brothers, when they saw me wearied out
With this long way, resolving here to lodge
Under the spreading favour of these pines,
Stepped, as they said, to the next thicketside
To bring me berries, or such cooling fruit

As the kind hospitable woods provide.
They left me then when the grey-hooded Even,
Like a sad Votarist in palmer's weed,
Rose from the hindmost wheels of Phœbus' wain.
But where they are, and why they came not back,
Is now the labour of my thoughts. 'T is likeliest
They had ingaged their wandering steps too far;
And envious darkness, ere they could return,
Had stole them from me. Else, O thievish Night,
Why shouldst thou, but for some felonious end,
In thy dark lantern thus close up the stars
That Nature hung in heaven, and filled their lamps
With everlasting oil, to give due light
To the misled and lonely travailler?
This is the place, as well as I may guess,
Whence even now the tumult of loud mirth
Was rife, and perfet in my listening ear;
Yet nought but single darkness do I find.
What might this be? A thousand fantasies
Begin to throng into my memory,
Of calling shapes, and beckoning shadows dire,
And airy tongues that syllable men's names
On sands and shores and desert wildernesses.
These thoughts may startle well, but not astound
The virtuous mind, that ever walks attended
By a strong siding champion, Conscience.
O welcome, pure-eyed Faith, white-handed Hope,
Thou hovering angel girt with golden wings,
And thou unblemished form of Chastity!
I see ye visibly, and now believe
That He, the Supreme Good, to whom all things ill
Are but as slavish officers of vengeance,
Would send a glistering guardian, if need were,
To keep my life and honour unassailed. . . .
Was I deceived, or did a sable cloud
Turn forth her silver lining on the night?
I did not err: there does a sable cloud
Turn forth her silver lining on the night,
And casts a gleam over this tufted grove.
I cannot hallo to my brothers, but
Such noise as I can make to be heard farthest
I'll venter; for my new-enlivened spirits
Prompt me, and they perhaps are not far off.

Song

Sweet Echo, sweetest Nymph, that liv'st unseen
  Within thy airy shell
By slow Meander's margent green,
And in the violet-imbroidered vale
  Where the love-lorn Nightingale
Nightly to thee her sad song mourneth well:
Canst thou not tell me of a gentle pair
  That likest thy Narcissus are?
    O if thou have
  Hid them in some flowery cave,
    Tell me but where,
  Sweet Queen of Parley, Daughter of the Sphere!
  So may'st thou be translated to the skies,
And give resounding grace to all Heaven's harmonies!

Comus. Can any mortal mixture of earth's mould
Breathe such divine inchanting ravishment?
Sure something holy lodges in that breast,
And with these raptures moves the vocal air
To testify his hidden residence.
How sweetly did they float upon the wings
Of silence, through the empty-vaulted night,
At every fall smoothing the raven down
Of darkness till it smiled! I have oft heard
My mother Circe with the Sirens three,
Amidst the flowery-kirtled Naiades,
Culling their potent hearbs and baleful drugs,
Who, as they sung, would take the prisoned soul,
And lap it in Elysium: Scylla wept,
And chid her barking waves into attention,
And fell Charybdis murmured soft applause.
Yet they in pleasing slumber lulled the sense,
And in sweet madness robbed it of itself;
But such a sacred and home-felt delight,
Such sober certainty of waking bliss,
I never heard till now. I'll speak to her,
And she shall be my Queen.—Hail, foreign wonder!
Whom certain these rough shades did never breed,
Unless the Goddess that in rural shrine
Dwell'st here with Pan or Sylvan, by blest song
Forbidding every bleak unkindly fog
To touch the prosperous growth of this tall wood.

Lady. Nay, gentle shepherd, ill is lost that praise
That is addressed to unattending ears.

Not any boast of skill, but extreme shift
How to regain my severed company,
Compelled me to awake the courteous Echo
To give me answer from her mossy couch.
    Comus. What chance, good Lady, hath bereft you thus?
    Lady. Dim darkness and this leavy labyrinth.
    Comus. Could that divide you from near-ushering guides?
    Lady. They left me weary on a grassy turf.
    Comus. By falsehood, or discourtesy, or why?
    Lady. To seek i' the valley some cool friendly spring.
    Comus. And left your fair side all unguarded, Lady?
    Lady. They were but twain, and purposed quick return.
    Comus. Perhaps forestalling night prevented them.
    Lady. How easy my misfortune is to hit!
    Comus. Imports their loss, beside the present need?
    Lady. No less than if I should my brothers lose.
    Comus. Where they of manly prime, or youthful bloom?
    Lady. As smooth as Hebe's their unrazored lips.
    Comus. Two such I saw, what time the laboured ox
In his loose traces from the furrow came,
And the swinked hedger at his supper sat.
I saw them under a green mantling vine,
That crawls along the side of yon small hill,
Plucking ripe clusters from the tender shoots;
Their port was more than human, as they stood.
I took it for a faery vision
Of some gay creatures of the element,
That in the colours of the rainbow live,
And play i' the plighted clouds. I was awe-strook,
And, as I passed, I worshiped. If those you seek,
It were a journey like the path to Heaven
To help you find them.
    Lady.   Gentle villager,
What readiest way would bring me to that place?
    Comus. Due west it rises from this shrubby point.
    Lady. To find out that, good Shepherd, I suppose,
In such a scant allowance of star-light,
Would overtask the best land-pilot's art,
Without the sure guess of well-practised feet.
    Comus. I know each lane, and every alley green,
Dingle, or bushy dell, of this wild wood,
And every bosky bourn from side to side,
My daily walks and ancient neighbourhood;
And, if your stray attendance be yet lodged,
Or shroud within these limits, I shall know

Ere morrow wake, or the low-roosted lark
From her thatched pallet rouse. If otherwise,
I can conduct you, Lady, to a low
But loyal cottage, where you may be safe
Till further quest.
    Lady.   Shepherd, I take thy word,
And trust thy honest-offered courtesy,
Which oft is sooner found in lowly sheds,
With smoky rafters, than in tapestry halls
And courts of princes, where it first was named,
And yet is most pretended. In a place
Less warranted than this, or less secure,
I cannot be, that I should fear to change it.
Eye me, blest Providence, and square my trial
To my proportioned strength! Shepherd, lead on. . . .

The Two Brothers

    Eld. Bro. Unmuffle, ye faint stars; and thou, fair Moon,
That wont'st to love the travailler's benison,
Stoop thy pale visage through an amber cloud,
And disinherit Chaos, that reigns here
In double night of darkness and of shades;
Or, if your influence be quite dammed up
With black usurping mists, some gentle taper,
Though a rush-candle from the wicker hole
Of some clay habitation, visit us
With thy long levelled rule of streaming light,
And thou shalt be our star of Arcady,
Or Tyrian Cynosure.
    Sec. Bro.   Or, if our eyes
Be barred that happiness, might we but hear
The folded flocks, penned in their wattled cotes,
Or sound of pastoral reed with oaten stops,
Or whistle from the lodge, or village cock
Count the night-watches to his feathery dames,
'T would be some solace yet, some little cheering,
In this close dungeon of innumerous boughs.
But, Oh, that hapless virgin, our lost sister!
Where may she wander now, whither betake her
From the chill dew, amongst rude burs and thistles?
Perhaps some cold bank is her bolster now,
Or 'gainst the rugged bark of some broad elm
Leans her unpillowed head, fraught with sad fears.

What if in wild amazement and affright,
Or, while we speak, within the direful grasp
Of savage hunger, or of savage heat!
  Eld. Bro. Peace, brother: be not overexquisite
To cast the fashion of uncertain evils;
For, grant they be so, while they rest unknown,
What need a man forestall his date of grief,
And run to meet what he would most avoid?
Or, if they be but false alarms of fear,
How bitter is such self-delusion!
I do not think my sister so to seek,
Or so unprincipled in virtue's book,
And the sweet peace that goodness bosoms ever,
As that the single want of light and noise
(Not being in danger, as I trust she is not)
Could stir the constant mood of her calm thoughts,
And put them into misbecoming plight.
Virtue could see to do what Virtue would
By her own radiant light, though sun and moon
Were in the flat sea sunk. And Wisdom's self
Oft seeks to sweet retirèd solitude,
Where, with her best nurse, Contemplation,
She plumes her feathers, and lets grow her wings,
That, in the various bustle of resort,
Were all to-ruffled, and sometimes impaired.
He that has light within his own clear breast
May sit i' the centre, and enjoy bright day:
But he that hides a dark soul and foul thoughts
Benighted walks under the mid-day sun;
Himself is his own dungeon.
  Sec. Bro.   'T is most true
That musing Meditation most affects
The pensive secrecy of desert cell,
Far from the cheerful haunt of men and herds,
And sits as safe as in a senate-house;
For who would rob a Hermit of his weeds,
His few books, or his beads, or maple dish,
Or do his grey hairs any violence?
But Beauty, like the fair Hesperian Tree
Laden with blooming gold, had need the guard
Of dragon-watch with uninchanted eye
To save her blossoms, and defend her fruit,
From the rash hand of bold Incontinence.
You may as well spread out the unsunned heaps
Of miser's treasure by an outlaw's den,

    And tell me it is safe, as bid me hope
Danger will wink on Opportunity,
And let a single helpless maiden pass
Uninjured in this wild surrounding waste.
Of night or loneliness it recks me not;
I fear the dread events that dog them both,
Lest some ill-greeting touch attempt the person
Of our unownèd sister.
  Eld. Bro.   I do not, brother,
Infer as if I thought my sister's state
Secure without all doubt or controversy;
Yet, where an equal poise of hope and fear
Does arbitrate the event, my nature is
That I encline to hope rather than fear,
And gladly banish squint suspicion.
My sister is not so defenceless left
As you imagine; she has a hidden strength,
Which you remember not.
  Sec. Bro.   What hidden strength,
Unless the strength of Heaven, if you mean that?
  Eld. Bro. I mean that too, but yet a hidden strength,
Which, if Heaven gave it, may be termed her own:
'T is Chastity, my brother, Chastity:
She that has that is clad in com'plete steel,
And, like a quivered nymph with arrows keen,
May trace huge forests, and unharboured heaths,
Infamous hills, and sandy perilous wilds;
Where, through the sacred rays of chastity,
No savage fierce, bandite, or mountaineer,
Will dare to soil her virgin purity.
Yea, there where very desolation dwells,
By grots and caverns shagged with horrid shades,
She may pass on with unblenched majesty,
Be it not done in pride, or in presumption.
Some say no evil thing that walks by night,
In fog or fire, by lake or moorish fen,
Blue meagre hag, or stubborn unlaid ghost,
That breaks his magic chains at curfew time,
No goblin or swart faery of the mine,
Hath hurtful power o'er true virginity.
Do ye believe me yet, or shall I call
Antiquity from the old schools of Greece
To testify the arms of Chastity?
Hence had the huntress Dian her dread bow
Fair silver-shafted Queen for ever chaste,

Wherewith she tamed the brindled lioness
And spotted mountain-pard, but set at nought
The frivolous bolt of Cupid; gods and men
Feared her stern frown, and she was queen o' the woods.
What was that snaky-headed Gorgon shield
That wise Minerva wore, unconquered virgin,
Wherewith she freezed her foes to con'gealed stone,
But rigid looks of chaste austerity,
And noble grace that dashed brute violence
With sudden adoration and blank awe?
So dear to Heaven is saintly chastity
That, when a soul is found sincerely so,
A thousand liveried angels lackey her,
Driving far off each thing of sin and guilt,
And in clear dream and solemn vision
Tell her of things that no gross ear can hear;
Till oft converse with heavenly habitants
Begin to cast a beam on the outward shape,
The unpolluted temple of the mind,
And turns it by degrees to the soul's essence,
Till all be made immortal. But, when lust,
By unchaste looks, loose gestures, and foul talk,
But most by lewd and lavish act of sin,
Lets in defilement to the inward parts,
The soul grows clotted by contagion,
Imbodies, and imbrutes, till she quite lose
The divine property of her first being.
Such are those thick and gloomy shadows damp
Oft seen in charnel-vaults and sepulchres,
Lingering and sitting by a new-made grave,
As loth to leave the body that it loved,
And linked itself by carnal sensualty
To a degenerate and degraded state.

Sec. Bro. How charming is divine Philosophy!
Not harsh and crabbed, as dull fools suppose,
But musical as is Apollo's lute,
And a perpetual feast of nectared sweets,
Where no crude surfeit reigns.

Eld. Bro.   List! list! I hear
Some far-off hallo break the silent air.

Sec. Bro. Methought so too; what should it be?

Eld. Bro.   For certain,
Either some one, like us, night-founded here,
Or else some neighbour woodman, or, at worst,
Some roving robber calling to his fellows.

Sec. Bro. Heaven keep my sister!
   Again, again, and near!
Best draw, and stand upon our guard.
   Eld. Bro.   I'll hallo.
If he be friendly, he comes well: if not,
Defence is a good cause, and Heaven be for us!

The Attending Spirit, *habited like a shepherd*

That hallo I should know. What are you? speak.
Come not too near; you fall on iron stakes else.
   Spir. What voice is that? my young Lord? speak again.
   Sec. Bro. O brother, 't is my father's Shepherd, sure.
   Eld. Bro. Thyrsis! whose artful strains have oft delayed
The huddling brook to hear his madrigal,
And sweetened every musk-rose of the dale.
How camest thou here, good swain? Hath any ram
Slipped from the fold, or young kid lost his dam,
Or straggling wether the pent flock forsook?
How couldst thou find this dark sequestered nook?
   Spir. O my loved master's heir, and his next joy,
I came not here on such a trivial toy
As a strayed ewe, or to pursue the stealth
Of pilfering wolf; not all the fleecy wealth
That doth enrich these downs is worth a thought
To this my errand, and the care it brought.
But, oh! my virgin Lady, where is she?
How chance she is not in your company?
   Eld. Bro. To tell thee sadly, Shepherd, without blame
Or our neglect, we lost her as we came.
   Spir. Ay me unhappy! then my fears are true.
   Eld. Bro. What fears, good Thyrsis?
      Prithee briefly shew.
   Spir. I'll tell ye. 'T is not vain or fabulous
(Though so esteemed by shallow ignorance)
What the sage poets, taught by the heavenly Muse,
Storied of old in high immortal verse
Of dire Chimeras and inchanted Isles,
And rifted rocks whose entrance leads to Hell;
For such there be, but unbelief is blind.
   Within the navel of this hideous wood,
Immured in cypress shades, a Sorcerer dwells,
Of Bacchus and of Circe born, great Comus,
Deep skilled in all his mother's witcheries,
And here to every thirsty wanderer

By sly enticement gives his baneful cup,
With many murmurs mixed, whose pleasing poison
The visage quite transforms of him that drinks,
And the inglorious likeness of a beast
Fixes instead, unmoulding reason's mintage
Charactered in the face. This have I learnt
Tending my flocks hard by i' the hilly crofts
That brow this bottom glade; whence night by night
He and his monstrous rout are heard to howl
Like stabled wolves, or tigers at their prey,
Doing abhorrèd rites to Hecate
In their obscurèd haunts of inmost bowers.
Yet have they many baits and guileful spells
To inveigle and invite the unwary sense
Of them that pass unweeting by the way.
This evening late, by then the chewing flocks
Had ta'en their supper on the savoury herb
Of knot-grass dew-besprent, and were in fold,
I sat me down to watch upon a bank
With ivy canopied, and interwove
With flaunting honeysuckle, and began,
Wrapt in a pleasing fit of melancholy,
To meditate my rural minstrelsy,
Till fancy had her fill. But ere a close
The wonted roar was up amidst the woods,
And filled the air with barbarous dissonance;
At which I ceased, and listened them a while,
Till an unusual stop of sudden silence
Gave respite to the drowsy-flighted steeds
That draw the litter of close-curtained Sleep.
At last a soft and solemn-breathing sound
Rose like a steam of rich distilled perfumes,
And stole upon the air, that even Silence
Was took ere she was ware, and wished she might
Deny her nature, and be never more,
Still to be so displaced. I was all ear,
And took in strains that might create a soul
Under the ribs of Death. But, oh! ere long
Too well I did perceive it was the voice
Of my most honoured Lady, your dear sister.
Amazed I stood, harrowed with grief and fear;
And "O poor hapless Nightingale," thought I,
"How sweet thou sing'st, how near the deadly snare!"
Then down the lawns I ran with headlong haste,
Through paths and turnings often trod by day,

Till, guided by mine ear, I found the place
Where that damned wisard, hid in sly disguise
(For so by certain signs I knew), had met
Already, ere my best speed could prevent,
The aidless innocent lady, his wished prey;
Who gently asked if he had seen such two,
Supposing him some neighbour villager.
Longer I durst not stay, but soon I guessed
Ye were the two she meant; with that I sprung
Into swift flight, till I had found you here;
But furder know I not.

  Sec. Bro.   O night and shades,
How are ye joined with hell in triple knot
Against the unarmèd weakness of one virgin,
Alone and helpless! Is this the confidence
You gave me, brother?

  Eld. Bro.   Yes, and keep it still;
Lean on it safely; not a period
Shall be unsaid for me. Against the threats
Of malice or of sorcery, or that power
Which erring men call Chance, this I hold firm:
Virtue may be assailed, but never hurt,
Surprised by unjust force, but not enthralled;
Yea, even that which Mischief meant most harm
Shall in the happy trial prove most glory.
But evil on itself shall back recoil,
And mix no more with goodness, when at last,
Gathered like scum, and settled to itself,
It shall be in eternal restless change
Self-fed and self-consumed. If this fail,
The pillared firmament is rottenness,
And earth's base built on stubble. But come, let's on!
Against the opposing will and arm of Heaven
May never this just sword be lifted up;
But, for that damned magician, let him be girt
With all the griesly legiöns that troop
Under the sooty flag of Acheron,
Harpies and Hydras, or all the monstrous forms
'Twixt Africa and Ind, I'll find him out,
And force him to restore his purchase back,
Or drag him by the curls to a foul death,
Cursed as his life.

  Spir.   Alas! good ventrous youth,
I love thy courage yet, and bold emprise;
But here thy sword can do thee little stead.

Far other arms and other weapons must
Be those that quell the might of hellish charms.
He with his bare wand can unthread thy joints,
And crumble all thy sinews.
    Eld. Bro.   Why, prithee Shepherd,
How durst thou then thyself approach so near
As to make this relation?
    Spir.   Care and utmost shifts
How to secure the Lady from surprisal
Brought to my mind a certain shepherd lad,
Of small regard to see to, yet well skilled
In every virtuous plant and healing hearb
That spreads her verdant leaf to the morning ray.
He loved me well, and oft would beg me sing;
Which when I did, he on the tender grass
Would sit, and hearken even to ecstasy,
And in requital ope his leathern scrip,
And shew me simples of a thousand names,
Telling their strange and vigorous faculties.
Amongst the rest a small unsightly root,
But of divine effect, he culled me out.
The leaf was darkish, and had prickles on it,
But in another country, as he said,
Bore a bright golden flower, but not in this soil:
Unknown, and like esteemed, and the dull swain
Treads on it daily with his clouted shoon;
And yet more med'cinal is it than that Moly
That Hermes once to wise Ulysses gave.
He called it Hæmony, and gave it me,
And bade me keep it as of sovran use
'Gainst all inchantments, mildew blast, or damp,
Or ghastly Furies' apparition.
I pursed it up, but little reckoning made,
Till now that this extremity compelled.
But now I find it true; for by this means
I knew the foul inchanter, though disguised,
Entered the very lime-twigs of his spells,
And yet came off. If you have this about you
(As I will give you when we go) you may
Boldly assault the necromancer's hall;
Where if he be, with dauntless hardihood
And brandished blade rush on him: break his glass,
And shed the luscious liquor on the ground;
But seize his wand. Though he and his curst crew
Fierce sign of battail make, and menace high,

Or, like the sons of Vulcan, vomit smoke,
Yet will they soon retire, if he but shrink.
   Eld. Bro. Thyrsis, lead on apace; I'll follow thee;
And some good angel bear a shield before us!

The Scene changes to a stately palace, set out with all manner of deliciousness: soft music, tables spread with all dainties. Comus appears with his rabble, and the Lady *set in an inchanted chair; to whom he offers his glass; which she puts by, and goes about to rise.*

   Comus. Nay, Lady, sit. If I but wave this wand,
Your nerves are all chained up in alabaster,
And you a statue, or as Daphne was,
Root-bound, that fled Apollo.
   Lady.   Fool, do not boast.
Thou canst not touch the freedom of my mind
With all thy charms, although this corporal rind
Thou hast immanacled while Heaven sees good.
   Comus. Why are you vexed, Lady? why do you frown?
Here dwell no frowns, nor anger; from these gates
Sorrow flies far. See, here be all the pleasures
That fancy can beget on youthful thoughts,
When the fresh blood grows lively, and returns
Brisk as the April buds in primrose season.
And first behold this cordial julep here,
That flames and dances in his crystal bounds,
With spirits of balm and fragrant syrups mixed.
Not that Nepenthes which the wife of Thone
In Egypt gave to Jove-born Helena
Is of such power to stir up joy as this,
To life so friendly, or so cool to thirst.
Why should you be so cruel to yourself,
And to those dainty limbs, which Nature lent
For gentle usage and soft delicacy?
But you invert the covenants of her trust,
And harshly deal, like an ill borrower,
With that which you received on other terms,
Scorning the unexempt condition
By all mortal frailty must subsist,
Refreshment after toil, ease after pain,
That have been tired all day without repast,
And timely rest have wanted. But, fair virgin,
This will restore all soon.
   Lady.   'T will not, false traitor!
'T will not restore the truth and honesty

That thou hast banished from thy tongue with lies.
Was this the cottage and the safe abode
Thou told'st me of? What grim aspects' are these,
These oughly-headed monsters? Mercy guard me!
Hence with thy brewed inchantments, foul deceiver!
Hast thou betrayed my credulous innocence
With vizored falsehood and base forgery?
And wouldst thou seek again to trap me here
With lickerish baits, fit to ensnare a brute?
Were it a draught for Juno when she banquets,
I would not taste thy treasonous offer. None
But such as are good men can give good things;
And that which is not good is not delicious
To a well-governed and wise appetite.

Comus. O foolishness of men! that lend their ears
To those budge doctors of the Stoic fur,
And fetch their precepts from the Cynic tub,
Praising the lean and sallow Abstinence
Wherefore did Nature pour her bounties forth
With such a full and unwithdrawing hand,
Covering the earth with odours, fruits, and flocks,
Thronging the seas with spawn innumerable,
But all to please and sate the curious taste?
And set to work millions of spinning worms,
That in their green shops weave the smooth-haired silk,
To deck her sons; and, that no corner might
Be vacant of her plenty, in her own loins
She hutched the all-worshiped ore and precious gems,
To store her children with. If all the world
Should in a pet of temperance, feed on pulse,
Drink the clear stream, and nothing wear but frieze,
The All-giver would be unthanked, would be unpraised,
Not half his riches known, and yet despised;
And we should serve him as a grudging master,
As a penurious niggard of his wealth,
And live like Nature's bastards, not her sons,
Who would be quite surcharged with her own weight ,
And strangled with her waste fertility:
The earth cumbered, and the winged air darked with plumes;
The herds would over-multitude their lords;
The sea o'erfraught would swell, and the unsought diamonds
Would so emblaze the forehead of the Deep,
And so bestud with stars, that they below
Would grow inured to light, and come at last
To gaze upon the Sun with shameless brows.

List, Lady; be not coy, and be not cozened
With that same vaunted name, Virginity.
Beauty is Nature's coin; must not be hoarded,
But must be current; and the good thereof
Consists in mutual and partaken bliss,
Unsavoury in the injoyment of itself.
If you let slip time, like a neglected rose
It withers on the stalk with languished head.
Beauty is Nature's brag, and must be shown
In courts, at feasts, and high solemnities,
Where most may wonder at the workmanship.
It is for homely features to keep home;
They had their name thence: coarse complexions
And cheeks of sorry grain will serve to ply
The sampler, and to tease the huswife's wool.
What need a vermeil-tinctured lip for that,
Love-darting eyes, or tresses like the Morn?
There was another meaning in these gifts;
Think what, and be advised; you are but young yet.

Lady. I had not thought to have unlocked my lips
In this unhallowed air, but that this Juggler
Would think to charm my judgment, as mine eyes,
Obtruding false rules pranked in reason's garb.
I hate when Vice can bolt her arguments
And Virtue has no tongue to check her pride.
Impostor! do not charge most innocent Nature,
As if she would her children should be riotous
With her abundance. She, good Cateress,
Means her provision only to the good,
That live according to her sober laws,
And holy dictate of spare Temperance.
If every just man that now pines with want
Had but a moderate and beseeming share
Of that which lewdly-pampered Luxury
Now heaps upon some few with vast excess,
Nature's full blessings would be well-dispensed
In unsuperfluous even proportion,
And she no whit encumbered with her store;
And then the Giver would be better thanked,
His praise due paid: for swinish Gluttony
Ne'er looks to Heaven amidst his gorgeous feast,
But with besotted base ingratitude
Crams and blasphemes his Feeder. Shall I go on?
Or have I said enow? To him that dares
Arm his profane tongue with contemptuous words

Against the sun-clad power of Chastity
Fain would I something say;—yet to what end?
Thou hast nor ear, nor soul, to apprehend
The sublime notion and high mystery
That must be uttered to unfold the sage
And serious doctrine of Virginity;
And thou art worthy that thou shouldst not know
More happiness than this thy present lot.
Enjoy your dear Wit, and gay Rhetoric,
That hath so well been taught her dazzling fence;
Thou art not fit to hear thyself convinced.
Yet, should I try, the uncontrollèd worth
Of this pure cause would kindle my rapt spirits
To such a flame of sacred vehemence
That dumb things would be moved to sympathize,
And the brute Earth would lend her nerves, and shake,
Till all thy magic structures, reared so high,
Were shattered into heaps o'er thy false head.
  Comus. She fables not. I feel that I do fear
Her words set off by some superior power;
And, though not mortal, yet a cold shuddering dew
Dips me all o'er, as when the wrath of Jove
Speaks thunder and the chains of Erebus
To some of Saturn's crew. I must dissemble,
And try her yet more strongly.—Come, no more!
This is mere moral babble, and direct
Against the canon laws of our foundation.
I must not suffer this; yet 't is but the lees
And settlings of a melancholy blood.
But this will cure all straight; one sip of this
Will bathe the drooping spirits in delight
Beyond the bliss of dreams. Be wise, and taste . . .

The Brothers *rush in with swords drawn, wrest his glass out of his hands, and break it against the ground: his rout make sign of resistance, but are all driven in. The* Attendant Spirit *comes in.*

  Spir. What! have you let the false Enchanter scape?
O ye mistook; ye should have snatched his wand,
And bound him fast. Without his rod reversed,
And backward mutters of dissevering power,
We cannot free the Lady that sits here
In stony fetters fixed and motionless.
Yet stay: be not disturbed; now I bethink me,
Some other means I have which may be used,

Which once of Meliboeus old I learnt,
The soothest Shepherd that ere piped on plains.
  There is a gentle Nymph not far from hence,
That with moist curb sways the smooth Severn stream:
Sabrina is her name: a virgin pure;
Whilom she was the daughter of Locrine,
That had the sceptre from his father Brute.
She, guiltless damsel, flying the mad pursuit
Of her enragèd stepdame, Guendolen,
Commended her fair innocence to the flood
That stayed her flight with his cross-flowing course.
The water-Nymphs, that in the bottom played,
Held up their pearlèd wrists, and took her in,
Bearing her straight to aged Nereus' hall;
Who, piteous of her woes, reared her lank head,
And gave her to his daughters to imbathe
In nectared lavers strewed with asphodil,
And through the porch and inlet of each sense
Dropt in ambrosial oils, till she revived,
And underwent a quick immortal change,
Made Goddess of the river. Still she retains
Her maiden gentleness, and oft at eve
Visits the herds along the twilight meadows,
Helping all urchin blasts, and ill-luck signs
That the shrewd meddling Elf delights to make,
Which she with pretious vialed liquors heals:
For which the Shepherds, at their festivals,
Carol her goodness loud in rustic lays,
And throw sweet garland wreaths into her stream,
Of pansies, pinks, and gaudy daffadils.
And, as the old Swain said, she can unlock
The clasping charm, and thaw the numbing spell,
If she be right invoked in warbled song;
For maidenhood she loves, and will be swift
To aid a virgin, such as was herself,
In hard-besetting need. This will I try,
And add the power of some adjuring verse.

Song

  Sabrina fair,
    Listen where thou art sitting
  Under the glassy, cool, translucent wave,
    In twisted braids of lilies knitting
  The loose train of thy amber-dropping hair;

> Listen for dear honour's sake,
> Goddess of the silver lake,
>   Listen and save!
> Listen, and appear to us,
> In name of great Oceanus,
> By the earth-shaking Neptune's mace,
> And Tethys' grave majestic pace;
> By hoary Nereus' wrinkled look,
> And the Carpathian wizard's hook;
> By scaly Triton's winding shell,
> And old soothsaying Glaucus' spell;
> By Leucothea's lovely hands,
> And her son that rules the strands;
> By Thetis' tinsel-slippered feet,
> And the songs of Sirens sweet;
> By dead Parthenope's dear tomb,
> And fair Ligea's golden comb,
> Wherewith she sits on diamond rocks
> Sleeking her soft alluring locks;
> By all the nymphs that nightly dance
> Upon thy streams with wily glance;
> Rise, rise, and heave thy rosy head
> From thy coral-paven bed,
> And bridle in thy headlong wave,
> Till thou our summons answered have.
>   Listen and save!

Sabrina rises, attended by Water-nymphs, and sings

> By the rushy-fringèd bank,
> Where grows the willow and the osier dank,
>   My sliding chariot stays,
> Thick set with agate, and the azurn sheen
> Of turkis blue, and emerald green,
>   That in the channel strays:
> Whilst from off the waters fleet
> Thus I set my printless feet
> O'er the cowslip's velvet head,
>   That bends not as I tread.
> Gentle swain, at thy request
>   I am here!

Spir. Goddess dear,
We implore thy powerful hand
To undo the charmèd band

Of true virgin here distressed
Through the force and through the wile
Of unblessed enchanter vile.
  Sabr. Shepherd, 't is my office best
To help insnarèd Chastity.
Brightest Lady, look on me.
Thus I sprinkle on thy breast
Drops that from my fountain pure
I have kept of pretious cure;
Thrice upon thy finger's tip,
Thrice upon thy rubied lip:
Next this marble venomed seat,
Smeared with gums of glutinous heat,
I touch with chaste palms moist and cold.
Now the spell hath lost his hold;
And I must haste ere morning hour
To wait in Amphitrite's bower.

Sabrina *descends and the* Lady *rises out of her seat*

  Spir. Virgin, daughter of Locrine,
Sprung of old Anchises' line,
May thy brimmèd waves for this
Their full tribute never miss
From a thousand petty rills,
That tumble down the snowy hills:
Summer drouth or singèd air
Never scorch thy tresses fair,
Nor wet October's torrent flood
Thy molten crystal fill with mud;
May thy billows roll ashore
The beryl and the golden ore;
May thy lofty head be crowned
With many a tower and terrace round,
And here and there thy banks upon
With groves of myrrh and cinnamon.
  Come, Lady; while Heaven lends us grace,
Let us fly this cursed place,
Lest the Sorcerer us entice
With some other new device.
Not a waste or needless sound
Till we come to holier ground.
I shall be your faithful guide
Through this gloomy covert wide;
And not many furlongs thence

Is your Father's residence,
Where this night are met in state
Many a friend to gratulate
His wished presence, and beside
All the Swains that there abide
With jigs and rural dance resort.
We shall catch them at their sport,
And our sudden coming there
Will double all their mirth and cheer.
Come, let us haste; the stars grow high,
But Night sits monarch yet in the mid sky.

The Scene changes, presenting Ludlow Town, and the President's Castle: then come in Country Dancers; after them the Attendant Spirit, with the two Brothers and the Lady.

Song

Spir. Back, Shepherds, back! Enough your play
Till next sun-shine holiday.
Here be, without duck or nod,
Other trippings to be trod
Of lighter toes, and such court guise
As Mercury did first devise
With the mincing Dryades
On the lawns and on the leas.

This second Song presents them to their Father and Mother

Noble Lord and Lady bright,
I have brought ye new delight.
Here behold so goodly grown
Three fair branches of your own.
Heaven hath timely tried their youth,
Their faith, their patience, and their truth,
And sent them here through hard assays
With a crown of deathless praise,
To triumph in victorious dance
O'er sensual Folly and Intemperance.

The dances ended, the Spirit epiloguizes

Spir. To the ocean now I fly,
And those happy climes that lie
Where day never shuts his eye,

Up in the broad fields of the sky.
There I suck the liquid air,
All amidst the Gardens fair
Of Hesperus, and his daughters three
That sing about the Golden Tree.
Along the crispèd shades and bowers
Revels the spruce and jocond Spring;
The Graces and the rosy-bosomed Hours
Thither all their bounties bring.
There eternal Summer dwells,
And west winds with musky wing
About the cedarn alleys fling
Nard and Cassie's balmy smells.
Iris there with humid bow
Waters the odorous banks, that blow
Flowers of more mingled hue
Than her purfled scarf can shew,
And drenches with Elysian dew
(List mortals, if your ears be true)
Beds of hyacinth and roses,
Where young Adonis oft reposes,
Waxing well of his deep wound
In slumber soft, and on the ground
Sadly sits the Assyrian queen;
But far above in spangled sheen
Celestial Cupid, her famed son, advanced,
Holds his dear Psyche sweet intranced,
After her wandring labours long,
Till free consent the gods among
Make her his eternal Bride,
And from her fair unspotted side
Two blissful twins are to be born,
Youth and Joy; so Jove hath sworn.

But now my task is smoothly done,
I can fly, or I can run
Quickly to the green earth's end,
Where the bowed welkin slow doth bend,
And from thence can soar as soon
To the corners of the Moon.

Mortals, that would follow me,
Love Virtue, she alone is free:
She can teach ye how to climb
Higher than the spheary chime:
Or, if Virtue feeble were,
Heaven itself would stoop to her.